THAT WAS ENTERTAINMENT

That Was ENTERTAINMENT

THE GOLDEN AGE OF THE MGM MUSICAL

BERNARD F. DICK

UNIVERSITY PRESS OF MISSISSIPPI · JACKSON

www.upress.state.ms.us

Designed by Peter D. Halverson

The University Press of Mississippi is a member of the
Association of American University Presses.

Photographs courtesy of Photofest/MGM unless otherwise noted

First printing 2018

∞

Cataloging-in-Publication Data

Names: Dick, Bernard F., author.
Title: That was entertainment : the golden age of the MGM musical / Bernard F. Dick.
Description: Jackson : University Press of Mississippi, [2018] | Includes bibliographical references
and index. |
Identifiers: LCCN 2017049132 (print) | LCCN 2017053326 (ebook) | ISBN 9781496817341 (epub
single) | ISBN 9781496817358 (epub institutional) | ISBN 9781496817365 (pdf single) | ISBN
9781496817372 (pdf institutional) | ISBN 9781496817334 (cloth : alk. paper)
Subjects: LCSH: Musical films—United States—History and criticism. | Metro-Goldwyn-Mayer.
Classification: LCC PN1995.9.M86 (ebook) | LCC PN1995.9.M86 D53 2018 (print) | DDC
791.43/6578—dc23
LC record available at https://lccn.loc.gov/2017049132

British Library Cataloging-in-Publication Data available

In Memoriam
Debbie Reynolds (1932–2016)

CONTENTS

ACKNOWLEDGMENTS

I would like to express my gratitude to Dr. Linda Harris Mehr, director, Margaret Herrick Library at the Fairbanks Center for Motion Picture Study, for creating such a friendly space for film research. I am indebted to the staff on whose expertise I have relied, especially Louise Hilton of Special Collections and Kristine Krueger of the National Film Information Service (NFIS). Special thanks to the Seattle Genealogical Society for providing me with valuable information about Arthur Freed and his family; everyone's favorite archivist, Ned Comstock of the University of Southern California's Cinematic Arts Library; and Phillips Exeter Academy archivist Edouard L. Desrochers, who verified Arthur Freed's brief stay at the academy. As always, I must acknowledge my debt to my wife, Katherine Restaino, for her encouragement and wisdom.

I would also like to single out two books that were enormously helpful to me: Hugh Fordin's *The World of Entertainment! Hollywood's Greatest Musicals* (Avon, 1975), reprinted as *MGM's Greatest Musicals: The Arthur Freed Unit* (Da Capo Press, 1996); and Earl J. Hess and Pratibha A. Dabholkar's *Singin' in the Rain: The Making of an American Masterpiece* (UP of Kansas, 2009). Both have drawn heavily on the Arthur Freed Collection at the University of Southern California, thus facilitating my own research.

My deepest gratitude to James Robert Parish for his meticulous reading of my manuscript and his suggestions for improvement, which I have implemented.

To cut down on needless repeating of documentation, unless indicated, all financial information (budgets, grosses, losses) come from the *Eddie Mannix Ledger* at the Margaret Herrick Library. (Mannix was MGM's troubleshooter, who knew how to cover up scandals that would detract from the studio's family-friendly image.) While the *Ledger* provides financial information for MGM films from 1928 to 1962 (production costs, domestic and international grosses, etc.), the figures only reflect revenues from a film's initial release, not from subsequent rentals. Still, the *Ledger* is the most reliable source of an MGM film's box office performance after its release.

THAT WAS ENTERTAINMENT

INTRODUCTION

In the 2015 Broadway musical, *Something Rotten!* set in Elizabethan England, the playwright Nick Bottom resents Shakespeare's widespread fame, while he labors in obscurity. "God, I hate Shakespeare," Nick sings. "I just don't get it, how a mediocre actor from a measly little town / is suddenly the brightest jewel in England's Royal Crown." He seeks out Nostradamus to see what the future holds for him. Nostradamus predicts a new theatrical form in which part of the story will be told in song. Nick is stunned: "An actor is saying his lines, and out of nowhere he just starts singing?" "What possible thought can the audience think other than this is horribly wrong?" Nostradamus replies that they will not think that because ... Cue for his big number, "A Musical," in which he foresees a type of stage presentation "with song and dance and sweet romance / and happy endings happening by happenstance." The lyrics explain the reasons audiences have gravitated to musicals: On a Saturday night, instead of attending a Greek tragedy and "see a mother have sex with her son" or a drama "with all that trauma and pain," try a musical "where crooners croon a catchy tune and limber leggy ladies thrill ya till ya swoon." *Something Rotten!* is essentially a tribute to the unique American art form, the stage musical, which may have derived from European operetta but which composers and lyricists such as Jerome Kern, George and Ira Gershwin, Richard Rodgers, Lorenz Hart, Oscar Hammerstein, Cole Porter, Jule Styne, Alan Jay Lerner and Frederick Loewe, John Kander and Fred Ebb, Sheldon Harnick and Jerry Bock, and Stephen Sondheim have turned into an indigenous art form.

Hollywood followed suit, creating a unique kind of film: the movie musical. In this regard, one studio eclipsed the others: MGM.

The MGM musical of the studio's golden years (the late 1920s through the end of the 1950s) typically glorified the America of yesteryear, inspiring nostalgia for a simpler and seemingly happier time (*Meet Me in St. Louis, Easter Parade, Two Weeks with Love*) when gender roles were clearly defined, and society was unashamedly patriarchal (*Meet Me in St. Louis*); it portrayed an America devoid of urban sprawl and social unrest, where adolescents lacked a libido (*Babes in Arms, Strike Up the Band, Little Nellie Kelly*); and adults who did expressed it in dance (the "Slaughter on Tenth Avenue" ballet in *Words and Music*) or song ("I Can Cook, Too," Betty Garrett's catalogue of her culinary—and other—skills in *On the Town*). The Soviet Union may have exploded its first atomic bomb in 1949, but one would never know it from MGM's musicals of that year which belonged to an age of moviemaking marked "golden," not "nuclear." Who cared about the bomb when Esther Williams was swimming in turquoise water in *Neptune's Daughter* as if she were the sea god's offspring? For the aquatically indifferent, there was the sexy "Baby, It's Cold Outside" duet with a suave Ricardo Montalban romancing a coy Williams, in contrast to an uninhibited Betty Garrett cozying up to a seduction-resistant Red Skelton. *Take Me Out to the Ball Game* posed the burning question of 1949: Will Gene Kelly remain a ballplayer and pair off with Esther Williams so Frank Sinatra can do likewise with Betty Garrett? There was no pairing off in *On the Town* with three sailors on a twenty-four-hour leave in New York. They do their wooing, have an adventure (no time for a fling), and return to their ship at 6:00 a.m.

The MGM musical confirmed audiences' belief in an America with strong family values, even if they interfered with social mobility. In *Meet Me in St. Louis*, the prospect of a father's uprooting his family and relocating to New York causes such consternation among his children that he decides to remain in his old job. The film's moral is simple: Home is where the heart is, especially when it is the site of the 1904 St. Louis Exposition World Fair.

No studio could compete with the dreamy lushness that Vincente Minnelli brought to a wisp of a film like *Yolanda and the Thief* (1945), in which a convent-schooled young woman (Lucille Bremer) imagines that a con man (Fred Astaire) is her guardian angel with dancing feet instead of wings. Minnelli was a master of the surreal baroque, flooding the screen with torrents of color, particularly red, often in combination with yellow, blue, and white. The "Coffee Time" sequence is a prime example of Minnelli's palette. The convent girls are in drab frocks with leggings in Minnelli's favorite colors: red, blue, and white (it's carnival time); Lucille Bremer, in a yellow skirt and white blouse; and Astaire, in a gray jacket and white pants. Clapping their hands, they move with a sense of decorum befitting a faux angel and his convent school partner, but with a hint of the sensual (Bremer can do a high kick)—all this on an art deco floor of wavy strips of black and white suggesting coffee with or without cream, dancing as if they were two bodies sharing the same soul. Shunned by audiences in its day because of its attempt to elevate the whimsical to the grand bourgois, *Yolanda* was the essence of musical pictorialism.

There had never before been a musical like Minnelli's *The Pirate* (1948) with Gene Kelly as a strolling player hypnotizing a sexually frustrated Judy Garland, who sheds her inhibitions as she breaks into "Mack the Black," preferring ravishment by Kelly (who she thinks is the pirate Macoco) to an arranged marriage to portly Walter Slezak (who turns out to be the title character).

Such was the MGM musical of the golden age. This book is a tribute to both its greatness and variety, which consisted of integrated musicals, admittedly rare, in which the musical sequences (song, dance, ensemble) are so inseparable from the action that their order cannot be rearranged without affecting the whole; revues, variety shows in disguise with a wisp of a story line; adaptations of Broadway shows, both faithful and altered, often refitted with new songs for a mass audience; biopics, mythicohistorical lives of composers and lyricists, impressarios, pop singers, and opera stars; original musicals; musical versions of works of fiction and theater; aquacades with Esther Williams; show business musicals revolving around the creation of a stage production; operettas with Jeanette MacDonald and Nelson Eddy; and celebrations of youth with Judy Garland, Mickey Rooney, Jane Powell, and Debbie Reynolds. No other studio could equal MGM's diversity.

TEANECK, NJ
APRIL 2017

THE MUSIC MAN OF MGM

In Hollywood's Golden Age, each of the studios—including Poverty Row's Republic, Monogram, and PRC—made musicals. MGM, the "Tiffany of studios," whose letterhead boasted of "More Stars than Are in the Heavens," was the gold standard. That might never have been the case if Arthur Freed had not become part of the MGM family in 1929, five years after the amalgamation of Metro Pictures, Goldwyn Pictures, and Louis B. Mayer Productions to form Metro-Goldwyn-Mayer, known to generations of moviegoers as MGM.

Arthur's life is a skein of dates and places, supplemented by news stories and production files. There are many lacunae, many questions never to be answered; there are also facts that are easily verified. His father, Max, was born in 1866 in Asszonyfa, Hungary, seventy-eight miles west of Budapest. Max emigrated to America in 1887; his future wife and Arthur's mother, Rosie Grossman (née Groseman), also Hungarian, emigrated in 1891. Rosie was either four or six years younger than Max. Census records give her birth year as 1872; her death certificate is more specific—August 1, 1870. Max and Rosie seem to have met in Charleston, South Carolina, which had been a major center of Jewish immigration before the Civil War but afterward was just a southern city with a small Jewish presence. Why Max and Rosie were in Charleston in 1894, the year they supposedly married, is unknown. Since postbellum Charleston Jews were merchants and peddlers, Max, who was, among other things, a zither salesman, may have thought that Charlestonians would be intrigued by the sound of the stringed instrument that was becoming increasingly popular in North America.

Since census data are never complete, the 1910 and 1920 census reports did not record the day and month of Max and Rosie's marriage. The month would be significant: Arthur was born on September 9, 1894. Initially, he bore his mother's surname, Grossman, probably because Rosie and Max had not yet married, although it is also possible that Max may not have been Arthur's biological father. Romantics might like to imagine Max and Rosie as lovers living in a garret where he played Hungarian folk melodies on a zither, legitimizing their union after Rosie became pregnant with Arthur; or getting married to legitimize Arthur, if he were another man's child. Either version would make a great woman's picture, a blend of fact and fiction complete with a tragic ending: Max's suicide in 1917 at age fifty-one, as Arthur was on the first leg of a journey that brought him to MGM twelve years later.

Within this skein of dates, places, and conjectures, there is one certainty: Arthur was his mother's son in every way and remained devoted to her until her death on March 11, 1957, in Los Angeles. At some point, Arthur was given his father's last name, Fried, which, according to *Polk's Seattle City Directory*, Max was still using in 1909 when he was working in real estate in Seattle. By 1910, "Fried" had vanished from the *Directory*, replaced by Freed, a variant of the family name (Max's father was Mordechai Moritz Fried). To Max, "Freed" seemed less ethnic (for example, Freed, West Virginia). The spelling apparently meant a great deal to Max, even though "Fried" and "Freed" are pronounced the same. "Freed" also went better with his new title. The listing in the 1910 *Directory* read, "Freed, Max, mngr, Max Freed & Co."

The mercurial Max did not remain in real estate for long. His business address changed frequently. In the 1913 *Directory*, he was listed as president of the Smyrna Valley Orchard Company. There was no listing for him in 1914, but there was one a year later. Max had switched from produce to hardware and was now manager of the Seattle office of Butler-Freed-Riley, a hardware manufacturing company with headquarters in Jersey City, New Jersey.

The Freeds were now living on a ranch in Bellevue, just across Lake Washington and accessible by boat or ferry from Seattle.

To census takers, Max Freed was a merchant, who began in art, antiques, and zithers, but soon branched out into totally unrelated businesses like furniture, real estate, fruit growing, and livestock. Max seemed happiest on the Bellevue ranch, which may have evoked memories of his Hungarian boyhood. *The Ranch* (April 1, 1914) carried an ad for an auction (cash only) at Max's ranch. Up for bidding were Holstein dairy cows, a Holstein bull, horses, a seven-passenger Garford touring car that cost $3,850, milk cans, and separators. "Max the Rancher" was just another role in an ever-growing repertoire. In the 1916 *Directory*, "Freed, Max" was followed by the names of two companies that he supposedly represented: Molloch Knitting Mills and the National Loan and Investment Co. There was no listing for him in 1917, only one for his wife, identified as "Rosie wid Max." After May 9, 1917, Rosie was a widow.

There was something about Max Freed that recalls Hubie in the Jule Styne–Betty Comden and Adolph Green Broadway musical, *Do Re Me* (1961). In his opening number, Hubie, whose wife calls him "a schemer, a dreamer," insists that "all that you need is an angle" to succeed. Max found enough of them to buy a ranch in Bellevue, Seattle's largest suburb. Until they settled permanently in Seattle around 1909, the Freeds lived a peripatetic existence. They moved regularly, their latest address determined by Max's latest angle. All of their children were born in different places: Arthur, 1894, in Charleston; Victor, 1896, in Denver; Hugo, 1897, in Boston; Sidney, 1900, somewhere in New Jersey; Walter, 1903, in Spokane; Ruth, 1906, somewhere in Washington State; Ralph, 1907, in Vancouver, British Columbia; Clarence Rupert, 1911 in Seattle. When Max felt successful enough to purchase the Bellevue property, he believed he could finally settle down and become a successful rancher, providing his family with a lifestyle befitting a gentleman farmer.

The Freeds were a musical family. Max was a tenor; Walter was an organist who later taught music; Sidney worked in the record business; Ralph and Ruth wrote songs, at first for amusement, and later for profit; and Arthur became a lyricist and world-class movie producer, whose Freed Unit at MGM was responsible for many of the world's best-loved musicals such as *Meet Me in St. Louis* (1944), *Easter Parade* (1948), *An American in Paris* (1951), and *Singin' in the Rain* (1952). Except for Victor, who was killed in World War I, all of Arthur's siblings relocated in Los Angeles, including Clarence Rupert, about whom the least is known. In the 1930 census, he identified himself as "employer" and listed his occupation as "packing company." He still described himself as "employer" in the 1940 census, but this time as "proprietor." Nothing else is known about him except that he married, enlisted in the army on April 29, 1944, was discharged in 1946, and died in Ventura, California, in 1988 at the age of seventy-seven.

Max Freed did not live to see his children embark on successful careers. Hugo became an orchid breeder and popular lecturer on orchids. In 1946, he and Arthur started Arthur Freed's Orchids in Malibu. Ruth took up songwriting professionally, sometimes under the pseudonym of Patty Fisher. As Ruth Freed, she wrote "Perhaps" and "Make a Circle," recorded, respectively, by Joni James and Kay Starr. As Patty Fisher, she wrote the lyrics for "An Old Love Letter," performed by Alice Lon, the "Champagne Lady," on the *Lawrence Welk Show* on March 29, 1958. She also wrote two numbers, including the title song, for the Doris Day movie, *The Tunnel of Love* (1958). Ruth's husband, Albert Akst, was a former musician who became a highly regarded film editor and cut a number of Arthur's films including *Meet Me in St. Louis, The Harvey Girls, Ziegfeld Follies, Till the Clouds Roll By, Good News, Words and Music, Easter Parade, Summer Holiday, The Barkleys of Broadway, Royal Wedding, The Belle of New York, The Band Wagon,* and *Brigadoon.*

Ralph also became a songwriter, not as famous as his older brother but more prolific. At fourteen, he left Seattle for Los Angeles; after graduating from Hollywood High School, he worked as a writer and lyricist at Paramount and Universal. He joined the American Society of Composers, Authors and Publishers (ASCAP) in 1931 and began collaborating with such composers

as Burton Lane and Sammy Fain. Ralph and Lane wrote the Oscar-nominat-
ed "How about You?" sung by Judy Garland and Mickey Rooney in MGM's
Babes on Broadway (1941), which Arthur produced. Notable artists such as
Shirley Bassey, Frank Sinatra, and Rosemary Clooney have recorded the song.
Since 1941, "How about You?" has been heard in a number of movies: *Ship
Ahoy* (1942), *Grand Central Murder* (1942), *The Youngest Profession* (1943), *A
Guy Named Joe* (1943), *All about Eve* (1950), *Don't Bother to Knock* (1952), *The
Young Lions* (1958), *The Good-bye Girl* (1977), and *The Fisher King* (1991). Alec
Baldwin even sang it on TV's *Saturday Night Live* in 2000. At least one critic
found Ralph's lyrics superior to Arthur's, "whose words stroll through their
clichés with a shrug."

Arthur was a June/moon type of lyricist whose rhymes were elementary:
"I walk down the lane / With a happy refrain" ("Singin' in the Rain"); "You
are my lucky star / I saw you from afar" ("You Are My Lucky Star"). Arthur's
rhymes are never intellectually teasing, unlike, say, Cole Porter's, which are.

Ralph's lyrics, however, have flashes of wit and clever internal rhymes: "I
like potato chips, moonlight and motor trips" ("How about You?"); "A rhyth-
mical campaign can do more than champagne" ("Swing High, Swing Low").

Between 1932 and 1962, Ralph wrote regularly for the movies, often uncredited. One of the films for which he received credit was Arthur's production of *Du Barry Was a Lady* (1943), based on Cole Porter's 1939 Broadway
musical. Ralph wrote the lyrics for three numbers: the title song and "Madame, I Like Your Crepes Suzettes" with Burton Lane and "I Love an Esquire
Girl" with Roger Edens. Although Ralph's lyrics did not evoke vintage Porter,
they captured one aspect of his style: the incongruous rhyme: "work of art"
/ "a la carte" ("Madame, I Like Your Crepes Suzettes"). Porter, of course, remains the indisputable master of the incongruous. Who else would rhyme
"sassy air" with "brassiere" ("I Jupiter, I Rex" in *Out of This World* [1951])?
Only two of Porter's songs from *Du Barry Was a Lady* made it into the movie: "Do I Love You?" and a laundered "Katie Went to Haiti." Gone were the
references to Katie's trade ("Practically all Haiti had Katie."). It was obvious
that the delectably bawdy "But in the Morning, No" would never make the
cut. It was a question and answer duet with Madame du Barry asking Louis
XV, among other things, if he uses the breaststroke, does double entry, and
likes third parties, to which he replies in the affirmative—"But in the morning, no." The finale, "Friendship," was interpolated from Porter's Broadway
show, *Anything Goes* (1934). At least a glimmer of Porter peeked through the
1943 MGM film.

Ralph may not have been a poet, but he was a superb craftsman. For the
Esther Williams–Van Johnson musical, *Thrill of a Romance* (1945), he wrote
"Please Don't Say No" with Sammy Fain.

The lines are of varying length, and there is no fixed meter. The rhyme scheme is unobtrusive, unlike Arthur's in "Singin' in the Rain." Note what Ralph does in the last two lines of the first stanza: "I've so much love to impart / It's making my heart overflow." There is nothing poetic about "impart," which is, literally, prosaic. Yet Ralph makes it poetic by having "part" rhyme with "heart." In the last line, the singer (in the film, operatic tenor Lauritz Melchior) must take a beat after "heart" to bring out the rhyme, so the song can end quietly with an anapest, "overflow."

Since Ralph wrote songs for a number of MGM films, one might assume that Arthur was responsible for his being hired. Although Arthur wielded great influence at MGM, the studio was not bringing on a movie industry newcomer. Ralph had written lyrics for twenty-nine films between 1932 and 1941 before joining MGM. Two of his best were "When Is a Kiss Not a Kiss" in *Champagne Waltz* and the title song in *Swing High, Swing Low* (both Paramount, 1937). "Swing High, Swing Low," sung by a chorus over the opening credits, has been recorded by Gertrude Niesen, the Ink Spots, Benny Goodman, and Artie Shaw, among others.

Ralph received a better high school education than Arthur, although one would never know it from the standard biographical sources. According to imdb.com, Arthur Freed was educated at Phillips Exeter Academy in Exeter, New Hampshire—a claim seconded by britannica.com, giving the impression that Max and Rosie, like many immigrant parents, wanted their son to have the kind of education they never received. Phillips Exeter archivist Edouard L. Desrochers discovered that Arthur—for some reason still bearing the surname "Fried"—had been enrolled as an upper-middle-class (third-year) student in fall 1911. His grades—Latin, D; English, C; Declamation, C; Math, French, and History, E (failure)—precluded his returning for the spring term, much less graduating from Phillips Exeter.

After the debacle at Phillips Exeter, Arthur returned to Seattle, where he completed his education at Broadway High School on the corner of Broadway and East Pine Street, the first building in Seattle specifically intended for secondary education. Since Broadway High no longer exists, one must assume that he graduated in 1912. That same year, the seventeen-year-old Arthur received his first notice in the *Seattle Daily Times* (May 24, 1912) as a cast member in *Arabian Nights*, a comedy presented by the Alumni Association of Temple De Hirsch, a Reform Jewish synagogue that played a major role in the city's religious and cultural life. As an alumnus, he would have been part of the congregation and perhaps attended the Temple's school. Arthur must have been gratified to read that the show "was well received by a large audience." He enjoyed performing, but songwriting took precedence.

Soon after graduating high school, Arthur set out for Chicago, determined to pursue a career as a songwriter. Chicago's appeal was understandable. Although it had not yet been christened the second city, it was the entertainment capital of middle America. Chicagoans embraced performers like Lillie Langtree, the Barrymores, Maud Adams, Lillian Russell, and Sarah Bernhardt, who responded in kind with return engagements. For the fledgling movie industry, Chicago was a major film distribution center. For Carl Laemmle, an immigrant from Laupheim, Germany, who went on to found the film company that became Universal Pictures, Chicago was the first stop on the road to Hollywood. Laemmle started in exhibition in 1906 with a nickelodeon, the White Front, on Milwaukee Avenue. Needing a piano player, Laemmle hired the thirteen-year-old Sam Katz, a barber's son; after realizing that all that was necessary to enter the nickelodeon business were a storefront, folding chairs, a projector, and film, Katz went the same route. For Katz, too, nickelodeons were just the beginning. He teamed up with the Balaban brothers—the most famous of whom was Barney, who became head of Paramount Pictures— to provide Chicagoans with their first movie palaces that looked like opera houses, where movies were not just accompanied by a piano but by a four-piece orchestra and a pipe organ.

Arthur was in Chicago at the right time. He first found a job as a song plugger in the Chicago office of the music publishing house of Waterman, Berlin, & Snyder. It was there that he met Irving Berlin, whose immigrant background and richly melodious songs resonated so deeply with him that one of his lifelong ambitions, which never came to pass, was to produce an Irving Berlin biopic, *Say It with Music*. Arthur soon realized that, as a song plugger, he would be sitting at the piano on the mezzanine of some department store, playing and singing other people's songs to sell other people's sheet music, while yearning for the day when someone would be doing the same for him. He attracted the attention of Minnie Marx, the mother and driving force behind the Marx Brothers, who had been living in Chicago since 1910. The standard biographies of the Marx Brothers do not mention Arthur, which is not surprising, since it seems that all he did was write special material for their act, in which he also sang. Arthur told the *Los Angeles Times* (June 1, 1946) that after "Mama Marx" heard him sing, she made him an offer: "You sing good, and how would you like to join the act?"

That was in 1916, according to his obituary in the *Hollywood Reporter* (April 13, 1973). Arthur did not remain with the act for long. By summer 1916, he was back in Seattle, where he received his second notice in the *Seattle Daily Times* (June 29, 1916), in which he was listed among the performers in a vaudeville program at the Hippodrome Theatre on Cherry Street.

Arthur was probably in Seattle on May 9, 1917, when his father took his life. One source described Arthur as having "assumed responsibility as the head of the family" after his father's death. On his draft registration form, dated June 5, 1917, Arthur identified himself as "head of the family" and gave as his occupation "fruit grower, self-employed." The Bellevue ranch had apparently become a fruit-producing property. Possibly the 1914 auction marked the end of Max's dabbling in livestock. Arthur was not head of the family for long. On June 15, 1917, two months after the United States entered World War I, he enlisted in the army, as his brother Victor had done earlier. Unlike Victor, Arthur remained stateside, staging military shows.

Victor, who had been a medical student at New York's College of Physicians and Surgeons before entering the service, died in France in 1918.

No one in the Freed family was prepared for what happened on May 9, 1917. That day, the *Oregon Daily Journal* carried a brief news item on the front page with a headline that read: "Max Freed, Seattle, Wealthy, Kills Self":

> Max Freed committed suicide here today by shooting himself in the head.
>
> Freed called his closest friend, Sol Friedenthal, Secretary-Treasurer of the Schwabacher Hardware company, on the telephone and said, "I'm going to kill myself. Meet my wife and son at the dock. They're coming to the city from across the sound." Freed leaves an estate valued at more than $100,000. No cause for his action was given. He leaves a widow, seven sons and a daughter.

The Seattle press was more informative. According to the *Seattle Star* (May 9, 1917), Max made his suicide call at 10:35 a.m., from his office in the Mutual Life Building. He then hung up and shot himself in the head. Friedenthal told reporters that he did not know Freed intimately and wondered why he was the one to receive the call. An evening paper, the *Seattle Daily News* (May 9, 1917), added further details. Intending to kill himself that morning, Max purchased a pistol before he went to his office. He left a note for Rosie, stating only that he was tired of life. The press intimated that the real reason was financial problems, which seems odd. Max had property in Vancouver valued at $50,000. He was able to buy a $50,000 ranch; hence, his $100,000 estate. At the time of his death he was a representative of the Standard Tire and Rubber Company, in whose office he committed suicide. He even had a new venture: making loganberry juice from the loganberries on his property. If, as Max told Rosie in his suicide note, he was tired of living—perhaps implying that he was tired of searching for the ultimate angle that continued to elude him—he may have been another Richard Corey, the man with supposedly everything in Edward Arlington Robinson's eponymous poem, who "one calm summer night /

went home and put a bullet through his head." One can only speculate on the reasons for Max's suicide. "Financial problems" is unsatisfactory; "tired of life" is more plausible. Hamlet, who was much younger than Max, suffered from *taedium vitae*, weariness of life. To Hamlet, life is "an unweeded garden / That grows to seed" (1, 2). Max would have agreed. How many business ventures can a man pursue in his half century on earth—zithers, art, antiques, real estate, furniture, livestock, hardware, fruit growing, and juice making—without feeling the crush of constant striving?

The son who arrived at the dock with his mother on that fateful morning was the seventeen-year-old Sidney. If Max's suicide affected Arthur, it did not result in probing, introspective lyrics. Arthur wrote upbeat songs and produced upbeat musicals. By the time he arrived at MGM, he had buried the past and shaken its dust from his shoes. Max Freed's suicide was absent from his MGM bio.

It also had no effect on Arthur's career plans. Arthur was discharged from the army with the rank of sergeant first class on January 27, 1919. He returned to Chicago for a few months; by May he was back in Seattle. The May 14, 1919, *Seattle Times* gave him an epithet: "Arthur Freed of Seattle fame," who would be introducing "Harold Weeks' latest song hit, A-MI-TI-YA" at the Masonic Wigwam. The "song hit" was forgettable; Harold Weeks was not. According to the *Discography of American Recordings*, between 1918 and 1921, seventeen of Weeks's songs, performed by various artists, had been recorded—eight for RCA Victor, and nine for Columbia Records. "A-MI-TI-YA" was not one of them. Two of his songs, the highly popular "Hindustan" with lyrics by Oliver G. Wallace and "Siren of a Southern Sea," are among the historical recordings in the National Jukebox at the Library of Congress. Arthur was moving in the right circles.

He had also become quotable. The *Seattle Times* (July 20, 1919) reported that during a gig in Vancouver, Arthur enjoyed a breakfast of Canadian eggs and bacon, which he "had not tasted . . . for a long time," meaning since 1907, the year his brother Ralph was born in Vancouver where Max had a furniture store, another short-lived venture that ended when the store burned down.

Nineteen twenty was Arthur's transformative year. First, he was asked to perform at the wedding of the Utah governor's son in the Louis XIV room of the new Washington Hotel, which the *Seattle Times* (February 16, 1920) described as a study in green and white, with "soft greens studded with white flowers." Amid such floral effusion, Arthur serenaded the couple with "At Dawning" and "I Love You, Truly." Three months after being a wedding singer, he was recognized as a songwriter. The *Seattle Times* (May 16, 1920) reported that Arthur and Oliver G. Wallace would be writing songs for "William Rock's Big Revue," scheduled to open that summer at George M. Cohan's Theatre on

West 43rd Street. Arthur and the English-born Wallace met in Chicago after Arthur was discharged; they immediately connected and collaborated on several songs including "Dance It Again with Me" (1919) and "Louisiana" (1920).

Arthur's lyrics are plain spoken and proudly unsophisticated. "Louisiana" is typical, with its images of robins singing, fields of sugarcane, and a first stanza that ends with an imperfect rhyme ("sunshine" / "again"). That Arthur had never been to Louisiana is irrelevant. Bertolt Brecht and Kurt Weill had never been to Alabama, but that did not stop Weill from setting Brecht's "Alabama Song" to music and incorporating it into the opera, *The Rise and Fall of the City of Mahagonny*. Arthur Freed's Louisiana was a state of mind, the idealized past reflected in so much American popular song (e.g., "Swanee River," "Old Kentucky Home," "Sidewalks of New York").

Even before Arthur met Wallace, he had made the acquaintance of William Rock, probably in Chicago in 1916 when Rock was costarring with Maude Fulton in *The Candy Shop*, which they first performed in New York in 1909. Rock, a former vaudevillian, was now a stage performer, who had appeared in the *Ziegfeld Follies of 1916*. He then turned to producing, but his first show, *Let's Go* (1918), only ran three weeks. Still, Rock had not given up. He was so impressed with "Dance It Again with Me" and "Louisiana" that he engaged Arthur and Wallace for *The Big Revue*, renamed *Satins and Silks* when it opened in New York on July 16, 1920. The *New York Times* (July 17, 1920) found the show "pleasing at times." It had a longer run than *Let's Go*: sixty performances. Unfortunately, *Satins and Silks* was Rock's last production. He died two years later.

Arthur and Wallace were not the only contributors to *Satins and Silks*. There were six other composers and seven other lyricists, including Rock. According to the playbill, two of Arthur and Wallace's songs were featured: "That Colored Jazzboray," which spoofed *Macbeth*, and "I've Got a Sentry (On the Beat of My Poor Heart)." At least Arthur could claim to have "gone legit." But he would not be returning to Broadway, except posthumously when his songs were resurrected for the musicals *Big Deal* (1988) and the stage version of *Singin' in the Rain* (1985).

Arthur and Wallace would both end up in Los Angeles but in different capacities. Wallace found a berth at the Walt Disney Studios, scoring numerous cartoons and animated features such as *Dumbo* (1941), for which he shared an Oscar with Frank Churchill, *Cinderella* (1950), and *Alice in Wonderland* (1951). Arthur first visited California when he accompanied Rock to Los Angeles in May 1920, presumably to work with him on his revue, suggesting that, initially, his involvement may have been greater than it turned out to be. Arthur still considered himself a songwriter in need of a composer. He was in the right place. Los Angeles had become the recording center of the West Coast.

Fortune always favored Arthur, bringing him in contact with those who could further his career. First, it was Minnie Marx; then, Oliver G. Wallace and William Rock. In 1921, it was the New Mexican–born Ignacio Herbert Brown, better known as Nacio Herb Brown. Like Arthur, Brown came from a musical family. His mother taught him to play the piano, which sparked his interest in composing. Realizing he needed a day job to pursue his vocation, Brown became a successful tailor with a clientele that included Rudolph Valentino and Charlie Chaplin. Arthur and Brown teamed up, and in 1921 their first song was published, "When Buddha Smiles," which sold a million copies after it was introduced by Paul Whiteman. The lyrics may seem purile and politically incorrect by contemporary standards: "So while [Buddha and Moonman] their watch they keep, / Chinaboy, go sleep." Arthur knew that for the sake of the rhyme, he needed an inversion in the third verse ("their watch they keep"), showing that he was becoming familiar with the tropes of the trade. The lyrics would become more intimate, and the rhymes more intricate. "You Are My Lucky Star" starts off with a six-syllable line: "You are my lucky star / I saw you from afar." Then Arthur expands the third verse to twelve syllables with internal rhyme ("eyes that were gleamin', beamin'"). He does the same in the third line of the second stanza ("heaven's portal," "poor mortal"). Unable to sustain the rhythmic flow, he resorts to a strained comparison, claiming that if God is "a glamourous creature," his lucky star is "a four-star feature." By forcing the rhyme, he has subverted the meaning. Since God lacks glamour, the "you" has lost her four-star rating.

In 1923, he scored a hit with "I Cried for You (Now it's your turn to cry over me)," which he composed with Abe Lyman, with lyrics by Gus Arnheim. The song was atypical of Arthur, who was more of a lyricist than a composer. "I Cried for You" has been recorded by such artists as Mildred Bailey, Kate Smith, Billie Holiday, and Sarah Vaughan. Judy Garland sang it in *Babes in Arms* (1939); Helen Forrest in *Bathing Beauty* (1944); Frank Sinatra in *The Joker Is Wild* (1957); and Diana Ross as Billie Holiday in *Lady Sings the Blues* (1972). It was also in 1923 that he married Renée Klein, a California native of German descent and a woman of striking beauty.

Arthur's life was not without scandal. One made the press during his lifetime; the other was revealed eighteen years after his death by America's favorite child star. The *Los Angeles Examiner* (August 15, 1955) reported that Mary Norris lodged a paternity suit against Arthur, alleging that he was the father of her daughter. Norris, a would-be actress, had become so bothersome that Arthur claimed that he paid her $14,000 "to let me alone." How the matter was resolved is unknown. MGM had its own way of covering up indiscretions. Publicity director Howard Strickling set up a network of informers in the police department who helped him keep career-damaging stories out of the papers. In her autobiography, *Child Star*, Shirley Temple recalled how she signed with MGM in 1941 after her Twentieth Century–Fox contract was not renewed. She was eleven at the time, and no longer a wunderkind. Her last Fox films, *Young People* and *The Blue Bird* (both 1940)—the latter, the studio's answer to *The Wizard of Oz*—performed poorly at the box office. Arthur explained how he could turn her into a musical comedy star and teach her to belt a song; in short, make her into another Judy Garland, who was then under contract at the studio. He then said, "I have something made for just you." Thereupon he opened his fly and exposed himself. The sight of his organ made Temple laugh, enraging Arthur, who threw her out of his office. Since Temple had already signed her contract, he could not punish her for failing to appreciate his endowment. But MGM proved to be a dead end. Temple made only one film for the studio, *Kathleen* (1941). Then she made the rounds: United Artists, Columbia, Warner Bros., and RKO. In 1948, Temple returned to her old studio, Twentieth Century–Fox, for *Mr. Belvedere Goes to College* (1949). She made a few more movies and then retired from the screen in 1949.

Arthur Freed was neither a sexual predator nor a pedophile; Temple had turned him momentarily into a dirty old man. He would never have behaved that way with Judy Garland, whom he worshipped. Even when she was a girl, Judy had a woman's voice. It was the voice and its owner that interested him. Temple had a kid's voice and a kid's demeanor that made her Daddy's Little Girl. She was a father's dream child. Few dads dreamed about Judy, whose voice seemed to come out of a body that was hers on loan; the best was yet to come. What the incident suggests is that Arthur Freed, like so many producers, wanted to be a star maker. He did not create stars; he couldn't because he was not a production head. The MGM stars were not Arthur Freed creations; they were studio contract players, whose image had been created before they appeared in an Arthur Freed film. He may have wanted to elevate Shirley Temple from child star to movie star by asserting his manhood, saying, in effect, "Me, Tarzan, You Jane." Each survived the experience, and Temple got a juicy tidbit for her autobiography.

Despite his indiscretions, Arthur loved Renée, even naming an orchid after her. He was also a devoted father to their only child, Barbara, who was born in 1924, a year that marked his venture into theatrical production with mixed results. He took over the old Walker Theatre in downtown Los Angeles, renaming it the Orange Grove, where he had limited success as a producer of musicals and straight plays, including Eugene O'Neill's *Desire under the Elms*, which was hardly mainstream entertainment. But Arthur Freed was in the right city at the right time. The movies would soon begin to talk, and the musicals he produced would be for the screen.

ALL TALKING, ALL SINGING, ALL DANCING, ALL EVERYTHING

In 1925, Sam Warner convinced his brothers Jack and Harry that the Vitaphone sound-on-disk system, in which sound recorded on 16-inch, 33 1/3 rpm disks is synchronized with the celluloid image, would prove a boon to their company, soon to be known as Warner Bros.–First National, and then simply as Warner Bros. Vitaphone was also a reasonable substitute for exhibitors unable to afford a pianist or an organist to provide musical accompaniment for their films, then silent (but not for long). Most important, Vitaphone was a vast improvement over the Edison Corporation's Kinetophone, an earlier sound-on-disk format beset with problems such as poor amplification, broken film, and groove-skipping needles. If synchronization was lost, anyone watching Enrico Caruso performing an excerpt from *Pagliacci* would question the tenor's stellar reputation.

Once the brothers Warner were in agreement, they knew they were inaugurating a new era. On Thursday evening, August 6, 1926, their first Vitaphone production, *Don Juan*, opened in New York at the Warners' Theatre. It was a gala affair; the New York Philharmonic played the overture to Wagner's *Tannhaüser*, followed by a series of eight musical shorts including Metropolitan Opera tenor Giovanni Martinelli singing "Vesti la giubba" from *Pagliacci*. The *New York Times* (August 7, 1926) was ecstatic: "Nothing like it had ever been heard in a motion picture theatre, and the invited gathering burst into applause such as is seldom heard in any place of amusement." Violinist Mischa Elman played Dvorak's "Humoresque" with "every note that came to one's ears synchronized with the gliding bow and the movements of the musician's fingers." When soprano Marion Talley sang "Caro nome" from Verdi's *Rigoletto*, "one heard her as if from a front seat in the Metropolitan Opera."

The revelation was the film itself with swords clashing, bells tolling, and lips kissing. This was the first time osculation was audible. And as the title character, John Barrymore, "lithe as ever," conjured up memories of Rudolph Valentino in his love scenes with Mary Astor as Adriana della Varnese.

But the talkies were really launched when *The Jazz Singer* premiered at the same theater on October 6, 1927. There were eight sequences with synchronized sound—ambient, spoken, and sung. The main attraction was Al Jolson, one of America's great showmen, as a cantor's son more interested in a career in show business than following in his father's footsteps. Musical numbers included "Blue Skies," "Mother of Mine, I Still Have You," a poignant "Kol Nidre" for his father, and the climactic "My Mammy." *New York Times* critic Mordaunt Hall (October 7, 1927) was even more impressed by *The Jazz Singer* than he was by *Don Juan*: "Not since [*Don Juan*] . . . more than a year ago at the same playhouse, has anything like the ovation been heard in a motion picture theatre."

The success of *The Jazz Singer* did not escape the attention of MGM mogul Louis B. Mayer, who loved musicals and always made a point of seeing the latest ones on his visits to New York. With the coming of sound, Mayer wanted to push MGM into the forefront of the movie musical. So did MGM's production head, Irving Thalberg, who had heard some of Arthur and Brown's songs at the Orange Grove. By 1929, the team was part of the MGM family. They differed from other songwriting teams like Rodgers and Hart and Rodgers and Hammerstein. Larry Hart would only write the lyrics after Richard Rodgers composed the music. When Rodgers teamed up with Oscar Hammerstein II, it was the opposite: Hammerstein, who rightly considered himself a poet, wrote the lyrics first, which Rodgers then set to music. Arthur and Brown, on the other hand, started with a title, for which Brown provided a musical setting; and Arthur, the lyrics. They wrote most of the songs—"You're My Everything" being the best known—for MGM's first sound musical, *The Broadway Melody* (1929), a backstage romance in which the leading man in a revue is engaged to one member of a sister act but attracted to the other. It was not an upbeat movie; neither sister finds the fame she hoped for. But at least it avoided the "star is born" cliché.

The Broadway Melody was only nominally a musical; it was really a backstage woman's film, derived from an original story by Edmund Goulding, who went on to become a director of woman's films—notably the Bette Davis vehicles, *That Certain Woman* (1937), *Dark Victory* (1939), and *The Great Lie* (1941). Despite the upbeat title song proclaiming that "Broadway always wears a smile" and that "no skies are grey on the Great White Way," there was little humor in *The Broadway Melody*, unless one found a stuttering agent, an alcoholic, and a prissy costume designer funny and could pick up on the homophobic reference to his costumes looking better in lavender.

The Broadway Melody suffered from the same faults as many early talkies: slow pacing, tinny sound, minimal fluidity, and reaction close-ups that harked back to the exaggerated look of apprehension that the less accomplished silent stars affected. Originally intended as a partial talkie, *The Broadway Melody*, under production head Irving Thalberg's supervision, "blossomed into the studio's first full-length talking picture." MGM was taking no chances; as a carryover from the silents, intertitles were added to indicate a change of location for moviegoers who had not yet transitioned out of the silent era. That the scene had changed from a music publishing house to "a theatrical hotel on W. 46th St., New York" is evident when a bellhop accompanies the sisters, Hank (Bessie Love) and Queenie (Anita Page), to their room. The title, "The birthday party at the girls' apartment," is similarly redundant, since the gathering, complete with a cake, could not have been anything else. The intertitles slowed down the narrative as a title was followed by a fade-in and a new scene. In a theater, it would have been like watching the curtain descend after a scene within an act, followed by a pause, after which the curtain would rise on a different set.

For all its implausibility, *The Broadway Melody* was a $4 million hit for MGM. The story would only make sense to those who believed that a mediocre sister act could end up in a *Ziegfeld Follies*–type revue; and that a songwriter (Charles King) could be cast in a leading role. Neither sister has much talent. Hank is the business manager, using Queenie of the virginal countenance to get the bookings. One must accept on faith the fact that Queenie became the toast of Broadway by standing semiclad (the film is decidedly pre-Code) on the prow of a ship. When Hank and Queenie finally unveil their act in the *Follies*, it is a tired routine that might have wowed them in the boondocks, but only made it to Broadway because of Queenie's dewy-eyed, if vapid, look of innocence that could still attract men on the lookout for farmfresh variety, not wilted produce.

Hank's devotion to her sister may seem mildly lesbianic. Although their kissing scenes suggest something other than sisterly affection, Hank is really the opposite of the mother unwilling to sever the silver cord; Hank is determined to reattach it, so that she and Queenie will be inseparable. If there is such a phenomenon as a "stage sister," Hank is the prime example. Yet the sisters cannot go big time because they cannot move beyond vaudeville, where their act might score with the locals, but not with discerning audiences. Queenie at least opts for marriage as a way out of one-night bookings on the vaudeville circuit; Hank, a trouper to the end, goes on the road as part of another sister act, doing the same routines that she did with Queenie. Still the dreamer, Hank promises her new partner that the next stop will be the Great White Way.

The Broadway Melody is significant for reasons other than its deglamorization of show business. First, the dancers were photographed in full shot, so that it was evident they were doing their own numbers. The full-shot dance sequence became a convention of subsequent musicals. Second, the film introduced what has since been known as "playback." When Thalberg saw the rushes of "The Wedding of the Painted Doll" sequence, he found it stagey. Since the film was already over budget, Douglas Shearer, Thalberg's brother-in-law and a recording engineer at MGM who became a pioneer in sound technology, suggested that the cast repeat the number more enthusiastically, with the previously recorded music played back on loudspeakers. Thus the practice of playback was born, with a prerecorded sound track that could be danced or sung to—the latter much trickier, since it required perfect coordination of mouth and lyric.

In *The Broadway Melody*, the numbers either advanced the plot or functioned as interludes. "You Were Meant for Me" was Eddie's declaration of love to Queenie, anticipating the love songs of later musicals that were the equivalent of sung dialogue. If the songs became standards, like "You Were Meant for Me," the context did not matter; the lyrics made sense on their own. *The Broadway Melody*, which won an Oscar for Best Picture, is a relic, but worth seeing both for itself and its pre-Code conventions. Morals are loose, décolletage is peek-a-boo cleavage, and lingerie is more exciting than outerwear. This was Hollywood before the Grinch—better known as the Hays Office, later the Breen Office, and the National Legion of Decency—hijacked it, purporting to read the minds of moviegoers who were apparently anti-cleavage and pro-twin beds for married couples. The loudmouths won; the others simply enjoyed the vicarious experience of a foreign but enviable lifestyle that would soon recede into subtext.

That same year, MGM released another sound movie, this time a revue—*The Hollywood Revue of 1929*, in which Arthur and Brown were represented by two of their best-known songs: "Singin' in the Rain" and a reprise of "You Were Meant for Me," lip-synched by Conrad Nagel to the voice of Charles King. Other collaborations followed: "Pagan Love Song" in *The Pagan* and "Should I?" in *Lord Byron on Broadway* (both 1929). Arthur shared story credit with Dale Van Every for *Those Three French Girls* (1930), which starred Fifi D'Orsay, who, to generations of moviegoers, personified the saucy French coquette, even though she was Canadian born.

The closest MGM came in the 1930s to the equivalent of the "book musical" were the eight Jeanette MacDonald–Nelson Eddy operettas (1935–1942) and *The Firefly* (1937), with MacDonald and Allan Jones. The last MacDonald-Eddy pairing, *I Married an Angel* (1942), had the airiness of operetta, although it derived from the Richard Rodgers and Larry Hart musical of the same name that opened on Broadway in May 1938. The movie was even sillier than the play. To prevent true believers, especially angelologists, from being offended, the hero (Eddy) only *dreams* he married an angel (MacDonald) and tries to find a way to make her less angelic. MacDonald, a lyric soprano with an almost three-octave range, also had a flair for the risqué, reacting to double entendres with virginal innocence. In *One Hour with You* (Paramount, 1932)—usually attributed to Ernst Lubitsch, although George Cukor "insisted [he] was the actual director"—Maurice Chevalier and MacDonald play a couple who keep their marriage alive by behaving like lovers. Embracing on a park bench, they are interrupted by a gendarme who informs them that they cannot make love there. Chevalier replies, "I can make love anywhere," and MacDonald heartily agrees. In the next scene, after Chevalier and MacDonald retire to their bedroom, Chevalier comes out, speaking directly to the audience: "I know what you think," but then adds that they are married and goes back in.

Thalberg was eager to add MacDonald to the MGM galaxy; so was Louis B. Mayer, for reasons both professional and personal. He was fascinated by MacDonald, as he was by any actress of "great style, presence, and reserve." Since MacDonald was then involved with her agent, Bob Richie, she had no time for Mayer, although she did sing "Ah, Sweet Mystery of Life" from *Naughty Marietta* at his 1957 funeral. MacDonald's tenure at MGM was free of double entendre. There would be no scenes like the one in *One Hour with You*, in which she and Chevalier are conversing in bed as Chevalier keeps turning off the light, while the demure MacDonald is continuing the conversation.

Her first MGM operetta, *The Cat and the Fiddle* (1934), was an adaptation of Jerome Kern and Otto A. Harbach's 1931 Broadway show of the same name. MacDonald was really the star, although Ramon Novarro, whose MGM contract was about to end and would not be renewed, was billed first. The film is significant for two reasons, first of which is the finale, photographed in three-strip Technicolor, with MacDonald, her hair fiery red, and an overly made-up Navarro singing "I Watch the Love Parade"; and second, the score, which came to the screen intact with some of the songs reassigned and included such favorites as "The Night Was Made for Love," which MacDonald sang exquisitely; and "She Didn't Say 'Yes' (She Didn't Say 'No')," a mildly suggestive "Will she or won't she?" number, which MacDonald clearly enjoyed singing. Although the original lasted for 395 performances on Broadway and enjoyed a successful London run, the film, despite favorable reviews, did not catch on with the public. MGM, however, must have been impressed by the way MacDonald looked in the Technicolor sequence. The studio's first three-strip Technicolor feature was *Sweethearts* (1938), Victor Herbert's operetta with some of the music but none of the book, as a vehicle for MacDonald and her favorite leading man, Nelson Eddy.

Another disappointment for MGM was *The Merry Widow* (1934), budgeted at $1.605 million and grossing only $861,000 domestically but performing somewhat better internationally. *The Merry Widow*'s mix of charm, sophistication, and cynicism was not the confection that audiences expected. As directed by Ernst Lubitsch, known for his smudge-free touch, the film is visually opulent and musically sublime. The black-and-white photography by Oliver T. Marsh evokes a Vienna *Konditorei* with dark chocolate, glazed cake, and *café mit schlag*. The widow's mansion resembles a tiered wedding cake; her boudoir, a pastry shell with cream-colored walls. When MacDonald appears in a black negligee, the stunning black-and-white contrast is palette enough. Then there is Franz Lehár's music, particularly "Vilia," which Mac-Donald sings as if she were spinning silver.

Thalberg had not given up. He was convinced there was an audience for operetta, not as subtly decadent as *The Merry Widow*, perhaps, but more accessible with the standard features of the genre: disguise, deception, romantic complications, and the occasional surmounting of class barriers. The end can be tragic with the hero dying in a duel (*Bitter Sweet* [1940]), or the lovers can be reunited in the hereafter where they stroll down a blossom-strewn path (*Maytime* [1937]). Death is no deterrent if the music provides the catharsis.

For an operetta cycle to work, MacDonald needed a leading man, and Mayer wisely chose Nelson Eddy, who had been under contract for two years and had a strong baritone voice that could have led to a career in opera. The first of their films was Victor Herbert's *Naughty Marietta* (1935), in which they both were ideally cast: MacDonald as a French princess, who flees an arranged marriage by joining a group of young women en route to New Orleans as prospective wives; Eddy as Captain Dick Warrington, the leader of a troop of mercenaries, who save the women from pirates, thus bringing him in contact with the disguised princess. Sparks fly between them, with Eddy getting a chance to show off his impressive baritone in the lusty anthem, "Tramp! Tramp! Tramp!" and the romantic "'Neath the Southern Moon," with which he serenades MacDonald. Eddy was never as impressive as he was as Warrington. Far from slim, he was not heavy set, singing with ease and assurance and projecting a masculinity that was more bravado than threat. The denouement is ridiculous, however. Defying class strictures, the princess and the mercenary are last seen supposedly on their way to California, singing, "Ah, Sweet Mystery of Life," with Warrington's men chanting, "Tramp! Tramp! Tramp!" in counterpoint.

The plot, considerably simplified from the original, is so hole-riddled that you reach a point at which you realize MacDonald and Eddy are so committed to their characters that you go along with the nonsense. The princess claims to have a special song that she will sing for Warrington at the ball, after which she must return to France. When the guests ask her for a song (her reputation has preceded her), she sings "Ah, Sweet Mystery of Life" on the staircase, resplendent in a white gown and a cotton-candy wig. Warrington stands at the foot of the stairs (how he knows the lyrics is never explained), so their voices can blend in a glorious duet, after which they run off and are last seen heading West. But this is operetta, in which anything is possible. And the public bought it. *Naughty Marietta* cost $782,000 and made $2.057 million at a time when the Great Depression was far from over.

Even more popular with audiences was *Rose Marie* (1936), which bore only the slightest resemblance to its source, the Rudolph Friml and Herbert Stroth-art operetta, *Rose-Marie* (1924), with book and lyrics by Otto A. Harbach and Oscar Hammerstein II. With Jeanette MacDonald in the lead, her character could no longer be an ordinary French Canadian in love with a miner, but an opera star, Marie de Flor, who eventually falls for a mountie, Captain Bruce (Nelson Eddy). Most of the score was eliminated, and the book was radically altered by Frances Goodrich and Albert Hackett, who made Rose-Marie's brother in the original an escaped convict. With James Stewart as the brother, revealing the underside of his genial persona on which Anthony Mann capitalized in a series of psychological westerns in the 1950s, *Rose Marie* (unhyphenated) is far more realistic than Friml and Strothart's creation. The revision also allowed MacDonald to do some acting; Marie is torn between love for her brother and an overwhelming desire to help him, and her attraction to Captain Bruce, who is determined to bring him in. Goodrich and Hackett had the difficult task of keeping the romance between Marie and Captain Bruce from deteriorating after the brother's capture. They found an easy solution: one final reprise of the most popular song in the movie, "The Indian Love Call."

The melody and lyrics are hypnotic. The song itself has a dreamlike effect, as if one were hearing it in an echo chamber: "When I'm calling you / Oo-Oo-Oo-Oo, Oo-Oo-Oo-Oo." When one lover begins the call, the other is inspired to reply, so that whatever separates them dissolves away as they yield to its spell. At the end, Marie starts the call, Bruce takes it up, and their voices unite. True love trumps fraternal devotion, which is no longer an impediment after the brother disappears from the plot. The love call is a unifier and an anodyne, bringing the lovers back together and banishing thoughts of the brother, who has been dropped in the discard bin of used-up plot devices.

MGM thought it had a cure for Depression blues: Jeanette and Nelson, who would waft you away for a couple of hours to the far side of paradise. It did not last long. By 1940, the similarity of the plots affected the box office. *New Moon* (1940) cost $1.487 million and grossed $1.290 million domestically. World War II also made operetta seem frivolous. By 1942, with *I Married an Angel*, their tenure as a screen team had ended.

In 1935, the year the MacDonald-Eddy operetta cycle began, Arthur Freed had not yet ascended to the producer's suite; that would happen five years later. Until then, he and Nacio Herb Brown kept turning out songs for MGM movies. For *Hold Your Man* (1933), they composed the title song, performed by Jean Harlow; for *Sadie McKee* (1934), "All I Do Is Dream of You," "I Looked in Your Eyes," "I'm Willing," and "Temptation," the last heard the year before in *Going Hollywood* (1933), sung by Bing Crosby in his characteristically laid-back style without any hint of danger. *Going Hollywood* also featured five new Brown and Freed songs, including the title song played during the opening credits and later sung by Crosby. One would have thought that in the Marx Brothers classic, *A Night at the Opera* (1935), excerpts from Verdi's *Il Trovatore* would have sufficed, yet they came up with a duet for Kitty Carlisle and Allan Jones, "Alone," which Harpo later played on his instrument of choice. Although *San Francisco* (1936) is primarily remembered for the famous earthquake sequence, the team provided Jeanette MacDonald with the classic "Would You?": "He holds her in his arms / Would you, would you?" It was a simple lyric that Brown turned into a waltz-like melody that MacDonald sang wistfully, as did Debbie Reynolds (or rather, Betty Noyes, who dubbed her voice) in *Singin' in the Rain* (1952), which was practically a Brown-Freed retrospective with no less than thirteen of their songs, along with one that Arthur had written with Al Hoffman and Al Goodhart, "Fit as a Fiddle," for the revue, *George White's Music Hall Varieties* (1932).

Arthur Freed had become ubiquitous, and his career was in the ascendant. He stood in awe of Louis B. Mayer, who saw in him not just an acolyte but someone who could revolutionize the movie musical. By 1933, Arthur was breakfasting with Mayer at his Bel Air home. The following year, he had become influential enough to bring pianist and arranger Roger Edens to MGM, launching Edens's Hollywood career, which spanned forty-five years. Edens was Judy Garland's best arranger, and according to Judy's daughter, Lorna Luft, "a second father" to her mother. For *Broadway Melody of 1938* (1937), Edens wrote the words to Judy's love letter to Clark Gable, "Dear Mr. Gable," which led into the James V. Monaco–Joseph McCarthy ballad, "You Made Me Love You," delivered with such unfeigned emotion that it was obvious that within this teenager there was a torch singer waiting to break loose.

Although Luft wrote that her mother could be homophobic at times, Judy did not seem to care that Edens was gay: "[Edens] came into [Judy's] life when she was only thirteen and remained in it until the day she died. . . . After my grandfather died, Roger was the only person in my mother's life that Mama completely trusted. . . . Small wonder, then, that to my mother, some gay men became symbols of love and trust."

Edens knew that Judy was a unique talent. For *Every Sunday* (1936), the musical short that launched her career, he wrote "Americana." For *Everybody Sing* (1938), Edens composed "Ever Since the World Began / Shall I Sing a Melody?" for her. Arthur felt similarly about Judy. For *Thoroughbreds Don't Cry* (1937), he and Brown wrote "Got a Pair of New Shoes," which Judy sang several times in the movie, first during the opening credits. Judy Garland was STAR from the very beginning; Arthur Freed and Roger Edens just increased the font size.

Broadway Melody of 1936 (1935) and particularly *Broadway Melody of 1938* (1937) convinced Mayer that Arthur Freed was not just another songwriter. In the former, two Brown and Freed songs were reprised ("All I Do Is Dream of You" in French, "Broadway Melody"), and five new ones were introduced: "Broadway Rhythm"; "You Are My Lucky Star," played on piano by Edens, sung by Frances Langford, and danced by Eleanor Powell; "I've Got a Feelin' You're Foolin'"; "Sing before Breakfast"; and "On a Sunday Afternoon." *Broadway Melody of 1938* was another mix of the old ("Broadway Melody," "Broadway Rhythm," "You Are My Lucky Star," "Got a Pair of New Shoes") and the new ("Your Broadway and My Broadway," "Follow in My Footsteps," "Yours and Mine," "Everybody Sing," and "I'm Feelin' Like a Million").

In 1938, Arthur felt confident enough to approach Mayer about becoming a producer, first by suggesting that Judy be given the star treatment after the great success of *Broadway Melody of 1938*. When Mayer told him to find a film for her, Arthur Freed entered the producers' circle. He felt L. Frank Baum's *The Wizard of Oz* (1900) would be the perfect vehicle for Judy, who was then pushing sixteen and could play Dorothy Gale if the character, who is nine in the novel, was rewritten as a teenager. Hugh Fordin has documented Arthur's involvement in the film in *The World of Entertainment! Hollywood's Greatest Musicals* (reissued as *M-G-M's Greatest Musicals: The Arthur Freed Unit*). In short, Arthur Freed, along with many others, was part of *The Wizard of Oz* team from its inception in February 1938 to its first preview on July 18, 1939. He made casting suggestions: Ray Bolger and Buddy Ebsen as the Tin Man and the Scarecrow, respectively, although their roles were later reversed, with Jack Haley replacing Ebsen, who had a violent reaction to the makeup. Arthur would have preferred W. C. Fields as the Wizard. When Fields declined, despite an offer of $150,000, Frank Morgan assumed the role. Casting Bert Lahr as the Cowardly Lion was E. Y. "Yip" Harburg's idea. Since Harburg had written the lyrics for two of Lahr's revues, *Life Begins at 8:40* (1934) and *The Show Is On* (1936), he knew Lahr would be the perfect Cowardly Lion. Harburg and Harold Arlen were entrusted with the score, which included what became Judy's signature song, "Over the Rainbow." Directors kept changing—Norman

Taurog, Richard Thorpe, George Cukor for two days, and finally Victor Flem-
ing, who had to move on to *Gone with the Wind*, leaving King Vidor to shoot
the Kansas sequences that begin and end the film.

No one at MGM quite knew how audiences would react to the movie version of a beloved classic, especially with a song like "Over the Rainbow," which
seemed more of an adult's yearning for a lost world than an adolescent's
dreaming of an earthly paradise. When *The Wizard of Oz* was first previewed,
audience response to "The Jitterbug" and "Over the Rainbow" was tepid. Arthur had no love for "The Jitterbug," which has been reinstated in the stage
version that is frequently performed around Christmastime. But "Over the
Rainbow" was special to him; it conjured up the same nostalgic mood that
made "You Are My Lucky Star" and "You Were Meant for Me" such favorites.
It may also have evoked the kind of world he imagined as a child when his
father was constantly changing jobs and residences. He fought for the song,
even threatening to leave the studio if it was cut. In fact, he was the one who
suggested to Harold Arlen that a song was needed "as a transition from Kansas to Oz." That song became "Over the Rainbow," which, in Arlen's first version, was, as Yip Harburg complained, "full of crescendos" and unsuited to his
lyrics. Arlen reorchestrated the song, making it a meditation and providing
Judy with the encore that fans expected at her concerts, always delivered with
great poignancy, if not always with richness of tone.

Arthur's notes on the first draft screenplay reflect an awareness that a visual medium like film calls for a "minimum amount of dialogue" and a carefully
planned "rhythm," especially in a movie conceived as a musical even though
a final decision had not been made about the composer and lyricist. (Jerome
Kern, Nacio Herb Brown, Harold Arlen; and Ira Gershwin, Dorothy Fields,
and Yip Harburg were under consideration.) There is by no means a "minimum amount of dialogue" in *The Wizard of Oz*. As Tom Dirks has shown in
his exhaustive scene-by-scene summary, there is a great deal of dialogue in
the film. Since the first full-length movie version of Baum's novel was a 1925
silent film; one could easily imagine a nonmusical *Wizard of Oz* with the right
combination of story and special effects. Freed did not succeed in minimizing the dialogue, which became didactic when it was time to spell out the
moral: We have the power within ourselves to achieve what we want when
circumstances arise to make it possible. By coming to Dorothy's aid when
she was imprisoned in the Witch of the West's castle, the Scarecrow proves he
has a brain; the Tin Man, a heart; and the Cowardly Lion, courage, none of
which each originally thought he possessed. If the film has such a strong appeal to young audiences, it is because it preaches the gospel of empowerment
for adolescents lacking in self-esteem, beset with anxiety, and misunderstood
by their elders.

The Wizard of Oz is nominally a musical, yet a good deal of plot transpires before there is even a song. It begins like a play (it had been dramatized), with Dorothy (Judy) making an entrance and complaining to her indifferent uncle and aunt that their neighbor Miss Gulch (Margaret Hamilton) mistreated her terrier, Toto. When she repeats the same story to two farmhands, Hunk (Ray Bolger) and Zeke (Bert Lahr), Hunk rebukes her for not having enough "brains" to let Toto onto Miss Gulch's property; Zeke, that she should have acted more aggressively. Another worker, Hickory (Jack Haley), who fancies himself an inventor, offers no advice. Aunt Em scolds Dorothy, telling her to find "a place where you won't get into any trouble." That place is "over the rainbow." At last a song, or rather *the* song, which is not so much a transition as a cue. If Arthur Freed was thinking of an integrated musical, in which the songs would fill in when the characters stopped speaking, The Wizard of Oz was a modest beginning.

"Over the Rainbow" became a standard that could be sung out of context—in a cabaret act, at a pop concert, or at a Harold Arlen tribute. The same could not be said of the other songs. Even before there is any more singing, another package of plot arrives. Fearing Miss Gulch will do violence to Toto, Dorothy leaves home with the terrier and encounters Professor Marvel (Frank Morgan), who may actually be clairvoyant, and persuades her to return home, just as a tornado is about to hit. Knocked unconscious, Dorothy spins away to fantasyland.

The first quarter of The Wizard of Oz is a model of construction in which setting, theme, and character are established within the first ten minutes. The main characters are introduced naturally, all of whom, except for Dorothy's aunt and uncle, take on other identities in the Land of Oz, the way familiar figures do in a dream where they appear in altered or transmogrified form: Hunk, the brainless Scarecrow; Zeke, the Cowardly Lion; Hickory, the (literally) heartless Tin Man; Miss Gulch, the Wicked Witch of the West; and Professor Marvel, the Wizard. Now one can appreciate the irony of Hunk criticizing Dorothy for not using her "brains" and Zeke for not standing up to Miss Gulch. Only Dorothy and Toto remain the same externally, although Dorothy undergoes a spiritual transformation that leaves her with a deeper appreciation of home and family.

One waits in vain for another "Over the Rainbow." Of course, a reprise at the end when Dorothy realizes there's no place like home would have muddied the message. Oz exists in the Technicolor world of the imagination; Kansas, in sepia tone, reddish brown like the earth. The decision to photograph Kansas in sepia, and Oz in color, was not arbitrary. It was a visual distinction between reality and fantasy. Dorothy started in sepia, landed in a world awash in color, and returned to sepia, coming full circle from a place where people make their living off the land to one "way above the chimney tops" and back to the good earth again. Having awakened from a dream in which adventure and peril overlap, Dorothy has a renewed appreciation for the familiar, which she had previously taken for granted.

The Oz sequences are rich in color and rife with drama, but musically thin. Dorothy does not have another solo, although one longs for something comparable to "Over the Rainbow." Upon her arrival in Oz, she is greeted as savior by the Munchkins after the house that was swept up by the tornado landed on the Witch of the East. Glinda, the good Witch of the North, reminds Dorothy to take the Witch of the East's ruby slippers, which later are found to have magical properties. The Munchkins sing "Ding Dong, the Witch Is Dead," which is difficult to perform out of context, except on occasions when a particularly loathsome person has passed on. To find her way back to Kansas, Dorothy must consult the Wizard, prompting the Munchkins to sing "You're Off to See the Wizard," a bouncing number that expresses musically what is already known. When Dorothy encounters the Scarecrow, the Tin Man, and the Cowardly Lion, each expresses his desire for a brain, a heart, and courage, respectively, in the same music but with different lyrics ("If I Only Had a Brain," "If I Only Had a Heart," "If I Only Had the Nerve"). That's pretty much the extent of the singing, except for chants, choruses, and Lahr's hysterical "If I Were King of the Forest" with its goofy rhymes ("elephant" / "cellophant").

For all the music in which the film abounds, including bits of Schumann, Mussoursky, and Mendelssohn, *The Wizard of Oz* is a one-song movie with a remarkable screenplay by many hands that is extraordinary in its blending of individual efforts into a seamless unity. But is it a musical in which song and dance advance the plot? The American Film Institute (AFI) thought so, ranking *Wizard* third among the twenty-five greatest musicals after *Singin' in the Rain* and *West Side Story*. There is no argument about the first two, but *The Wizard of Oz*, beloved though it be, is an elaborately plotted fantasy with music, in which the screenplay is more satisfying than the score.

Although Arthur Freed deserved the title of associate producer for his contributions to *The Wizard of Oz*, his name does not appear in the credits. Even when the film incurred a $1.1 million loss in its initial release, Mayer did not tell him to go back to writing songs; instead, he put him in charge of his own unit "for no good reason other than he had a hunch." The hunch paid off. Like Mayer, Arthur knew how to court talent. As John Waxman, son of the great film composer Franz Waxman, put it: "Freed and Mayer were cut from the same cloth. . . . Hire the best people and leave them alone."

- 3 -

"I WANNA BE A PRODUCER"

Arthur Freed, producer, occupied a corner suite with private bath on the second floor of the four-story art deco Thalberg Building on the MGM lot. An avid art collector, he decorated the walls with paintings by Renoir, Chagall, Rouault, Dufy, and Utrillo. But, as Murray Schumach noted in the *New York Times* (February 16, 1964), it was still a working office with a piano and a desk piled with books, manuscripts, and scores. That was Arthur Freed's public self, his creative self. But to others he was a vulgarian with dirty fingernails who mispronounced words, spewed food while talking, and was, in short, "a slob," according to award-winning costume designer Irene Sharaff. He may have been ill mannered, but he knew talent when he saw it. And he also knew that the way to cultivate it was not by micromanaging.

He became a full-fledged producer with *Babes in Arms* (1939), which is hardly the film by which any producer would want to be remembered, despite its spectacular performance at the box office; budgeted at $748,000, it brought in $3.335 million when first released, resulting in a profit of $1.542 million. He had seen the Rodgers and Hart musical, *Babes in Arms*, at some point during the Broadway run in 1937, a year before he became involved in *The Wizard of Oz*. Even before *The Wizard of Oz* wrapped up, Arthur approached Mayer about buying the rights to *Babes in Arms*, which were quite reasonable: $21,000. The show was moderately successful, lasting for 289 performances; it was also impossible to film without a makeover.

Babes in Arms was an unusual musical for Rodgers and Hart, who wrote both the score and the book; the latter was overtly political, as were the two 1930s films for which they composed the scores: *The Phantom President* (Paramount, 1932) and *Hallelujah, I'm a Bum* (United Artists, 1933). The former starred George M. Cohan in the dual role of a banker whom a political machine has put up for president, only to discover that the public finds him a dullard; and his lookalike, a fast-talking medicine man, whom the machine uses to get the votes, planning to ship him off to the Arctic after the election. As it happens, the banker is the one who is packed off to the North Pole with a seal for a companion, while the charlatan takes up residence at 1600

Pennsylvania Avenue. The message was obvious: the country needs a dynamo in the White House, which is exactly what it got in Franklin Delano Roosevelt the following year.

The latter was a vehicle for Al Jolson, speaking in rhyming couplets as the "Mayor of Central Park," an honorific for the kind-hearted head of the park's homeless. *Hallelujah, I'm a Bum* took an unusual view of the Great Depression, celebrating the freedom of life on the road while at the same time depicting the plight of those deprived of life's amenities. Jolson is especially touching in his affection for a young woman (Madge Evans), whom he saves from drowning and then must stand by as she transfers her affections to a real mayor, the mayor of New York (Frank Morgan).

When Rodgers and Hart were working on the stage production of *Babes in Arms* in 1936, they knew they were living in an imperiled world. Civil War had erupted in Spain with the Soviet Union aiding the Loyalists; and Italy and Germany, the Nationalists. The Nazi Party had become Germany's only legal party; Hitler remilitarized the Rhineland; Italy was using poison gas against Ethiopians; the persecution of German Jews had begun, first with legislation denying employment to anyone with a Jewish grandparent; and Japan had withdrawn from the League of Nations after it was censured for its aggression toward China. In the United States, the radio priest, Father Charles E. Coughlin, was preaching anti-Semitism on the air; the Silver Shirts were doing the same at rallies; and the pro-Nazi German American Bund had just come into existence. As Jews, Rodgers and Hart knew they could never write a musical about a world teetering on the brink of war, but they could write one about teenagers banding together as a self-proclaimed army, muting their militarism ("They call us babes in arms / But we are babes in armor") in the best musical comedy tradition of boy and girl and the rough path they must traverse until fortune cooperates so they can "put on a show."

Taking advantage of their parents' absence, the kids produce their own show. Brimming with confidence, they launch into a marching song, in which they declare a "new day" when everyone will hear "a rising war cry." "Youth will arrive," and woe to those who think "they must direct us"; instead, "we'll make them all respect us." In the MGM adaptation, directed by Busby Berkeley, the kids led by Douglas McPhail (who looked every bit of twenty-five) sing the title song marching through the streets with torches, picking up crates as they go along, which they pile up and set on fire. To anyone who recalls the torchlit Nuremberg rallies and the 1933 book burnings in Nazi Germany, the scene can be disquieting. Whether Berkeley intended a parallel or was suggesting how easily enthusiasm can lead to destruction is unclear. Regardless, one would not want to be in the neighborhood when this teenage juggernaut comes barreling through.

Shortly before *Babes in Arms* closed in December 1937, *Pins and Needles*, a pro-labor satirical revue featuring members of the International Ladies Garment Workers Union premiered, poking fun at everything from the German American Bund, Hitler, and Mussolini to anti-Semites, racists, and the Daughters of the American Revolution (DAR). A month earlier, on November 2, 1937, another Rodgers and Hart show, *I'd Rather Be Rich*, arrived starring George M. Cohan as President Roosevelt. Larry Hart and George S. Kaufman's topical book, along with Hart's irreverent lyrics, found humor in the plight of a young couple who cannot marry until the prospective groom is given a raise, which depends upon the president's being able to balance the budget. Unlike the polio-stricken president, Cohan sings and dances and eventually tells the couple that he cannot help them, but encourages them to marry anyway and show their faith in America. Nothing is sacred: the Supreme Court; the Federal Theatre; the WPA; even the president's mother, Sara. The First Lady remained unscathed, except for some gentle ribbing.

I'd Rather Be Rich ended on a genial note, with Cohan delivering a fireside chat in the best FDR tradition. The wittiest number is "Off the Record," which James Cagney brought to the screen in the biopic *Yankee Doodle Dandy* (Warner Bros., 1942). "Off the Record" is essentially the president's catalog of complaints, among which is the White House food: "If Eleanor would stay at home, I'd have a decent meal. / But that's off the record."

If Rodgers and Hart seem to have been politically minded in the 1930s, so was Broadway. In Sidney Kingsley's *Dead End* (1935), a tenement faced a high rise in a cul de sac, a grim reminder of the economic disparity caused by the Great Depression. The Socialist grandfather in Clifford Odets's *Awake and Sing* (1935) urges his grandson to "go out and fight so life shouldn't be printed on dollar bills." Although Leonie in S. N. Behrman's *End of Summer* (1936) leads a privileged existence, she is aware of the gross inequities of unchecked capitalism and is almost grateful for the radicals who vow to reform the system. Lorna Moon in Odets's *Golden Boy* (1937) yearns for "some city where poverty's no shame—where music is no crime!—where there's no war in the streets." In John Howard Lawson's *Marching Song* (1937), disaffected employees cause a citywide power outage, from which arises a coalition of white and black workers. Playwrights were making allusions to fascism, veiled and overt. In *End of Summer*, a radical complains of "house painters and minor journalists" becoming "dictators of great nations," an obvious reference to Hitler and Mussolini. A German Communist in Odets's *Till the Day I Die* (1935) describes his treatment at the hands of the Nazis. Torture leads to "numbness," and "the mind begins to wander." Worst of all, there is "no possible contact with party members." The Party is family for which there is no substitute.

Babes in Arms, the stage musical, was political, but not militant except for the title song, whose lyrics can be disturbing, depending upon the staging. To prove that vaudeville is not dead, a group of old-timers go on tour, leaving their teenage children to fend for themselves. Eager for careers in show business, the kids forego anything as mundane as school and put on a show, hoping it will succeed so they will not be sent to a work farm. Although the show flops, even life on the work farm does not deter them. When a French aviator makes a forced landing on the grounds, the kids use the occasion to stage a variety show, which this time is so successful that they are able to build a youth center, which naturally will become their theater until Broadway beckons.

Since radicals, both Socialists and Communists, had become characters in such plays as Behrman's *Biography* and *End of Summer*; Odets's *Waiting for Lefty*, *Awake and Sing*, *Till the Day I Die*, and *Golden Boy*; and Lillian Hellman's *Days to Come*, Rodgers and Hart thought there was room for at least one in their musical, as well as a Nietszche-quoting adolescent and the son of a southern racist. That was as far as Rodgers and Hart were willing to go. The Communist was played for laughs. He is all in favor of "sharing the wealth" until he wins the Irish sweepstakes. After suffering a financial loss from a bad investment, he goes back to preaching—but not practicing—Marxism.

It was half a century before *Babes in Arms* was performed as written. George Oppenheimer, the noted critic-playwright-screenwriter-publisher, rewrote and depoliticized the book, making it the story of teenagers trying to save a summer theater from demolition. That was the version used until 1988 when the Cincinnati College of Music mounted *Babes in Arms* as Rodgers and Hart had conceived it, minus some of the racial references.

Like Oppenheimer's revision of Rodgers and Hart's book, the movie version of *Babes in Arms* underwent a makeover of a different sort. The kids still put on their show; in fact, they put on two, the first of which is rained out. The work farm is a threat that never comes to pass. There is no Communist firebrand, southern racist, or stranded aviator. However, there is an extended blackface number that today would be problematic for any sensitive viewer, who would find nothing entertaining about the portrayal of African Americans as tar babies on parade—smiling, wide-mouthed, and eye-rolling.

Babes in Arms (1939) was an evisceration of the original, retaining only the plot pivot of teenagers staging their own show while their parents are off trying to drum up interest in a moribund form of entertainment. Yet the film's opening augured well, suggesting a musical that would juxtapose the death of vaudeville with the birth of the talkies, illustrated by clips from MGM's first musicals, *The Broadway Melody* and *The Hollywood Revue of 1929*, both of which contained ample selections from the Arthur Freed song book, as did his production of *Babes in Arms*.

Because of the success of the Andy Hardy movies, Mickey Rooney was touted as the star, dominating the film and leaving little room for Judy Garland, who at least had two decent numbers, "Good Mornin'" and "I Cried for You," both with lyrics by Arthur Freed. Rodgers and Hart's score was winnowed down to two songs: the title song and "Where or When," with "The Lady Is a Tramp" as background music when Rooney is trying to figure out which fork to use while having dinner with June Preisser. Harold Arlen and Yip Harburg contributed the flag-waving finale, "My Country"; Roger Edens, "I Like Opera / I Like Swing" and "Figaro," in which Judy parodied *The Barber of Seville*, while Betty Jaynes sang a bit of the sextet from *Lucia di Lammermoor*; and the nadir, "My Daddy Was a Minstrel Man," a blackface routine with Judy and Mickey as Mr. Tambo and Mr. Bones, end men in a minstrel show who answer the interlocutor's questions with jokes.

Until that point, *Babes in Arms* has been making some sense. Mickey is producing, directing, writing, and starring in a show that seems to be a boy-girl musical (or so the ballad, "Where or When," leads one to suspect); it also includes a takeoff on *Antony and Cleopatra* with Mickey doing imitations of Clark Gable and Lionel Barrymore. But by opening night, the show had become a blackface revue with Mickey and Judy performing Stephen Foster's "De Camptown Races," "Swanee River," and "Oh! Susanna." A hurricane arrives midway in the performance, causing a mass exodus, but fortunately a New York producer is in the audience who gives Mickey a second chance. In record time, Mickey whips up a show called "Babes in Arms," which must have amused its creators, since all that we see of it is "My Country," with music and lyrics not by Rodgers and Hart but by Arlen and Harburg. The number begins with Mickey conducting the orchestra and the cast popping up from the pit, marching up the aisle and back on to the stage with a Capitol building backdrop. "My Country" was particularly relevant; *Babes in Arms* went into release in September 1939, two weeks after Hitler invaded Poland. The audience is urged to "give a hand for your land," where "every man is his own dictator." MGM gets a thumbs up, too: "We've got no Duce, we've got no Führer / But we've got Garbo and Norma Shearer." The sequence ends with Mickey and Judy imitating FDR and Eleanor, with Judy doing the better job in mimicking the First Lady's flutey voice. Perhaps moviegoers needed a "feel good" movie in times that were growing increasingly parlous. *Babes in Arms* would not be shown in France until after V-E Day. It was never shown commercially in Germany, but only on television for the first time in 1995.

Arthur Freed produced three more Mickey and Judy musicals: *Strike Up the Band* (1940), *Babes on Broadway* (1941), and *Girl Crazy* (1943). He also produced five with Judy without Mickey (*Little Nellie Kelly* [1940], *Meet Me in St. Louis* [1944], *The Harvey Girls* [1946], *Easter Parade*, and *The Pirate* [both

1948]); one with Mickey without Judy (*Summer Holiday* [1948]); and another that reunited them briefly for the last time, the Rodgers and Hart biopic, *Words and Music* (1948), in which they sang "I Wish I Were in Love Again" from the original *Babes in Arms* score. Perhaps Arthur thought it was time to make amends, since "I Wish I Were in Love Again" was omitted in the movie version of *Babes in Arms*, as was "Johnny One Note," which Judy finally had a chance to belt in full—and awesome—voice in *Words and Music*.

Since *Babes in Arms* was such a megahit, Arthur immediately planned a follow-up, with the same director (Busby Berkeley), a similar plot, and a hybrid score. Instead of putting on a show, Mickey and Judy are putting together a band; hence, the title, *Strike Up the Band* (1940), which rewarded MGM with a profit of $1.229 million. The score consisted of one classic, the title song by George and Ira Gershwin from their 1927 musical of the same name, which bore no resemblance to the 1940 movie. Most of the other songs were composed by Roger Edens, with Arthur supplying the lyrics for "Drummer Boy" and "Our Love Affair," which received an Oscar nomination. Arthur was not one for self-effacement. Supposedly, he was finding it difficult to come up with a rationale for "Our Love Affair," which he especially liked. Vincente Minnelli, who was two years away from directing his first picture, was on the set the day Arthur asked for his advice. In his autobiography, Minnelli recalls how he looked at the set, noticing a bowl of fruit on a table. He suggested that Mickey regard "each piece of fruit as if it were a musical instrument . . . apples for fiddles, oranges for brass, bananas for woodwinds." Mickey would conduct, and the fruit would become puppet-like musicians. It was a charming sequence, but unnecessary.

Mickey has written a new arrangement for "Our Love Affair," which he wants Judy to introduce. It is an unusual number for a movie about two adolescents hoping to raise enough money to enter a talent contest sponsored by Paul Whiteman. The lyrics suggest neither puppy love nor hormonal attraction, but an idealistic view of married life, in which love prevails despite quarrels and tears. Mickey sings a bit of the song at the piano, but when Judy takes over, she invests the words with the feeling of someone who went over the rainbow as an adolescent and came back as an adult.

After the song, Mickey asks if there is any more chocolate cake left. As they head for the kitchen, Mickey stops at the dining room with its fruit-laden table. He imagines himself conducting at Carnegie Hall, arranging the pieces of fruit as if they were instruments in an orchestra. There is a quick cut to fruit-headed mechanical toys in a Lilliputian orchestra led by a conductor with a cluster of grapes for hair. "Our Love Affair" was sufficiently motivated and in no need of a cartoonishly clever add-on.

During the filming, Rooney was a randy twenty-year-old, bedding anyone who was available. He married Ava Gardner, his first wife, in 1942; a year earlier, on July 27, 1941, the twenty-year-old Judy married songwriter David Rose ("The Stripper," "Holiday for Strings"), her first husband. Neither Mickey nor Judy enjoyed stable marriages. Mickey was married eight times, Judy five. Their on-screen image gave no indication of what lay ahead.

Arthur Freed was not thinking of Mickey and Judy's future, except in terms of box office. He had hit upon a formula: the youth-centered musical which Universal replicated with its Donald O'Connor–Peggy Ryan–Gloria Jean movies in the 1940s after Judy and Mickey grew up, each going his and her own way. Meanwhile, youth must be served, and Arthur was MGM's maître d'. *Babes on Broadway* (1941) reverted to the "let's put on a show" story line, this time one whose proceeds would be used to send orphans, including British refugee children, to the country for two weeks. Again we have teenage vaudevillians waiting for their big break; director Busby Berkeley's dazzling crane shots; Rooney doing imitations (this time of Harry Lauder, George M. Cohan, and a priceless Carmen Miranda); another minstrel show with the principals in blackface; and a richly diverse score with contributions from Burton Lane, Roger Edens, Harold Rome, and George M. Cohan. The Freed in the credits is not Arthur, but his lyricist brother Ralph, who contributed the standard "How about You?" "Anything Can Happen in New York," and "Hoe Down." MGM had another winner that cost $955,000 and did $3.8 million worth of business. If you can get past the racism—Mickey, face blackened and lips blubbery, and a bronzed Judy, both dressed in white and strutting their way through "Waiting for the Robert E. Lee"—there are some standout moments: Mickey channeling George M. Cohan in "Yankee Doodle Boy," and especially Judy's moving rendition of "Chin Up, Cheerio, Carry On," Burton Lane and Yip Harburg's tribute to a Britain under siege, which she sings over the air to the parents of the British children who have been evacuated to America, making every word count and reminding them that "the sun's sure to smile / on your tight little isle" and to "hang on to your wits / and you'll turn the Blitz on Fritz." Opening in New York three weeks after Pearl Harbor, *Babes on Broadway* took on even greater meaning as America also had to gird itself for what lay ahead and "be a stout fella" with "a stiff upper lip."

The last of the Mickey and Judy backyard musicals was *Girl Crazy* (1943), the second of three screen versions of George and Ira Gershwin's 1930 Broadway musical of the same name that made stars of Ginger Rogers and Ethel Merman, each of whom had songs that were forever associated with them: "Embraceable You" with Rogers and "I Got Rhythm" with Merman. RKO produced the first version in 1932 with Bert Wheeler and Robert Woolsey, which was budgeted at $552,000 but only brought in $555,000, adding to the studio's $10 million deficit that year. The third incarnation of *Girl Crazy* was MGM's *When the Boys Meet the Girls* (1965), filmed in Metrocolor with Connie Francis and Harve Presnell and special appearances by Louis Armstrong and Liberace, who make the film watchable.

As a Broadway musical, *Girl Crazy* had a memorable score that compensated for the middle-drawer book by Guy Bolton and John McGowan about a father who sends his playboy son to manage a property in Arizona, which the son turns into a dude ranch with Broadway entertainers. The mildly bawdy "Sam and Delilah," which Merman delivered with an earthy brashness, would never make it past the Motion Picture Production Code office. The opening lyrics spelled deletion: "Delilah was a floozy / She never gave a damn."

Arthur thought *Girl Crazy* would be perfect for Judy in the Ginger Rogers role, except for the book. Judy's character would remain a mail carrier, like Ginger's Molly Gray—but not with the same first name. Someone, probably screenwriter Fred F. Finklehoffe, had heard of the then-famous night during the Broadway run when Allen Kearns, the leading man, drew a blank, and instead of saying, "Molly, I love you," said, "Ginger, I love you." So Judy became Ginger, delivering the mail, not at a dude ranch but at Cody College somewhere out West where her grandfather is dean. Since *Girl Crazy*, released in November 1943, was shot at the height of World War II, the decision to change Danny Churchill (Mickey) from a man about town to a student at a mining and agricultural college was a way of saying that although Danny is not serving his country, he is getting an education, despite Cody's curriculum that seemed more equestrian than scholastic. Ironically, Mickey was drafted the year after *Girl Crazy* premiered and spent the rest of the war entertaining the GIs.

Girl Crazy got off to a bumpy start. Busby Berkeley, who had helmed the other backyard musicals, was slated to direct. He decided to film the finale first, which proved to be a blessing, since he envisioned a wind up with "I Got Rhythm" as a western jamboree complete with geometric deployments of dancers; and Mickey and Judy hoofing away like the vaudevillians they once were. Judy and Berkeley had a falling out for reasons that have never been fully explained, even though *Girl Crazy* was her fifth film with him—the others being *Babes in Arms*, *Strike Up the Band*, *Babes on Broadway*, and *For Me and My Gal*. It may have been a combination of his drinking and temper. He was "a bad drunk," as Howard Keel recalled, and notoriously uncivil. Arthur replaced Berkeley (who received a credit for staging "I Got Rhythm") with Norman Taurog. Seven of the original songs remained, but not as they were performed on stage; as for the others ("Sam and Delilah," "Barbary Coast," "Boy!

What Love Has Done to Me," and "When It's Cactus Time in Arizona")—just some of the music, but no lyrics. Ethel Merman's number, "Treat Me Rough," a masochist's credo, was sung at the beginning of the film by June Allyson at a nightclub where she shed her demure persona and worked the room, mussing men's hair and patting the heads of those who had none. The song swelled into a production number with Mickey dragged on stage and roughed up by the chorus girls. His antics made the papers, giving his father a reason to ship him off to a men's college. One could imagine Merman delivering the same "debase me" lyrics in such a way that no one would dare mess with her.

Then there was Judy with a guitar and some students doing a laid-back "Bidin' My Time" as if life were one extended yawn, and then breaking into a hoedown. Naturally Judy would be entrusted with "Embraceable You," which Ginger Rogers performed with Allen Kearns, who was thirty-seven at the time, as compared to Rogers, who was nineteen. However, the song works best as a solo, which was the case in the movie. The students stage a birthday party for Judy (one cannot think of her as Ginger Gray, since characterization is not the point here) and present her with a white piano. She begins "Embraceable You" at the piano and then makes a round of the table where the students are seated as the camera slowly tracks her. The tempo, at first enticingly slow, accelerates; the number ends with Judy atop the piano, which the students move around the floor. Charles Walters received a credit for staging the sequence, which also allowed him to dance joyously with Judy.

The context for "But Not for Me," the quintessential song of resignation, is also different. "Rags" Ragland (born John Lee Morgan Beauregard Ragland), whose character does not appear in the Gershwin musical and is simply identified as "Rags" in *Panama Hattie* and *Girl Crazy*, asks the despondent Judy for a song. Her upswept hair gave her a grown-up look, but her virginal gown with a cluster of daisies suggests that she is still little girl blue. She sang the words with the subdued emotion known only to the broken hearted who are too proud to express their disillusionment full voice: "They're writing songs of love, but not for me. / A lucky star's above, but not for me."

Screenwriter Fred F. Finklehoffe realized that *Girl Crazy* needed some kind of a situation-complication-resolution plot to accommodate all the musical numbers, especially the finale, which might not necessarily come out of the story but should at least have some connection with it. The situation had already been established: Don Juan Jr. goes to college. Finklehoffe arranged a disastrous meet cute in which Mickey manages to get Judy's jalopy running, after which she drives off without him. Mickey is forced to walk to the college, which seems to be on an alien time zone with wake up at dawn and lights out at nine-thirty. Finklehoffe had to smooth the path to true love, first by strewing it with obstacles, chief of which is the imminent closing of the college because of low enrollments. Solution: a show, but since this is the West, it will be a rodeo with a young woman crowned as queen, an event that will make Cody College one of 1943's "best bets," no longer single sex but coed. This was a wise plot device in light of the military draft. Still the lothario, Mickey promises the title to a number of young women, including the governor's daughter. Since the governor's approval is essential for the college's continuation, Mickey has no other choice but to crown the daughter, much to Judy's dismay. Finklehoffe got the idea from *Babes in Arms*, in which Mickey, after promising Judy the lead in his show, had to renege and give it to a former child star. When the star's father intervenes, Mickey recalls Judy, who, trouper that she is, goes on, as does the show. In *Girl Crazy*, Judy's disappointment is a perfect segue into "But Not for Me," the only motivated song in the film. Of course, Mickey and Judy reconcile in time for the finale, at which the rodeo queen should have been crowned, except that it would have made "I Got Rhythm" an anticlimax.

The sequence is Berkeley at his most symmetrical: dancers moving in various configurations (rows, columns, circles) as Judy in white boots and a fringed vest and skirt, and Mickey looking like a pint-sized buckaroo but dancing like a pro, throw themselves into the music with a kind of rapture. It is a thrilling ending, made ominous when a cannon juts into the frame and fires, resulting not in carnage but in a two-shot of Judy and Mickey singing, "Who could ask for anything more?" Whether the cannon bit was Berkeley's way of alluding to a war in which cannons were a common form of artillery or ending with a bang is debatable. The number itself is more frenzied than joyous, more of a military exercise than a sporting event. This is ironic since "I Got Rhythm" was a triumph for Ethel Merman, who in her autobiography described the audience's response to the song on opening night, October 14, 1930: "When I held the C note for sixteen bars, an entire chorus, while the orchestra played the melody, the audience went a little crazy. . . . And that was the song that made me." Judy sustained the note for a bit, but not for sixteen bars. Each artist was unique in her own way. "I Got Rhythm" was never meant for Judy's character, but she performed it creditably. And Merman, extraordinary as she was, could never have sung "Embraceable You" and "But Not for Me" with Judy's plaintiveness.

Girl Crazy was Judy's movie, and Finklehoffe and Arthur knew it. Since Mickey needed a number of his own, an overly orchestrated and jazzed-up "Fascinating Rhythm" by Tommy Dorsey and his Orchestra was added, with Mickey pounding away at the ivories. Mickey had a duet with Judy, "Could You Use Me?" but not a solo. Neither did Allen Kearns in the original, just

"Could You Use Me?" and "Embraceable You," both with Ginger Rogers. Since Mickey's character drives the plot, such as it is, he is shoehorned into "Treat Me Rough," "Fascinating Rhythm," and the finale. He is also given an opportunity to imitate a sportscaster covering a tennis match and a fight. His staccato delivery is authentic, but the bit is pure filler. Judy had the best songs, even though Mickey's name preceded hers in the main title.

- 4 -

JUDY WITHOUT MICKEY

In April 1943, seven months before the release of *Girl Crazy*, another Judy movie (this time without Mickey) appeared, *Presenting Lily Mars*, which revealed a more mature Judy Garland, so that anyone who saw the films back to back, in whatever order, would wonder which is typical of the real Judy: the aspiring actress in *Presenting Lily Mars* or the sweetheart of Cody College in *Girl Crazy*. Both have one plot point in common: In each, Judy experiences disappointment but accepts it as one of life's many reversals. In *Presenting Lily Mars*, it is not a tinsel crown but the opportunity to play the lead in a Broadway musical for which, unfortunately, she is not ready. She must content herself with playing the maid, a common role for an aspirant or even for an old-timer like the "Broadway Baby" in Stephen Sondheim's *Follies* (1971) who confesses, "Heck, I'd even play the maid to be in a show."

Presenting Lily Mars's producer was not Arthur Freed, but the Hungarian-born Joe Pasternak, who introduced Deanna Durbin to the public in a series of operetta-like musicals at Universal. He was chosen because a compatriot of his, the soprano Marta Eggerth, known as the "Callas of operetta," had been cast as the star of the musical in which Lily has a walk-on. When Eggerth detects a blossoming romance between Lily and the producer-playwright (Van Heflin), she exits the show, leaving him no other choice but to put Lily on in her place. But unlike Judy Garland, Lily Mars is not yet a star. When Eggerth is coaxed into rejoining the company, Lily goes back to playing the maid—but not for long. In record time, as can only happen in the movies, she marries the producer, who makes her the toast of Broadway.

Since *Presenting Lily Mars* was Pasternak's first MGM movie, it was not his fault that it lacked the lightness it might have had with Durbin. Judy was not a classically trained soprano like Durbin. There was also no way of connecting the two plot lines. The first had Lily trying to convince the producer that she is a dramatic actress; the second had her taking over the lead in an operetta. Norman Taurog was not the type to direct in waltztime, especially since there was nothing Straussian about the script, except perhaps for Eggerth's three songs. Basically, *Presenting Lily Mars* is "What Price Broadway?"

meets "Cinderella," in which a wannabe's ego is bruised but healed by Prince Charming, who also doubles as Pygmalion.

Judy and others involved in the production felt that *Presenting Lily Mars* needed a grand finale, not the patriotic "Paging Mr. Greenback," a pitch for buying war bonds that Judy was slated to sing and did so with patriotic fervor: "Uncle Sam is looking for a fella / hiding with his bundle in the cellar." The lyrics were defiantly unsubtle. Mr. Greenback is "a moron [who] doesn't know there's a war on." The movie required an ending that proved Lily achieved stardom, not that Judy Garland could sell bonds. "Paging Mr. Greenback" was dropped, and Roger Edens substituted Brown and Freed's "Broadway Rhythm," which showed Lily as a musical comedy star. Dressed in black, looking more womanly than ever before, and dancing on a circular platform with Charles Walters in a tux, Judy is a revelation. Lily Mars had disappeared, leaving only Judy Garland, whose rapport with Charles Walters made "Broadway Rhythm" more of a joyous celebration than a fairy-tale ending. Walters was primarily an MGM dance director, who had choreographed *Girl Crazy*, in which he danced with Judy in the "Embraceable You" sequence, bringing high style to what otherwise would have been just another song. But when he partnered with Judy in *Girl Crazy*, the mood switched from a birthday tribute to an exhibition in dance; and when Judy sang out, "Everybody dance," in the *Presenting Lily Mars* finale, everyone did. But for moviegoers there were only two people on the screen, Judy and Walters, doing some classy stepping, with Judy flashing some leg as well. Walters's dancing days were coming to an end; in a few years, he would be behind the camera, making his directorial debut in *Good News* (1947) and directing Judy the following year in *Easter Parade*. In the "Broadway Rhythm" sequence, Judy danced with a freedom she had never exhibited before, perhaps because she had more in common with Walters than she did with Mickey, to whom she was just a pal. But to Walters, she was an equal.

MGM had no idea how to market Judy. It was not certainly Arthur Freed's idea to cast her in *Ziegfeld Girl* (1941), opposite Lana Turner and Hedy Lamarr, the studio's reigning sex symbols—something Judy never was at any point in her career. It must have been Mayer's or Pandro S. Berman's inspiration. Berman had just moved to MGM from RKO, where he produced, among other films, all the Astaire and Rogers musicals except for their first, *Flying down to Rio* (1933), which was produced by Merian C. Cooper. *Ziegfeld Girl* was Berman's first MGM production, which, if it had been made in 1938, as planned, would never have involved himself or Judy, but rather the same team responsible for its predecessor, *The Great Ziegfeld* (1936): screenwriter William Anthony McGuire, director Robert Z. Leonard, and producer Hunt Stromberg. But McGuire contracted uremia and died in September 1940. At least he received a story credit, although his concept—the interconnected lives of three stars from the *Follies*—was substantially changed over the next two years. Stromberg's goal was to become an independent producer; dissatisfied with his MGM contract, he left the studio in 1941. Yet even before his departure, he was more interested in producing prestige films (*The Women, Susan and God, Northwest Passage, Pride and Prejudice*) than revisiting *The Great Ziegfeld*. Stromberg's indifference and McGuire's illness created a vacuum, which required a rethinking of the project that was supposed to have starred Joan Crawford, Virginia Bruce, and Eleanor Powell. After *The Women*, which was an ensemble piece, Crawford returned to costarring vehicles, sharing the spotlight with male actors (Frederic March in *Susan and God* [1940], Clark Gable in *Strange Cargo* [1940], Robert Taylor in *When Ladies Meet* [1941], Melvyn Douglas in *A Woman's Face* [1941]). One could not imagine a marmoreal Crawford descending a winding staircase in an iridescent gown and a plumed headdress.

Despite Virginia Bruce's fine performance in *The Great Ziegfeld*, in which she at least looked like one of Flo Ziegfeld's discoveries, MGM could not make her into a star. By 1939, Bruce was freelancing. Eleanor Powell, who would have been wasted in a decorative role, appeared to better advantage in *Broadway Melody of 1940* and *Lady Be Good* (1941). Regardless, MGM was determined to continue the Ziegfeld saga, but with a different concept: a movie that does not revolve around Ziegfeld (he does not even appear) but around three women from the *Follies*, whose lives are affected by sudden fame. Marguerite Roberts and Sonya Levien took over the screenplay, creating what was essentially a woman's film—or at least one with which women could identify. Both were atypical screenwriters. In 1938, Roberts married novelist John Stanford (né Julian Lawrence Shapiro), who joined the Communist Party a year later, as did his more moderate wife, who left in 1947 just as the House Un-American Activities Committee began its investigation into the alleged Communist subversion of the movie industry. Blacklisted in 1951, Roberts was unemployed for the next decade until she was hired by Columbia to adapt Peter Gilman's novel, *Diamond Head* (1963).

Roberts came to MGM in 1939, receiving her first credit for the anti-Nazi film, *Escape* (1940), although she contributed in an uncredited capacity to *They Shall Have Music* (1939), a Samuel Goldwyn production released by United Artists, in which a gang member's life is transformed when he attends a Jascha Heifetz recital. Russian-born Sonya Levien was a highly regarded screenwriter, who was at home in a variety of genres: historical dramas (*In Old Chicago, Drums along the Mohawk*), literary adaptations (*The Hunchback of Notre Dame, Valley of Decision*), biopics (*The Great Caruso, Interrupted Melody*), and musicals (*The Student Prince, Oklahoma!*). Politically, she and

Roberts were kindred spirits, although Levien was more circumspect, even refusing to comment on her daughter's and son-in-law's membership in the Communist Party.

Since they envisioned a film about the dark side of show business, they punched up the dialogue, making it sound pulpy at times, much to the displeasure of Joseph Ignatius Breen, who, as the enforcer of the Production Code, wanted "lousy," "tramp," "paddle in the rear," and the line, "She gave me a life—if you know what I mean," deleted. "Tramp" remained; it was used effectively by Jimmy Walters (Dan Dailey, then Dan Dailey Jr.), an ex-prizefighter, who hits on a down-and-out Sheila in a dive. When she rebuffs him, he strikes her, calling her a "tramp," which, sadly, is what she has become. Breen was also disturbed by the suggestiveness of "You look good and defrosted. But you're still on ice if you know what I mean" (Walters), to which Sheila replies, "I'm twenty degrees cooler than you think. You don't have to defrost me." "But you're still on ice" was cut; however, the rest remained. What the dialogue showed was that Sheila could trade metaphors with any sleazebag and decode his subtext as well.

Despite their leanings, Roberts and Levien produced a politically neutral script, which, to its credit, did not gloss over the fact that the "girls" were objects of the male gaze. Ziegfeld or one of his lieutenants would spot a performer at a third-rate venue or an employee in a department store who looked as if she could be made over into a moon goddess, swathed in sequins and satin, walking down a gleaming staircase and into men's fantasies. In the film, the unseen Ziegfeld catches a father and daughter act (Charles Winninger and Judy) mugging their way through Roger Edens's "Laugh? I Thought I'd Split My Sides," a recreation of the sock-it-to-'em number complete with corny jokes, beloved by old-school vaudevillians who would give their all when less was better. Ziegfeld saw nothing in the father but envisioned a bright future for the daughter, who still seemed too much of an adolescent to pass as a showgirl. Even when Judy paraded with the others, dripping with silvery strands that looked like oversized icicles, she was striking but out of place. Ziegfeld was committed to "glorifying the American girl." Judy was an American girl, but did not need Ziegfeld's, or anyone else's, magic wand. Her magic came from within; like a diamond, it just needed the right setting, and it was not on a staircase awash in glitter.

But once Judy was cast in the film, Roberts and Levien had to flesh out her character, the only one of the three who remains in the *Follies*. Knowing that Judy was born into a family of vaudevillians and made her debut at the age of two, they created a close relationship between Judy's character, Susan Gallagher, and her father, which mirrored the one between Judy and her own father, Frank Gumm. (Judy admitted that his death was "the most terrible event in her life.") And just as Frances Gumm went from performing with her siblings in a sister act to Hollywood stardom with a name change along the way, Susan went from the two-a-day to the *Follies* and retained her own name. The writers did the same with Lana Turner's character, Sheila Regan, who is discovered while operating an elevator in a swank department store. Lana herself was discovered by the *Hollywood Reporter* founder and editor, William R. Wilkerson, while she was sipping a Coke at the counter of the Top Hat Malt Shop across from Hollywood High. Wilkerson gave her his card with director Mervyn LeRoy's name written on it. Lana reported to the studio and was immediately cast in a small role in LeRoy's *They Won't Forget* (1937). In both the film and real life, all it took was a chance encounter for a career to take off.

The credits—with James Stewart top billed over Judy, Turner, and Lamarr—were misleading. Stewart's character, Gil Young, a trucker engaged to Sheila, is a typical blue-collar male, who presents his future wife with an ultimatum, saying in effect: "Quit your job (even though she is bringing in the dough) and be a wife and mother, or the marriage is off." Stewart did what he could with the role, which required him to succumb to the lure of easy money and work for a bootlegger. (It's Prohibition, although one would never know it from the wardrobe, which is unmistakably 1940–1941.) Billing Stewart over the women was MGM's way of rewarding him for his Oscar nomination as best actor in *The Philadelphia Story* (1940), in which he costarred with Katharine Hepburn and Cary Grant. Hepburn was also nominated, losing to Ginger Rogers in *Kitty Foyle*; Grant was bypassed, as he generally was throughout his career. Stewart won for what was really a secondary role, like his character in *Ziegfeld Girl*.

It was difficult for Roberts and Levien to allocate equal screen time to Stewart and the three women. Gil Young weaves in and out of the plot, which initially seemed to be tripartite, until it becomes evident that the main character is Sheila. The ethereally beautiful Hedy Lamarr played Sandra Kolter, a violinist's wife, who is discovered waiting in the wings while her husband is auditioning for a place in the orchestra. He doesn't get the job; she does, but not one she even sought. But what does it matter if it puts food on the table? It does to her husband, who presents her with the now standard dilemma: the *Follies* or me. She chooses the *Follies*, but only temporarily. Marriage must win out at any cost, including plausibility. Sandra quits and rejoins her husband, now a virtuoso about to make his Carnegie Hall debut.

Since neither Turner nor Lamarr was a singer but could descend a staircase with grace and ease while looking enigmatically alluring, Judy and Tony Martin were entrusted with the musical chores. Judy became her old wistful self with "I'm Always Chasing Rainbows," which she infused with the same yearning that she brought to "Over the Rainbow" and "But Not for Me." She also had to don brownface and native dress for "Minnie from Trinidad," a faux Caribbean frolic that was less offensive than MGM's other ventures into minstrelsy. Since Sandra has left the *Follies*, and Susan stayed on to see her name in lights, that left Sheila, who did neither, yet she was the one who merits the audience's sympathy because Roberts and Levien had steered the plot in her direction. The lush life goes to Sheila's head; she overspends, becomes an alcoholic, messes up a production number, and is fired. She hits the skids, is brutalized by an ex-boxer (a creepy Dailey), and develops a heart condition. And as if that were not enough, she leaves her sick bed and dons a symbolically black gown to attend the opening night of a new *Follies*, even if it means sitting in the balcony. Unable to stay for the entire performance, she descends the staircase with the same elegance and style that she once exhibited on stage, this time unchoreographed and poignantly natural, only to collapse at the foot of the stairs.

Roberts and Levien provided Lana with a deathbed scene that so disturbed preview audiences that they decided to leave the ending ambiguous, allowing optimists to think that with Gil's help she will recover; or realists to infer from Lana's moving performance that, if she did not die, she at least "expired." Lana expires literally, breathing her last, although Pollyannas will insist that she is just taking a breath. Roberts and Levien modeled their ending on *The Great Ziegfeld*'s, in which the frail impressario passes away without any fanfare or sobbing. Of course, Sheila dies, regardless of what one calls the ultimate reality. If expiration is good enough for Ziegfeld, it's good enough for a Ziegfeld girl.

The production numbers, staged by Busby Berkeley, are what one might expect: flamboyant without turning gaudy. It is the costumes that widen the eye. Adrian, MGM's premier costume designer, allowed his imagination to run rampant. Unsatisfied with satin, sequins, and chiffon, he dressed some of the women in plant and animal accessories, as if they came from a world where they were part of the fauna and flora. One had a swan wrapped around her; another, pigeons on her arms. There was even one who looked as if orchids were growing over her. Lana was decked out in a costume with flowers rising from behind her neck. High camp, perhaps. Ziegfeld never courted excess; MGM did, but audiences loved it. *Ziegfeld Girl* cost $1.468 million and brought in over $3 million. The public had spoken.

Judy was not so much miscast as implausibly cast in *Ziegfeld Girl*, in which she was spared the embarrassment of looking like a flower garden or an aviary. *For Me and My Gal* (1942) was a much better fit; it was also Gene Kelly's film debut. This time Judy's name preceded the title, followed by George Murphy and Gene Kelly, who did not get an "Introducing Gene Kelly" credit. It was as if he were part of the MGM family, as he would be for the next fifteen years. Although Arthur Freed was interested in bringing Kelly to MGM after seeing him in the supporting role of Harry, the aspiring comic, in William Saroyan's *The Time of Your Life* (1939), it was not until Rodgers and Hart's *Pal Joey* (1940), with Kelly as the amoral title character—and everyone but the ingenue, on the make—that he became a star. After Mayer saw *Pal Joey*, he knew instinctively that Kelly belonged at MGM. To work Kelly into a film that was to have starred song-and-dance man George Murphy, the writers—Richard Sherman, Fred F. Finklehoffe, and Sid Silvers—had to revert to Howard Emmett Rogers's original story about an entertainer involved with two women, one of whom he marries and then dumps. When Stella Adler—who had been cast in a minor role in MGM's *Shadow of the Thin Man* (1941) and had yet to become one of the theater's greatest acting teachers—read Rogers's story at Arthur's request, she suggested that the two women be conflated into one, played by Judy Garland as Jo Hayden, with Kelly taking over the role originally planned for Murphy. Kelly's character, Harry Palmer, is brash and oily with occasional flashes of charm but nonetheless a narcissist. There's enough of Joey in Harry Palmer for those who saw Kelly in *Pal Joey* to make the connection; for the rest, Palmer was just another smooth talker who finds the core of his humanity in a regenerative action.

Both Kelly and Judy were in their element as vaudevillians—she as part of a company headed by Jimmy Metcalf (George Murphy); he, as solo performer. Theirs is a meet frosty, with Jo ignoring Palmer's aggressiveness, until he proposes that they team up, insisting that she is too good for Metcalf, whose routines have grown stale. Oddly, the reverse seems to be the case. In his solo act, Palmer appears as a bearded baggy-pants hobo with a bulbous nose, a cross between Dickens's Fagin and Jimmy Durante, who gets laughs for his antics and applause for his athleticism. From what we see of Metcalf's act, in which he and Jo offered the old standbys, "Oh, You Beautiful Doll" and "By the Beautiful Sea," the sheen was still there, although the act could stand a polish job, which it obviously received, enabling Metcalf to play the Palace, the dream of every vaudevillian, before Harry and Jo.

Although *For Me and My Gal* overflows with familiar songs that flood the fissures in the plot, the integration of the title song with the story line suggests that the writers thought of it as a plot point, not as another addition to the sound track. Palmer pays a conductor $50 for the orchestration of a song that had been promised to Metcalf. The song is "For Me and My Gal," which would have been perfect for Metcalf and Jo, but not for Palmer's hobo-clown—unless Palmer was thinking of changing his act. When a contrite Palmer explains what he has done, Jo seems unconcerned, now that they are a team. At this point, it is impossible to think of Kelly as Palmer. He is Gene Kelly, who sits down at a piano and starts playing "For Me and My Gal." Immediately, Kelly and Judy begin singing as if they were born with infused knowledge of the lyrics, and then dance like pros. However, the other numbers Judy and Kelly perform on their way to the big time ("When You Wore a Tulip, and I Wore a Big Red Rose," and "Ballin' the Jack") could easily have been handled by Judy and Murphy. The exception is "After You're Gone," which no one else could have sung but Judy. First she does an upbeat version, bouncy and care-free, with total disregard for the end-of-the-affair lyrics. Then, leaning against the proscenium arch, she sings it as a blues number, somewhere between a prophecy and a lament. Her knowing eyes belied her conviction that her lover would repent of his ways ("There'll come a time when you'll regret it"). One will never know what Judy was thinking, but she looked as if she were longing to cross over that rainbow bridge again.

For Me and My Gal is a show biz musical, in which all the principals are vaudevillians, whose material, for the most part, is interchangeable. It is also a historical artifact, beginning in 1916, two years after World War I broke out in Europe, as we are reminded by newspaper headlines flashing across the screen accompanied by newsreel footage. But the vaudevillians are oblivious to the war, which is not covered in *Variety*. It is not until Palmer receives his draft notice that he is even aware that the United States has entered the war. Earlier in the film, director Busby Berkeley included a shot of the open lid of a trunk, which dominates the frame, intimating that it will take on greater importance later. Hitchcock did the same with such objects as a glass of milk (*Suspicion*), a wine bottle (*Notorious*), eye glasses (*Strangers on a Train*), and an envelope (*Saboteur*). Unwilling to jeopardize his chance to play the Palace, Palmer brings the lid down on his hand, thus becoming ineligible to serve. His lack of patriotism is abhorrent to Jo, whose brother has enlisted and will die in battle. But before that happens, Lucille Norman sends him on his way with a stoically poignant "Till We Meet Again" that becomes a predated re-quiem. When Jo is handed a telegram, we know that it will begin, "We regret to inform you."

To regain Jo's respect, Palmer tries to enlist, only to be rejected because of his hand. Eventually, the main characters end up in Paris near the end of the war—Metcalf in the army; Jo and Palmer as entertainers. Palmer has an opportunity to redeem himself when he drives a jeep through enemy lines to warn ambulance drivers to return to their base while, at the same time, throwing a grenade into a German machine-gun nest. Exactly how he could drive with a bum hand is beside the point. In 1942, MGM could hardly release a movie in which its latest discovery plays a draft dodger, despite his sudden change of heart. An act of heroism was required, and Palmer delivered.

Meanwhile, Jo, the consummate entertainer, is lifting the troops' spirits with "How Ya Gonna Keep 'Em Down on the Farm (After They've Seen Paree?),"

"It's a Long, Long Way to Tipperary," and "Pack Up Your Troubles." She is back in the States for the finale, starring at the Palace and singing "When Johnny Comes Marching Home," when she spots a spiritually renewed Palmer in the audience. He joins her onstage as they launch into the title song, bringing the film full circle. Tacked on to "The End" was a then familiar appeal: "America Needs Your Money. Buy War Bonds At This Theater."

For Me and My Gal was released in mid-October 1942; it was a huge moneymaker, $4.37 million. Yet with the battle scenes and entertainers at the front, one cannot help but think of a war that, for Americans, was not even in its first year. Fall 1942 did not bode well. A few days after Pearl Harbor, Guam fell to the Japanese, followed by Wake Island; and early in 1942, Singapore. By the time the film opened, Manila had been declared an open city, and Bataan and Corregidor were under Japanese control. The Japanese defeat at Midway in June 1942 may have been decisive, but Japan's Asian conquests offered little hope of an easy victory. Thus *For Me and My Gal* seems less of a World War I movie than one about the war in progress. Such is the power of historical displacement; like a palimpsest, the present emerges out of the past, so that what was, now is.

There was no historical displacement in *Meet Me in St. Louis* (1944), which remains Judy's most popular film after *The Wizard of Oz*. When it was released in November 1944, World War II was in its final stage. The film offered war-weary moviegoers a chance to revisit the past where the din of battle was absent, and spend some time with the Smith family at 5135 Kensington Avenue in turn-of-the-twentieth-century St. Louis, where the overwhelming question is whether Mr. Smith will accept a job in New York, thus uprooting his family, or make everyone happy by staying put. *Meet Me in St. Louis* spanned the period from summer 1903 to spring 1904, climaxing with the St. Louis World's Fair, which historians prefer to call the Louisiana Purchase Exposition of 1904.

If *Meet Me in St. Louis* had been made when its source—Sally Benson's stories, "5135 Kensington Avenue,"—began appearing in the *New Yorker* between June 14, 1941, and May 23, 1943, it probably would have starred Judy and Mickey. Fortunately, MGM waited until after Benson turned the stories—partly autobiographical vignettes about growing up in the Sherman Park neighborhood of St. Louis—into a novel. Originally, there were eight stories, to which Benson added four more, one for each month from 1903 to 1904. Knowing that Random House planned to bring the novel out at the end of 1942, MGM bought the rights in January 1942 for $25,000. Since the film would be called *Meet Me in St. Louis*, that became the book's title as well, although it is also known as *The Kensington Stories*.

Benson had been assigned to write the screenplay for the Arthur Freed production, working on it from March 30 to May 9, 1942. Arthur was unimpressed with the result. The problem was that there was not much of a plot, which was never a priority in musicals, except for those with a real trajectory like *For Me and My Gal*. When Gene Kelly deliberately injured his hand to escape the draft, the plot could have gone off in several different directions: Judy could have returned to her former partner, George Murphy; Kelly could have become a star and a self-loathing alcoholic; or Judy could have gone her way by herself and become the toast of Broadway. America's involvement in World War II required the plot to take the turn that it did, although any of the above scenarios would have been plausible.

Meet Me in St. Louis does not admit of any such divergences. It is a period piece like *Life with Father* that makes up in charm for what it lacks in drama. In fact, Arthur originally thought that Howard Lindsay and Russel Crouse, who coauthored *Life with Father* (1939), then in its fourth season on Broadway, would be the ideal adapters of Benson's novel. But they politely declined, although one could understand why they were considered. The plot pivot in each is a "Will he or won't he?" Will Clarence Day agree to be baptized (*Life with Father*), and will Alonzo Smith take the job in New York (*Meet Me in St. Louis*)? In between there is a series of episodes that distract the viewer from wondering if anything momentous is going to happen. In *Life with Father*, there are other issues, admittedly not compelling, besides the patriarch's baptism, which include the oldest son's getting a suit of his own before going off to Yale; a budding romance between him and a young visitor (Elizabeth Taylor in the 1947 movie version); and a potentially deadly medicine that his brother puts in their mother's tea, resulting in a literal tempest in a teapot.

Similarly, a series of domestic crises occurs in *Meet Me in St. Louis* before Mr. Smith (Leon Ames) announces that he is moving the family to New York. The older sister, Rose (Lucille Bremer), is waiting for her beau to propose, while the younger, Esther (Judy), is pining for John Truett (Tom Drake), the boy next door. Interspersed between young love and the denouement are a Halloween prank that takes an ugly turn and nearly wrecks the relationship between Esther and Truett; Truett's failure to pick up his tuxedo in time to take Esther to the Christmas ball, requiring her to go with her grandfather, who disappears behind a Christmas tree as Truett appears from the other side, thus saving the evening; and three classic numbers by Hugh Martin and Ralph Blane: "The Trolley Song," which Judy usually sang in her concerts; "The Boy Next Door," which could have come off as torchy except that Judy turned Esther's longing into wistfulness; and "Have Yourself a Merry Little Christmas," perhaps the most rueful song ever composed about the "season of comfort and joy." Not to worry. Father announces that he will not accept the New York offer, even though it means a promotion, so that everyone can stay in St. Louis "'til we rot" and attend the World's Fair in the spring.

Filming began in November 1943, but did not go smoothly. In his BFI Film Classics monograph, Gerald Kaufman has summarized everything there is to know about the troubled production of one of the world's most cherished films. First, Judy thought that her character, Esther Smith, was just another ingenue. At twenty-one, she would be playing the seventeen-year-old younger sister of Lucille Bremer, who was about the same age as herself. Esther also has two younger sisters: Agnes (Joan Carroll) and the five-year-old Tootie (Margaret O'Brien). Judy knew how children can steal scenes, particularly Margaret O'Brien, who could cry on cue as she showed in *Journey for Margaret* (1943) and again in *Meet Me in St. Louis* after Judy tried to console her with "Have Yourself a Merry Little Christmas." Joan Carroll was no slouch, either. She attracted considerable attention when she played Ginger Rogers's younger sister in *The Primrose Path* (RKO, 1940). That same year, she appeared with Ethel Merman in Cole Porter's *Panama Hattie* (1940), in which they sang "Let's Be Buddies."

Judy's then lover, Joseph L. Mankiewicz—an MGM producer, soon to be one of the industry's greatest writer-directors—told her to pass on the movie. The director, Vincente Minnelli, disagreed. According to Minnelli, Judy confronted him with the script, insisting it was not particularly good, which it probably wasn't in its early drafts. He tried to convince her that, in his hands, she would shine. Still dubious, Judy sought out Louis B. Mayer, who initially sided with her until Arthur Freed argued that Judy and the film were a perfect match. Mayer yielded to Freed, bragging, "I've taken this boy and I've made a great producer out of him." The great producer prevailed, Judy acquiesced, and the headaches began.

Benson's stories were vignettes that recalled pictures with captions in a family album—nostalgic mementos for a rainy afternoon in need of a narrative arc. Victor Heerman, his wife, Sarah Y. Mason, and William Ludwig, were brought in to provide one. Plot complications—blackmail, kidnapping, various romantic entanglements—were considered and abandoned; so were secondary characters such as a set of grandparents and a bigamous family. What finally appeared on the screen was the work of Irving Brecher and Fred F. Finklehoffe, both of whom had solid MGM credentials. Although, supposedly, each had worked on *The Wizard of Oz*, neither is mentioned in Aljean Harmetz's *The Making of* The Wizard of Oz (1977), suggesting that what they contributed was never used or that it was not significant enough to merit a credit. Brecher, however, received sole screenplay credit for the Marx Brothers comedies, *At the Circus* (1939) and *Go West* (1940), and *Du Barry Was a Lady*

(1943); and coscreenplay credit for *Shadow of the Thin Man* (1941) and *Best Foot Forward* (1943), the latter with Finklehoffe, who was no stranger to Judy Garland movies, having been involved in the scripts of *Strike Up the Band* (1940), *Babes on Broadway* (1941), *For Me and My Gal* (1942), and *Girl Crazy* (1943). The *Meet Me in St. Louis* screenplay was essentially "theirs," in the sense that Brecher and Finklehoffe were the chief architects of a script that may have borne traces of the work of others, but not enough to overshadow their own.

Once the script had reached final draft stage, production began. So did the problems, which caused numerous delays and sent the film over budget. Judy had developed the habit of calling in sick or claiming some kind of indisposition. During the filming of *Girl Crazy* she missed seventeen days; sixteen, during the *Meet Me in St. Louis* shoot for various reasons including an ear infection, a tooth extraction, a sinus condition, swollen eyes, oversleeping, and the common cold. Joan Carroll had an emergency appendectomy and was out for two weeks; Mary Astor, for three weeks with sinusitis; Margaret O'Brien, for thirteen days with hayfever, influenza, and "nervous spells," all of which necessitated her leaving rainy Los Angeles to recuperate in Arizona. With all the absences and layoffs, the film, originally budgeted at approximately $1.708 million, came in at around $1.885 million. It was worth it; in its original release, it grossed $6.566 million.

Meet Me in St. Louis was the perfect companion piece to two shows that were then on Broadway: *Life with Father* (1939) and *Oklahoma!* (1943). Neither became an MGM movie. *Life with Father* closed on July 12, 1947, after an eight-year run; a month later, Warner Bros. released the movie version, budgeted at $4.7 million and grossing $6.45 million. Rodgers and Hammerstein's *Oklahoma!* was not even a year old when *Meet Me in St. Louis* started filming. The movie version would not be made for another decade, and not by MGM. *Oklahoma!* (1955) was a Magna Theatre Corporation production, photographed in Todd A-O, a widescreen process requiring projection in 70 mm for road-show engagements, although most moviegoers would have seen it in the 35 mm CinemaScope format.

To Richard Barrios, author of the superb *Dangerous Rhythm: Why Movie Musicals Matter* (2014), *Meet Me in St. Louis* "was to movies what *Oklahoma!* was on the stage—an unprecedented jolt of Americana that let song and script move each other along in near radical ways." It is true that in each the songs propel the story; it is also true that both share the same homespun qualities and respect for traditional values, while showing at the same time how an ordered world can be overturned by irrational behavior, as seen in the Halloween sequence in *Meet Me in St. Louis*, which Arthur Freed wanted deleted, arguing that it did not advance the plot. Actually, it did, but not linearly. It was retained, since it was revelatory of another side of Tootie's character and that of the neighborhood kids, who regard the Eve of All Hallows as the equivalent of the Witches' Sabbath.

Tootie and Agnes, dressed in grotesque costumes (Tootie wears a nose-piece that makes her look like the folkloric trickster), have targeted the local misanthrope, Mr. Braukoff, who, they believe (or have convinced themselves), beats his wife with a hot poker and poisons cats and burns them in his furnace. By this time, it is evident that Tootie has an overripe imagination. She gives her dolls deadly diseases and then buries them in the garden in cigar boxes. It is not just an ordinary Halloween. The kids have made a bonfire out of what one would like to assume is discarded furniture. There is menace in the air, which, when it turns to mayhem, attracts the police. The kids plan to visit the homes of people they dislike and throw flour in their faces. Because of Mr. Braukoff's reputation, they decide to bypass his house. Desperate to prove herself, Tootie volunteers to go up to the Braukoffs and throw flour in Mr. Braukoff's face. For her courage, she is crowned "the most horrible." At some point in the evening, the police became involved; in the next scene, Tootie is hysterical, claiming that she had been attacked by John Truett. Perhaps not in 1944, but in a pedophilia-aware age, such an allegation is bound to unnerve some viewers seeing the film for the first time, especially since the alleged "attack" takes place off screen, which may have been a mistake. This should have been a case of show and tell, not just tell. Brecher and Finklehoffe needed a scene to bridge the end of the Halloween sequence and Tootie's allegation, one that would dramatize what happened when Truett tried to shield the girls from the police. In the process, Tootie pulled a lock of hair from Truett's head, which convinced Esther that Tootie had been attacked. Despite her innocent exterior, Tootie inhabits a dark world of her own making. She revels in the morbid and the violent; she is also on the verge of becoming thoroughly amoral. She and Agnes see nothing wrong in placing an effigy on the trolley tracks that could have caused a derailment and physical injury. As the youngest, she was probably pampered and mildly scolded instead of being punished. The Smith family seems to think Halloween pranks are harmless fun. Tootie's grandfather (Harry Davenport) even gives her the bag of flour, telling her that if it is wet, it is harder to remove. The Smiths appear to be a conservative household of indulgent liberals.

And yet there is such a disparity between the angelic Tootie—or one should say angel-faced Margaret O'Brien—when she and Esther perform a cakewalk while singing "Under the Bamboo Tree" and the Tootie who reveals her shadow self in the Halloween revels. But that may have been Minnelli's purpose: to keep *Meet Me in St. Louis* from becoming a nostalgia trip by refusing to depict a world of unalloyed innocence that would make audiences pine for "the good old days" at the expense of a realistic portrayal of an early twentieth-century American family, warts and all, in which children are not cherubs.

To recast Richard Barrios's comparison between *Meet Me in St. Louis* and *Oklahoma!* one might say that Tootie is to Minnelli's film what Jud is to Rodgers and Hammerstein's musical. Each casts a pall over the action—Tootie less so than Jud—which is eventually lifted, so young love can triumph. In *Oklahoma!* Jud is a farmhand who lives alone in the smokehouse with pictures of naked women as substitutes for the virginal Laurey, for whom he lusts. Jealous of Curly, his rival, he is unsuccessful in his attempt to induce Curly to look through the "Little Wonder," a handheld peep show with a concealed blade that pops out at the eye. A character like Jud either has to be dispatched or banished from the community. Jud, however, is not the type to go gently. He lunges at Curly with a knife and accidentally falls on it. *Oklahoma!* went further than anything Freed or Minnelli ever imagined. And yet the musical has been produced worldwide—in revivals in New York, regional theaters, colleges, and even high schools. Although Jud's character suggests a sexual predator, *Oklahoma!* has always been a family musical with a manly hero, a virtuous heroine, a disturbed villain, and a righteous community. One suspects that if MGM had bought the rights to *Oklahoma!* with Arthur Freed producing, the movie would have had the same fireside warmth as *Meet Me in St. Louis*; and that Jud's dark side would have been brightened by a few lumens.

What is amazing about *Meet Me in St. Louis* is the art with which Vincente Minnelli endowed it, particularly since the plot is lacking in suspense until Mr. Smith announces the impending move to New York. But you can become so taken with the film's style and grace that you go along with the story, even though under ordinary circumstances you could care less about how sweet or sour the ketchup is, whether Rose Smith gets a phone call from her boyfriend in New York, or whether John Truett catches the trolley to the fairgrounds. In Minnelli's hands, what seems so ordinary is transformed into art.

Although the film may seem episodic, Minnelli has given it a discernible structure: a four-part narrative, reminiscent of a quadtych with each panel in the form of a greeting card sketch of the Smith's Victorian house that first takes on color, and then springs to life, as the action spans the four seasons— from summer 1903 to spring 1904. In the first, the Smith family is introduced. Alonso Smith Jr. rides his bike onto the property where, inside the house, his mother (Mary Astor) is making ketchup, scrutinized by their fastidious cook (Marjorie Main). Agnes returns from a swim and starts singing the title song, which is taken up by her grandfather and brought to a close by Esther, who has returned from playing tennis with her friends. Next, Tootie arrives after accompanying the ice deliverer on his route; then Rose, and finally the patriarch, Alonso Smith. Without the audience's being aware of it, the background has been filled in, and the title song introduced.

Meet Me in St. Louis is a movie of privileged moments, one of which has a rare kind of poignancy. You are moved and at the same time remain ineffably still. After Father Smith announces the move, the children decline to eat their cake and leave the table. Their mother sits down at the piano and begins playing "You and I," a song that Nacio Herb Brown and Arthur Freed had written, which expresses the deep feeling the couple has for each other. Arthur also worked himself into the number by dubbing Leon Ames's singing voice. After hearing the song, a confirmation of conjugal love, the others slowly file into the room and begin eating their cake, as if they were partaking in a ritual of renewal. But their acceptance of the move is only temporary. After Esther sings "Have Yourself a Merry Little Christmas" to Tootie, which is not exactly a song to bolster one's spirits, Tootie charges off into the yard and hacks away at the snow family she had created, crying that, since she cannot take them to New York, she would rather see them destroyed. Minnelli intended the incident not as just another example of Tootie's impulsiveness, but a way of effecting Mr. Smith's change of heart. He witnesses the scene and then, after saying goodnight to Agnes, descends a staircase past a wall bereft of pictures into a parlor cluttered with crates filled with everything that made 5135 Kensington Avenue a home instead of a house. Minnelli has just motivated Alonso's epiphany: it will be a home again. He assembles the family and breaks the news that they will not be moving—the segue into the fourth and shortest section: the Exposition, in which everyone realizes, like Dorothy in *The Wizard of Oz*, that the bluebird of happiness is right in your own backyard.

Meet Me in St. Louis is Arthur Freed's first truly integrated musical, in the sense that the songs flow from the action, either advancing or sharpening it, but always in the interest of the story. When Rose realizes that Esther has a crush on John Truett, she remarks imperiously, "My dear, when you get to be my age, there are more important things than boys," which is the cue for "The Boy Next Door." "The Trolley Song," the film's best-known number, is more of an interlude. Esther is waiting for Truett so they can take the trolley together to the fairgrounds. When he fails to arrive on time, she boards without him. The passengers—mostly female with picture hats—begin singing, "Clang, clang, went the trolley, / Ding, ding went the bell" as Esther works her way up to the top deck, so she can look for Truett. She takes up the song, as if to explain her anxiety by recounting an experience she once had (perhaps in her imagination, but not in real life), dramatizing it so vividly and singing so exuberantly that anyone would think it actually occurred. Describing herself "in a high-starched collar" with "high-topped shoes," and "hair piled high upon my head," she recalls the mythical trolley ride that ended with "his hand holding mine to the end of the line." Esther, however, is not wearing a high-starched collar, but a white lace one; and her hair is not in an upsweep, but flowing like a silken fold down her back. But it did not matter. When Truett hops on board, Esther has just finished singing and settles back in the seat like an ordinary passenger, having returned to reality from fantasyland. Judy delivered the lyrics so convincingly that you could picture the young man in the song tipping his hat, sitting down, asking her name, and then taking her hand. And yet there is a slightly neurotic edge to her delivery as if she were narrating the story of her trolley romance, line by line, anxiously waiting for Truett to arrive and verify it. He joins her, sitting next to her to the end of the line. The two of them look a bit awkward—Esther, because she had been such an exhibitionist; Truett, because he should have skipped basketball practice and accompanied her.

"The Trolley Song" can be interpreted in various ways, the most obvious being a song intended specifically for the trolley sequence and nothing more. It also reveals another aspect of Esther's character: a seventeen-year-old so eager for Truett's affection that she envisions what would have happened if they had met on a trolley. Minnelli saw something in Judy that made him understand what she could do with a song: act it out, as if she were living it, revealing more about herself than the character. He capitalized on her innate sense of drama in the "Mack the Black" number in their next—and last—musical together, *The Pirate* (1948), which is one of the best examples of neurosis set to music.

- 5 -

THE ACTRESS

On November 21, 1946, anyone tuning into the CBS series, *Suspense*, "Radio's Outstanding Theatre of Thrills," would have experienced the equivalent of culture shock. The story that night was "Drive-In," written by Mel Dinelli, who demonstrated the art of calibrating suspense in his scripts for *The Spiral Staircase* (1946) and *The Window* (1949), and later in his play *The Man* (1950), filmed as *Beware, My Lovely* (1952) with Ida Lupino and Robert Ryan as a widow and the handyman who terrorizes her. *Suspense* generally starred dramatic actors such as Rosalind Russell, Joseph Cotten, Charles Laughton, Loretta Young, Orson Welles, Chester Morris, Humphrey Bogart, and Agnes Moorehead, whose nerve-fraying monologue, *Sorry, Wrong Number* (1943), ranks with Orson Welles's *The War of the Worlds* (1938) as one of radio's towering achievements. The star that November evening was known almost exclusively for musicals, although anyone who saw *The Clock* (1945) the year before would not have been surprised that Judy Garland could act without singing a note.

In "Drive-In," Judy played a carhop at a Hollywood drive-in, whom a coworker coaxes into serving the last customer. There is something odd about him. When she hands him the tray through the car window, she feels something sticky. It is blood. The man claims to be a doctor; the blood, that of a patient he brought to the hospital. Eager to catch the last bus home, she inadvertently puts a pepper shaker in her pocket, little knowing how useful its contents will be. The man offers her a lift to the bus stop, but when he passes it and heads toward Laurel Canyon, terror begins to creep into Judy's voice. Since she is also functioning as narrator, her voice had been tremulous from the start. But as the car speeds along and she realizes her life is in danger, her voice becomes even more agitated, but never hysterical. The man is a psychopath, who, after being institutionalized and released, murdered his wife and the doctor who put him away. When the car is stuck in a mudslide atop a cliff, he demands her raincoat for traction. Then, as he is about to push her off the cliff, she feels the shaker in her pocket. The top had come off, and she throws the pepper in his eyes, causing him to fall to his death.

It was a flawless performance, a half hour of compelling drama, which, apparently, no one at MGM heard (after all, radio is a nonvisual medium). Even in her movie musicals, Judy was always convincing, although the demands made of her came more from the production numbers than the scripts, which rarely varied from the boy-girl-complication-resolution model.

More than anyone else at MGM, Vincente Minnelli saw the actress within the singer. Judy had entrusted herself to Minnelli after *Meet Me in St. Louis*. They had become lovers and would marry on June 15, 1945, seven months after the film's release. Earlier, Judy had become aware of an MGM property, *The Clock*, about a secretary and a soldier on a forty-eight-hour leave in New York. It was a straight dramatic role, and Judy campaigned for it. Getting it was easy; getting the right director was not. She was delighted with Robert Nathan and Joseph Schrank's screenplay but not with director Fred Zinnemann, who could make a harrowing World War II movie like *The Seventh Cross* (1944), but had no feeling for the story of a soldier (Robert Walker) and a secretary (Judy), who meet when the heel of her shoe gets caught in the escalator at New York's Penn Station. Judy went to Arthur Freed, begging him to replace Zinnemann with Minnelli, who understood that, for the film to work (it turned a modest profit for a nonmusical, $2.78 million), there had to be an innocence about it, which distinguished it from other films about a whirlwind romance in wartime. Minnelli delicately plotted the trajectory of their relationship from initial hostility to love, and finally to marriage—all within the space of forty-eight hours. There is a deeply spiritual moment as the two stop by what is obviously St. Patrick's Cathedral to exchange their vows, believing that pledging their fidelity to each other would be more meaningful in a church than it was in city hall where they were married. Two solitaries found each other through a providential reordering of time and place that began and ended in Penn Station, where they first met and where they take their leave as he is about to report for active duty. In between, they lose each other in the subway, reconnect under the clock at the Hotel Astor, help a milk deliverer with his rounds, manage to get a marriage license despite the bureaucracy, marry, and enjoy a wedding breakfast before parting.

Having made his reputation in New York, graduating from costume and set designer to stage director, Minnelli knew how to bring the city to life on an MGM soundstage, so that everything—Penn Station, the escalator, the subway, the Hotel Astor lobby, and especially the hallowed interior of St. Patrick's Cathedral—seemed palpably real. Judy would have a few more opportunities to demonstrate her acting skills, winning Oscar nominations for *A Star Is Born* (1954) and *Judgment at Nuremberg* (1961), losing to Grace Kelly (*The Country Girl*) and Rita Moreno (*West Side Story*), respectively. After *The*

Clock, it was back to musicals, except that Minnelli had one in mind that, if it worked, would establish Judy as a singing actress.

Of all the MGM musicals of the golden age, *The Pirate* (1948) is the most problematic. Inspired by S. N. Behrman's 1942 play of the same name, which was an adaptation of the similarly named 1912 comedy by the German play-wright Ludwig Fulda, *The Pirate* opened on Broadway on November 25, 1942, for a run of 177 performances. The stars were the legendary couple, Alfred Lunt and Lynn Fontanne, with Lunt performing magic tricks and walking a tightrope. MGM had no intention of replicating the original; there was no one at the studio of the Lunts' stature and, more important, no audience for a so-phisticated comedy involving seduction. The film version would be a musical, reuniting Gene Kelly and Judy Garland, who had not appeared together since *For Me and My Gal* (1942) and retaining the names of the principals (Manu-ela, Serafin, Aunt Inez, with Don Bolo becoming Don Pedro) and the story line: a woman who succumbs to the blandishments of an actor pretending to be a pirate, and, after discovering the deception, succeeds in unmasking the real pirate, who, in the play, happens to be her husband. Obviously, this would not pass muster with Joseph Ignatius Breen, who enforced the Production Code as if it were holy writ. The woman (Manuela) must be unmarried, and her relationship with the actor-pirate must carry no hint of seduction, which was quite the opposite in the original.

The Pirate had a long gestation period. Minnelli became involved with the project in November 1945. The film was special to him; he thought of it as Judy's metamorphosis from girl to woman, especially a woman for whom sex and gender were distinct. He scrutinized the treatments, expressing his unhappiness to Benny Thau, MGM's casting director: "Boy-Girl story still doesn't play." And it never would, since it was not about a dewy-eyed adoles-cent and the boy next door, but an impressionable young woman awakening to her sexuality through the machinations of a traveling player, who is some-thing of a stud.

When the screenplays of Joseph L. Mankiewicz and Anita Loos proved un-filmable, *The Pirate* was entrusted to the screenwriting team of Frances Hack-ett and Albert Goodrich, perhaps with the blessing of Freed and Minnelli, who conceived the film as a vehicle for Judy (Manuela), billed above Kelly (Serafin). What could have been the first psychological musical—something to which *Lady in the Dark* (Paramount, 1944) aspired but failed to achieve—became a thoroughly disjointed movie with a middling Cole Porter score and set pieces that, with one exception, did little to advance the plot. Part of the reason was Judy's bouts of depression, weight fluctuation, despondency over a crumbling marriage (it was over by December 1950), and perhaps postpartum depression (she had given birth to Liza in 1946, a year before *The Pirate* went into production on February 17, 1947), causing her to miss 99 of 135 shooting days. The budget soared to $3.765 million; although *The Pirate* took in $15,795 on opening day, May 24, 1948, at Radio City Music Hall, it never caught on with the public, grossing only $2.656 million domestically. Because of Judy's frequent absences, Kelly became the star by default, and Behrman's satiric comedy landed somewhere between a rape fantasy and a clown show.

The movie opens with a close-up of a red leather-bound book with the title, *The Pirate*, in gold lettering. What follows is not a reenactment of the book but a reading session in which Manuela entertains her friends with stories about the pirate Macoco, aka Mack the Black, as she envisions him swooping down on her "like a chicken hawk" and carrying her off—to where is irrelevant. Manuela insists that wherever he takes her, she would be treated like a queen. ("The Pirate Ballet" suggests otherwise.) Manuela is an orphan with an unfettered imagination, whose financially strapped relatives have arranged for her to marry the corpulent Don Pedro (Walter Slezak), the real Macoco and hardly her dream lover. The arranged marriage solved the problem in terms of the Production Code. Since Manuela is unmarried, there will be neither adultery nor seduction, just a woman shedding her inhibitions and a man assisting her in the process. If feminists protest that this is the classic case of a man bringing out the woman in the girl, playing Pygmalion to her Trilby, they would be right. But this was the 1940s when women did not control their sex life because they needed a man to tell them they had one.

Instead of exploring the tension between the real and the illusory, which admittedly would require an almost complete overhauling of Behrman's play, Hackett and Goodrich stayed with the deception theme, pursuing it to the limit, so that it is only a matter of time before the masquerade is over and reality, or some semblance of it, sets in. It might have been different if the controversial "Voodoo" number with Judy and Kelly had been retained. It was so erotic, with the stars' libidos in full gallop, that Louis B. Mayer demanded it be cut. And yet *The Pirate* is all about sex, sublimated and otherwise.

Serafin, the head of a troupe of itinerant players, is a preening lothario who wears his masculinity like a cod piece, as he reveals in "Nina," ogling women passing by, climbing up balconies, dancing on ledges, walking a flower-entwined tightrope like Lunt, and sliding down candy-striped poles. He immediately senses that Manuela is sexually repressed. Judy's Manuela is a confused virgin, with a limited knowledge of carnality, knowing only that it is something she would rather avoid but finding it difficult to do so. When the players perform in the square beneath her hotel room, the music and the oppressive heat prevent her from sleeping. As if drawn to their world, she does not even bother to change out of her shift. She throws on a red skirt, dons a cloak, and joins the spectators. Serafin spots her in the crowd and makes her part of the act. He hypnotizes her, ridding her of her inhibitions, as she launches into "Mack the Black," enumerating his exploits with abandon, as if she were experiencing them. Judy threw herself into the number, as if she were truly liberated by the music. She sways as if in a trance, bringing the song to a frenzied climax, her eyes staring wildly like someone possessed. "Mack the Black" is a superb example of characterization through song, as Manuela releases her inner self, sheds her cloak, and literally lets her hair down. It is also sung at such a fever pitch that it's possible to overlook an unusual example of Porter's wit: "Mack the Black, around the Caribbéan / Mack the Black, or Caríbbean Sea." By shifting the accent from the é to the í, Porter is making allowances for either pronunciation and at the same time having some linguistic fun.

Once the number is over, it's story time again. Manuela believes Serafin is Macoco; when she learns otherwise, she pelts him with crockery. Complementing "Mack the Black" and visually surpassing it, is "The Pirate Dance" (really a ballet), Kelly's shining hour and the movie's high point. Manuela's ode to Macoco and the ballet share the same music—"Mack the Black," first sung by Manuela and then danced by Serafin. But in "The Pirate Dance," the music is lavishly orchestrated. One could be at a performance of a ballet like Khachaturian's *Spartacus* and feel the same thrill. It is hard to tell if the ballet is Manuela's or Serafin's fantasy. Perhaps it is a shared one. We know Manuela has a rich inner life, but what about Serafin? Standing in the square beneath Manuela's window, Serafin spots a donkey. He is intrigued by the donkey's ears. When Manuela looks out of the open window, there is an almost imperceptible dissolve to Serafin as a pirate in an abbreviated black outfit looking like Douglas Fairbanks. Wielding a scimitar, he dances before a cowering woman (Manuela?), who sways back and forth as he menaces her. She wears a white head wrap braided on either side like pointed ears, a surreal evocation of the donkey's that set off the fantasy. Serafin swings his scimitar, cutting off the earlike braids as the woman topples over like a discarded puppet. Serafin and his fellow pirates advance like a marauding band, twirling their scimitars as if they were doing the Sabre Dance. He grabs hold of a female captive, and just when you think they will go into a dance, he throws her on the deck. Is this the rough stuff that Manuela secretly desired but dared not admit? Amid swirling smoke and fiery explosions, Serafin/Mack, lusting for booty, scoops up a tangle of jewels from a treasure chest, as if loot was all he really wanted. When the ballet ends, Kelly looks as if he has awakened from a reverie. Was he imagining himself as Mack? If so, was the ballet his fantasy? Manuela was looking down from the window, but at whom or what? Serafin? The donkey? Her puzzled expression suggests a reaction shot. But a reaction to what? If this was her vision of a pirate's life, there is no motivation for it—no dreamy dissolve or mesmerized look. Whether Judy even knew the context is doubtful.

She and Minnelli had violent rows during the shoot, with Judy snarling at him at one point. Minnelli may have framed her at the window and told her to look curious. She obeyed. He was the director. At the time he was also her husband. Judy must have sensed it would be the last time she and Minnelli would work together. And it was.

The rest of the film is an anticlimax with a silly denouement. Don Pedro gives himself away, and Manuela joins Serafin's troupe. In the grand finale, Manuela and Serafin, or rather Judy and Kelly, dressed as circus clowns with matching makeup, urge the audience, and by extension ourselves, to "be a clown." It was the only time in the film that Judy looked happy. She was not Judy Garland any longer, troubled movie star fed a diet of uppers and downers to get through a shoot, but Frances Gumm, the vaudevillian, beholden to no studio and cavorting like a trouper on the Orpheum circuit. Judy would do a few more musicals, but, except for "A Couple of Swells" in *Easter Parade* (1948), she would never seem as relaxed as she was in "Be a Clown." Minnelli may have wanted to unveil a new Judy Garland, but what he succeeded in doing was showing us the old Judy, who knew the freedom of performance before Hollywood robbed her of it.

Minnelli had great hopes for the film. It had a few highlights, including the first time "Be a Clown" is sung by Kelly and danced by the extraordinary Nicholas Brothers in their last major screen appearance as a team. The brothers combined athletic grace with astonishing leaps, splits, and tumbles; sadly, their art was not seen in movie theaters in the South, where scenes with African American performers like Dorothy Dandridge and Lena Horne were excised as if they were excrescences. After seeing a rough cut, Minnelli wired Arthur Freed, who was staying at New York's Hampshire House, calling *The Pirate* the "best thing any of us has done." Not really. There were too many ideas being tossed about, which invariably happens during a production. Choreographer Robert Alton argued for "violent emotional transitions" with Serafin at one point throwing daggers, but at what or whom? He never specified. But what Minnelli wanted he could not achieve: a film that would define the essence of Judy Garland. Instead, he got a great solo piece from each star and an astonishing performance by the Nicholas Brothers. Kelly would go on to greater heights in *An American in Paris* and *Singin' in the Rain*; Garland, to her finest role in *A Star Is Born*, directed by George Cukor, who, like Minnelli, was gay, but understood her and her artistry perhaps even better than Minnelli did.

- 6 -

JUDY'S LAST YEARS AT MGM

Arthur Freed's dream was a musical biopic of Irving Berlin, a composer whom he admired and with whose immigrant background he identified. Although he never achieved his goal, he did the next best thing: he produced *Easter Parade* (1948), whose score consists entirely of Berlin's songs, making the film a tribute to the composer. The main title said it all: "Irving Berlin's *Easter Parade*," followed by the names of Judy Garland, Fred Astaire, and Peter Lawford, with Ann Miller heading the supporting cast in a role that was hardly supporting. Paramount had paid a similar homage to Berlin in *Holiday Inn* (1942) and *Blue Skies* (1946), both of which *Easter Parade* surpassed in style, casting, and screenplay. *Holiday Inn* was an excuse to introduce the classic "White Christmas," sung as only Bing Crosby could. But the plot—a New England inn that is only open on holidays, causing one to wonder how it could survive, even with classy floor shows—is rather silly. The Crosby–Marjorie Reynolds romance never ignited, leaving only the sound track with Crosby's introspective versions of "White Christmas" and "Be Careful, It's My Heart." *Blue Skies* included more Berlin favorites ("A Pretty Girl Is Like a Melody," "Puttin' on the Ritz," "Heat Wave," "Always," "You Keep Coming Back Like a Song," and the title song). But the triangular plot—Crosby and Astaire in love with Joan Caulfield—veered off into melodrama when Astaire's character falls from a ledge during a performance, bringing an end to his dancing career. The trio is reunited at the end when Caulfield, who disappeared from the plot, returns, followed by a shot of an azure sky for those who take movie titles literally.

The *Easter Parade* sound track was in a class by itself, a mix of the old and the new, so carefully worked into the plot that the songs seemed to spring out of it, either moving it forward or touching it up. Whatever the case, they were an easy fit. There was never the feeling of songs getting squeezed into the narrative. Peter Lawford sings "A Fella with an Umbrella" after paying a street vendor for his umbrella so he can protect Judy from the rain. Astaire addresses "It Only Happens When I Dance with You" to Ann Miller, reminding her of their onstage chemistry after she tells him she is leaving their act to star on Broadway. The title song is naturally reserved for the Fifth Avenue Easter Parade.

Other songs in *Easter Parade* came from Berlin's Tin Pan Alley days: "Snooky Ookums" (1912), "When the Midnight Choo Choo Leaves for Alabam'" (1912), "I Want to Go Back to Michigan" (1914), "I Love a Piano" (1915), and "The Girl I Love Is on a Magazine Cover" (1916). Judy was singing "I Want to Go Back to Michigan" the night Astaire chose her as Miller's replacement; "I Love a Piano," when she auditioned for Astaire; "Snooky Ookums" when she and Astaire were headlining in vaudeville; and "When the Midnight Choo Choo Leaves for Alabam'" when they auditioned for Ziegfeld. "The Girl I Love Is on a Magazine Cover" was a *Ziegfeld Follies* number danced by Miller, sung by sweet-voiced Richard Beavers, and featuring tastefully dressed cover girls coming to life, this time without floral or feathered accessories.

Two songs came from Broadway: "Shaking the Blues Away," introduced by Ruth Etting in *Ziegfeld Follies of 1927*, and performed by Miller, waving a red feather fan and dancing with such abandon that she seemed to be ridding herself of whatever "unhappy news" had been plaguing her; and the title song, introduced by Marilyn Miller and Clifton Webb in *As Thousands Cheer* (1933)—a song that Berlin intended as "conversation set to music," which is exactly how Judy delivered it. When Judy sang "Easter Parade" at the end of the film, she treated it as musical dialogue as she prepared Astaire for the grand procession along Fifth Avenue, describing how they would join the fashionably dressed participants and perhaps find themselves in the rotogravure. Judy interpreted "Better Luck Next Time" the same way, but as a soliloquy set to music. Seated at the bar of the saloon where she used to perform, and wearing an emerald-green velvet gown with matching earrings and necklace, she muses on her fate, convinced that Astaire prefers his former partner to her. Give Judy a rueful song and she can turn it into a confession without mea culpas. Resigned and with just a hint of regret, she made the lyrics into a credo. In real life, Judy was a recent mother with a fraying marriage and a history of depression that would eventually lead to the parting of the ways with MGM. Oddly, she had better luck next time, with her legendary *Judy at the Palace* (1951, 1957); concerts, including the spectacular one at Carnegie Hall on April 23, 1961; her own television show (1963–1964); and her frequent appearances as a talk-show guest where she revealed a wicked sense of humor that MGM never exploited.

Except for "Better Luck Next Time," most of Berlin's new songs for the film were not intended for Judy. Astaire had most of them, including the first three: "Happy Easter," "Drum Crazy," and the best, "It Only Happens When I Dance with You," his attempt to convince Miller that he would be lost without her. It was also the kind of song that could transport audiences to dreamland.

Astaire teaches it to Judy, who plays it dutifully on the piano, but it is not her song. Astaire and Miller later dance to it, leaving Judy wondering if her partner would ever be able to free himself of her rival.

Since the first three songs in *Easter Parade*—the second of which was a bravura dance number—were Astaire's, it looked as if he might be taking over the film as Gene Kelly did in *The Pirate*. The three other principals—Astaire, Miller, and Lawford—had all made their appearance before Judy. *Easter Parade* begins on the Saturday before Easter 1911 with Don Hewes (Astaire) sauntering down Fifth Avenue, extending a musical greeting to passersby ("Happy Easter") and then going on a shopping spree that concludes with a visit to a toy store where he spots a rabbit that a young boy has already claimed. Determined to get the rabbit as another surprise present for Nadine Hale (Miller), he distracts the boy by doing an intricate dance while beating on toy drums and then skipping out of the store with the rabbit, after giving the kid a lesson in the art of the con through dance. Nadine is reluctant to accept his presents, informing him that she has had an offer to star in a show. He counters with "It Only Happens When I Dance with You," reminding her that she was the catalyst that sparked their act. Judy has to wait until Astaire bets that he can replace Nadine with the first woman he sees and make her into a pro. Naturally, it's Judy's character, Hannah Brown, after she delivers the nostalgic "I Want to Go Back to Michigan."

The Frances Goodrich and Albert Hackett screenplay, with additions by Sidney Sheldon, was another show biz musical about a team's breakup and its reconstitution. Eventually, Don and Hannah have a crack at the *Ziegfeld Follies*, until Don discovers that Nadine is starring and instead signs with Charles Dillingham, a rival producer. We see only the last two numbers of the Dillingham production: "Steppin' Out with My Baby," another original for Astaire, which, for some reason, he performs in brownface, which is at odds with his attire: a straw hat with a red band, a red vest, and two-toned shoes; and the priceless "A Couple of Swells," with Don and Hannah as hobos in dented top hats and ragged tuxes—and Hannah with a missing front tooth—lamenting having to "walk up the avenue" because they have neither trolley fare nor any means of transportation. Astaire was mocking his image as an impeccable dresser, and Judy was reveling in her raffish persona that was at odds with her usual self. Deck her out with a caved-in hat and a beat-up tux, and she becomes an endearing clown, having as much fun with Astaire as she did with Kelly in the "Be a Clown" finale of *The Pirate*.

The denouement is what one might expect. Nadine reenters Don's life, Hannah gets miffed, but everything works out, so that Don and Hannah can promenade along Fifth Avenue on Easter Sunday 1912. The closing shot is art directors Cedric Gibbons and Jack Martin Smith's masterful soundstage replica of New York's Fifth Avenue between 49th and 50th Streets with St. Patrick's Cathedral looming in the background, which allows the film to end on a note of majestic awe that some might even find spiritual.

Easter Parade was pure entertainment. There was no political subtext, no complications other than the usual romantic ones, and no straining of credulity. The sets and costumes—except for Miller's, which are forties chic—are what one would expect in a film that spans the 1911–1912 period. The *Easter Parade* released in July 1948, however, was not the one that either Arthur Freed or MGM originally planned, which was supposed to have reunited Judy and Gene Kelly, with Cyd Charisse as Kelly's onetime partner and love interest. Minnelli had been scheduled to direct; and the husband and wife team of Francis Goodrich and Albert Hackett commissioned to write a screenplay based on Berlin's memories of vaudeville. Judy had recovered, at least temporarily, from a nervous breakdown, attributed both to her grueling schedule at MGM, where she went from picture to picture; and to Minnelli, who proved not to be the father figure she was seeking. After *The Pirate*, Judy began to think of Minnelli as an antagonist, not a collaborator. She informed Arthur Freed that she no longer wished to work with him. The marriage was beyond repair, and two years after *Easter Parade* was released, they initiated divorce proceedings. Freed complied with her request, leaving Minnelli in a state of confusion, wondering why Judy had not discussed her dissatisfaction with him personally.

Pleased with Charles Walters's direction of *Good News* (1947), Freed put him in the director's chair, which delighted Judy, who had danced with Walters in *Girl Crazy* and *Presenting Lily Mars*. After both Kelly and Charisse had accidents that affected their mobility, they were replaced by Astaire and Miller, both MGM newcomers but with impressive resumes. After making his last RKO musical with Ginger Rogers, *The Story of Irene and Vernon Castle* (1939), Astaire began freelancing, stopping off at MGM to costar with George Murphy and Eleanor Powell in *Broadway Melody of 1940* (1939), in which he and Powell danced a ravishing "Begin the Beguine," the only time these two extraordinary talents appeared together. He moved over to Columbia for two movies with Rita Hayworth: *You'll Never Be Rich* (1941), with a mediocre score by Cole Porter; and the far better *You Were Never Lovelier* (1942), with a classic score by Jerome Kern that included the title song and "Dearly Beloved." He went back to RKO for perhaps the strangest film of his career, *The Sky's the Limit* (1943), in which he played a former member of the Flying Tigers who sneaks off to New York for some fun before reporting for duty. After having deceived, romanced, and alienated a newspaper photographer (Joan Leslie), Astaire in a faux tux—black jacket and bow tie with a white carnation and a fedora in place of a top hat—goes bar hopping while singing the Johnny

Mercer–Harold Arlen standard, "One for Me Baby (and One More for the Road)" as a boozy monologue, delivered piecemeal to indifferent bartenders. At the last bar, frustrated by his inability to court the photographer in proper fashion, he throws himself into a furious dance, leaping up on the bar and tapping away his self-loathing. When the dance does not do the trick, he smashes rows of glasses and hurls a chair at the mirror behind the bar, as if he cannot bear to see his reflection. He addresses the last line to the bartender ("So make it one for my baby and one more for the road / That long, long road"), laying out some bills for the drinks and the damage, picking up his hat from the floor with his walking stick, and exiting as if nothing had happened, except a display of regret and vandalism by a man who is completely clueless when it comes to women. Astaire did not so much sing as act out the song as if it were a monologue that should have been an interior one except that it sneaked out of the unconscious in an attempt to find a sympathetic ear.

The sequence is significant for other reasons. Astaire, playing a character named Fred, choreographed it himself. Apparently Mercer changed one of the final lines to include his character's name: "Don't let it be said that little Freddie can't carry his load." Whether the addition is revelatory of Astaire's character, Fred Atwell, or of Astaire himself, is for biographers to ponder. Astaire was then forty-four and perhaps was thinking of retiring from the screen, where he had been carrying his "load" since he made his film debut in *Flying down to Rio* (RKO, 1933). By 1946 he felt ready to retire. Freed had lured him back to MGM for *Ziegfeld Follies* (1946), which had been in production from April 1944 to February 1945; and *Yolanda and the Thief* (1945), which began filming on January 15, 1945, and six months later was ready to be previewed. The preview audiences were enthusiastic, but *Yolanda and the Thief* proved too weirdly fey for most tastes and incurred a loss of $1.64 million in its initial release.

The failure of *Yolanda and the Thief* was a sobering experience for both Astaire and his costar, Lucille Bremer. Although Astaire seemed to have found an ideal partner in Bremer, with whom he danced in both *Yolanda and the Thief* and *Ziegfeld Follies*, stardom was unimportant to Bremer, who left the business in 1948. Astaire thought of doing the same after making *Blue Skies* (Paramount, 1946). But after *Blue Skies* brought in $5.7 million in rentals, Astaire had second thoughts. So did Arthur Freed. It took a chance incident—Gene Kelly breaking his ankle playing touch football—for Astaire to return to MGM in *Easter Parade*, a box office phenomenon ($5.803 million), which marked the beginning of his glorious second act.

Ann Miller had previously been at RKO (1936–1940) and Columbia (1941–1945), before making her MGM debut in *Easter Parade* and remained at the studio until 1956. Never a superstar, she shared Eleanor Powell's title as the Queen of Taps and could always be counted on for a showstopper.

Believing that the Goodrich-Hackett script needed a lighter touch, Freed brought in Sidney Sheldon, who had won an Oscar for his original screenplay, *The Bachelor and the Bobby Soxer* (RKO, 1947), although it is hard to determine what he contributed. Regardless, it was a seamless script that resulted in a grand musical, which came off better than one would have imagined.

Judy's last two MGM movies, *In the Good Old Summertime* (1949) and *Summer Stock* (1950), were less memorable. Because of the success of *Easter Parade*, she was scheduled to play opposite Astaire again in *The Barkleys of Broadway* (1949), but the demons that plagued her had returned and she was replaced by Ginger Rogers, who had not danced with her former partner since *The Story of Irene and Vernon Castle* (1939). The Betty Comden and Adolph Green script was a variation on the "breaking up of the act" plot, in which Ginger decides she wants to branch out on her own and do serious drama. In the intervening years, Ginger had won an Oscar for *Kitty Foyle* (1940) and revealed her versatility in both drama (*The Primrose Path* [1940], *Tender Comrade* [1943], *I'll Be Seeing You* [1944]) and comedy (*The Major and the Minor* [1942], in which she played a twelve-year-old for most of the picture; *Roxie Hart* [1942], *It Had to Be You* [1947]). She was far more assured than she had ever been before and now was every bit Astaire's equal. Ginger could hold the stage on her own, as she proved when she replaced Carol Channing in *Hello, Dolly!* in 1966. Less flamboyant than Channing, she sang an electric "Before the Parade Passes By," believing every word of it as she vowed to "get some life back into my life."

While *The Barkleys of Broadway* had been earmarked for Judy, *In the Good Old Summertime* was meant for June Allyson. Joe Pasternak felt there was operetta potential in *The Shop around the Corner* (1940), Ernst Lubitsch's near-perfect romantic comedy about two employees in a Budapest gift shop who can barely tolerate each other, unaware that they are anonymous pen pals carrying on an epistolary romance. *In the Good Old Summertime* was not the operetta Pasternak had in mind. The potential was there but was never realized until *The Shop around the Corner* was turned into a stage musical, *She Loves Me* (1963), with a score by Sheldon Harnick and Jerry Bock, which proved there was an audience for an operetta with a cast that looked as if it had stepped out of 1930s Budapest into 1960s Broadway. Like *The Shop around the Corner*, *She Loves Me* did not gloss over a sales clerk's affair with his employer's wife. In operetta, however, people do not have sex; they have liaisons. And eventually, the bounder gets bounced, and the pen pals discover that their workplace hostility is the flip side of love.

Originally, June Allyson and Frank Sinatra were slated for *In the Good Old Summertime*. Since Allyson and her husband, Dick Powell, had already adopted a daughter when the film went into production in fall 1948, Allyson preferred motherhood for the time being, returning the following year for *The Statton Story* (1949). Sinatra would have been out of his element as a music store employee at the turn of the twentieth century; since his character originally had no songs, they would have to be drawn from period music, which was not Sinatra's specialty. After *The Kissing Bandit* disaster, Sinatra went into *Take Me Out to the Ball Game* and *On the Town* (both 1949), which, along with *High Society* (1956), were his best MGM musicals. Allyson and Sinatra were replaced by Judy and Van Johnson in the roles originated by Margaret Sullavan and James Stewart in the Ernst Lubitsch original, which would later be assumed by Tom Hanks and Meg Ryan in the second remake, Nora Ephron's *You've Got Mail* (1998), in which the antagonists correspond by e-mail.

For *In the Good Old Summertime*, the Budapest gift shop in *The Shop around the Corner* became a Chicago music store in the early decades of the twentieth century so Judy could sing "Meet Me Tonight in Dreamland" while trying to sell a harp; "Put Your Arms around Me, Honey"; and Eva Tanguay's declaration of independence, "I Don't Care," which Judy made her own as she flaunted her indifference to public opinion.

Some plot points remained the same: the cool-to-each-other workers but ardent pen pals; and the restaurant rendezvous when they decide to meet in person, with Judy bringing a red rose and a copy of Elizabeth Barrett Browning's sonnets, as opposed to Margaret Sullavan's red carnation and copy of *Anna Karenina*. There is no adulterous employee, and therefore no cuckolded employer who attempts suicide. The names have become anglicized (Veronica Fisher and Andrew Larkin vs. Klara Novak and Alfred Kralik), but the resolution occurs again on Christmas eve when Andrew reveals his identity by quoting from one of his letters. But the movie can't end there. Audiences were promised summertime, even though most of the action takes place in December. Cut to a summer scene a few years later when Andrew and Veronica, now married, are strolling in the park with their daughter, played by the almost three-year-old Liza Minnelli. The film was a wonderful experience for Judy, even though it is one of her lesser ones. Everyone made her feel at home, and she enjoyed great rapport with Van Johnson, who, when Louis B. Mayer asked how Judy managed to get through the shoot without any problems, told him that "we made her feel wanted and needed." The nurturing showed in Judy's performance, especially in her delivery of "I Don't Care," in which she danced around the floor in a red gown, throwing herself into the number and, temporarily, throwing out the neuroses that went with them.

Judy's tenure at MGM did not end in a blaze of glory, but in a spectacular finale that bore no relationship to the film in which she starred, and, in fact, was shot several months after its completion. Someone at MGM—perhaps Joe Pasternak, the producer, or Louis B. Mayer—came up with the idea of a final backyard musical, *Summer Stock* (1950), which would reunite Judy and Mickey, with Judy as the owner of a farm that has seen better days; and Mickey as the star-writer-producer of a show that Judy's stage-struck sister (Gloria DeHaven) hopes to put on in Judy's barn after it has been converted into a summer theater. Judy agrees, on the condition that the cast earn their keep by performing farm chores. Mickey was freelancing and no longer a box office draw, particularly after the failure of *Summer Holiday* (1948), which seems far more innovative today with its rhyming dialogue and subjective camera sequence than it was when first released. Since Judy and Gene Kelly had already made two films together, *For Me and My Gal* and *The Pirate*, Kelly seemed an ideal costar, who could also be her protector-therapist-confidant when she had panic attacks, caused by her insecurity and sense of alienation after three months at Peter Brent Brigham in Boston, where her health was restored, albeit temporarily, along with a weight gain of twenty-five pounds. Fortunately, Judy was surrounded by a caring cast—Kelly, Phil Silvers, Marjorie Main, Gloria DeHaven, and Eddie Bracken—and a supportive director, Charles Walters, whom she regarded as a friend and ally.

Judy donned overalls in the early scenes, which made her look dumpy, but she seemed ebullient as she drove a tractor, singing "Howdy, Neighbor! Happy Harvest!" She and Kelly squared off in "Portland Fancy," a contra dance in which they challenged each other step for step, as if they were contestants. The writers, George Wells and Cy Gomberg, went back to *Babes in Arms*, *Presenting Lily Mars*, and *Easter Parade* for the creaky plot point of the star's replacement. After DeHaven walks out, someone has to walk in—and who better than Judy? But the film was lacking a real finale. When Charles Walters informed Judy that she would have to return to the studio to shoot it, she agreed, provided it would be Harold Arlen and Ted Koehler's "Get Happy," which Ruth Etting had introduced in *The Nine-Fifteen Review* (1930). Judy wanted a spectacular finish, perhaps thinking that "Get Happy" might be her last. It certainly was for MGM, but a greater one awaited her: the "Born in a Trunk" sequence in *A Star Is Born* (Warner Bros., 1954), in which her character, Vicki Lester, chronicled her rise to stardom from vaudeville and tab shows to supper clubs and Broadway. It was the ultimate bravura piece; "Get Happy" came close.

What immediately catches the eye is Judy's androgynous look: She is wearing a tuxedo jacket, sheer tights that made her legs look sculpted, black pumps, and a sporty fedora. Audiences could have seen her in a similar costume in *Easter Parade*, in which she was supposed to sing Irving Berlin's "Mr. Monotony," except that the number was cut but can be seen on YouTube. Berlin must have been fond of "Mr. Monotony," which he had originally composed for *Miss Liberty* (1949), his unsuccessful Broadway musical about a reporter's attempt to locate the model who posed for the Statue of Liberty. Realizing it had no place in *Miss Liberty*, Berlin thought Judy could get it to work in *Easter Parade*. It was not a question of Judy's weaving her old black magic; the problem was the lyrics, which were too suggestive for a family musical. Mr. Monotony is a slide trombone player whose lack of rhythm extends to his love life: "Any pleasant interlude that would mean a change of mood / Didn't go with Mr. Monotony." As a result, when a clarinetist comes along, Mrs. Monotony changes instrumentalists. Berlin still had not given up; he inserted it into the score of *Call Me Madam* (1950) for Ethel Merman as a celebrated Washington hostess sent as an ambassador to a mythical European country. "Mr. Monotony" was dropped during the out-of-town tryouts of that show, too, but was reinstated forty years later in *Jerome Robbins' Broadway* (1989), a retrospective of excerpts from musicals Robbins choreographed, which included *Miss Liberty*, the song's original destination.

If "Mr. Monotony" had survived the cut in *Easter Parade*, the costume would not have created the sensation that it did in *Summer Stock*. When Judy came back to MGM for "Get Happy," she had slimmed down considerably. Gone was the woman in overalls and conservative dresses. Here was a true icon with no focal point. You didn't know where to look: the playful eyes, the snapping fingers, the sexy legs, or the fedora that she played with, teasing you with every tug of the brim.

Against an abstract pink backdrop dabbed with fragments of clouds, eight dark-suited men move in a circle. One stands with his arms apart, as if shielding someone. He drops to the floor, revealing Judy, whose appearance energizes the men. They seem transported, as if they were at a revival meeting with Judy as the bringer of good news: Judgment Day is not a day of wrath, but an opportunity to go across the river to the peaceful other side. One would never know she was singing about the sweet by-and-by. In fact, the song is so jubilant that you can't wait to make the crossing, as long as Judy is on board, moving her hips—a thrust here, a thrust there—and toying with the brim of her fedora, pulling it down over her right eye on arrival. Forget the joyous death-wish lyrics and watch an artist make light of the ultimate reality, which Judy experienced nineteen years later on June 22, 1969, when she went to the other side.

- 7 -

THE REVUE, HOLLYWOOD STYLE

A revue has been defined as "a form of entertainment so designed that it doesn't matter when you get there." There was no plot, perhaps just a theme, but always a mix of specialty acts, witty skits, songs that were at least hummable and a few perhaps that were memorable, at least one knockout solo, long-limbed dancers, and a grand finale. The revue was, for a time, a Broadway perennial. In Hollywood, it was a hothouse plant. The Broadway revue was a high-toned variety show, topical and sophisticated, with sketches interspersed with musical numbers. The more lavish ones were Florenz Ziegfeld's *Follies*, George White's *Scandals*, and Earl Carroll's *Vanities*. There were also classics such as *Blackbirds of 1929* with an African American cast including Bill "Bojangles" Robinson and Leslie Uggams's mother, Eloise; *Pins and Needles* (1937), a pro-labor revue performed by members of the International Ladies Garment Workers Union (ILGWU); *Sons o' Fun* (1941) with Carmen Miranda in totemic splendor with platform shoes and a fruit-bursting headdress, which became her calling card during her Hollywood career; and *Call Me Mister* (1946), in which Betty Garrett delivered a deliciously suggestive "South America, Take It Away," as she enumerated the orthopedic problems caused by the conga, rhumba, and samba ("I've a great big crack in the back of my sacroilliac").

Revues reveled in topical satire that flattered theatergoers who prided themselves on being au courrant. Bette Davis's withering impersonation of Tallulah Bankhead in the short-lived revue, *Two's Company* (1951), would have been lost on anyone unaware of the frosty relationship between the two after Davis landed the roles in *Dark Victory* (1939) and *The Little Foxes* (1941), which Bankhead originated on stage. And anyone unfamiliar with W. Somerset Maugham's short story "Rain," or the movie versions with Jeanne Eagels and Joan Crawford as Sadie Thompson, would not have appreciated Davis's take on Sadie and her complaint that men are always trying to convert her, but not immediately: "Lord, make her a good girl / But not right now." *Two's Company* could not be accused of pandering to the marketplace.

Moviegoers, who only knew Bert Lahr as the Cowardly Lion in *The Wizard of Oz* (1939) and bought tickets for the revue *Two on the Aisle* (1951) on the strength of his name, might have wondered why audiences cheered the first act finale, "Vaudeville Ain't Dead / Catch Our Act at the Met," with music by Jule Styne and lyrics by Betty Comden and Adolph Green, in which Lahr and his costar, Dolores Gray, played two vaudevillians spoofing the efforts of Metropolitan Opera's general manager, Rudoph Bing, to unfetter a tradition-bound art form: "[Bing] dressed up the stage and undressed the soprano." And if you didn't know Donizetti's opera, *Lucia di Lammermoor*, the exchange between Gray and Lahr—"I'll play Lucia" (Gray), to which Lahr replies, "And I'll play sextet"—would make no sense. The reference is to the great sextet in the second act. But it gets better: Lahr: "By Don Ameche"; Gray, "No, Donizetti." This is the kind of wit that characterized the Broadway revue, but not the Hollywood equivalent—unless it originated on Broadway like *New Faces of 1952*, which was rarely the case.

New Faces of 1952 was the exception; the 1954 movie version—retitled *New Faces*, produced by Twentieth Century–Fox and available on YouTube and DVD—was a duplicate of the original with the same cast, except for a trivial story line (a revue in need of an infusion of cash to keep from closing) that was grafted on to give it the semblance of a movie musical. Still, it is the only example on film of what a Broadway revue was like with the musical numbers and sketches following each other in quick succession, and the wit never faltering for an instant. There was Alice Ghostly lamenting the impossibility of finding romance in puritanical Boston ("Boston Beguine"); Eartha Kitt lolling around on divans in "Monotonous," voicing her boredom with everything including a gift of the Black Sea as her personal swimming pool; and the hoedown, "Lizzie Borden" ("You can't chop your mama up in Massachusetts even if you're tired of her cuisine"). There was always room in a revue for a pensive song, more ironic than satiric. *New Faces* had two of them: "Penny Candy," in which an affluent woman pines for the days when she could go to the local grocery store for penny candy; and "Guess Who I Saw Today?" in which a suburban wife stops at a cafe one afternoon and sees her husband at a table with another woman. Two sketches were standouts: "The Explorer," with Paul Lynde with a crutch and his arm in a sling, describing a disastrous safari and declaring that "Africa is not the nicest place in the world"; and Ronny Graham impersonating an effete Truman Capote in "Oedipus Goes South," best appreciated by those who had read Capote's *Other Voices, Other Rooms*. *New Faces of 1952* epitomized the classic Broadway revue.

Another outstanding example of the Broadway revue was *John Murray Anderson's Almanac*, which opened in late 1953 and starred Hermione Gingold and Billy De Wolfe, with an outstanding supporting cast that included Harry

Belafonte, Orson Bean, Carleton Carpenter, and Polly Bergen. "Which witch?" was Gingold's droll inquiry about which witch she would be playing in a production of *Macbeth*. Gingold and De Wolfe in drag did a hilarious bit as two middle-aged women who get increasingly tipsy on port. But the highlight was Jean Kerr's irreverent parody, "Don Brown's Body," inspired by a staged reading of Stephen Vincent Benét's epic, *John Brown's Body* (1928), performed on Broadway in 1953 by Tyrone Power, Raymond Massey, and Judith Anderson. "Don Brown's Body" is done in the style of Mickey Spillane, lurid and pulpy ("So I kicked him in the mouth and his teeth dropped all over the sidewalk like marbles."). And the familiar "John Brown's body lies a-mouldering in the grave" became "Don Brown's body lies a-moulderin' at the 'Y.'"

No movie revue had that kind of wit, certainly not MGM's *The Hollywood Revue of 1929*, which was vaudeville with big-name stars. Jack Benny, painfully unfunny, was the master of ceremonies; the dashing Conrad Nagel, the interlocutor, had to do shtick with Benny, neither of whom was comfortable with the material. The highlights were Arthur Freed and Nacio Herb Brown's "Singin' in the Rain" played over the opening credits, later sung by Cliff "Ukelele Ike" Edwards and danced by the rain-coated ensemble; Joan Crawford in her flapper phase dancing a more genteel Charleston than the one she did on a tabletop in *Our Dancing Daughters* (1928); and Norma Shearer and John Gilbert enacting the balcony scene from *Romeo and Juliet* in the grand manner and then switching to the vernacular for a mass audience.

The low points of *The Hollywood Revue of 1929* include Marie Dressler looking menacingly imperious as she sang "I'm a Queen," which would have caused any sane subject to emigrate; and Laurel and Hardy as bumbling magicians in a sketch requiring Hardy to slip on a banana peel and toss a cake into the wings that you know will encrust someone's clothes—in this case, Benny's. Unless a revue is thoroughly cinematic, with the numbers following each other seamlessly, it comes off as a movie without a plot. Fluidity is everything, but that is exactly what was lacking in the cumbersome *Hollywood Revue of 1929*.

During World War II, the revue became the equivalent of a studio showcase with a wisp of a plot for those who prefer a story line, however tenuous. In *Star-Spangled Rhythm* (Paramount, 1942), a guard at Paramount Pictures leads his son in the navy to believe that he is a studio producer and can put on a show for the sailors with Paramount's top stars such as Bing Crosby, Bob Hope, Dorothy Lamour, Veronica Lake, Paulette Goddard, Ray Milland, and Fred MacMurray. In true fairytale fashion, the performance comes off with the Paramount regulars recreating the kind of variety show that GIs would have seen on army bases during the war. There was no attempt at art or sophistication; this was entertainment for the undiscerning. The skits included Fred MacMurray, Franchot Tone, and Ray Milland imitating women whose card game is interrupted when they see a mouse; Dorothy Lamour, Paulette Goddard, and Veronica Lake mocking their screen personas in "Sweater, Sarong, and Peekaboo Bang"; Alan Ladd in a trench coat parodying his "tough guy" image in "Scarface"; and the Harold Arlen–Johnny Mercer classic, "That Old Black Magic," sung by Johnny Johnson and danced by a fairy-like Vera Zorina. Bing Crosby ended the show (and the movie) with "Old Glory," which he sang with such patriotic fervor that one could imagine some moviegoers stopping to buy war bonds in the lobby.

Not to be undone, Warner Bros. responded with two revues: *Thank Your Lucky Stars* (1943) and *Hollywood Canteen* (1944). Both had plotlines that were simply excuses for appearances by the Warner regulars. In *Thank Your Lucky Stars*, Eddie Cantor hijacks a fundraiser and is about to turn it into his own show when Dennis Morgan and Joan Leslie intervene and restore order. The highlight was a jaded Bette Davis lamenting that "They're Either Too Young or Too Old" by Frank Loesser and Arthur Schwartz, as she bemoans the shortage of available men ("What's good is in the army / What's left will never harm me."). *Hollywood Canteen* had more of a wartime feeling. A corporal (Robert Hutton) drops into the Hollywood Canteen on Cahuenga Boulevard, hoping to see his favorite actress, Joan Leslie. With some help from Jack Carson, he succeeds. The highlights are Roy Rogers on loan from Republic Pictures singing Cole Porter's uncharacteristic "Don't Fence Me In" as if he were an old cowhand from the Rio Grande; and Carson and Jane Wyman teaming up in "What Are You Doin' the Rest of Your Life?" which revealed Wyman's flair for musical comedy that, for some reason, eluded Warner Bros.

There were not enough stars on tap at Columbia for a revue, although the studio attempted something of the sort in *Stars on Parade* (1944), whose stars—Larry Parks, Lynn Merrick, and Judy Clark—were known only to fans of B movies. Republic did its bit with *Hit Parade of 1941* (1940) and *Hit Parade of 1943* (1943), neither of which had anything to do with World War II, although the latter is worth seeing for appearances by the great Dorothy Dandridge and Count Bassie. *Hit Parade of 1947* and *Hit Parade of 1951* (1950) followed, but the series never enjoyed the popularity or the longevity of the radio show that inspired it: *Your Hit Parade* (1935–1953), later a popular television program.

Universal may have been one of the Little Three (the others being Columbia and United Artists), but it managed to come up with an extravaganza, *Follow the Boys* (1944), drawing on its contract players (Susanna Foster, Grace McDonald, Maria Montez, Peggy Ryan, Donald O'Connor, Evelyn Ankers, Lon Chaney Jr., the Andrews Sisters) and outside talent (Jeanette MacDonald, Orson Welles, Sophie Tucker, Vera Zorina, and the renowned pianist Arthur

Rubinstein). The star-studded cast was crammed into a plot about a dancer (George Raft) who, after being classified 4-F, served his country—you guessed it—by staging a show for the armed forces. Jeanette reprised "Beyond the Blue Horizon," which she introduced in *Monte Carlo* (1930) and made GIs less lonely with a reassuring "I'll See You in My Dreams." The Andrews Sisters performed a medley of their hits including "The Beer Barrel Polka" and "The Boogie Woogie Bugle Boy of Company B"; Sophie Tucker sang her old stand-by, "Some of These Days"; Dinah Shore offered a reflective "I Walk Alone" and "I'll Get By"; Orson Welles sawed Marlene Dietrich in half in a magic act; and Arthur Rubinstein played Liszt's Liebestraum. At 122 minutes, *Follow the Boys* was studio surfeit.

The closest Twentieth Century–Fox came to a wartime revue was *Stormy Weather* (1943), a fictionalized and truncated "life" of Bill "Bojangles" Robinson (renamed Bill Williamson), with some extraordinary African American performers: Lena Horne, on loan from MGM; Fats Waller, Cab Calloway, Katherine Dunham and her dancers, the Nicholas Brothers; and, of course, Bojangles himself. Like *Star-Spangled Rhythm*, there was a plot thread (love story of dancer [Robinson] and nightclub singer [Horne]), but what mattered were the artists. Horne performed the title song like a torch singer, with a greater emphasis on the music than the lyrics. When she starred on Broadway in her one-woman show, *Lena Horne: The Lady and Her Music* (1981), she repeated the studio-authorized version and later sang it the way it should be done, with all the passion and heartbreak implicit in the lyrics. By 1981, the storm had passed, and Horne, not Hollywood, was in command.

While the other studios made their wartime revues in black and white, MGM went for color in *Thousands Cheer* (1943), which bears no relationship to the Irving Berlin revue, *As Thousands Cheer* (1933). MGM bought the title and dropped the "As," just as it bought *Lady, Be Good*, and dropped the comma. Leave it to MGM to come up with a movie that is half feature (romance between a GI and an aspiring singer, whose divorced parents reconcile at the end) and a variety show hosted by Mickey Rooney, with MGM stars Judy Garland, Margaret O'Brien, Virginia O'Brien, Eleanor Powell, Red Skelton, June Allyson, Gloria DeHaven, and Donna Reed. Grayson was entrusted with the ending, "United Nations on the March," which she sang in uniform, as if she were at the head of a column. She was, nominally, the star, who had a chance to show off her coloratura in "Sempre libera" from Verdi's *La Traviata*. Horne did a sultry "Honeysuckle Rose," and Garland enlivened the overlong (125 minutes) movie with "The Joint Is Really Jumpin' in Carnegie Hall."

The least self-congratulatory wartime revue was *Stage Door Canteen* (United Artists, 1943), a tribute to the historic basement club at New York's

44th Street Theatre that had been a speakeasy during Prohibition. The canteen, sponsored by the American Theatre Wing, opened in 1942 and attracted large numbers of servicemen passing through New York or stationed there. Actresses, some from Hollywood but mostly from stage and radio, served as hostesses and danced with the GIs; actors volunteered as waiters, busboys, and dishwashers.

Producer Sol Lesser envisioned a film about the Canteen and paid the American Theatre Wing $50,000 for use of the title. *Stage Door Canteen* generated a true wartime ambience with a plot that, unlike *Hollywood Canteen*, did not require a suspension of disbelief. An aspiring actress (Cheryl Walker) volunteers at the Canteen, hoping to be discovered. Instead, she falls for a soldier (William Terry) and disobeys the "no fraternizing" rule by becoming engaged. When she is dismissed, big sister/hostess Katharine Hepburn brings her back to the fold after her fiancé ships out to "destination unknown." *Stage Door Canteen* was a different type of star-sprinkled revue. Over eighty actors and actresses appeared in the film, many in mere walk-ons (Arlene Francis, Virginia Grey, Sam Jaffe, Cornelia Otis Skinner); others in cameo roles with some dialogue (Tallulah Bankhead, Ina Claire, Alfred Lunt, Lynn Fontanne, Judith Anderson, and a shirtless Johnny Weissmuller washing dishes). Then there were the entertainers: Gracie Fields sang a reverential "Lord's Prayer"; Ethel Merman belted "Marching through Berlin"; Gypsy Rose Lee did a ladylike strip; Edgar Bergen gave voice to Charlie McCarthy; Yehudi Menuhin played Schubert's "Ave Maria" and Rimsky-Korsakov's "Flight of the Bumble Bee"; and Ray Bolger sang and danced his way through Rodgers and Hart's "The Girl I Love to Leave Behind."

What is impressive about *Stage Door Canteen* is not its length (originally 132 minutes) but the naturalness of the performers. It was not a splashy "send in the stars" revue. In fact, while many of the stars would have been known to moviegoers (for example, Judith Anderson, Dame Mae Whitty, Ethel Waters, Helen Hayes), they were not on the order of Bette Davis, Judy Garland, Mickey Rooney, Bing Crosby, and Bob Hope. Katharine Hepburn was the exception, but she was both a stage and screen star. The year before *Stage Door Canteen* premiered, she was on Broadway in Philip Barry's *Without Love* (1942). Katharine Cornell, who, along with Helen Hayes, has often been dubbed "First Lady of the American Theatre," made her only screen appearance in *Stage Door Canteen*. When a lonely GI (Lon McCallister) tells her he played Romeo in a high school production of *Romeo and Juliet*, the years drop away, and Cornell, then fifty, becomes the young Juliet as they enact the balcony scene— McCallister with callow earnestness, and Cornell with a femininity that could only have come from within. Cornell had played Juliet in New York in 1934 opposite Basil Rathbone as Romeo. She was then forty-one; according to John

Mason Brown in the *New York Post* (December 21, 1934), hers was "the most lovely and enchanting Juliet that our present day theatre has seen."

Once World War II ended in 1945, the revue became the equivalent of army surplus. MGM made one last attempt in *Ziegfeld Follies* (1946), Arthur Freed's homage in lush Technicolor to the variety shows of his youth and the showman who brought the revue to its zenith, if not in wit, at least in spectacle. His tribute to the great Ziegfeld would be a mélange of highbrow, middlebrow, and lowbrow entertainment, very much in the Ziegfeld tradition. There were comedy sketches with Fanny Brice, Keenan Wynn, and Red Skelton; the drinking song from the first act of *La Traviata* sung by James Melton and Marion Bell; satire (Judy Garland imitating a screen diva deigning to grant an interview); elegantly choreographed dance numbers with Fred Astaire and Lucille Bremer; a sadly underutilized Lena Horne; and a grand finale with Kathryn Grayson rhapsodizing about beauty.

Dance aficionados remember *Ziegfeld Follies* as the first and only time Fred Astaire and Gene Kelly danced on screen together—the latter admitting in *That's Entertainment!* (1974) that Astaire was his favorite dancing partner, depressing news for fans of Rita Hayworth, Judy Garland, Vera-Ellen, Cyd Charisse, and Leslie Caron, and questionable in light of Kelly's admission that "when I danced with Fred, I felt terribly uncomfortable because we don't dance alike." One would never know it from "The Babbit and the Bromide," in which Fred and Gene performed as a team, making it impossible to determine who was whose partner.

Ziegfeld Follies was intended to be more extravagant than the real *Follies*, which could never have featured Esther Williams swimming underwater. But MGM's soundstage 30 functioned as her personal swimming pool where cameras could capture Williams's graceful maneuvering between clusters of coral. *Ziegfeld Follies* was opulence (and budget) run riot; in production from April 1944 to February 1945, it ended up costing MGM over $3 million but managed to turn a modest profit. Although the movie is often cited as "Vincente Minnelli's *Ziegfeld Follies*," Minnelli directed five sequences: the two Astaire-Bremer dance numbers ("This Heart of Mine" and "Limehouse Blues"); Judy's "A Great Lady Has an Interview," although one can also see Charles Walters's hand in the choreography; "The Babbitt and the Bromide"; and the finale with Kathryn Grayson reminding us that beauty is everywhere, as if we didn't know it from the intoxicating spectrum that drugged the senses. Other directors working on *Ziegfeld Follies* were Lemuel Ayers ("Love," sung by Lena Horne in Kay Thompson's thrilling arrangement that allowed her to attack the number with feral intensity); Roy Del Ruth (the Fanny Brice–Hume Cronyn sketch, "A Sweepstakes Ticket"); Robert Lewis ("Number, Please" with Keenan Wynn becoming so frustrated trying to make a phone call that he ends up eating the telephone); George Sidney ("Here's to the Girls," the opening number; and two sketches, "Pay the Two Dollars" with Edward Arnold and Victor Moore; and "When Television Comes" with Red Skelton).

By September 29, 1944, a sequential order had taken shape:

Ziegfeld Days, a prologue with Fred Astaire and puppets recreating Ziegfeld's glory days	**Retained with revisions.**
"Meet the Ladies," the opening number with Astaire and Lucille Ball	**Changed to "Here's to the Girls"**
"Death and Taxes," a comic sketch with Jimmy Durante as himself	**Discarded**
"If Swing Goes, So Do I," with Astaire and Lucille Bremer	**Discarded**
"The Burglar," with Fanny Brice as her radio character, Baby Snooks, in which Snooks drives a burglar to distraction with her literal interpretation of his argot (Burglar: "I'm on the lam"; Snooks: "Are you a sheep?")	**Discarded**
"Love" with Lena Horne	
"This Heart of Mine" with Astaire and Bremer	
"We Will Meet Again," with Esther Williams and James Melton	**Discarded**
"The Interview" with Judy Garland	**Retitled "The Great Lady Has an Interview"**
"When Television Comes" with Red Skelton	
"The Babbitt and the Bromide" with Astaire and Kelly	
Another Fanny Brice sketch, "The Ice Box," in which Snooks, failing to understand why the light goes off in the refrigerator when the door is closed, climbs into it and is unable to determine if the light was off because "it was too dark."	**Discarded**

Throughout the shoot, old routines were scrapped, and new ones added. Two that were considered and then dropped contained the kind of inside references for which Broadway revues were famous. One was a Mickey

Rooney–Judy Garland duet, "Will You Love Me in Technicolor (As You Do in Black and White)?" with allusions to House of Westmore makeup (the Westmores were Hollywood's leading makeup artists) and Natalie Kalmus (MGM's Technicolor consultant at the time). Another was "Life with Junior," which would have amused moviegoers who had seen the Broadway hit, *Life with Father* (1939), which was still running when *Ziegfeld Follies* was released in April 1946. *Life with Father* revolved around a wife's efforts to persuade her husband to get baptized. In "Life with Junior," the title character, lacking a first name, refuses to acquire one through baptism. After the father informs Junior that in ancient Rome unbaptized children were thrown to the lions in the Circus Maximus, the boy acquiesces.

When the original cut of *Ziegfeld Follies* ran close to three hours, the Garland-Rooney duet and "Life with Junior" were eliminated, along with Fanny Brice's Baby Snooks bits. Since radio is the theater of the imagination, listeners had their own image of the mischievous child from *The Baby Snooks Show*, and it was not that of the forty-seven-year-old Fanny Brice. *The Baby Snooks Show* was still on CBS radio when *Ziegfeld Follies* opened in spring 1946 and stayed on until 1951. Brice died two days after the show went off the air.

At least Brice's "Sweepstakes" sketch was preserved. Brice and Hume Cronyn play a couple who offer a sweepstakes ticket to their landlord as partial payment for the rent and resort to devious means to recover it when they learn they hold the winning ticket. Other sketches that went by the wayside included routines by Jimmy Durante and, sadly, "Liza," which Avon Long, who played Sportin' Life in the 1952 revival of *Porgy and Bess*, sang to Lena Horne.

Ziegfeld Follies had more of a point of view than a plot. In the heavenly prologue, the late Florenz Ziegfeld (William Powell) in a silver-striped red dressing gown is ensconced in his celestial digs, MGM's equivalent of an impresario's hereafter. He yearns for another *Follies*, knowing this time it will be a movie. Ziegfeld recalls his first venture, *The Follies of 1907*, recreated with puppets as first nighters and performers—one of the few creative touches in the film.

He envisions an opening in pink and, lo! it is. In "Here's to the Girls," Fred Astaire in a tux with a pink boutonniere introduces the beautiful ladies, who enter appropriately dressed in pink, with Cyd Charisse, MGM's resident ballerina, demonstrating the art of the dance, and thus adding some class to a number that is hopelessly kitsch. The beautiful ladies revolve on a carousel, flashing radiant but frozen smiles. Then, for some reason, Lucille Ball in killer pink makes her unsmiling entrance, cracking a whip like a ringmaster, and releasing panther-like women from their cages, who pose no threat to the unflappable Ball. If the number had a hidden meaning, only a deconstructionist could uncover it. The sequence invites self-parody when Virginia O'Brien enters on a horse wearing a knockoff of Ball's pink effusion, hoping someone will "bring on the wonderful men."

When the film was finally released, it consisted of

1. The Heavenly Prologue
2. "Here's to the Girls"
3. James Melton and Marion Bell in the "Brindisi" from *La Traviata* with couples in black and white waltzing around as if they were in old Vienna and not at a Parisian courtesan's soiree
4. Keenan Wynn in "Number, Please"
5. Esther Williams in "A Water Ballet," swimming amid coral and emerging with her face encircled by water lilies
6. Victor Moore and Edward Arnold in "Pay the Two Dollars," a rather dark sketch in which Arnold, as Moore's lawyer, refuses to give his client two dollars to pay a fine, threatening instead to appeal and causing Moore's incarceration and ultimate bankruptcy
7. "This Heart of Mine," sung and danced to Arthur Freed's lyrics and Harry Warren's music with Astaire as a jewel thief who crashes a party, romances the wealthy Lucille Bremer, and filches her bracelet. Knowing his kind, she offers him her necklace as well and departs. He realizes that while he has her jewelry, he does not have her, which, apparently, means more to him than the gems. He looks pensive, then turns to the left as Bremer comes rushing toward him, suggesting that thievery pays off if there is chemistry between thief and victim. Astaire sings the lyrics seductively, and the two dance romantically, inviting audiences to speculate on the outcome with its various permutations of the "Will they or won't they?" resolution. They will, but in a way no one could have anticipated, except those who believe that being taken by a con artist is preferable to being fleeced by an amateur.
8. Fanny Brice and Hume Cronyn in "The Sweepstakes Ticket"
9. Lena Horne in a green and white gown singing "Love" in a Caribbean dive
10. "When Television Comes," an overlong sketch with Red Skelton as an announcer getting progressively drunk while promoting Guzzler's Gin, perhaps suggesting a connection between alcoholism and TV commercials
11. "Limehouse Blues," which brought back Astaire and Bremer—he, looking eerily Asian as a dockworker; and she, sleekly Eurasian as a mystery woman. Noticing her interest in a fan in a shop window, Astaire is about to procure it for her when thieves smash the window and make off with all the merchandise except the fan, which Astaire retrieves and is then shot. Cue for a reverie in which he and Bremer engage in a bit of stylized chinoiserie, as they open and close their fans simultaneously in an extraordinary demonstration of ritual dance. The reverie ends with Astaire on his death

bed in the shop. Bremer and her Chinese protector (one assumes she is a high-class call girl) stop by. She notices the fan, picks it up, and drops it when their eyes meet. The sequence is a brilliant evocation of the song, "Limehouse Blues," which ends with a fitting description of Bremer's enigmatic character: "Rings on your fingers and tears for your crown / That is the story of old Chinatown."

12. "The Great Lady Gives an Interview," with Judy Garland doing an imitation of a screen diva, sounding like Bette Davis with her affected pronunciation and announcing that her next film will be the story of Madame Crematon, the inventor of the safety pin. Audiences who sensed that Garland was parodying Greer Garson and the noble characters she played in *Mrs. Miniver* (1942), *Madame Curie* (1943), and *Mrs. Parkington* (1944) would have smiled wryly. Actually, the sketch was originally intended for Garson. When her then husband, Richard Ney, who was considerably younger (he played her son in *Mrs. Miniver*), learned that Garson would be parodying her persona, he vetoed it. What the sketch revealed was Garland's devastating sense of humor, which was amply displayed later on when she started appearing on talk shows.

13. Astaire and Kelly in "The Babbitt and the Bromide," as two pillars of the community who, whenever they encounter each other, exchange platitudes and are destined to do the same in the hereafter

14. The finale, "Beauty" with music by Harry Warren and lyrics by Arthur Freed, featuring Kathryn Grayson in pink chiffon and dancers emerging from swirling suds. You almost expected Esther Williams to rise out of the foam and dive into a pool of emerald green water. The movie had to end somehow, and it was fitting that it did with an ode to beauty and Grayson in front of a sparkling *Ziegfeld Follies* marquee.

Even before *Ziegfeld Follies*, MGM had not abandoned the revue format, believing it would work if it were threaded with a plot, like a "book revue," Ethan Mordden's term for a Broadway show like *Follow the Girls* (1944), which was basically a tame burlesque show masquerading as a musical comedy. MGM adopted the book revue format for the three *Broadway Melody* films (1936, 1938, 1940) showcasing the studio's talent in the hybrid form of a revue with a show business plot, in which a show either needs a star (1936), money (1938), or a leading man (1940).

Since a movie about a Broadway revue is bound to feature musical numbers, it makes no difference whether they move the plot along or are just excuses for a song and dance routine. *Broadway Melody of 1936* (1937) was a revue that could pass as a musical with a plot about an aspiring performer (Eleanor Powell), who reconnects with a high school beau, now a Broadway producer (Robert Taylor), and is so eager to snag the lead in his revue entitled—what else?—*Broadway Rhythm*—that she poses as a French artiste, La Belle Arlette. When the producer stages a reception for "Arlette," Powell materializes instead, dancing on a circular platform to the distinctly un-French "Broadway Rhythm" in a glittering tux that looks as if it could set off sparklers any minute. Powell's dancing and Francis Langford's warm rendition of "You Are My Lucky Star" were the film's highlights. Regular moviegoers would have already heard "Broadway Rhythm," "You Are My Lucky Star," and "Broadway Melody" in *The Broadway Melody* and *The Hollywood Review of 1929*. That did not matter; the songs were like old wine in new bottles. Audiences experienced a movie with a Broadway-themed plot and repeats from the past adjusted to the tastes of the present, proving that some songs can span the years.

Powell could dance on anything and anywhere. In *Rosalie* (1937), Powell, as a Vassar-educated princess, danced down a winding arrangement of what looked like circular hassocks and onto a performing space as part of a festival in her mythical country. No one could take the film seriously, but it was always a pleasure to watch Powell go into her dance and hear Nelson Eddy sing "In the Still of the Night" without programming himself into the operetta mode, as he did when he costarred with Jeanette MacDonald. In *Honolulu* (1939), Powell, a nightclub performer sailing to Hawaii with Gracie Allen as her ditzy sidekick, dances on the deck of the ship. Later, at a "Come as Your Favorite Movie Star" evening, Allen arrives as Mae West, performing a silly routine with faux Marx Brothers; Powell blackens her face for a tribute to the legendary African American entertainer and superb tap dancer, William ("Bojangles") Robinson. Her impersonation might strike some as racist, but it was really a tribute from one artist to another that could not have been paid in any other way.

Broadway Melody of 1938 found Taylor playing another producer, this time in need of money that is raised by betting on a horse appropriately named Stargazer, who naturally comes in first, so Powell can star in the show. The now familiar "Broadway Melody" and "You Are My Lucky Star" were played over the credits. Moviegoers who did not despair of the American Dream during the Great Depression would have had no difficulty believing that Sally Lee (Powell), a horse trainer, could metamorphose into a Broadway star; the others would have been so dazzled by the array of talent—Sophie Tucker, the sixteen-year-old Judy Garland, Buddy Ebsen, and George Murphy—that they would have forgotten about Sally's profession, which was simply an ID tossed into the discard bin after it served its purpose. Sophie Tucker would perform her signature song, "Some of These Days," on television variety shows in the 1950s, but the 1938 version is one for the archives. Judy, looking dumpy but with a voice that belied her years, sang her fan letter to Clark Gable, "Dear Mr.

Gable," that segued into a torchy "You Made Me Love You." The song might have struck some viewers as cute, but there was something unsettling about a teenager with the voice of a bandstand artist who could plumb the depths of a song as if she knew the lyrics implied more than what they said. And when she belted "Everybody Dance" in a formless dress that made it seem she had no waistline and a white collar that gave her a schoolgirl look, her eyes lit up in wild abandon that was at odds with her appearance. This was a kid ordering adults to shake the blues away and go into a dance—a kid who worked the room like a seasoned performer. There were times when Judy looked transported, as if the freedom and the authority implied by the lyrics had taken hold of her and turned her into a martinet. She was thrilling, but scary—a harbinger of things to come.

Powell, of course, was given the finale, "Got a Pair of New Shoes." She was dressed in a black tux, hat, and white gloves, affecting a masculine persona—hands in pockets, jaunty walk, and a happy-go-lucky swagger softened by a feminine gracefulness that remained intact even when she was tossed around by male dancers, sending her into a split with a cartwheel windup. "Got a Pair of New Shoes" may not have been the greatest of finales, but it attested to Powell's unique combination of dance and athleticism, rivaled only by Gene Kelly and justifying her title as "Queen of Taps" that should have been amended to "Queen of Dance."

Broadway Melody of 1940 was the best of the lot. A dance team (George Murphy and Fred Astaire) breaks up when Murphy is mistakenly hired to play opposite Eleanor Powell in a Broadway revue. Although in real life Murphy was an accomplished dancer, in the film Astaire is the one the producer wants. When Murphy gets drunk on opening night, Astaire goes on to great acclaim. The same pattern occurs in the next show, with Astaire substituting for an incapacitated Murphy. This time, however, Murphy is only faking inebriation, so that his friend can get the recognition he deserves, along with Powell.

Broadway Melody of 1940 was the only pairing of Astaire and Powell. Astaire was meant for costars (Ginger Rogers, Cyd Charisse, Judy Garland, Jane Powell, Lucile Bremer, Vera-Ellen) with whom he could have a cool rapport, so that when they danced together, she was his partner, not his competitor. This time, Astaire was top billed on the basis of his hugely successful RKO musicals with Ginger Rogers; the trailer anointed Astaire and Powell as "The King of Rhythm" and "The Queen of Taps." Powell suppressed the fire within when she danced with Astaire, although she could not help but usurp a spotlight that was not meant to be shared. In the "Juke Box Dance," Astaire and Powell are in an Italian restaurant, when Astaire asks her to demonstrate a step that intrigues him. Powell obliges, and the two begin dancing away like teenagers. Astaire brought out the rarely seen girl in Powell—the woman had already been on view—and the two behaved as if they just came out of the local soda fountain and danced onto the street after sharing an ice cream soda with two straws. They demonstrated their art again in "I Concentrate on You," which gave Powell, in a white wig and black tutu, a chance to play prima ballerina with Astaire as her partner. Astaire's name may have preceded Powell's in the credits, but her art, undiminished and unsurpassed, came through with blinding force.

The highlight was Cole Porter's "Begin the Beguine." The three-part sequence opens in a Latin American setting with the lush-voiced Lois Hodnott (uncredited), dressed in a low-cut, art deco gown, delivering the lyrics as if she were spellbound by their sensuousness and the "nights of tropical splendor" they evoked. The camera tilts up to a stage, at first diaphanously curtained and then exposed, where dancers in shimmering white gowns sway to music that renders them oblivious to the outside world. For the moment, we are nowhere in particular—certainly not in the Caribbean but in some mythical realm where eroticism meets discretion—the latter giving way to dance, which provides a substitute for sex.

Suddenly Powell emerges in a long white dress that flows down her slender frame, joining the ensemble and at one point gracefully tracing an arc by swinging her leg clockwise and creating a momentary swirl of white. In the distance the figure of a man appears, dressed like a matador. It is Astaire, who becomes her partner. But, in a sense, neither is the other's partner. They just dance together, alternating between ballroom and flamenco—hands behind back, hands in motion. They have absorbed each other's rhythms—their movements coordinated as if each is the other's alter ego.

After the segment with Powell and Astaire is over, the four Music Macs come on, jiving up "Begin the Beguine" for those preferring the jukebox version. Then Powell and Astaire return for the finale, all in white and casually attired. It's sheer tap—no story, no subtext, just two supremely talented people exulting in the symbiosis of the dance, where partners can retain their individuality with neither eclipsing the other. When Powell and Astaire danced together in their only on-screen appearance, the chemistry was artistic, not sexual; theirs was neither a mating nor a courtship dance, but an occasion for two professionals to demonstrate their art without posturing or feigning physical attraction.

Despite top billing, the character Powell played in *Lady Be Good* (1941)—which bears no resemblance to the George and Ira Gershwin musical, *Lady, Be Good!* (1924)—contributed nothing to the plot. Since Powell is playing a musical comedy star, she is given an opportunity to perform her specialty twice; first, tapping away to the title song with Buttons, a dog that Powell had trained herself. Buttons did not upstage her; in fact, he held his own, showing a mastery of show biz, canine style. Buttons moves between Powell's legs and jumps through the space she forms with her arms; he even gets to dance on his hind legs. Powell alternates between cartwheels and splits, working her way to the sofa where she collapses, with Buttons jumping on her lap in a perfectly timed finish. It is a great piece of showmanship that has nothing to do with the story of two songwriters (Ann Sothern and Robert Young) who cannot achieve the same harmony as a married couple that they once could as professionals. The film's finale, "Fascinating Rhythm," at least bears a tenuous relationship to the Broadway original, in which it was performed by Fred and Adele Astaire and Cliff ("Ukelele Ike") Edwards. On Broadway, "Fascinating Rhythm" was just one of several numbers in the first act. In the film, it is a showpiece for Powell, who is starring in a musical for which Sothern's character has written the lyrics. Purists will have to keep repeating to themselves, "George and Ira Gershwin wrote the music and lyrics of 'Fascinating Rhythm,' not two fictional songwriters."

A similar misappropriation occurred earlier when Sothern sang a deeply felt "The Last Time I Saw Paris," a lament for the city then under Nazi occupation. Ironically, "The Last Time I Saw Paris" was not written for any film, much less for *Lady Be Good*. Oscar Hammerstein, devastated by the fall of France, showed the lyric he had written to Jerome Kern, "who composed a melody that captured the pictures Hammerstein described." Equally ironic is "The Last Time I Saw Paris" winning the Oscar for best song even though it was not written for *Lady Be Good*, which only included two songs from the Gershwins' musical: the title song, "Oh! Lady Be Good" and "Fascinating Rhythm." The others were by Nacio Herb Brown and Roger Edens (music) and Arthur Freed (lyrics). MGM bought a title, changed the punctuation, kept two songs, and added others. It would have been difficult for MGM to produce a faithful movie version of *Lady, Be Good!* since the plot revolved around a brother and sister, played on the stage by real siblings, Fred and Adele Astaire. In 1941, Fred was long past playing male ingenues, and Adele retired from the stage in 1932. But in September 1941, when *Lady Be Good* arrived, audiences were more interested in being entertained, given what was happening in Europe, than in parsing its fidelity to a Broadway musical that few of them would have seen.

At least "Fascinating Rhythm" was not jettisoned, since it provides one of the best examples of Powell's extraordinary art. The number begins with the orchestra in silhouette and a singer in an iridescent gown (Connie Russell) belting out the song and getting a well-earned close-up at the end. Then the Berry Brothers come dancing in, performing cartwheels and splits. The Brothers were a talented African American trio, whose contribution to the film, brief as it is, was cut in the pre–civil rights South, where artists like Lena

Horne and the Nicholas Brothers suffered the same fate. The Berry Brothers move off stage (the sequence suggests a Broadway revue rather than a book musical), followed by a shot of Powell's dancing feet. Then she emerges in a shiny tuxedo—top hat, striped pants, and white tie, tapping on to a runway, then onto a stage and flipped over the heads of two rows of men, landing upright in time for an ecstatic close-up, with her fingers tightening her bow tie in triumph.

With America's entry into World War II, Powell's popularity began to wane. *Ship Ahoy* (1942) and *I Dood It* (1943) were part of an espionage cycle (Universal's *Saboteur*, Warner Bros.' *All through the Night*, Paramount's *Lucky Jordan*, RKO's *The Fallen Sparrow*, Twentieth Century–Fox's *They Came to Blow Up America*) that portrayed an America swarming with spies and fifth columnists. In *Ship Ahoy*, Powell was a Broadway performer on a cruise ship, duped into becoming a courier for the Nazis; when she discovers the truth, she taps out a message in Morse Code to alert an American agent in the audience. Since it was impossible to believe that anyone was in danger, much less Powell, one could forget the plot and enjoy the musical numbers. In "I'll Take Tallulah"—the song refers to Powell's character, Tallulah Winters, not actress Tallulah Bankhead—she taps to a conga, doing cartwheels and somersaults, dancing on tables and leaping off of them, shaking a hip, kicking a leg, getting tossed around, and always landing on her feet. In *I Dood It* (1943), again with Skelton, she swung a lariat as if she were roping cattle all her life, sometimes even dancing within it. *I Dood It* was another Red Skelton musical with a saboteur plot, with Powell's character as a plot point and a featured attraction. That same year, dressed in an unflattering black outfit with silver applique, she did a brief boogie-woogie tap in *Thousands Cheer* (1943), a wartime revue with a bit of plot and guest appearances by members of the MGM family. Then Powell and MGM parted ways.

Powell starred in one more movie, *Sensations of 1945* (United Artists, 1944), in which she may have been top billed, but the main attraction was the supporting cast: W. C. Fields, Sophie Tucker, Woody Herman and His Band, Cab Calloway, and the great African American jazz pianists Dorothy Donegan and Gene Rodgers in a revue with a negligible plot about a PR whiz (Powell) with a flair for wacky publicity stunts. For the finale, Powell clones leap off of one platform and land in a split on the other, replicating the technique that Powell had perfected. Then the lady herself appears in tights, top hat, and a spangled jacket, leading a horse that pranced to the beat of her taps. A charming moment, but a bittersweet end to the career of one of the greatest female dancers in movies.

She returned to her old studio for a cameo in the Esther Williams–Van Johnson musical, *Duchess of Idaho* (1950). At a nightclub, the bandleader

(Johnson) spots her and asks her to perform for the audience. Dressed in a light-blue gown, she begins moving with the studied grace of a ballroom dancer until Johnson, irritated by her feigned propriety, orders her to "go to work." She obliges, detaching the lower half of her gown that leaves her in fringed tights with a sparkling top, as she executes a boogie-woogie tap dance with a spotlight lovingly encircling her. Despite the brevity of the number, she rehearsed so strenuously that her feet bled. One wished that somehow the script could have been rewritten to star Powell, with Williams doing one of her water ballets. But Johnson and Williams were still box office draws, and *Duchess of Idaho* brought in $2.815 million domestically and $1.385 million internationally.

- 8 -

THE MGM ORIGINALS

At the March 20, 1952, Academy Awards ceremony, the Oscar for best picture was expected to go to either *A Streetcar Named Desire* or *A Place in the Sun*. Instead, it went to *An American in Paris*. Rarely were musicals honored in that category. Only twice before was a musical voted Best Picture: *The Broadway Melody* (1929) and *The Great Ziegfeld* (1936), both MGM releases and derived from original screenplays. *An American in Paris* was also an original musical, with a screenplay by Alan Jay Lerner, creator of the book and lyrics of one of Broadway's best-loved musicals, *Brigadoon* (1947), which MGM would film in 1954 with Gene Kelly and Van Johnson as two Americans who get lost while hunting in Scotland and stumble upon the lost village of Brigadoon on the one day it has emerged from the mist, which it does once every hundred years. Unlike the Broadway musical, the MGM movie version of *Brigadoon* was not a hit; it cost over $3 million, but only grossed $2.36 million domestically. *Brigadoon* may have struck moviegoers as too whimsical. Broadway audiences reacted differently. They understood the need for a retreat from reality after the horrors of a world war and could accept the ending in which the hero (David Brooks in the original, Gene Kelly in the film) chooses to return to Brigadoon, where he found true love (Marion Bell in the original, Cyd Charisse in the film), even if it means experiencing life as he knew it for only one day every hundred years.

By 1952 Alan Jay Lerner's name had become familiar. The previous year, *Paint Your Wagon* opened on Broadway with book and lyrics by Lerner and a thrilling score by his collaborator, Frederick Loewe. The musical enjoyed a moderately successful run during the 1951–1952 season but was turned into an abominable movie with Clint Eastwood in 1968. In March 1951, MGM's *Royal Wedding* (1951) arrived with story, screenplay, and lyrics by Lerner and music by Burton Lane.

March 20, 1952, was a memorable night for Lerner. "Too Late Now" from *Royal Wedding* was nominated for Best Original Song but lost to "In the Cool, Cool, Cool of the Evening" from Frank Capra's *Here Comes the Groom*. In addition to winning for Best Picture, *An American in Paris* also won for Best Story and Screenplay, both of which were Lerner's. Although *An American in Paris* lacked the charm of *Singin' in the Rain* (1952), it inspired the same format: an original screenplay with an unoriginal score—George Gershwin's in *An American in Paris*; songs for the most part by Nacio Herb Brown and Arthur Freed in *Singin' in the Rain*.

In *An American in Paris*, Gene Kelly and Oscar Levant play expatriates— Jerry Mulligan (Kelly), an aspiring painter; Adam Cook (Levant), a concert pianist without a career. Milo Roberts (Nina Foch), a mysteriously wealthy American who seems to know everyone in the Paris art world, is drawn to both the painter and his paintings, intending to make Jerry her protégé and, if she succeeds, her lover. At the time, Kelly was thirty-eight; Foch, twenty-six, although she was cast as the older woman, with the elfin Leslie Caron as Lise, her competition, requiring Kelly to play older man to Caron's younger woman; and their dancing to take on a purity and innocence that was discreetly erotic in accordance with their age difference. *An American in Paris* marked Caron's film debut; she was nineteen, looking fifteen but revealing a talent for the dance that made her a perfect partner for Kelly. Her cool and sculpted movements, balletic yet sensuous, inspired Kelly to ease up on the bravura and convey the ambivalence of love at first sight—closeness and withdrawal; the moving toward and away from each other, suggesting physical attraction and inner conflict, as if so perfect an experience might not last in an imperfect world. The "Our Love Is Here to Stay" sequence is not so much a courtship dance as a mating ritual. Kelly and Caron draw close, then separate and sway dreamily, their hands behind their backs, until the preliminaries are over, and the tensions are resolved.

The Gershwin material is inserted into, rather than integrated with, the plot. The numbers work because they are staged Broadway style, with the sequences calculated to end with applause; and routines timed to a finish, with the performer exiting on the last tap, gesture, or pose. Since a decision was made to incorporate one of Ethel Merman's signature songs, "I Got Rhythm," into the plot, director Vincente Minnelli realized that Kelly's invitingly soft voice was no match for Merman's trumpet. The song was staged as a teaching tool in which Kelly instructs some French children to say, "I got," after which he adds "rhythm," then "music," completing each verse while making the kids both students and spectators, even putting on a show for them in which he impersonates a soldier, a cowboy, and Charlie Chaplin. Without their realizing it, Kelly keeps moving closer to his apartment building where he pauses, bids good-bye, and enters, as if he had maneuvered his way from stage right to stage left and then disappeared into the wings. Theatergoers would have broken into applause. Moviegoers could only marvel at Kelly's timing.

The most famous moment in the film is the climactic "dream ballet" choreographed by Kelly and performed to the music of Gershwin's 1928 tone poem, *An American in Paris*, rearranged with additional music by Saul Chaplin. That it was neither pure Gershwin nor the entire score did not matter to 1951 audiences, who were treated to a spectacle second only to the eponymous ballet in *The Red Shoes* (1948). By its very nature, a dream ballet is not part of the onward thrust of the narrative, but rather a representation of a character's inner state—a fantasy acted out in his or her imagination. In both the stage and screen versions of Rodgers and Hammerstein's *Oklahoma!* "Out of My Dreams," Laurey's expression of joy at finding her dream lover in Curly, is followed by a ballet in which she imagines Curly and Jud vying for her affections, with Jud winning and carrying her off. The ballet, which seems to be taking place in a bordello in keeping with Jud's taste in women, does not advance the plot; it mirrors Laurey's ambivalence about the unstable Jud and her fear of rejecting him in favor of the gentlemanly Curly. When the ballet ends (it is not performed by the leads, but by dancers representing them, identified as Dream Laurey, Dream Jud, and Dream Curly), Laurey feels obliged to keep her promise and attend the box social with Jud, bringing the first act to an unsettling close.

Similarly, the pas de deux in *On the Town* (1949), both on stage and screen, is an enactment of Gaby's (Gene Kelly) fantasy about Ivy Smith (Vera-Ellen), who he thinks is a celebrity (she is really a hooch dancer in Coney Island). As they dance, their movements are purged of anything that would moor them to earth. Gaby and Ivy are transported by dance to a place where time has stopped for them and where there is only bliss and never disillusionment. Coney Island is disillusionment; the pas de deux is the redemption of reality, if only for a while.

There is a dream—or rather, a day dream—sequence in *An American in Paris* in the form of a wish fulfillment reverie: the granting of a wish that could only occur in the fantasist's imagination. Oscar Levant was too well known a pianist (who had also known George Gershwin personally) to function merely as Gene Kelly's sidekick. Levant needed something to justify being in a film with so little to do. Audiences expected to see Levant at the piano playing something by Gershwin, such as the *Concerto in F*, which he performed in the Gershwin biopic, *Rhapsody in Blue* (Warner Bros., 1945). Minnelli added a sequence in which Levant's character imagines himself at the keyboard, performing Gershwin's *Concerto for Piano and Orchestra* and playing some of the instruments as well. Whenever Levant played the piano in a movie, one always wanted more—in this case, the complete concerto, not just the third movement.

The *American in Paris* ballet is another matter. It is the climax of a two-part finale, the first of which is narrative; the second, a fourteen-minute dance sequence without a word of spoken dialogue. Part one is the Beaux Arts ball, a black-and-white revel inspired by Picasso's monochromatic paintings. Lise informs Jerry that she can no longer see him; she is engaged to Henri, a famous French entertainer (George Guetary). Dejected, Jerry tears up a sketch he had made of La Place de l'Étoile. The pieces are caught up with confetti from the ball—the cue for Jerry's entry into fantasyland.

The climactic sequence is generally referred to as a "dream ballet." "Fantasy" is the better word, a fantasy unfolding in Jerry's unconscious. In his autobiography, Minnelli explained his intentions: "The hero is at the lowest point of his life. It is an emotional nightmare which alternates with moments of great joy. Then he returns to the same reality. He thinks of life without the girl. . . . He finds her for a moment, and then loses her again. All of Paris has lost its color and excitement. The ballet doesn't reflect what's happened in the picture so far. It shows instead the conflict within the hero."

What Minnelli has described is story told in dance, which is not really what happens in the film. The ballet is clearly an attempt to rival the one in *The Red Shoes* (1948), suggested by Hans Christian Andersen's tale of a pair of red shoes that, once worn, are unremovable and take on a will of their own, forcing the wearer (in Andersen, a young woman; in the movie, a ballerina) to remain in a state of perpetual motion that ceases only in death. In the tale, even amputation cannot rid the wearer of the shoes, and it is only through divine intervention that her suffering ends with her entrance into heaven. In the film, the ballet dispenses with the amputation, but the dancer's ordeal is no less grueling, with peace coming only with the removal of the shoes and her death. Initially, Minnelli may have thought of a story ballet, but Gershwin's tone poem does not lend itself to linear narrative, despite the title. The ballet in the film is as impressionistic as the paintings it evokes; it is a musical extravaganza in which boy keeps meeting and losing girl in a shape-shifting Paris.

Since the ballet is nonnarrative, it cannot be summarized like *Swan Lake* or *Giselle*. The episodes in the *American in Paris* ballet do not unfold like pieces of a story but like a series of images evoking different painting styles and familiar Paris settings. Jerry picks up a rose, the symbol of the eternal feminine, that Lise had dropped. Suddenly women in white appear, causing him to drop it. The women are not representative of Lise; if anything, in their cool whiteness, they recall Milo. Next, a corps of women in red arrive, perhaps to tempt him. Jerry avoids them, rushing into a cityscape that comes to life, vibrant and bustling, almost operetta-like, with gendarmes marching in like a troupe out of Gilbert and Sullivan. While everyone is dressed colorfully, Jerry is in black with a white collar; he is still in the monochrome mode of the Beaux Arts ball. He sees Lise in white (she will wear the same costume in the finale), but the women in red come between them, and Lise vanishes. The scene then changes to a flower market. Jerry selects a red rose, savoring it. Lise appears, dressed enticingly. They dance, he with longing; she somewhat somnambulistically, suggesting a simulacrum or a ballerina moving gracefully but without passion—a study in form without feeling. She, too, disappears; in the hands that had held her is a bouquet of flowers that Jerry lets fall to the ground. Another illusion, another loss.

Lise undergoes various transformations in different costumes, compared to Jerry, who changes from his basic black and white twice. Some GIs try to cheer him up; they head into a men's store and come out as hoofers—with Jerry in a red jacket, white pants, and a straw hat with a red band. Cavorting like a vaudevillian leaves him in a better frame of mind. When he sees Lise again, now looking like a schoolgirl, he draws her into the dance. Lise follows the tapping Kelly (forget Jerry) en pointe, making it seem so astonishingly effortless. For the moment, the mood is joyous, but then it changes, becoming bluesy as Lise and Jerry, silhouetted, approach each other in a yellow haze. When the haze turns blue, they are no longer in silhouette, but man and woman revealing their yearning in discreetly sensuous movements, as their bodies grow close, but not to the point that desire turns to passion. Kelly was a master at expressing rarefied passion. In *Cover Girl* (Columbia, 1944), he and Rita Hayworth danced to Jerome Kern's "Long Ago and Far Away," as if they were bringing the lyrics to life ("Long ago and far away / I dreamed a dream one day"). Their dancing brings the dream to life, as if they had given birth to it.

The episodes in the ballet follow no more logically than they would in a dream. It's not a question of connecting the narrative dots, since there are none to connect, unless "narrative" is defined as a series of tableaux vivants in music and dance in which boy keeps finding and losing girl, who, like Silenus, keeps changing type—sometimes ingenue; other times, slinky dancer. Better to fall under the spell of a city brought to painterly and musical life than pursue the elusive anima. Essentially, the finale is a showcase for Kelly and, to a lesser extent, Caron, an accomplished dancer who was not limited to ballet and could even be convincing in films that drew on her talent as an actress (*Glory Alley, Gaby, The L-Shaped Room, Fanny*). But it is really Kelly's shining hour. There was little reason for Toulouse-Lautrec's painting, *Chocolat dansant dans un bar* to come to life, except for Kelly to do a perfect imitation of the clown "Chocolat." Since political correctness was not in fashion in 1951, it did not matter that "Chocolat" (Rafael Padilla) was black. To Minnelli's credit, Kelly did not appear in blackface, unlike Irene Dunne in *Show Boat* (1936) and Bing Crosby in *Dixie* (1943). Kelly-Chocolat does not merely assume the clown's signature pose. His Chocolat goes off to the Moulin Rouge and frolics with the Can-Can dancers.

The ballet must end, and Minnelli decided it should with Lise in white and Kelly in his monochrome duds, dancing on the Fountain of the Rivers at the Place de la Concorde. The women in red reappear, now unthreatening, but when the music reaches its climax, Jerry finds himself alone, back where the fantasy began—on a street that looks like a stage with a black-and-white backdrop, which is Minnelli's way of saying that fantasy is theater, and that film—or at least his idea of film—is theater on frames of celluloid that, when projected, replicate the excitement of a live performance. Jerry spots the rose; he picks it up, holding it for a close shot and thus bringing the sequence full circle. The rose, dropped at the beginning, is retrieved at the end. Lise, lost at the beginning, is restored—not at the end of the ballet, but at the end of the film, as Henri, realizing that she belongs to Jerry, sets her free. There is no dialogue. It is as if the final scene is an epilogue, with the now liberated Lise rushing into Jerry's arms, achieving what could not be accomplished in the ballet, where boy loses girl. In the hypothetical "real" world, a man sends a woman back to her true love without benefit of song and dance. Sometimes, words are unnecessary.

An American in Paris is Kelly's (and Minnelli's) homage—and perhaps challenge—to *The Red Shoes*, which ends with the shoemaker displaying the toe shoes in a chilling close shot. In *An American in Paris* Jerry does the same with a rose, the symbol of the lost (but not for long) Lise. Minnelli's film at least has a happy ending, preceded by a ballet—call it what you will, dream or fantasy, nonlinear or circular—that is unique in the history of the American musical film.

A few movie musicals transferred to Broadway with varying degrees of success. The standout was *42nd St.* (1980); *Seven Brides for Seven Brothers* (1982), *Singin' in the Rain* (1985), *White Christmas* (2008), and *Holiday Inn* (2016) never matched the appeal of the originals. Then there is *An American in Paris* (2015), directed and choreographed by British dancer-choreographer Christopher Wheeldon with a book by Craig Lucas (*Prelude to a Kiss*) that ran on Broadway for over a year and won four Tony awards. Working from Alan Jay Lerner's screenplay, Lucas adhered to the basic story line (painter and composer in postwar Paris, dancer torn between two men; climactic ballet that is not the dream fantasy it was in the film; but one of the composer's own creations). Three of the main characters remained unchanged: Jerry, the painter; Lise, the dancer; and Milo, the art patron. The composer's surname was changed from Cook to Hochberg; Henri Baurel is not a music hall performer, but the son of a textile manufacturer, aspiring to become one. The

Gershwin selections are not the same as the film's. Wheeldon only kept "I Got Rhythm," "'S Wonderful," "But Not for Me," and "I'll Build a Stairway to Paradise," which starts with Henri trying out the number in a club until his imagination takes over, and he is performing it at Radio City Music Hall with a chorus of beautiful women. Wheeldon added "The Man I Love," "Shall We Dance?" "Who Cares?" "For You, for Me, for Evermore," "They Can't Take That Away from Me," and "Liza," which Jerry sings to Lise, preferring to call her by that name, and then deftly turns the song into a wooing. Wheeldon's real achievement was his transformation of the vibrantly cinematic finale with its set pieces into an extended pas de deux danced to Gershwin's blues-inflected music. Wheeldon's version is dance in its most basic form, desire distilled into delicately carved movement, unencumbered by anything that would moor it to plot and prevent it from taking flight into a world where passion, purged and aestheticized, is all that matters.

By setting the action immediately after the liberation, Lucas was able to recreate a Paris ridding itself of the detritus of the occupation. Nazi flags are torn down, and a collaborator is hounded off the street. These realistic touches are part of Lucas's fleshing out of Lise's character. In the film, Lise feels indebted to Henri Baurel (George Guetary) for sheltering her during the war. Lerner never explains why Lise had to be hidden, but Lucas makes it clear: Lise is a Jew, and it was not Henri, but his parents who hid her. Thus, Lise feels obliged to marry Henri because his family saved her from being shipped off to Auschwitz. As in the film, Henri graciously yields to Jerry, knowing that he is Lise's true love. Lucas has also made the ballet part of the plot. Earlier, Milo commissioned Adam to compose the score and Jerry to design the sets for a ballet starring Lise called *An American in Paris*. Thus we are watching a performance, not Jerry's fantasy. Lucas's book differs from Lerner's screenplay in another respect: it becomes a tale of lost loves and rejected lovers. Milo is less predatory than she was in the original. Although attracted to Jerry, she accepts the fact that he belongs to Lise. But Adam, crippled from a war injury, is also in love with Lise. In the show's final number, the three men—Jerry, Adam, and Henri—stand alone on stage and sing "They Can't Take That Away from Me"—Adam and Henri resigned to living with their memories, and Jerry in possession of the real thing. The Wheeldon-Lucas *An American in Paris* is an outstanding example of the conversion of a film musical into a stage musical that respects its source and is also a work of art in its own right.

Unlike *An American in Paris*, an original movie musical that had an afterlife on Broadway, *Summer Holiday* (1948) originated as a play, which was turned into an MGM film, then into an MGM musical, and finally into a Broadway show. The source for each was Eugene O'Neill's *Ah, Wilderness!* (1933), his idyllic portrait of a family that bore no resemblance to his own, with a cast headed by George M. Cohan as Nat Miller, the head of a Connecticut household, whose middle son, Richard, discovers Socialism and Charles Algernon Swinburne at the same time. *Ah, Wilderness!* is atypical O'Neill with its evocation of a bygone era when a father could explain the facts of life to his son by telling him that "certain natural feelings" can only be gratified in marriage, not with "a certain class of woman." The speech is beautifully euphemistic, and to ears accustomed to the vernacular, strangely poignant. MGM produced the movie version in 1935 with Lionel Barrymore as Nat Miller, Eric Linden as the poetry-spouting Richard, and Mickey Rooney as the youngest son, Tommy. Arthur Freed believed *Ah, Wilderness!* could work as a musical; the result was Rouben Mamoulian's *Summer Holiday* with a score by Ralph Blane and Hugh Martin and a cast that featured Walter Huston and Mickey Rooney, now in his mid-twenties, as Nat and Richard. But that was not the end of *Ah, Wilderness!* The last iteration was the Broadway musical, *Take Me Along*, with a score by Bob Merrill and starring Walter Pidgeon as Nat, Robert Morse as Richard, and Jackie Gleason as the hard-drinking Uncle Sid. Gleason was the main attraction, and to his credit, he created a character quite different from Ralph Kramden of *The Honeymooners*, delighting audiences for 448 performances during the 1959–1960 season.

Summer Holiday was a lace-edged valentine to storybook America, circa 1906, with girls in frilly white dresses, young men in spiffy suits, mischievous boys, chiding mothers, and fathers, who, if they did not know best, knew how to counsel their hormonally confused sons. In his desire to combine Americana with operetta, Mamoulian had the writers, Frances Goodrich and Albert Hackett, occasionally resort to rhyming dialogue, similar to his earlier film, *One Night with You* (Paramount, 1932), minus the innuendo. Fortunately, the actors let the lines fall naturally on the ear: "Will you marry me?" / "We'll see"; "owe to it" / "Connecticut"; "Feel better, my pet?" / "You bet." Like *Ah, Wilderness!* a play of character in which nothing momentous happens, *Summer Holiday* has some rich characterizations but lacks the trajectory of a plot-centered film. As Walter Huston announces in "Our Home Town," every day is pretty much the same. To provide some sort of narrative buildup, Mamoulian resorted to set pieces, notably a Fourth of July picnic that typifies the way the sexes were demarcated in turn-of-the-twentieth-century America. The men engage in a beer-drinking contest; the women in white and pastel dresses play a ladylike game of croquet and set up the food tables; the kids go swimming, and the young folks dance on the green. That may have been a typical picnic in 1906, but by mid-century, holiday celebrations had become less segregated, as Joshua Logan showed in the brilliant Labor Day sequence in *Picnic* (1956).

Mamoulian did not have the same feeling for the material that Minnelli had for *Meet Me in St. Louis*. However, like Minnelli, he knew that he could not present a pristine America of imaginary gardens without real toads. At one point he seemed to suggest that we should step back and look at another image of small-town America. In the graduation sequence, Mamoulian arranged a series of tableaux inspired by Grant Wood paintings, including *American Gothic* (1930) with its humorless couple, a woman in colonial garb and a man with a pitchfork. One might have laughed or smirked; if the latter, it was because the puritanical pair seem to be looking askance at the film's mythic America, as if to say, "We're more representative of the country in 1906 than anyone in this movie."

Mamoulian went further than O'Neill did in the scene in which Richard is induced into going to a dive, where he pairs off with a chorus girl, Belle, played with menacing allure by Marilyn Maxwell. As Richard gets progressively drunk, Belle, who has been wearing a pale-pink dress and pink hat, suddenly morphs into the proverbial scarlet woman—her dress and hat now rose colored. She exposes a leg and draws Richard to her, like an earth mother cradling a lost soul. Her lips are blood red, and her jewelry is blinding. Richard tries to reform her in rhyme: "You're one of the nicest girls I ever met / You're going to get yourself in debt." Belle retaliates, telling the bartender: "One way to get him to hush / Give him the brush." When she sidles up to another customer, Richard sees her as she is—in the pale-pink outfit. He had been seeing her through a drunken haze, with everything visually intensified—the dress darker, the lips redder, the beauty mark more prominent, and the eyes more hypnotic. The scene is a brilliant example of subjective camera, reflecting Richard's woozy perception of Belle. It is also incredibly sexy.

Take Me Along was the better musical treatment; unlike Mickey Rooney, who played Richard as an older Andy Hardy, Robert Morse was a dreamy aesthete like the young O'Neill, before he ventured into the dark side of family life in *Mourning Becomes Electra* and *Long Day's Journey into Night*.

MGM made its share of stage musicals (*Babes in Arms, Girl Crazy, On the Town, Brigadoon, Kiss Me, Kate, Kismet*), it also produced several extraordinary original ones, notably *An American in Paris, Singin' in the Rain, Seven Brides for Seven Brothers*, and *It's Always Fair Weather*—the last written by Betty Comden and Adolph Green, who also coauthored the screenplay for *Singin' in the Rain*. Comden and Green scored their first success with the book and lyrics for Leonard Bernstein's *On the Town* (1944), which ran for 462 performances on Broadway. From then on, they were bicoastal, but New Yorkers to the core, traveling between MGM in Culver City and Broadway, writing book and lyrics for such shows as *Wonderful Town, Bells Are Ringing, Do Re Mi, Subways Are for Sleeping, Hallelujah, Baby*, and *The Will Rogers Follies*. When Comden and Green first came to MGM, it was to refurbish the twenty-year-old Broadway musical, *Good News* (1947), as a vehicle for June Allyson and Peter Lawford. MGM was also the natural studio for *On the Town*; and Comden and Green, the logical choice for the adaptation. *On the Town* came to the screen relatively intact, except for songs that were considered too introspective ("Lonely Town") or reminiscent of a nation still at war ("Some Other Time").

For their next project, Arthur Freed gave the team a title, "Singin' in the Rain," instructing them to begin with fade-in and "not stop until you come to 'That's all, folks.'" The concept was an original musical without an original score but rather a sound track consisting mostly of Brown and Freed songs from earlier MGM films such as "You Were Meant for Me," "Good Mornin'," "You Are My Lucky Star," and the title song. "Moses Supposes" was a novelty number with music by Roger Edens and lyrics by Comden and Green, created for Donald O'Connor and Gene Kelly to add a bit of the zany to a boy-girl plot, except that boy and girl are in the movie business, where the real and the illusory are never distinct, because in the movies, the illusory is always real, sometimes more so than reality itself.

Singin' in the Rain is also a model of integration with the musical numbers advancing the plot as dialogue does in a play. O'Connor's attempt to cheer up a despondent Kelly leads into "Make 'Em Laugh." A diction coach proudly illustrates his enunciation skills by reciting "Moses supposes his toeses are roses." Kelly and O'Connor then jazz up the tongue-twister, turning it into a dance routine that transforms the coach's office into a performing space and the coach into a captive spectator.

Kelly and O'Connor were known quantities, but the revelation was Debbie Reynolds, who proved she could hold her own in "Good Mornin'," dancing and clowning with two pros. That her voice was dubbed by Betty Noyes in "Would You?" did not detract from the way she delicately phrased questions to a lover, asking if he would do the same as the "he" in the song. Reynolds also had a transcendent moment when Kelly brings her into a stage on the lot, setting the scene as if he were shooting a movie. He simulates a sunset, conjures up a mist, turns on a fan to provide a breeze, and floods the stage with light. Unable to provide a balcony, he places Reynolds on a stepladder and serenades her with "You Were Meant for Me." When she steps down, they dance together with such grace as to make one believe that somewhere in the world there is a place untainted by original sin. What is ironic about the sequence is that Kelly is showing Reynolds "how illusions are created in Hollywood, and then proceeds to create one of his own . . . which reveals the real emotion he feels for her." Like true cinematic art, "You Were Meant for Me" is at the crossroads of artifice and reality.

The Broadway Melody sequence near the end of the film is a hybrid; it is not a dream ballet like the climax of *An American in Paris*, but Kelly's proposal for the grand finale of a talkie. Like all the numbers in *Singin' in the Rain*, the sequence is not original but a conflation of two songs from *Broadway Melody of 1936*, "Broadway Melody" and "Broadway Rhythm"—the latter a showcase for Eleanor Powell in white pants with glittering stripes and a rhinestone-studded hat, jacket, and bow tie, showing how the song, sung earlier by Frances Langford, lended itself to tap. Kelly went further, illustrating how a synthesis of the two songs could tell a story.

Singin' in the Rain is set in 1927 when Hollywood was in a state of transition from the silent to the sound era; and when an unattractive voice could spell the end of a career. In the film, once the studio head (Millard Mitchell) decides that *The Dueling Cavalier* needs music, the title is changed to *The Dancing Cavalier*. Kelly envisions a big production number at the end—a song-and-dance sequence tracing a hoofer's rise from obscurity to fame, with Cyd Charisse—who possessed the longest and slinkiest legs ever to dance across a screen—as the unattainable object of his desire. Such a ballet would only have been possible much later in the evolution of the movie musical; in the early days of sound, no studio could have staged the Broadway Melody ballet as it appears in the film, where it is a showcase for Kelly. Even the studio head has doubts about such a number: "I can't quite visualize it." Nor could anyone in 1927. Still, it is a brilliant sequence. From the moment Charisse in an emerald-green dress extends a leg horizontally across the frame, turning it into an erotic appendage, Kelly is in her thrall. But she is in the thrall of a coin-flipping hood (think George Raft in *Scarface*) and goes off with him. Meanwhile, the hoofer ascends the show biz ladder from burlesque to the Palace and then to big time in the *Ziegfeld Follies*. At a swank party, he meets the femme fatale again, this time dressed in white with (at least) twenty-five feet of voile trailing behind her. This part of the ballet is the hoofer's fantasy, a pas de deux like the one in *On the Town*, as Kelly and Charisse move into a realm where time stands still. But the lady is a tramp, albeit a classy one, despite her deceptively emblematic white dress. Her handler intrudes, again flipping a coin. She does the same, leaving Kelly with the coin as a memento, which he in turn gives to a hatcheck girl. Then another hopeful arrives, shouting, "Gotta dance!" having apparently heard that "no skies are gray on the Great White Way." The Broadway Melody sequence, sometimes referred to as "The Broadway Ballet," is the present imposed on the past, suggesting what MGM would be capable of achieving once the sound era was underway.

The famous title song, however, is truly motivated. Kelly bids good night to Reynolds, who reminds him to stay out of the rain. Kelly replies, "From where I stand, the sun is shining all over the place." He goes on to the street with an umbrella, then closes it, jauntily putting it over his shoulder. The flooded street becomes his private stage; and "Singin' in the Rain," a musical soliloquy, quite unlike Judy Garland's bouncy rendition in *Little Nellie Kelly*. Oblivious to the downpour, he opens the umbrella again, this time holding it in front of him; too smitten to care about being drenched, he kicks up the water, jumping from curb to sidewalk and even onto a lamp post, holding on to it with one hand and brandishing his umbrella in the other with a look of "excelsior!" on his face. Noticing that a police officer is viewing him suspiciously, he sheepishly saunters away, handing the umbrella to a passerby in need of one.

"Singin' in the Rain" is a touchstone moment in the musical film, with Kelly using an umbrella not as a prop but a reflection of the lyrics, which describe someone who can "laugh at clouds so dark up above" because "the sun's in my heart and I'm ready for love." The umbrella is an objectification of his euphoria. Realizing he has no need for it, he holds it in front of himself as if he were keeping the elements at bay, and sloshes around in the water to show his indifference to nature's mood spoiler. The real mood spoiler occurred when the Academy of Motion Picture Arts and Sciences announced its 1952 nominations. *Singin' in the Rain* was ignored in the top categories (picture, director, actor, actress, screenplay) and only received nominations for supporting actress (Jean Hagen) and scoring. One of the most-honored films of all time won no Oscars. Voted best picture of 1952 was *The Greatest Show on Earth*, an ironic choice when one of the greatest shows was shunned.

At least the American Film Institute recognized the film's greatness. In its list of the twenty-five greatest musicals, *Singin' in the Rain* ranks first; *An American in Paris*, ninth. Someone at MGM, perhaps screenwriter-producer George Wells, thought that O'Connor and Reynolds could be a team, the way O'Connor and Peggy Ryan were at Universal in the 1940s. But the studio was taking no chances. *I Love Melvin* (1953), with an original screenplay by Wells, who doubled as producer, ran a mere seventy-two minutes and opened at New York's Loew's State, which was not known as the house of musicals. The film started out promisingly. On an MGM soundstage, Judy Leroy (Reynolds) in a lavender gown that allows for an exposed leg is dancing with eight men in evening attire (top hats, tails, and capes), enumerating her preferences in jewelry and lingerie ("The Lady Loves"). When the number is over, the star, after accepting accolades from the adoring crew, spots Robert Taylor (the actor, not a lookalike). They embrace, at which point you suspect something is not quite right. Just as he confesses that he has something to tell her, the alarm goes off, and Judy wakes up. She is only in the chorus of *Quarterback Kelly*, a Broadway show in which she literally plays a football, getting tossed, thrown, and everything but kicked. Into her life comes Melvin Hoover (O'Connor), a fledgling photographer for *Look* magazine.

It is not exactly love at first sight (they collide with each other in Central Park), but who can resist Debbie Reynolds's incandescence and buoyancy?

In an effort to win her, Melvin puts her picture on the cover of a fake copy of *Look*, setting off a series of complications. But the film has to end somewhere, and the publisher comes to the rescue so that young love can triumph. O'Connor's hyperkinetic performance does not come as a surprise to anyone who had seen him in his Universal programmers or even for the first time in *Singin' in the Rain*. At one point, he leaps on to a lamp post, holding on with one arm and extending the other in imitation of, or homage to, Gene Kelly. He even tap dances on roller skates. In one overlong sequence, "I Wanna Wander," he dances with a feather duster and twirls a cane, showing that he can use props as effectively as Fred Astaire. But O'Connor does not overshadow Reynolds. In his lukewarm *New York Times* review (April 10, 1953), Bosley Crowther wished she had a "more substantial script." Although she was truly O'Connor's costar (second billing to his first), in her subsequent MGM musicals—*Give a Girl a Break* (1953), *Athena* (1954), and *Hit the Deck* (1955)—she was third, second, and third billed, respectively. If Reynolds had been born ten years earlier, she might have been Judy Garland's successor. But when she arrived at MGM, the studio was not grooming musical comedy types. They had their sopranos—Kathryn Grayson, Jane Powell, and briefly Ann Blyth; a prima ballerina who could act and lip-synch, Cyd Charisse; and, for a short time, a Broadway belter, Dolores Gray—but no young women in their twenties to star in musicals.

Reynolds arrived at MGM in 1950, after spending two years at Warner Bros. Louis B. Mayer's tenure was coming to an end; he left the studio in 1951, replaced by Dore Schary, who had little use for musicals. She was, however, a trouper in the Garland tradition, but without the encumbering medical history. Anyone who saw Debbie Reynolds on Broadway in *Irene* during the 1973–1974 season discovered what she could do with a torch song like "You Made Me Love You," and then turn wistful in "Alice Blue Gown," which, fortunately, can be heard on the original cast album. It was not until *The Unsinkable Molly Brown* (1964) that moviegoers realized what they had missed.

Lovely to Look At (1952) is virtually an original musical, despite its origins—a Technicolor makeover of the black-and-white *Roberta* (RKO, 1935) with a backstage story line: A trio (Howard Keel, Gower Champion, Red Skelton) has difficulty getting backing for a musical until Skelton inherits half of Roberta, his aunt's dress shop in Paris. The idea of Red Skelton having a famed couturiere as an aunt requires its own form of disbelief. But the pairing of the three males with three females (Keel with Kathryn Grayson, Champion with his then wife Marge, and Skelton with Ann Miller) allowed for a tidy resolution in the best movie tradition. With the roles evenly distributed, there was no star in *Lovely to Look At*, even though Grayson was top billed. (Someone had to be.) The plus side was that everyone had a solo; and, in some cases, more. Ann Miller in lavender tights belted out "I'll Be Hard to Handle" while fending off chorus boys with wolf masks and doing a few bumps (no grinds) before going into her customary tap dance. Keel performed the title song in his rich baritone. Skelton did a comic routine at a piano whose lid kept falling down, eliciting a smile from Champion, who looked as if he were posing for a toothpaste commercial (or perhaps cueing the audience to respond in kind). Grayson spun some silvery pianissimi in "Yesterdays," growing reflective when she mused about the "olden days, golden days." Her voice was still supple, but she was not the ingenue she was in *Anchors Aweigh*. Grayson could wear a dress that looked like spun gossamer flecked with gold without being in the least desirable. She was just, literally, lovely to look at. Grayson was not beautiful, but attractive in an unassuming way. She and Keel were the 1950s equivalent of MacDonald and Eddy, turning *Lovely to Look At* into an operetta with shtick (Skelton), tap (Miller), and, best of all, dance, with the Champions.

MGM knew who the real stars were: the Champions, whom the studio tried to promote as its new dance team. In 1952, Fred Astaire was in his early fifties and still had a few more musicals in him. Gene Kelly was forty, with more dancing to do (*It's Always Fair Weather, Brigadoon, Les Girls*). Champion was a boyish thirty-three and looked ten years younger; Marge was the same age but could pass for late twenties. Gower embodied the masculine grace acquired from his early years as a ballroom dancer; Marge possessed the technical perfection that came from classical ballet, which made her the perfect partner. They complemented each other, sharing the spotlight without either hogging it. Marge and Gower turned "I Won't Dance" into a courtship ritual (he wants to, she doesn't) in the dress shop's workroom that becomes their personal stage where everything—a stool, a measuring tape, dress mannequins—is part of the number. Marge, swearing she won't dance, wards off the persistent Gower as they move the mannequins around like buffers. Ducking under a dress rack to avoid contact does her no good. He toys with a measuring tape, which she puts around a mannequin, indicating that it belongs on the dummy, not around her. Marge taps away sitting on a stool, which Gower whirls around, lifting her from it.

The two are also acting out the lyrics; she refusing, he insisting, until Marge brings the number to an end by imposing a mannequin between them. What is unique about the sequence is Marge's expressing her refusal to dance through dance. But her body language belies her protestations; she clearly enjoys being pursued, alternating between feigned annoyance and genuine interest. When Marge gets to "For heaven rest us, I'm not asbestos," she sounds as if she'd like to be combustible if Gower would light the metaphorical match. What started as a protestation becomes a declaration, leading to an impasse with a "To Be Continued" ending.

Their second number is a divertissement; the plot is put on hold as the scene changes to a star-strewn dance floor in the heavens, where the Champions perform "Smoke Gets in Your Eyes" as a celestial pas de deux. What is supposedly the highlight of *Lovely to Look At* is a fashion show-revue, Runway meets Broadway. Although Mervyn LeRoy is credited as the film's director, the fashion show sequence was staged by Vincente Minnelli, who brings it to a close with a red-themed dance number featuring Gower as a jewel thief and Marge as his canny prey, who snatches back her bracelet every time he filches it. The number was Minnelli's self-homage (or perhaps, self-reference) to "This Heart of Mine" in *Ziegfeld Follies*, in which Astaire was the thief, and Lucille Bremer, his quarry, who knew his kind too well and was more than willing to cooperate.

One could see why MGM thought Gower could be Astaire's successor. He was as nimble as Astaire; he was also heart-throb handsome, which Astaire was not. Gower could express a greater range of moods, including a sexy aggressiveness that eluded Astaire, who knew his strengths and preferred to play to them. But what is equally impressive in the fashion show sequence is Marge's ability to affect a stylized sexiness, the kind a ballet-trained dancer can manage, so that sex becomes an exercise in pure form. When she executes an awesome high kick, one marvels at the technique without being in the least excited by it. The Champions were never shown to better advantage than they were in *Lovely to Look At*. One wished they had a better showcase.

Since *Lovely to Look At* is an overhaul of *Roberta* (1935), comparisons are inevitable, with the public preferring the original with its iconic stars, Fred Astaire and Ginger Rogers. *Roberta* is closer to the Jerome Kern–Otto A. Harbach 1933 musical, while *Lovely to Look At* is practically an original screenplay. *Roberta*, however, was not a pure stage-to-screen transfer. Screenwriters Jane Murfin, Sam Mintz, and Allan Scott took liberties with the book, conflating two characters into the one played by Fred Astaire and promoting another from supporting cast to female lead for Ginger Rogers. Astaire and Rogers, like the Champions in *Lovely to Look At*, eclipsed the star, Irene Dunne. The story line remained the same: An American band, the Wabash Indianians, has been booked into a Paris nightclub on the assumption that they are Native Americans able to provide exotic entertainment. Despite being out of a job, the bandleader (Astaire) is determined to stay in Paris once he learns that his friend's (Randolph Scott) aunt Minnie (Helen Westley) is the owner of Roberta, the city's leading dress shop. Scott falls in love with the shop's manager (Dunne); Astaire reconnects with an old flame (Rogers), who has reinvented herself as a Polish chanteuse. Unlike *Lovely to Look At*, Aunt Minnie appears as a character who dies peacefully from heart failure, lying on a sofa with one arm dangling over the side. Minnie's death by metaphor is not so much an intrusion of reality into a basically unrealistic film as a plot point: Scott inherits Roberta and, in love with Dunne, wants her as his business partner and future wife.

Astaire and Rogers outshone Dunne, despite her exquisite renditions of "Yesterdays" to guitar accompaniment and "Smoke Gets in Your Eyes," better remembered as a dance number with Astaire and Rogers. In the climactic fashion show, which is far more tasteful than the one in *Lovely to Look At*, Rogers enters all in black, wearing a coat with a winged collar like an Elizabethan standing ruff. Astaire helps her off with the coat, singing a bit of "Lovely to Look At"; the orchestra breaks into "Smoke Gets in Your Eyes," which they transform into a study in stylized passion, the music complementing their movements that range from ballroom style and soft shoe to sweepingly lush. The sequence is a tribute to their awesome versatility, partly the result of much rehearsing, but also of their mysterious affinity for an art form that requires the enactment of moods and emotions without words, unless there were lyrics. But even then, the song was the introduction to the dance.

"I Won't Dance," acted out by the Champions in *Lovely to Look At*, is largely an Astaire solo in *Roberta*. The number seems on the verge of becoming a duet for himself and Rogers, until Astaire takes "I won't dance, madame, with you" literally and performs an amazing celebration of self.

"I'll Be Hard to Handle" gave Rogers a chance to sing, but, unfortunately, it was in her faux Franco-Polish accent. Astaire applauds and they relax, reminiscing about the old days when she was plain Lizzie Gatz. She drops the accent; he drops his guard, and the two tap away, with Astaire trying to outdo Rogers, who will not play second fiddle to anyone. They behave like lovers who quarrel, make up, and reunite as equals, not rivals.

Rogers knew she had competition in Astaire, but refused to think of herself as a subordinate. She fought to become his equal. In the finale, they reprised "I Won't Dance," with Rogers proving that, even with Astaire, she could shine on her own. She let loose with a vengeance and nearly upstaged him.

Grayson and Keel were unhappy with *Lovely to Look At*, regarding it as a B movie in A trappings. Keel stayed on at MGM for more films, including the classic *Seven Brides for Seven Brothers*, and the gloriously sung but dramatically inert *Kismet*. Nineteen fifty-three seemed like Grayson's vintage year. She made her last film for MGM, *Kiss Me Kate* (no comma in the movie version); and costarred with Gordon MacRae in a stodgy version of *The Desert Song* at

Warner Bros., where she also had a chance to play opera star Grace Moore in *So This Is Love*, which may have been a bittersweet experience, since an operatic career is what she once envisioned for herself.

Another stage derivative that underwent a sea change is *Broadway Rhythm* (1944), which illustrates the lengths to which MGM went to fashion a vehicle out of a Jerome Kern musical for second-tier stars (Ginny Simms, Charles Winninger, George Murphy, Gloria DeHaven, Ben Blue, Nancy Walker, Eddie "Rochester" Anderson), and Tommy Dorsey and his Orchestra. Lena Horne was stuck with another throwaway role as a nightclub performer, who at least had a chance to sing "Brazilian Boogie" and "Somebody Loves Me"; the latter, the kind she could have delivered with more longing except that longing was not an emotion MGM wanted expressed by an artist of color.

Originally, *Broadway Rhythm* was to have been another *Broadway Melody* movie with Gene Kelly, Eleanor Powell, and Lena Horne. That changed when Louis B. Mayer became infatuated with Ginny Simms, who was given the star treatment. Simms had been a singer with Kay Kyser's Orchestra and in films since 1939. She had a mellow, soothing voice and a smiling face, but was not much of an actress. Her acting meant nothing to Mayer, who only wanted her as a mistress. But Mayer repelled Simms; she mocked him within hearing distance of Gerald Mayer, his nephew, who was shocked that his uncle "was courting her . . . and she was demeaning him in public."

Broadway Rhythm (1944) ran for 115 minutes with a total of sixteen musical numbers that kept audiences from asking, "Haven't we seen all this before?" They had, if they had seen the backyard musicals with Mickey and Judy; or if they had caught Jerome Kern and Oscar Hammerstein's *Very Warm for May* (1939), at one of its fifty-nine performances. The screenwriters, Dorothy Kingsley and Henry Clark, scrapped most of Kern's score and worked over Hammerstein's book, leaving only the character of a stage-struck young woman cast in a summer theater production that becomes a Broadway hit. But at least the show's most memorable song, "All the Things You Are," survived the transmogrification. What was *Very Warm for May* became *Broadway Rhythm*, the story of a show business family, the Demmings—father Sam (Charles Winninger), daughter Patsy (Gloria DeHaven), and son Johnny (George Murphy). Sam is a former vaudevillian; Patsy, an aspiring musical comedy star; and Johnny, a successful producer, eager to branch out into artistic (i.e., highbrow) musicals and leave behind the world of middle-class entertainment from which he came. The plot gets slightly, but not impossibly, complicated, with the appearance of Helen Hoyt (Simms), a fading movie star planning to revitalize her career by appearing in a Broadway musical, but not in anything as arty as Johnny's. Meanwhile, Helen, Sam, and Patsy convert a barn into a playhouse and plan to stage their own show, a more traditional one that Johnny had written and discarded. Johnny is tricked into acting as play doctor; once he realizes that their show is superior to his, he brings it to New York in record time, so that the show can end, along with the film, with an extravagant production number centered around "All the Things You Are."

Every seven or eight minutes there is a musical number, minimizing ennui and giving the cast ample opportunity to display their talent. Nancy Walker and Ben Blue perform a hilarious "Milkman, Keep Those Bottles Quiet," with Walker as a welder coming home from the night shift, and Blue as a noisy milk deliverer. Dean Murphy does clever impersonations of Joe E. Brown, James Stewart, Clark Gable, Bette Davis, and FDR. Winninger and Tommy Dorsey play a duet with trombones, "I Love Corny Music," in which Dorsey tries to bring Winninger into the age of jive by changing the pitch, but finally gives up and settles for cornball.

For the knowledgeable, there is a scene in which Johnny arrives at Helen's hotel suite, which happens to have a grand piano and the score of *Very Warm for May* on the stand. He sits down and turns the pages, singing bits of "In Other Words, Seventeen" and "That Lucky Fellow." As he begins to sing "All the Things You Are," Simms materializes in a gossamer-like green gown and completes the song, which she reprises in the finale with the same masklike smile, the result of plastic surgery that had been performed by Dr. Joel Pressman, Claudette Colbert's husband. Unique among big band singers, Simms had a voice of unusual sweetness and purity, like a honey-coated purr; she made no attempt to dramatize the lyrics, but was always faithful to the melody, which is why her version of "All the Things You Are" is so easy on the ear, but not in the least poetic. She may have been singing, "You are the promised kiss of spring time," but you never felt it on your lips.

Vincente Minnelli's *The Band Wagon* (1953) also comes across as an original movie musical which, perhaps unintentionally, owes more to the 1931 Broadway show of the same name than anyone thought at the time. *The Band Wagon* (1931), unlike the film, was never conceived as a book musical; it was a revue with music and lyrics by Arthur Schwartz and Howard Dietz and sketches by George S. Kaufman, starring Fred and Adele Astaire in their last appearance together; Helen Broderick, Frank Morgan, and Tilly Losch, which ran for 260 performances during the 1931–1932 season. Typical of the show's wit and style was the opening number, the self-spoofing "It Better Be Good," in which the entire cast expresses the thoughts that cross many theatergoers' minds before the curtain goes up on a new show. The 1953 film retained three of the songs: "I Love Louisa," "New Sun in the Sky," and "Dancing in the Dark," and added others by the same team of Schwartz and Dietz: "I Guess I'll Have to Change My Plan" from *The Little Show* (1929); "A Shine on Your Shoes" and "Louisiana Hayride" from *Flying Colors* (1932); "You and the Night and the

Music" from *Revenge with Music* (1934); and "By Myself" and "Triplets" from *Between the Devil* (1937).

Having poked fun at Hollywood grappling with the advent of sound in *Singin' in the Rain*, Comden and Green returned to their home turf, the New York theater, for *The Band Wagon*, a more sophisticated film with songs that were Broadway classics, not pop chart favorites. With such a disparate collection of music at their disposal, Comden and Green managed to interweave the songs with the story without making it seem that they are interrupting the narrative flow to make way for a musical number. When Fred Astaire's character, who had not been in New York for ten years, notices the changes that have occurred in Times Square, including an arcade with a pinball machine and shoe-shine stand, he sits down in the chair and launches into "A Shine on Your Shoes." The stand's owner, played by LeRoy Daniels, who worked as a bootblack between acting gigs, joins in, and what was just a jaunty tune became a joyous romp.

Since Astaire and his sister performed "Dancing in the Dark" in the original *Band Wagon*, Comden and Green devised a way in which Astaire could dance it with Cyd Charisse, his costar in a Broadway-bound show. They skip a rehearsal and take a carriage ride through Central Park, stopping at a secluded spot where they express in dance the emotional ambivalence of a couple on a first date. Only the music is heard, not the lyrics, which Astaire could have sung, but that would have detracted from the dance, which conveys the tentativeness that two people feel when they experience mutual attraction for the first time. The number is a study in white and black—each is dressed in white, dancing against a darkened sky. Charisse is wearing flats so that she does not look taller than Astaire, a concern that his character has—and Astaire himself had—when he learned who his costar was. Charisse initiates the dance, and he follows, first with hands behind his back as they face each other, starting and stopping, enacting a courtship ritual in which a false move can be disastrous. There is a cautiousness in their movements, as if they are trying to hold their emotions in check by observing the codes of decorum. While they may be dancing in the dark, they have dispelled whatever darkness had adumbrated their relationship, which boded ill at the beginning—Astaire wanting nothing to do with a ballet dancer, and Charisse feeling the same about a hoofer. But once the music ends, and the date is over, the couple return to the carriage for the ride home—now lovers as well as fellow artists.

Like *Singin' in the Rain*, *The Band Wagon* has its share of self-reflexive satire within a plot filled with show business tropes: an out-of-town flop that is reworked into a hit; the male lead (Astaire) who takes over the troubled show; the classical ballerina (Charisse) who must adapt to a different mode of dance; and the director (Jack Buchanan), whose ego is matched by the grandiosity of his productions.

The Band Wagon's ideal audience are moviegoers who also patronize the theater and appreciate show music. You do not have to be a regular moviegoer to enjoy *Singin' in the Rain*, whose appeal is universal. The songs are familiar, the plot is undemanding, and the joy it radiates is infectious. *The Band Wagon* is filled with inside references; songs with introspective lyrics like "By Myself" and "I Guess I'll Have to Change My Plan"; sleek dancing, partly balletic, partly Broadway razzle dazzle; and a number Schwartz and Dietz wrote especially for the film, "That's Entertainment," which, even better than Irving Berlin's "There's No Business Like Show Business," levels the distinction between high-, low-, and middlebrow entertainment, insisting that any show—musical or straight play, tragedy or comedy—is entertainment if it "sends you out with a kind of a glow." The glow is what matters, whether it is the catharsis of tragedy or the airborne buoyancy of a musical. The show can be a classic like *Hamlet* and *Oedipus*, a burlesque routine, or a nineteenth-century melodrama. Genre is irrelevant. One doubts, however, that the average moviegoer would find *Hamlet* entertaining or appreciate the pun on "meet" ("A ghost and a prince meet / And everyone ends in mincemeat." How many would even have gotten the reference, or the one to *Oedipus Rex*, in which a chap's killing his father "causes a lot of bother"? The pervasive cleverness and lack of a Cliff Notes screenplay were the reasons for *The Band Wagon*'s lack of popular appeal. Although it has been added to the Library of Congress's National Film Registry of historically, aesthetically, and culturally significant motion pictures, in its original release it lost $1.85 million. The American Film Institute ranked *The Band Wagon* seventeenth among the twenty-five greatest musicals, placing it between *Funny Girl* (#16) and *Yankee Doodle Dandy* (#18), but nowhere near the top three: *Singin' in the Rain*, *West Side Story*, and *The Wizard of Oz*.

A similar situation occurred in 1959 when *Gypsy* opened on Broadway in the same season as *The Sound of Music*, the movie version of which ranks fifth among AFI's top twenty-five. To the cognoscenti, *Gypsy* is the better musical, yet it never had the cachet of *The Sound of Music*, which racked up 1,443 performances as opposed to *Gypsy*'s 702. *Gypsy*'s main character, Momma Rose, a stage mother who lives vicariously through her daughters, was far from empathetic. But those wanting a bravura performance (Ethel Merman), a book structured as a play rather than a libretto (Arthur Laurents), and one of the greatest scores in musical theater (Jule Styne) were not disappointed. The movie version of *Gypsy* (Warner Bros., 1962), although superbly acted by a vocally challenged Rosalind Russell, never made AFI's golden circle.

The Band Wagon belongs to the subgenre of the backstage musical, or the movie about the making of a musical (*The Broadway Melody, 42nd St., Babes on Broadway, Kiss Me Kate*). It was also a daring film for Astaire, who was fifty-four when *The Band Wagon* was released in August 1953, and would make three more musicals, exclusive of the disastrous *Finian's Rainbow* (1968), which was beneath him: *Daddy Long Legs* (Twentieth Century–Fox, 1955), *Funny Face* (Paramount, 1957), and *Silk Stockings* (MGM, 1957). Of these, only *Daddy Long Legs* turned a modest profit. *Funny Face* cost $2.6 million and brought in $2.5 million; *Silk Stockings* incurred a $1.369 million loss. Both the subject matter (the world of high fashion in *Funny Face*, a Communist's conversion to capitalism in *Silk Stockings*) and the teasingly urbane scores (George and Ira Gershwin and Cole Porter, respectively) only attracted die-hard fans of the movie musical.

By 1957, Astaire had been on the screen for almost a quarter of a century. He was also fifty-eight. In the early 1950s, Astaire was alternating between hits and flops. Of his two 1950 films, *Three Little Words* and *Let's Dance* (Paramount), the former was successful, although not especially memorable; the latter, with Betty Hutton, who was in no way a suitable partner, was a failure. *Royal Wedding* (1951), which proved extremely popular, was followed by *The Belle of New York* (1952), which was not. In accepting the role of Tony Hunter, in which he gave one of his greatest performances, Astaire must have known audiences would forge parallels between himself—an artist whose glory days were over, and his character, a stage-turned-screen-star in the same predicament. The opening title said as much. The credits come on against the image of a top hat on a stand under which is a silver-tipped cane and a pair of white gloves. This was not merely a clever way of beginning a Fred Astaire movie by featuring his signature accessories. At the start of the film, the hat, cane, and gloves are about to be auctioned off as memorabilia. No one is bidding. The auction was a perfect metaphor for Hunter's career in dire need of resuscitation. Hunter arrives in New York, hoping to return to the theater, long the refuge of unbankable movie stars.

To establish Hunter's character as a survivor, Comden and Green had him sing "I'll Go My Way by Myself" before his train pulls into Grand Central Station. Astaire sings it as a monologue, resignedly and without the slightest trace of self-pity and in a kind of parlando. He is met by Lily and Lester Marton (Nanette Fabray and Oscar Levant), a writing and performing team, whom Comden and Green modeled after themselves: lyricists-authors-performers, very much like the team responsible for both the book and lyrics of the Broadway musical *On the Town* (1944), in which they appeared in major roles—the only difference being that the Martons are a married couple, while Comden and Green were married, but not to each other.

Since Lester is also a composer, he and Lily have created a comeback vehicle for Tony as the author of children's books who writes lurid thrillers on
the side, and sells his soul to the devil to achieve success. They have found an
actor-director, Jeffrey Cordova (Jack Buchanan), who, like the Martons, can
also sing and dance (the script requires it) and is so famous that he currently
has three shows on Broadway, starring in one of them. Cordova was supposedly modeled after José Ferrer, whose ego was not as jumbo sized as that of
Orson Welles, who also comes to mind, but of lesser proportions. Buchanan
played Cordova as if he were the fop in a Restoration comedy, affected without being effeminate and theatrical without being hammy. Buchanan and Ferrer were both talented performers, creatures of the stage, for whom no other
medium was as liberating or indulgent. Each could scale down his persona
for the screen, but the reduced dimensions of the performing space in no way
diminished their theatricality.

In 1953, José Ferrer had replaced Orson Welles as a Broadway wunderkind,
a title that Welles owned when he reigned supreme as head of the Mercury
Theatre. But in 1953, the Mercury Theatre was defunct. Welles returned to
New York in 1956 in a production of *King Lear* at the New York City Center,
performing in a wheelchair for most of the run because of a leg injury. In 1953,
he was working in England and had not been on the New York stage since the
ill-fated Cole Porter musical, *Around the World* (1946).

The 1953–1954 season was dominated by Ferrer, who directed and starred
in revivals of *Charley's Aunt* and *Cyrano de Bergerac* at the New York City
Center, where he also appeared in the title role of *Richard III*, staged by Margaret Webster, and in a revival of Joseph Kramm's Pulitzer Prize–winning drama, *The Shrike*, for which he won a Tony the previous year. *My 3 Angels*, which
Ferrer directed, was in its fifth month at the Morosco Theater when *The Band
Wagon* was released.

One could imagine Ferrer behaving in much the same way as Cordova,
who decided to transform the Mortons' script into a "modern musical morality play," elaborately staged with expressionistic sets in red and black and a
hell more sulfurous than fiery. The audience is spared anything of the production, except for a bit of the dress rehearsal with miscued explosions of colored
smoke. *Variety* would have reported that the show "laid an egg"; Minnelli preferred to show a giant egg on the screen.

Tony comes to the rescue, assuming the dual role of director and star,
much to the relief of Cordova, who is content to be one of the cast. Tony
had intended to return to the Mortons' original concept, but scenes from the
out-of-town tryouts in Philadelphia, Boston, Washington, DC, and Baltimore
make it clear that he has created something much closer to the original *Band
Wagon*: a revue, not a book musical. In Philadelphia, Charisse in a spangled

gold dress (yellow and red were among Minnelli's favorite colors) rapturously envisions a new beginning ("New Sun in the Sky"), which sums up the turn the show has taken. In Boston, Astaire and Buchanan (one can't think of them as Tony and Cordova) in matching tuxes and walking sticks do a soft shoe to "I Guess I'll Have to Change My Plan," which seems to have more to do with what has happened to the production than with losing a lover. In Washington, Nanette Fabray and the company perform a sprightly "Louisiana Hayride," which could make the PC patrol bristle, especially since the singers are white while the lyrics are decidedly not ("Get goin', we all is ready! / No use for callin' de roll"). Who would ever be singing such a song in a musical about a Faustian bargain? The best number, "Triplets," is from the Baltimore run, in which Astaire, Fabray, and Buchanan, dressed in baby clothes, sitting in high chairs, and even performing on their knees with prostheses, lament their fate, each wishing for "a wittle gun" to shoot the other two.

By the time the show reaches New York, it bears the same title as the 1931 revue, *The Band Wagon*. Minnelli has bridged the gap between Broadway and Hollywood by making a movie about the genesis of a stage musical with the same title as his own musical, which gives off the same sparks and oscillates with the same electricity as a theatrical production, yet retains its own identity as a film.

The finale of both the revue and the movie, "Girl Hunt: A Murder Mystery in Jazz," is at the center of the Broadway-Hollywood axis. It is a ballet that, as choreographed by Michael Kidd, is wildly cinematic with optical effects (circular flip wipes), hardboiled voiceover narration, and a film noir plot: private eye meets femme fatale. Shots of the audience and the orchestra confirm the setting, a Broadway theater, except that what unfolds is theater as film: a ballet that could have been performed on stage, but not in the same way as on the screen.

The curtains part, revealing the lurid cover of a pulp novel, *Girl Hunt*, with a one-sentence teaser, "She had to die." Everything that follows is theater as cinema. Bullets riddle the cover, setting the tone of the ballet in which bullets fly freely. This is the world of Mickey Spillane and his series detective, Mike Hammer, the sleazy shamus of *Kiss Me Deadly*, which begins when a woman in a trench coat is caught in the headlights of Hammer's car that nearly runs her over. *Girl Hunt* proceeds from the same premise: the encounter between a detective and an imperiled blonde in a trench coat. Rod Riley (Astaire in a blue shirt, white suit, and tie) is no Mike Hammer, but a middleweight version of Raymond Chandler's Philip Marlowe, who plays tough but looks harmless. Riley is walking along a deserted New York street ("The city was asleep. The joints were closed."). The only sound is a trumpet's lonely moan. A blonde in a yellow trench coat rushes up to him, glancing behind her as if she is being pursued and indicating by her agitated movements that she is in danger, or so he is led to believe. *Girl Hunt* is not exactly story ballet like *Giselle* or *Swan Lake*, but a dream narrative in dance that makes sense as images dredged up from the unconscious, which is indifferent to the laws of logic. A man stealthily approaches and picks up a glass that is later revealed to contain glycerine. There is an explosion; the blonde does a disappearing act (she will do so again), and Riley is roughed up by some hoods. All that remains of this strange interlude is, as Riley notes, "a rag and a bone and a hank of hair."

Rudyard Kipling characterized a woman who has a destructive hold on men as "a rag and a bone and a hank of hair" in his poem "Vampire" (1897), in which a fool worshiped "the woman who did not care," calling her "his lady fair," while she was nothing but "a rag and a bone and a hank of hair." The rhymes are elementary, but the concept of woman as succubus is folkloric. Like a true private eye, Riley assumes the three relics are clues to solving the mystery of the blonde in the trench coat. The "rag," an unusual fabric, brings him to a salon where models parade before blank-faced society matrons. The femme fatale slinks in from behind a curtain, presumably a model or another incarnation of the mystery woman—the dark side of the anima as a brunette in a rhinestone-sprinkled black gown. She lures Riley into the storage area, where he is again attacked by thugs. It seems that wherever she goes, trouble follows. She disappears again—or someone in a black hat and coat with an umbrella does. Riley pursues the mysterious figure into a Times Square subway station, where she (or he) disappears. Like a replacement, the imperiled blonde slides onto the platform as if she were making an entrance, this time clad in a diaphanous bluish-white dress and wearing toe shoes, indicating that it is ballet time—an erotic pas de deux with Riley and the blonde dancing out their longing, oblivious to a gunfight in the background. The platform becomes their stage as they dance to Schwartz's Wagnerian music, brimming with yearning and suggesting a possible Liebestod. If either or both were killed, it would be perfect music for a love-death. But the elusive lady disappears again. The "hank of hair" leads nowhere except to a baroque apartment where someone, presumably a female in a golden mask, is lounging in a bath. Since *Girl Hunt* straddles the divide between the phantasmagoric and the surreal, the symbolism—if there is any—of the lady in the gold mask is anybody's guess. Again, a false lead, and again Riley gets beaten up.

The bone, the last clue, brings Riley to the Den Bones Café. The sequence is a masterpiece of stylized dance, in which Kidd has created an atmosphere where syncopation takes on human form, and the rhythm of life has a jazz beat. It is a zoot suit world, where flamboyance is the essence of cool, and wide-cut suits are regulation attire. The cafe is smoky and menacing. Everyone seems to have a past. People either move nervously or robotically, as if they were on a high or coming off of one. Riley enters, affecting the walk of a habitué. After knocking over some thugs who try to bar his way, he spots the mystery woman at the bar, the same brunette from the salon, draped in a gray cloak that she sheds, revealing a red spangled gown. They dance out their encounter, but there is nothing sensuous about it. The dance is like a duel in which the two compete in seeing who can move and kick the best. Even when she plays the role of the partner willing to accept her inferior status as woman, she still has the upper hand—and the legs to go with it. But theirs is an unfinished dance. Violence breaks out again, and Riley (Astaire at his best) has to fend off his attackers, even kicking them over the bar. Wherever the femme fatale is, so are the goons. Riley now has a eureka moment, recalling how the note from the trumpet shattered the glass with the glycerine. A similar glass is on the bar, which he pushes to the end, causing an explosion. Now Riley must confront the figure in black again, whom he shoots, only to discover that it is the mystery woman, the blonde in the see-through dress with whom he danced the almost-but-not-quite Liebestod on the subway platform. Case solved. Riley is back on a deserted street and is about to light his cigarette when a black-gloved, braceleted hand does it for him. She is the brunette from the cafe in the snazzy red dress. The same pulpy voiceover narration at the beginning is repeated: "She was bad. She was dangerous. I wouldn't trust her as far as I could throw her. She was my kind of woman." The two walk off stage; the curtains close and then part for the stars to take their bow. Minnelli preserved the conceit to the very end, making *The Band Wagon* the definitive Broadway-meets-Hollywood movie.

What Kidd has accomplished is equally awesome: He has captured the essence of film noir in dance. A noir plot can have a linearity in which the narrative proceeds inexorably, like *Double Indemnity* (1944), with every incident a link in a fatalistic chain; or it can be a series of episodes that follow each other without necessarily being interconnected. That kind of noir is exemplified by *The Big Sleep* (1946) and *The Lady from Shanghai* (1948), in which logic slowly dissipates like incense, leaving the viewer trapped in a wild dream that can be described but not explained in terms of cause and effect. *The Big Sleep* is making sense until a black sedan is hauled out of the water at the Lido pier, after which the plot starts to crumble, and the fun begins. *The Lady from Shanghai* begins simply enough: Orson Welles, who rescues Rita Hayworth from a band of hoodlums, is hired by her husband, whose business associate offers him $5,000 (big bucks in 1948) to fake his murder, after which the business associate is murdered by, of all people, Rita, who shoots it out with her husband in a funhouse where they kill each other, dying amid shards of broken glass. The first part—the rescue that comes with a job offer—is believable. The rest is a roller-coaster ride. *Girl Hunt* is the same kind of noir narrative with a plausible beginning, an improbable middle, and a surprise ending. The beginning is not that different from *Kiss Me Deadly*; it is the hardboiled version of the meet cute: the meet dangerous. Everything that follows is, to quote Yeats, out of context, a crazy salad.

Seven Brides for Seven Brothers (1954)—filmed in Ansco Color, which was less expensive than Technicolor, lensed in CinemaScope, produced by Jack Cummings, directed by Stanley Donen, and spectacularly choreographed by Michael Kidd—is another original with a tenuous connection to the work that inspired it: Stephen Vincent Benét's "The Sobbin' Women." The score by Gene De Paul (music) and Johnny Mercer (lyrics) is so artfully fitted to the screenplay that every musical sequence flows out of the action, stopping only for the plot to continue as spoken dialogue and then resuming when it's time for the spoken word to hold its tongue and yield to song and/or dance. Adam Pontipee (Howard Keel), the oldest of seven unmarried brothers, strides into a town in the Oregon Territory in 1850 in search of a wife. Unused to the sight of women, he marvels at this strange but delightful species ("Bless Your Beautiful Hide"), sizing them up like cattle for auction. But the song also establishes his character: a mountain man who thinks of women as beef on the hoof. Millie (Jane Powell) agrees to marry him, at first behaving like a new bride ("Wonderful, Wonderful Day"). Once Millie realizes that Adam expects her to play nanny to his uncivilized brothers, she bars him from the bedroom and sends him off to sleep in a tree outside her window, from which she sings "When You're in Love," revealing her unabashedly romantic nature. When she takes Adam back, it is on the condition that he and the brothers learn proper etiquette.

The famous barn-raising sequence is not a set piece but a continuation of the plot through dance. The brothers, whom Millie has groomed into gentlemen (or so she thinks), compete for the local lasses with the (so-called) well-bred men of the community in a lively courtship dance, with the brothers engaging in the kind of athleticism usually seen in competitions. Kidd's choreography is so unselfconsciously virile that what is really ballet comes off, in terms of plot, as athletic prowess. But the barn raising is also a competition between the brothers and their rivals, who treat them as interlopers, harassing them to such an extent that they square off at each other, causing the barn to collapse.

Branded as pariahs and denied the right to court the women properly, the brothers abduct them—an action that might strike contemporary viewers as abhorrent. However, the brothers are really enacting their version of "The Sobbin' Women," inspired by Adam's rousingly discreet song about the Rape of the Sabine Women, a (probably mythical) part of Rome's prehistory, in which the Roman settlers carried off women from the Sabine tribe, taking them as their wives. "Rape" does not necessarily denote sexual violence, although that has become its primary meaning. In a different context, it can also mean "carry off" as in the theft of a lock of hair in Alexander Pope's mock epic, *The Rape of the Lock*. But there is no denying that the brothers have committed a criminal offense by kidnapping the young women, even though the National Legion of Decency rated *Seven Brides for Seven Brothers* A-II (Morally Unobjectionable for Adults and Adolescents), as if an abduction is a harmless prank.

An avalanche prevents the outraged parents from reclaiming their daughters, who are confined to the Pontipee home until the spring thaw. It is at this point that the film, which could have turned unsavory, veers off into feminism. Furious about the kidnappings, Millie banishes the brothers to the barn; Adam, equally unwelcome, retires to a cabin, leaving the women to themselves as they set up their own household with Millie as matriarch/confidante/surrogate mother/big sister. Through the miraculous compression of time for which film is famous, winter melts into spring, inspiring hope in the women—not for returning to their homes but for marrying the brothers ("June Bride"). There are weddings as well as a birth, Millie and Adam's daughter. The brides-to-be link up with their prospective husbands—the cue for "Spring, Spring, Spring," a celebration of nature's awakening and overall renewal. By this time, the audience has forgotten the abductions and settled in for the windup.

Seven Brides for Seven Brothers is a totally integrated musical; in no way can the numbers be rearranged without affecting the narrative. At Oscar time, unlike *Singin' in the Rain*, *Seven Brides for Seven Brothers* was nominated for Best Picture, losing to *On the Waterfront*. It ranks twenty-first among AFI's twenty-five greatest musicals.

- 9 -

FILM AS THEATER, THEATER AS FILM

Some musicals are theatrical in their own way, conveying the semblance of a live performance; others are theatrical in the sense that they originated on Broadway and seem like Manhattan transfers—stage musicals brought to the screen. Although *Annie Get Your Gun* (1950) was adapted from the 1946 stage hit that ran for 1,147 performances, the only vestiges of its origins were Irving Berlin's score, not all of which was used, and the plot, which pretty much remained intact. Even the set pieces—"Doin' What Comes Natur'lly," "There's No Business Like Show Business," "I Got the Sun in the Morning"—seemed typical of a movie, not a stage, musical. Certainly, the last image, a wide shot of riders parading in concentric circles at Buffalo Bill's Wild West Show, could never have been staged in any Broadway house. Yet the *Annie Get Your Gun* finale is theater, but a special kind: a filmed spectacle as kinetically thrilling as any live performance. Those who saw *Annie* on the stage and on the screen saw different versions of the same show: Broadway audiences saw Ethel Merman in person as Annie; film audiences saw Betty Hutton on celluloid, who sounded just as real, so much so that no one would think of saying, "Hutton's not live and lip-synching her prerecorded songs." They accept conventions even though they may not know what they are and experience reality in their own half state as a live enactment recorded on film, which, with the right director and cast, can seem as if the performers had sprung to life.

The musical is not just another genre like the crime film or the western; it holds a special place in film history. For many moviegoers, the Hollywood musical was the closest they would ever get to Broadway. Some MGM musicals had the feel of live theater, with numbers that ended with a stage-worthy exit. In *High Society* (1956), Bing Crosby and Frank Sinatra retire to the study rather than mingle with the guests at a stuffy party where they feel out of place. They parody the guests' genteel gossip in "Well, Did You Evah," interpolated from Cole Porter's earlier show, *Du Barry Was a Lady* (1939), in which they trade anecdotes about "dear Blanche [who] got run down by an avalanche" and "Mimsie Starr [who] got pinched in the Astor Bar." Since Porter wrote the lyrics (and the score) for *High Society*, the exchanges between

Crosby and a slightly inebriated Sinatra were far wittier than what was transpiring among the Newport bluebloods. With the concluding verse, "What a swellegant, elegant party this is," Crosby and Sinatra exit arm in arm, about to join the guests; then, realizing the boredom in store for them, they dash back to the study for another drink (and an encore), as they dance out of the room, each going his own way—one exiting right, the other left (think stage right and stage left), and leaving the audience in such a euphoric state that a burst of applause would not have been inappropriate.

Occasionally a performer is featured in a musical who is unmistakably from Broadway and seems to have crash landed in Hollywood, finding herself in the midst of an alien tribe. Such was Ethel Merman, whose outsized personality and thunderous voice was hemmed in by the confines of the screen. She toned down her Sally Adams in the movie version of *Call Me Madam* (Twentieth Century–Fox, 1953), giving audiences an indication of how she performed the role on stage where it was brassier, bawdier, and broader. Merman was Broadway; the rest of the cast—George Sanders, Vera-Ellen, Donald O'Connor—was Hollywood. Betty Grable's movie fame was behind her when she returned to Broadway in 1967 as one of Carol Channing's replacements in *Hello, Dolly!* Channing was another performer who lit up Broadway but who lost wattage in Hollywood. As Dolly Gallagher Levi, Grable brought Hollywood to Broadway, giving a performance that audiences expected of a one-time film star, who even exposed one of her Lloyds of London–insured legs when she sang, "Wow, wow, wow, fellas / Look at the old girl now, fellas!" And we did—and marveled. The "old girl" still had it.

Joan McCracken, Bob Fosse's second wife, was a trained ballet dancer and stage actor, equally at home in drama (*The Big Knife, Galileo*) and musicals (*Oklahoma!, Bloomer Girl, Billion Dollar Baby*). Neither striking in appearance nor endowed with a great voice, she could command a stage and the screen, too, as she demonstrated in her two film appearances—but only in specialty numbers, not for the duration of the film. Her "Ballet in Jive" (*Hollywood Canteen*, Warner Bros., 1944) made you wonder where this creature came from; her movements were so classically controlled yet uninhibited that she seemed to belong to an unclassified species, which set her apart from the rest of the cast that consisted of familiar names: Jack Carson, Jane Wyman, Dennis Morgan, Joan Leslie, the Andrews Sisters, and Roy Rogers and the Sons of the Pioneers.

MGM hired McCracken for *Good News* (1947), Betty Comden and Adolph Green's revitalization of the 1927 Broadway musical and the first of seven films they did for Arthur Freed. In the opening number, "Good News," McCracken led a chorus of collegians who went through the motions while she, despite a voice that was far from evangelical, brought such vitality to the number that one kept looking at *her* and not at the others. With McCracken, it was not business as usual, but show business as always. It was the same with "Pass That Peace Pipe," the ice cream parlor number by Roger Edens, Hugh Martin, and Ralph Blane, which was not in the original. McCracken was fortunate to have Ray McDonald as her partner, who, like herself, came from Broadway via vaudeville. (He and his sister Grace did the show-stopping "I Wish I Were in Love Again" in Rodgers and Hart's *Babes in Arms* on Broadway in 1937.) Together, McCracken and McDonald momentarily brought a conventional musical to life in a number that had little to do with the plot. But MGM had no place for McCracken, so it was back to Broadway and television drama, which was then in its infancy. McDonald lasted longer in the movies, but died tragically at thirty-eight, never having achieved the recognition he deserved. But neither did McCracken, who was too quirky for leading roles unless they were written with someone like her in mind. Her situation was complicated by diabetes, which contributed to her death at forty-three.

To recreate the experience of a stage musical, *Top Banana* (United Artists, 1954), with Phil Silvers in his Tony award-winning performance as a television star with a giant-sized ego (think Milton Berle), was shot on a specially constructed stage at the Motion Picture Center, a rental studio on North Cahuenga Boulevard in Hollywood. No one could mistake *Top Banana* for a Hollywood musical. The cast included members of the original production that premiered on November 1, 1952. The sets were the same, and the actors entered and exited on cue; the boy-girl subplot surfaced for a ballad and then disappeared so that Silvers and his cronies could revive some of burlesque's classic skits. *Top Banana* was never a great show, and the movie transcript, available on YouTube, might make contemporary viewers wonder why it lasted for 350 performances. The answer is "Phil Silvers," who introduced a new generation to the lost world of burlesque.

I have attended screenings at which audiences applauded after "On the Atchison, Topeka and Santa Fe" (*The Harvey Girls* [1946]) and Maurice Chevalier's "I'm Glad I'm Not Young Any More" (*Gigi* [1958]). In *The Harvey Girls*, a contingent of young women travel by train to Sand Rock, New Mexico, to work as waitresses at the Harvey House. The train's approach is greeted lustily by the locals; when the train pulls in, the rhythm changes, slowing down, as Judy Garland is helped off the last carriage, imagining the new life that awaits her. She slowly wends her way among the crowd that sways back and forth, as if affected by her graceful movements. When the conductor yells, "All aboard!" Judy and Ray Bolger rush to the head of the line that has formed alongside the train, extending their arms and pulling them back in imitation of the locomotive as it chugs along. The sequence culminates with a close-up of Judy at her radiant best, deserving a moment of awe; and the sequence, meriting applause for Robert Alton's staging.

At the end of *Gigi*, Maurice Chevalier is lunching in the park musing on his nephew's complicated love life. He sings "I'm Glad I'm Not Young Anymore" almost in its entirety while seated at the table, his eyes twinkling wickedly and his head tilting knowingly, as he enumerates the joys that come with age, particularly affairs that end, relieving both parties of the burden of pretense. Although seated, Chevalier uses his body so artfully that the song takes on a momentum of its own. Just before the last verse, he gets up, leaving money for the bill, and walks off singing, "Oh, I'm so glad that I'm not young anymore," elongating the syllables ("gl-ad," "I-m") and exiting smoothly on "anymore," as if he knew that applause would follow, as indeed it did.

Gigi has been called the cinematic equivalent of Alan Jay Lerner and Frederick Loewe's stage hit, *My Fair Lady* (1956). Lerner, who wrote the book and lyrics for *My Fair Lady*, was not a Hollywood novice, having written the original screenplay of *An American in Paris*, for which he won an Oscar, and the screenplay and lyrics for *Royal Wedding*. But his collaborator, Frederick Loewe, had never composed for the screen. When Lerner finally convinced Loewe that it would be practically the same as creating a Broadway musical, he signed on once he realized they could approach Colette's novella, *Gigi*, the same way they did Shaw's *Pygmalion*, which they turned into *My Fair Lady*. This time, they did not have to change the title. Gigi became a Parisian Eliza Doolittle. While Eliza was being tutored in standard English by Professor Henry Higgins, Gigi was being groomed to be a courtesan by her great-aunt; and Gaston, the jaded playboy for whom she is intended, became a Higgins type who realizes that Gigi has transformed him from a ladies' man to an ardent wooer, ready to propose marriage—a state to which he had previously been averse. Thus what could easily have been the sordid tale of a young woman raised to be a wealthy man's mistress became an edifying story of experience charmed by innocence, or, in the case of *My Fair Lady*, age humanized by youth. When love-struck Gaston (Louis Jourdan) breaks into the title song, half-singing, half-speaking it, as he tries to sort out his feelings for someone whom he had dismissed as just a "girl," one cannot help but think of Henry Higgins expressing similar sentiments in "I've Grown Accustomed to Her Face," recalling how Eliza has been so much a part of his life that he is adrift without her. *Gigi* is musical theater, conceived first as a film musical and then in 1973 converted with little tinkering into a stage musical, which was revived in 2015. Neither stage production cast the same spell as the movie, which proves that *Gigi* reached its level of excellence on the screen.

Not all musicals of this era were so theatrical. Sometimes the musical sequences functioned as diversions; the action would stop to feature a performer who may or may not figure prominently in the plot, but who had
a special talent that needed showcasing. This was certainly true of Eleanor
Powell, whose legs were capable of an astonishingly high kick and who had a
style that was uniquely her own: tap with a touch of the balletic. Since Powell
was not an actress (although she delivered her lines convincingly), MGM
had no reason to cast her in dramatic roles, but it knew how to capitalize on
her art, even when she was cast opposite other virtuoso dancers like George
Murphy (*Broadway Melody of 1938*) and Fred Astaire (*Broadway Melody of
1940*).

By 1948, another great tap dancer had joined the MGM family, Ann Miller. In the stage version of Leonard Bernstein's *On the Town* (1944), Claire
De Loone (Betty Comden), an anthropologist, confesses to Ozzie (Adolph
Green), one of the three sailors on leave, that she becomes so immersed in
her work that she gets "carried away," which is also the title of her big number.
"Carried Away" with its tricky vocal shifts would not have been a good fit
for Miller, cast in the role that Comden originated on Broadway. Not only
was the character's name changed to Claire Huddesen ("Claire De Loone"
may have sounded too much like a musical joke), but "Carried Away" was replaced by "Prehistoric Man," which, like "Carried Away," is sung in a museum.
With Miller in the role, a song was not enough; she also offered a demonstration of the art of tap. MGM provided Miller with a similar opportunity in
Kiss Me Kate when "Too Darn Hot," sung and danced in the original stage
production by a trio of men in the alley outside the stage door, was refashioned as a solo for her on screen.

MGM musicals had some extraordinary finales that either functioned as
plot resolutions or, if the plot had already been resolved, provided a splashy
coda, like a bonus track on a CD. The reasoning was best expressed in the lyrics of "That's Entertainment" from *The Band Wagon*: "A show that is really a
show / Sends you out with a kind of a glow." Leaving the audience aglow was
the goal, whether the finale flowed directly from the plot or was tacked on as
musical plumage. *The Pirate* (1948) ends with Gene Kelly and Judy Garland
wearing the motley while they urge the audience to "Be a Clown." Perhaps
the point is that Judy has now joined Kelly's strolling players. But logic does
not apply here. It's a grand number in a movie that did not have many of
them. Musically, *The Pirate*, which was no *Meet Me in St. Louis* (and did mediocre box office), needed a rousing windup to justify the audience's sitting
through a 102-minute movie about a fantasist who had been able to repress
her desires until an itinerant performer entered her life.

Musicals set in the entertainment world, especially the theater, operate by a different logic. In an adaptation of a Broadway musical, the numbers generally followed the same order as they did in the original, unless one of them was considered too risqué or erudite for a mass audience. In *Annie Get Your Gun* (1950), "Doin' What Comes Natur'lly" is Annie's first number, just as it was in the original. It would have made no sense for Annie to sing "Moonshine Lullaby" first (that comes third), since "Doin' What Comes Natur'lly" sums her up: she is an earthy woman, disarmingly unsubtle and endowed with a zest for life, about whose facts she is more than knowledgeable, as she admits in lyrics that were omitted in the movie, in which she explains how her baby brother distinguished between the sexes by looking. "Moonshine Lullaby," with its lyrics about a whiskey still, was cut; singing children to sleep with a song about a father at his distillery was not the average filmgoer's idea of a lullaby. The poignant ballad "I Got Lost in His Arms" was also dropped, perhaps because it was considered too romantic for Annie's character, particularly as played by the effervescent Betty Hutton. In the original, Ethel Merman sang it with great feeling, revealing a more feminine Annie than her clothes and demeanor suggested.

MGM's most atypical musical of the 1940s was *Cabin in the Sky* (1943). Until then, there had not been an all-black film from a major studio since *The Green Pastures* (Warner Bros., 1936), which also derived from a stage play—Marc Connelly's similarly named 1930 Pulitzer Prize winner. Richly ethnic and deeply religious, *The Green Pastures* was a Sunday School retelling of biblical stories made meaningful to African Americans in the rural South (Adam and Eve, Cain and Abel, Noah and the Flood, Moses and Aaron) and culminating in a moral: suffering is redemptive, as Dr. Martin Luther King Jr. proclaimed in his "I Have a Dream" speech and as De Lawd (Rex Ingram) preaches in *The Green Pastures*, urging those who have suffered injustice to link their sufferings with Christ's.

Cabin in the Sky, filmed in sepia tone, is also a folktale, specifically a folk musical in the form of a morality play about the battle for the soul of "Little Joe" Jackson (Eddie "Rochester" Anderson) waged by the forces of good and evil: the General (Kenneth Spencer) and Lucifer Jr. (Rex Ingram), whose minions have hornlike tufts of hair. On Broadway, *Cabin* ended with the death of "Little Joe" and his wife, Petunia (Ethel Waters), who are then seen ascending the staircase to paradise in white robes to dwell in their cabin in the sky. The movie version ends differently. In 1942, audiences wanted something from a musical other than death and transfiguration, particularly in the second year of America's entry into World War II.

When *Cabin in the Sky* (1940) opened on Broadway for a run of 156 performances, it could only boast of one big name, Ethel Waters. The show was not a hit, closing at a loss of $25,000. Thus the rights were cheap—$40,000. Arthur Freed was determined to make a profit, despite objections from the black press that the musical portrayed African Americans condescendingly. The press was right, but one could say the same about *The Green Pastures* and even *Porgy and Bess*, which featured characters of far greater humanity than those in many films set in white America, whose values were the norm against which those of other cultures were measured.

As often happens, most of *Cabin in the Sky*'s original score by Vernon Duke and John Latouche was scrapped, except for the title song, "Taking a Chance on Love," which Waters sang as an easy-going jazz ballad, reprising it at the end with the same dreamy wonder, and "Honey in the Honeycomb," sung by both Waters and Lena Horne. Streamlining the original score was getting to be commonplace at MGM, where within three years, three Broadway musicals with good but not great scores arrived in the theaters minus most of the original songs: *Lady Be Good*, *Panama Hattie*, *Du Barry Was a Lady*, and now *Cabin in the Sky*. The exception was *Best Foot Forward* (1943), in which ten of the fourteen songs from the 1941 Broadway original survived the transfer.

Cabin in the Sky was originally entitled *Little Joe*. However, Ethel Waters, then the reigning black artist on Broadway known for her impeccable diction and expressive singing, objected, arguing that the title implied that Joe, not his wife, Petunia, was the central character. Even when the musical was renamed *Cabin in the Sky*, Waters reluctantly signed on, ambivalent about the show's depiction of Uncle Remus–like blacks and especially the implied liaison between Joe and the local vamp (Katherine Dunham in the original, Lena Horne in the film).

Despite Waters's objections to the portrayal of southern blacks as naifs and prey to get-rich-quick schemes, she was ideally suited to the role of Petunia, who, after Little Joe, a compulsive gambler, is seriously wounded in a craps game, prays fervently for his recovery. Skeptics need only look at Waters's pleading eyes to see the meaning of faith. The white-suited General, a stand-in for the archangel Michael, agrees to a six-month reprieve so Joe can redeem himself and he and Petunia can be ensconced for all eternity in their cabin in the sky, the sharecropper's equivalent of the house of many mansions, as Jesus described the place he has prepared for his disciples (John 14:2). Petunia responds to the good news by singing "Happiness Is Just a Thing Called Joe," which Harold Arlen and E. Y. "Yip" Harburg had written for her and which she delivered with the subdued joy born of gratitude and humility, making the song seem almost like a prayer.

For a woman as religious as Waters, Joe's attraction to the hooker Georgia Brown was a problem even after the lyrics and dialogue had been sanitized. The National Legion of Decency imposed a "B" (Morally Objectionable in

Part for All) rating on the film, citing "suggestive lines and situations." It is easy to infer that Georgia and Joe are—or were—lovers from the scene in which she spies him lying in a hammock. Stopping to pluck a magnolia from a tree, she sashays toward him as if she were about to make an unrefusable offer. And with Horne in a two-piece skirt and blouse with an exposed midriff, resistance is difficult. Joe is clearly torn between Georgia's sensuousness and Petunia's maternalism, making Petunia seem more of a mother figure than a wife.

But with Eddie "Rochester" Anderson as Joe, known to moviegoers as Rochester of radio's *Jack Benny Program*, on which he played Benny's butler, it is virtually impossible to envision him having an affair with someone like Lena Horne. One could, however, easily accept him as the husband of Ethel Waters, who projected the image of a born-again earth mother.

Horne enters the film late, doing relatively little except to sing "Life Is Full of Consequences" with Anderson, who performs the number in speech song, punching out the syllables as if they were typewriter keys. Horne has a solo in the fantasy sequence, "Honey from the Honeycomb," which Waters then reprises while doing a wicked dance, complete with high kicks.

Cabin in the Sky was Vincente Minnelli's directorial debut. There was little Minnelli could do with the fable-like screenplay and its faux naifism, with the personifications of good and evil attired in white and black, leaving no doubt about which section of the hereafter each occupied. But he did create a disturbingly realistic climax that turns out to be a fantasy. Because of Lucifer Jr's machinations, Joe wins the sweepstakes and becomes a big spender, whose prodigal ways even inspire Petunia to get dolled up in a sparkling hooded gown and dance up a storm at Jim Henry's Paradise. A brawl breaks out between Joe and the gambler Domino Johnson (John W. Sublett), who shoots both Joe and Petunia. A tornado arrives like the biblical whirlwind, blowing the roof off of the Paradise and bringing the ceiling down on the fleeing patrons. As spirits, Joe and Petunia mount the stairway to heaven where Petunia is welcomed, but Joe is not until Lucifer Jr. learns to his dismay that Georgia Brown has repented and donated her share of the sweepstakes to the church, thus making Joe redeemable. Petunia and Joe walk up the heavenly staircase amid swirling clouds, as an off-screen chorus sings "Cabin in the Sky," which would have brought the film, as it did the play, to a sublimely spiritual close. But MGM decreed otherwise. Just as Petunia and Joe are about to relocate in their cabin on a cloud, Joe awakens. Everything, from the time Joe was brought home wounded to the ascent to heaven, was a dream. Joe recovers and has Petunia burn his sweepstakes ticket and dice. And Waters does a reprise of "Taking a Chance on Love," which has little to do with his regeneration, but few would quibble about a chance to hear Waters once more.

Minnelli had a penchant for infusing the surreal with an air of menace, which appears for the first time in *Cabin in the Sky* and would manifest itself later in the Halloween sequence in *Meet Me in St. Louis*, "Mack the Black" in *The Pirate*, and "The Girl Hunt" in *The Band Wagon*. In the Paradise nightclub, everyone seems to be on display, pretending to have a good time while knowing there is something lurking in the room that calls for cautious gaiety, which gives way to raucousness, as if the collective loss of inhibitions can keep impending violence at bay. That we are in the middle of a dionysian fantasy that turns apocalyptic is evident in Petunia's transformation from a fervent believer to a regular at the sinners' paradise with her eye on Joe's sweepstakes money. And whoever thought Ethel Waters could kick with such sass and abandon or that Lena Horne could act instead of sing, posing against a pillar?

Minnelli's *Brigadoon* (1954) and *Kismet* (1955) are more representative of MGM's approach to Broadway musicals, but less interesting. Despite its somber theme—a Scottish village that comes to life for one day every hundred years and is now threatened with extinction by the defection of a rejected suitor—the Broadway production of *Brigadoon* (1947) included "My Mother's Weddin' Day," Meg Brockie's rollicking account of her parents' nuptials that degenerated into a drunken free-for-all when the groom failed to arrive on time. Frederick Loewe set Alan Jay Lerner's "list song" lyrics with their head-spinning catalog of names ("MacGregor, MacKenna, MacGowan, MacVitie, MacNeil an' MacRae, MacVicker, MacDougall, MacDuff, an' Mac Coy") to an equally dizzying reel, with Meg and the chorus describing what happened when the men, tired of waiting, hit the rye; and the women, the gin. The song may have humanized the villagers and momentarily demythologized them. But the depiction of the wedding—much less the final verse which suggests a couple legitimizing their union in the presence of their daughter—would have caused the pious to frown. "My Mother's Weddin' Day" was a comic interlude, indicating that Meg knew the facts of life, even though nobody else in Brigadoon seemed to. It never had a chance in the movie; Freed knew that once Production Code czar Joseph Ignatius Breen read the lyrics, he would have immediately called for the song's elimination.

Although Minnelli wanted to shoot *Brigadoon* in Scotland, Dore Schary, then MGM production head, vetoed the idea, citing expense. Filming *Brigadoon* in CinemaScope was expensive enough; it would also have to be distributed in the regular format for theaters in small towns that were not equipped for widescreen. Nor was Technicolor an option; *Brigadoon* would be photographed in inferior Ansco Color. There was another problem that eluded Schary: the casting. While Cyd Charisse was a perfect Fiona speaking her lines like a true Scot and lip-synching to Carol Richards's vocals, Kelly's wispy singing voice could not do justice to the score. On Broadway, the leads were the soprano Marion Bell and the lyric baritone David Brooks. Kelly managed "Almost Like Being in Love," but the powerful ballad, "There but for You Go I," was cut because vocally it was out of his range. Fortunately, the original cast recording exists, so it is possible to hear Brooks's rendition, along with other songs that were cut, such as "Love of My Life" and "From This Day On."

But the chief problem with *Brigadoon* is the ending, which comes in the form of a death wish, although few filmgoers in 1954 would have interpreted it that way. Yet if Tommy (Gene Kelly) is to possess Fiona, he must relinquish his world for hers, which only materializes once every hundred years. Unable to forget her, Tommy flies back to Scotland, even though he knows that Brigadoon will not be there, having disappeared into the highland mists. If faith can move mountains, it can also alter destiny. Awakened by the sound of Tommy's voice, the village sage, Mr. Lundie (Barry Jones), explains that if you love someone, anything is possible, even a miracle. Tommy is searching for the peace that passeth understanding and has found it in Brigadoon, which is now ready to receive him. If dying to the world—his world—is the only way of achieving deathless love, Tommy is willing to enter an alternate world that operates on centennial time. Minnelli did not—or chose not to—bring out the darker aspects of the Lerner and Loewe musical, preferring to settle for a "happy ever after" ending with the lovers reunited. But the darkness is there for those who can penetrate it.

When *Kismet* (1955), filmed in CinemaScope and single-strip Eastman Color, reached the screen, there was virtually no laundering of the highly suggestive—but deliciously subtle—lyrics. The Arabian Nights setting and the movie's lineage—a hoary melodrama that had served as a vehicle for Otis Skinner—suggests a cross between a fable and a relic. Even the National Legion of Decency, which slapped "B" (Morally Objectionable in Part for All) ratings on movies with suggestive sequences, dialogue, costumes, and situations, classified *Kismet* A-II (Morally Unobjectionable for Adults and Adolescents). In "Not since Nineveh," Dolores Gray extolled the pleasure dome that Baghdad has become ever since "Babylon turned to mire / for a sin of a kind we never mind here" and "that village near Gomorrah got too hot for Lot." "Rahadlakum" also survived, despite the fact that it celebrates the powers of an aphrodisiac in lyrics meant for decoding, particularly when Gray describes her method of handling an errant mate by preparing a dish that will "drive him out of his Mesopotamian mind."

Edward Knoblock's *Kismet*—produced by the Waldorf Film Corporation in a 1920 silent version with Otis Skinner; by Warner Bros. in 1930 with Otis Skinner and Loretta Young, now considered a lost film; and in lush Technicolor by MGM in 1944 with Ronald Colman and Marlene Dietrich with her legs painted gold for one scene—inspired the 1953 Broadway show, set to the music of Alexander Borodin by George Forrest and Robert Wright, who had performed a similar service for Edvard Grieg in *Song of Norway* (1944). The MGM adaptation is unusually faithful to the Forrest and Wright musical. The daughter (Ann Blyth) of a mendicant poet (Howard Keel) is abducted and ensconced in the Wazir's harem. The Wazir's unfulfilled wife (Gray) is attracted to the poet, who is not indifferent to her charms. The poet's drowning of the Wazir in his own pool is somewhat jarring for a musical, but it paves the way for a happy ending, with the union of his daughter and Caliph (Richard Kiley on Broadway, Vic Damone in the movie); and the poet, accepting as punishment for the murder, banishment to an oasis, where the Wazir's widow plans to pay him frequent visits, bringing along, one supposes, her famous rahadlakum.

MGM incurred a loss with *Kismet*, which cost about $3 million but only grossed $1.87 million. It occasionally appears on Turner Classic Movies (TCM), but a stage revival in the twenty-first century would be chancy. Even though the setting is the mythical Middle East, the opening verse of "Not since Nineveh"—"Baghdad, don't underestimate Baghdad"—would have to be cut. If it were kept, it would either generate nervous laughter or provoke a snicker. No one can ever underestimate Baghdad.

Minnelli does not discuss *Kismet* in his autobiography; it was not a film he wanted to direct. Stanley Donen, in fact, directed some of it, uncredited. Minnelli only agreed if his next MGM project would be the Vincent van Gogh biopic, *Lust for Life* (1956), in which he indulged his pictorial sense as he had never done before. The direction in *Kismet* may seem desultory, but the performers make up for it with outstanding vocalism and musical comedy savvy—Gray keeping the witty double entendres from turning singular; and Keel, Blyth, and Damone bringing out the rich poetry of "And This Is My Beloved," "Stranger in Paradise," and "Sands of Time."

Except for *Kiss Me Kate* (1953) and perhaps *Silk Stockings* (1957), MGM did not do well by Cole Porter. *Panama Hattie* (1942) was a makeover of the 1940 musical that starred Ethel Merman as Hattie Maloney, a nightclub owner and singer in the Panama Canal Zone in love with a navy officer, who has to win over his eight-year-old daughter, in addition to contending with a rival for the officer's affections. The plot was ridiculously complicated (there was even an averted attempt at sabotage), but the score included a few standards, "Let's Be Buddies," which Merman sang with the daughter (Joan Carroll, Agnes in *Meet Me in St. Louis*); and "Make It Another Old Fashioned, Please," which Ann Sothern (Hattie) was supposed to sing in the film. The number was filmed, but, inexplicably, cut, possibly because someone figured out that it was about a former drinker who became so disillusioned in love that she went "off the wagon"—not exactly encouraging news for recovering alcoholics. The movie was tailored to Red Skelton's brand of slapstick, resulting in the reduction of Porter's sixteen songs to three: "I've Still Got My Health," "Let's Be Buddies," and "Fresh as a Daisy" (belted by Virginia O'Brien); and the updating of the script to include the unmasking of Nazi agents. Before it was released in September 1942, a finale was appended to reflect the country's mood after Pearl Harbor, as the cast vowed revenge on "The Son of a Gun Who Picks on Uncle Sam," one of Burton Lane and Yip Harburg's ephemera.

Nazis were big at MGM in 1942, even in films in which they seemed to have no place, such as *Rio Rita*, which bore hardly any resemblance to Ziegfeld's 1927 musical and, in fact, only included two songs from the original. Just as *Panama Hattie* was outfitted for Red Skelton, *Rio Rita* was tailored to the comedic talents of Bud Abbott and Lou Costello embroiled in a Nazi spy ring at a Western resort. Nazis were even aboard a cruise ship in *Ship Ahoy*, with Eleanor Powell tapping out a Morse Code alert to a government agent during her performance. Jeanette MacDonald could not even escape them in *Cairo*, in which journalist Robert Young is convinced that MacDonald, an opera-star-turned-nightclub-performer, is a Nazi spy. According to Hollywood, in 1942 Nazis could be in your own backyard—or at least in New York, as evidenced in *Saboteur, Lucky Jordan*, and *All through the Night*.

There was no way Nazis could be worked into Porter's *Du Barry Was a Lady* (1943), with Red Skelton and Lucille Ball in the roles created on Broadway by Bert Lahr and Ethel Merman. The plot, if one could call it that, remained basically the same, except for the bawdy humor, which even now is surprisingly unsubtle, particularly in "But in the Morning, No," with its references to getting one's ante up, enjoying third parties, doing breaststrokes and double entry, filling inside straights, selling one's seat, and owning a Pekinese that crosses its Q's and P's. The book by Herbert Fields and B. G. "Buddy" DeSylva was one of Porter's weakest: A nightclub coatroom (washroom in the original) attendant (Skelton), in love with a performer (Ball), consumes a drugged drink intended for a rival and dreams he is Louis XV and Ball is Madame du Barry. A faithful screen replica was impossible. Even in 1939, *New York Times* drama critic Brooks Atkinson (December 7, 1939) felt that the show "struck a dead level of Broadway obscenity." Interestingly, *Times* critic Ben Brantley felt similarly about a concert version at the New York City Center (February 17, 1996), noting that "But in the Morning, No" "still has the power to draw blushes." In the movie, what passes for risqué is Burton Lane and Ralph Freed's "Madame, I Love Your Crepes Suzettes," in which Skelton as Louis XV informs Ball as du Barry that he does not "mean to be rude," but he's "not in the mood for food" and proceeds to chase her around the boudoir.

Porter's last Broadway show, *Silk Stockings* (1955), was the musical version of Ernst Lubitsch's *Ninotchka* (1939) with a book by George S. Kaufman and

Debbie Reynolds as the title character in *The Unsinkable Molly Brown* (1964) singing "Belly Up to the Bar, Boys."

Arthur Freed (*right*) with Judy Garland and her then husband Vincente Minnelli on the set of *The Harvey Girls* (1946).

Judy Garland urging everyone to "Get Happy" in *Summer Stock* (1950).

Debbie Reynolds and
Carleton Carpenter
performing "I Wanna Be
Loved by You" in *Three
Little Words* (1950).

The glamorous Arlene Dahl singing "I Love You So Much" in *Three Little Words*.

Kathryn Grayson and Howard Keel in 3-D at the end of *Kiss Me Kate* (1953).

Eleanor Powell and Fred Astaire dancing to Cole Porter's "Begin the Beguine" in *Broadway Melody of 1940*.

Marge and Gower Champion describing "Life Upon the Wicked Stage" in *Show Boat* (1951).

Gene Kelly singing "You Were Meant for Me" to Debbie Reynolds in *Singin' in the Rain* (1952).

Fred Astaire dancing on the ceiling in *Royal Wedding* (1951).

Luise Rainer as Anna Held in
The Great Ziegfeld (1936).

Gene Kelly and Fred Astaire in "The Babbitt and the Bromide" in *Ziegfeld Follies* (1946).

Judy Garland taking the iconic trolley ride in *Meet Me in St. Louis* (1944).

Fred Astaire and Cyd Charisse in the Girl Hunt ballet in *The Band Wagon* (1953).

Frank Sinatra and Gene Kelly in *Anchors Aweigh* (1945).

Judy Garland and Mickey Rooney in *Babes in Arms* (1939).

Lena Horne in *Till the Clouds Roll By* (1946).

The three female costars
of *On the Town* (1949), *left
to right*, Betty Garrett, Ann
Miller, and Vera-Ellen.

Ricardo Montalban telling Esther Williams, "Baby, It's Cold Outside" in *Neptune's Daughter* (1949).

Nelson Eddy and Jeanette MacDonald in *Naughty Marietta* (1935).

Esther Williams after swimming the English Channel and Fernando Lamas, also an excellent swimmer, in *Dangerous When Wet* (1953).

Esther Williams in a water ballet in *Easy to Love* (1953).

Janis Paige illustrating the appeal of fancy lingerie in *Silk Stockings* (1957).

Cyd Charisse as the Soviet envoy Ninotchka discovering the perks of capitalism in *Silk Stockings*.

Debbie Reynolds and Donald
O'Connor in *I Love Melvin* (1953).

Jane Powell and Ann Sothern, daughter and mother, in *Nancy Goes to Rio* (1950).

Judy Garland as Dorothy
in *The Wizard of Oz* (1939).

Judy Garland and Charles Walters in the finale of *Presenting Lily Mars* (1943).

Leslie Caron and Gene Kelly in the flower market sequence in *An American in Paris* (1951).

Matt Mattox in the barn-raising sequence in *Seven Brides for Seven Brothers* (1954).

Left to right, Michael Kidd, Gene Kelly, and Dan Dailey dancing on trash-can lids in *It's Always Fair Weather* (1955).

Ava Gardner as the tragic Julie in *Show Boat* (1951).

Leueen McGrath. The producers, Cy Feurer and Ernest Martin, eager to maintain their track record of hits (*Where's Charley? Guys and Dolls, Can-Can*), engaged in such micromanaging that Kaufman was fired, although he was still credited for his contribution. Abe Burrows was brought in for the rewrites, thus getting a credit for himself. The playbill read: "Music and Lyrics by Cole Porter, Book by George S. Kaufman, Leueen McGrath, and Abe Burrows." On Broadway, the star was Don Ameche in the Melvyn Douglas role, changed from a count to a movie producer; and as the Soviet commissar, Ninotchka, one of Greta Garbo's best characterizations, the German actress, Hildegarde Neff, whose husky delivery of the lyrics was pleasantly melodic for speech song, proving that there is an alternative to the Rex Harrison school of accented delivery made famous in *My Fair Lady*, which is closer to speech than song. Although Neff received excellent reviews, she dismissed the show in her autobiography, *The Gift Horse* (1970), charging Feuer and Martin with making "hash" out of Kaufman's "souffle." The show was neither souffle nor hash, but more of a cherries jubilee. Naturally, many of the songs—for example, "All of You," in which Ameche expressed his desire to tour the east, west, north, and the south of Neff—were centered around sex.

Interestingly, "All of You" remained intact in the MGM movie version, suggesting that what was anatomy to a fantasist is geography to a literalist. However, "Stereophonic Sound," which spoofed Hollywood's latest technological innovation, was doctored. "The customers don't like to see the groom embrace the bride / Unless her lips are scarlet and her bosom's five-feet wide" necessitated a change from "bosom's" to "mouth is"—same idea, different body part. Janis Paige's sexy "Satin and Silk," in which she did a discreet strip while celebrating the fetishistic appeal of fancy lingerie, required some substitutions but no major alterations. "You cannot expect a lady to exert that certain pull / if she's wearing cotton stockings and her panties are made of wool" stayed except that "bloomers" replaced "panties"—an odd substitution since bloomers had long been passé. And yet, references to a burlesque queen's bra and G-string were retained. There was no rationale behind the changes, proving that all dirty minds do not think alike.

On Broadway, the male lead of *Silk Stockings* was a well-known movie star with a strong baritone (Don Ameche), not a dancer. Although Fred Astaire was the male lead in the film, the best dancing was done by his costar from *The Band Wagon*, Cyd Charisse, as Ninotchka, sporting a splendid Russian accent and doing some sexy dancing in the title number when she discovers the feel of silk against her legs. But Astaire needed his spotlight. "Stereophonic Song"—originally a solo performed on Broadway by Gretchen Wyler as a swimming star (think Esther Williams) about to go dramatic in a movie version of *War and Peace*—became a song-and-dance number for Paige and

Astaire. They shared the lyrics and did some hoofing, vaudeville style, that had them sliding and dancing on a conference table; for their finish, they grabbed on to a chandelier, swinging down to the floor and landing on their knees with outstretched arms like a couple that had given their all and expected applause in return. Astaire could have been a formidable partner for Paige, a natural musical comedy performer who, during her six years at Warner Bros., rarely had a chance to sing. At least, in *Silk Stockings*, her singing voice was not dubbed, unlike Cyd Charisse's. Costarring on Broadway with John Raitt in *The Pajama Game* (1954), Paige emerged as a true musical theater artist, as she proved to moviegoers in her character's three numbers in *Silk Stockings*: "Stereophonic Sound," "Satin and Silk," and "Josephine." Thus when she had to share "Stereophonic Sound" with Astaire, Paige was not out of her element as Joan Fontaine was when she danced with him in *Damsel in Distress* (1937). Paige was Astaire's partner who took what he gave—and vice versa—so that they came off as a team.

Astaire needed a standout like "Satin and Silk." He thought he had it in "The Ritz Roll and Rock," which Porter had written especially for the film and was intended to show that Astaire was still in touch with the music of the day. Astaire, who was nearing the end of his dancing career—although he would continue as an actor, winning a Best Supporting Actor nomination for *The Towering Inferno* (1974), losing to Robert DeNiro for *The Godfather, Part II*—asked Porter to compose a number that would show that his art had not deserted him. Watching "The Ritz Roll and Rock" has the effect of a double exposure, with the younger Astaire as a shadowy presence performing "Puttin' on the Ritz" in *Blue Skies* (Paramount, 1946) while his older self is trying to convince audiences that, at fifty-seven, he is still relevant. But he was not at the top of his game.

In *Blue Skies*, Astaire was his old self in top hat and tails, cravat, bouton-niere, and white spats, twirling and dancing with his cane, as if it were his partner. In *Silk Stockings*, he is back in a tux, this time more regal with a red sash across his dress shirt. But he was royalty only to his devotees. He was still limber, but the body could not do what it did a decade earlier; and the cane is just part of the act. At one point in "Puttin' on the Ritz," he danced along with miniature reflections of his image, as if he were performing with his own emanations. But it was still Astaire in his greater and lesser forms. In *Silk Stockings*, he had to compete with male dancers who could kick higher. It was the old Astaire repackaged for a generation that may have known who he was from their parents but who found real rock 'n' roll more to their taste. Cole Porter was as deaf to rock 'n' roll as Jerry Lee Lewis was to Broadway show music. No need to lament. "The Ritz Roll and Rock" was not "Puttin' on the Ritz" nor did it detract from Astaire's genius; it was high-class funk—art without the artist able to achieve what he once did, but leaving behind a facsimile of what it was and hoping his fans would know the difference.

MGM's most successful adaptation of a Broadway musical is *Kiss Me Kate* (1953), for which Kathryn Grayson returned to her home studio for one final partnering with Howard Keel, giving her best performance as Lili Vanessi, a Broadway diva playing Katherine in a musical version of Shakespeare's *The Taming of the Shrew*, called *Kiss Me Kate*, opposite her ex-husband, Fred Graham (Howard Keel), as Petrucchio. They play members of an acting troupe performing the musical—a device taken directly from Shakespeare's comedy, which is really a play within a play, here complicated by a backstage-onstage subplot. Backstage, Fred and Lili try to rekindle their old romance that fizzles when Lili receives flowers that she assumes Fred had sent to her, but were really intended for Lois Lane (Ann Miller). Then, two emissaries from the mob arrive to collect on a gambling debt that they believe Fred has incurred.

On stage, Lili throws herself into her character, known for a fierce temper. (In the play, Gremio calls her a "wildcat.") She trounces Graham every chance she gets; the two move in and out of character—their offstage sparring now part of the onstage battle of the sexes, reaching a point that so infuriates Graham that he spanks Lili in full view of the audience, who thinks it is part of the performance. Lili threatens to leave the show after the first act, but returns for the final scene in which Katherine delivers her "I am ashamed that women are so simple" speech, which must have made feminists cringe when she concludes with "Then vail your stomachs, for it is no boot, / And place your hands below your husband's foot; / In token of which duty, if he please, / My hand is ready, may it do him ease" (*The Taming of the Shrew*, 5, 2).

Kiss Me, Kate (the stage musical had a comma) came to the screen relatively unaltered. There was an omission ("Another Op'nin', Another Show"), an interpolation ("From This Moment On," dropped from Porter's 1951 musical *Out of This World*), and a reassignment ("Too Darn Hot," sung and danced by stage hands in the original and given to Ann Miller in red tights and a black fan, tapping her way around the room). The dialogue was laundered ("louse" replaced "bastard"), and the lyrics were purged of suggestiveness. In "I Hate Men," "mother had to marry father" became "mother deigned to marry father." When Katherine warns against marrying a businessman, "the business is the business that he gives his secretary" became "his business is the business with his pretty secretary." As for traveling salesmen: "'Tis he who'll have the fun, and thee, the baby" was tweaked to read, "When he's away in Mandalay, it's thee who'll have the baby."

George Sidney preserved the original concept of a dual audience—moviegoers watching the opening of a Broadway musical called *Kiss Me Kate*. To preserve the illusion of a show in progress, Sidney incorporated long shots of the theater audience, so that there is no doubt that this is a movie about the opening night of a musical with a backstage subplot. Sidney is even able to open up the cramped backstage area in "Wunderbar," as Lili and Graham recall their days in operetta, waltzing in and out of dressing rooms, as if backstage were a performing space unto itself. Grayson and Keel were at their peak; the blonde Grayson never sounding better and never looking so much at home in a role she was destined to play; and Keel, the ultimate alpha baritone, boasting of his conquests in "Where Is the Life That Late I Led?" and going into high testosterone mode with "Were Thine That Special Face." Keel had the most virile baritone in movies; it seemed to come out of the recesses of a libido that had been classically trained like his voice, so that there was no sleaze, just art.

Kiss Me Kate was filmed in both the increasingly passe 3-D and the then-standard 1:33:1 aspect ratio for a rectangular screen that was about 1 1/3 wider than high. If you saw *Kiss Me Kate* in 3-D, you might have ducked when Grayson tossed a tankard that looked as if it were heading straight for you. Other gimmicks included kicking a bouquet at the camera, cracking a whip at it, and, at the end, Grayson in Keel's embrace coming onto the screen and into your lap.

The one disquieting note in the film is the appearance of Cole Porter as a character in the first scene. As played by Ron Randell, a fine actor but hardly a Porter look-a-like, the composer was uncharacteristically mobile. That was not the case with the historical Porter, who was left disabled from a 1937 horse-riding accident. Although Porter was in constant pain when he was composing *Kiss Me, Kate*, one would never know it from Randall's hale and hearty characterization. MGM was apparently counting on an audience that was unfamiliar with the Porter biography; or, if they were, had forgotten about the date of an accident that occurred sixteen years earlier.

It seemed natural that Grayson would end her movie career in an operetta, this time at Paramount, which had developed its own form of wide-screen projection, Vista Vision. But even that could not save *The Vagabond King* (1956). Trapped in a cheesy production, Grayson, looking much slimmer than she had in the past, shouldered on, her voice as limpid as ever. *The Vagabond King* marked the film debut of her costar, Oreste (the Maltese tenor, Oreste Kirkop), as François Villon in his only American screen appearance. It was also Grayson's last feature, after which came the national tour of *Camelot*, summer theater, and television.

Like *Kismet*, Jerome Kern and Oscar Hammerstein's *Show Boat* (1927) had been filmed twice before MGM released its version in 1951. Universal made *Show Boat* first as a silent in 1929 with "song and dialogue added" and then in 1936 as a loving reproduction of the original. Universal's *Show Boat* (1936), which is more faithful to the Kern and Hammerstein musical than MGM's, has the texture of a stage work made cinematic by director James Whale, who came from the theater but who also knew how to use the camera as if it were a participant in the story. When the *Cotton Blossom* arrives, Whale uses a tracking shot to bring the audience into the action. The *Cotton Blossom* is indeed a show boat, where the box holders, photographed at a high angle, watch the melodramas enacted on the stage. When Joe (Paul Robeson) sings "Ol' Man River," the camera slowly encircles him, stopping with a close shot of his face. Believing that the audience should see the travails that Joe is enumerating, Whale renders each back-breaking activity visually ("tote that barge, lift that bale"), so that the song—really an aria—is a dramatized litany of woe.

Another reason Universal's *Show Boat* is a theatrical, not just a cinematic, experience is that the principals—Irene Dunne (Magnolia), Allan Jones (Gaylord Ravenal), Helen Morgan (Julie), Paul Robeson (Joe), and Charles Winninger (Cap'n Andy)—had appeared in various productions, including the original with Winninger and Morgan, whose interpretation of "Can't Help Lovin' Dat Man" and "My Bill" afford some idea of the way she sang them on stage. Dunne toured with the show for seven months; Jones appeared as Ravenal in a revival at the St. Louis Municipal Opera in 1934; Robeson played Joe in the 1928 London premiere, in a sense creating the role for British audiences. He can also be heard on the original London cast recording, which has been reissued on CD. For the *Show Boat* veterans, the roles had become second nature. The 1936 version also adhered closely to Hammerstein's book, which covers three generations of the Hawks family: Cap'n Andy and his wife, Parthy; their daughter Magnolia, who marries Gaylord Ravenal; and their daughter, Kim, a flapper on the cusp of stardom as the musical ends. In between, Ravenal deserts Magnolia and Kim, reappearing at the end, white haired and chastened.

For the 1951 MGM remake, which is really an abridgement, producer Arthur Freed did not want the story line to be a family dynasty. Two generations were enough, with an emphasis on the second, in which only one character interested him who was not even a Hawks—Julie LaVerne. Magnolia and Ravenal have some lovely songs ("Make Believe," "Why Do I Love You?" "You Are Love"), but as characters they are simply an ingenue forced to face reality when her husband leaves her; and a gambler who later repents of his improvident ways and rejoins his family. With an actress like Ava Gardner as the alcoholic, biracial Julie LaVerne, who could possibly care about Magnolia and Ravenal, especially when it was inevitable that the family would be reunited?

Although Grayson was billed over Gardner, Julie ended up being the main character who alone merits our sympathy after she is forced to leave the *Cotton Blossom* because she is part black. (This was a time when one-eighth

African American blood would make one a "Negro.") Julie hits the skids, disappearing from the plot, only to return at the end, her face still beautiful but sickly, to blow a kiss to the departing *Cotton Blossom*, with Magnolia, Ravenal, and Kim on board, whose reunion Julie has brought about. With that haunting close-up of Gardner, her face shining with the joy of one ready to leave the world after having accomplished something for others that they could not have done for themselves, the movie ends. And a *movie* is what MGM's *Show Boat* is, in which the only theatricality comes from the high-stepping Marge and Gower Champion, who seemed to know what they were singing about in "Life Upon the Wicked Stage." But there is only one *Show Boat* as theater repackaged for moviegoers without loss of immediacy: James Whale's.

Gardner should have received an Oscar nomination for Best Supporting Actress. It was bad enough that MGM had done her a disservice. For Julie's two songs, "Can't Help Lovin' Dat Man" and "My Bill," her voice was dubbed by Annette Warren. However, Gardner's own, equally effective renditions can be heard as outtakes on the Turner Entertainment sound track CD. Gardner experienced the same fate earlier in Universal-International's *One Touch of Venus* (1948), a musically anemic mangling of the Kurt Weill and Ogden Nash Broadway show that was a triumph for Mary Martin in 1943. Since the studio considered Weill's score and Nash's lyrics too highbrow for filmgoers, most of it was discarded. "Speak Low," the most famous song in *One Touch of Venus*, was retained with new lyrics by Ann Ronell and lip-synched by Gardner to Eileen Wilson's vocal. It was evident that Gardner had been classified as "actress, non singing." One only wishes that Arthur Freed allowed her to sing her own numbers in *Show Boat*, which would have added greater depth to her characterization, especially when she sang "My Bill."

- 10 -

LIVES IN MUSIC

The MGM musical biopic was a blend of fact, fiction, and fancy. When facts failed or were insufficiently dramatic, fiction took over in the form of invented plots and characters. And when the facts proved elusive, sketchy, or troublesome, the writers' imagination filled in the ellipses. All that was needed was a disclaimer in the form of a prologue: "We have dramatized the spirit rather than the facts of his life" was an accurate description of *The Great Waltz* (1938), a mostly fanciful life of the "Waltz King," Johann Strauss Jr. (1825–1899), as MGM would have had him live it. The biopic—musical or nonmusical—is the stepchild of historical fiction, itself a hybrid. Like Robert Frost's bifurcating road, fact and fiction diverge but then meet at the crossroads of truth and story. As Aristotle noted in the *Poetics*, history depicts the particular; tragedy, and by extension, fiction, the universal. But when the two intermingle, the result is history romanticized, fictionalized, or embellished, sometimes at the expense of the life that inspired it but generally a grander version of what may not have been so grand. The biopic is more a story of a life than an account of it—a story with all the narrative conventions—verisimilitude, linear plotting, collapsing of time, dramatic foreshadowing, rising/falling action, and denouement—on which storytelling draws. Story and truth, fiction and fact are at odds with each other until a truce is declared, and an amalgam of the two is forged, which rarely produces an equal distribution of fact and fancy, but usually a preponderance of the latter.

All one can say about the historical accuracy of MGM's *The Great Waltz* is that there was a Johann Strauss Jr., some of whose music is heard in the film ("Tales from the Vienna Woods," "On the Beautiful Blue Danube," *Die Fledermaus*); that he took part in the revolutions of 1848, which brought Emperor Franz Josef I to the throne (although the revolutionaries were far more nationalistic than those in the film); and played his first concert at the Café Dommayer on the outskirts of Vienna in 1844. The concert, however, was never the bacchanal in triple time that erupted on the screen. Entranced by the music ("I'm in Love with Vienna") emanating from within, the locals assemble outside the cafe, some dancing in the square, and others surging through the door and taking over the dance floor. It was a brilliant sequence, enlivened by Julien Duvivier's roving camera that caught the frolicsome spirit and drew the audience into the action without leaving them dizzy from all the circular movement. Later, Duvivier achieved a similar effect with couples dancing more decorously with gowns swaying in a swirl of satin and lace, personifying the essence of the waltz: couples moving in three-quarter time, responding to music that is discreetly sensuous like an invitation in a calligraphic hand that asks for more than the pleasure of one's company.

Although the historical Strauss was married three times, he has only one wife in the film, the fictitious Poldi (Luise Rainer of the soulful eyes). None of Strauss's wives was named Poldi, nor was there an operatic diva, Carla Donner (Miliza Korjus), with whom he became infatuated and for whom he would have left Poldi. Rainer does the only real acting in the film, proving that her back-to-back Oscars in 1937 and 1938 for *The Good Earth* and *The Great Ziegfeld*, respectively, were not a fluke. She had to play two extremely difficult scenes: a wife informed that her husband is involved with another woman, and who then confronts her rival, offering to step aside so he can be with someone better able to advance his career. The writers—Samuel Hoffenstein and Walter Reisch, whose screenplay derived from an original story by Gottfried Reinhardt—must have felt that since *The Great Waltz* would appeal mainly to women, why not make it a woman's picture, suggesting the possibility of adultery but, in the end, keeping the hero monogamous to avoid the ire of the Production Code Administration and the National Legion of Decency?

In one of the finest examples of controlled grief in film, Poldi must listen as Count Hofenfried (Lionel Atwill) delicately informs her that her husband's involvement with Donner is common knowledge. The lighting is low key, the kind one would expect in film noir when some dark deed or revelation is about to occur. In fact, when the Count appears at the door of the Strauss home, he is enshrouded in darkness. It is only when he enters that his face becomes discernible. Rainer—her back stiffened as if to ward off any blows, and her face expressionless except for eyes bespeaking pain that she will not articulate—plays the scene as if it were high tragedy. She is the embodiment of self-enforced decorum as she informs the Count that he can tell her nothing that she does not already know and bids him good night. Rainer is a study in unaffected graciousness in her meeting with Donner when she agrees to give up her husband just as he and Donner are about to embark on a life of sin. Donner turns magnanimous (a switch from her earlier home-wrecker image, dictated no doubt by someone's realization that the plot was heading toward adultery) and releases her hold on Strauss, who returns repentant to the forgiving Poldi.

In an epilogue fifty years later, a visibly aged Strauss and Poldi slowly make their way into the presence of Emperor Franz Joseph I, their faces powdered into whiteness, which was MGM's idea of aging. The emperor brings them onto the balcony, where it seems that half of Vienna has assembled to serenade them with "On the Beautiful Blue Danube" sung to Oscar Hammerstein's anachronistic lyrics. Superimposed over the crowd is the image of Donner, suggesting either that she was still the love of his life or that someone at MGM felt that their new discovery needed an encore, at least as a presence. *The Great Waltz* was Korjus's only Hollywood film. The Polish soprano, who, oddly, won a Best Supporting Actress Oscar nomination, had a bright but metallic voice. If aluminum could sing, it would sound like Miliza Korjus.

The Great Waltz introduced a convention that writers have seized upon to illustrate how a song is born. Usually, the lyricists are trying to hammer out the words (*Lady Be Good, Three Little Words*). In *The Great Waltz*, it is the composer. Escaping from the revolutionaries who have blockaded the streets, Strauss hails a carriage that transports himself and Donner through the Vienna Woods. The clickety-clack of the carriage wheels, which the coachman mimics on his harmonica, and the woods themselves provide Strauss with the melody, which, in true cinematic style, bursts forth on the sound track. "Tales from the Vienna Woods," however, was not composed in a carriage with Strauss and an opera singer. But it's a magical moment in a less than magical film.

The life of Jenny Lind (1820–1887), the "Swedish Nightingale" with an extraordinary vocal range, had the makings of a major biopic with historical figures like Hans Christian Andersen, Felix Mendelssohn, Robert and Clara Schumann, and Hector Berlioz, all of whom were fans, but none of whom appeared in *A Lady's Morals* (1930), a provocative title for a movie that only provokes dismay at MGM's failure to do justice to Lind's extraordinary life. In place of a smitten Andersen, Lind is given a fictitious lover, whose blindness poses no obstacle to a happy ending. The only historical figure who survived was P. T. Barnum (Wallace Beery), who arranged Lind's spectacular American tour. The film's chief asset was its star, Metropolitan Opera soprano Grace Moore, who appeared to greater advantage in her Columbia films, especially *One Night of Love* (1934) and *The King Steps Out* (1936). Arthur Freed had just arrived at MGM when *A Lady's Morals* went into production. Interestingly, Moore sang "Oh Why," which Freed had written with Harry Wood, an indication that Freed was on his way to becoming one of Louis B. Mayer's favorites. Audiences, however, paid scant attention to "Oh Why"; they came to hear Moore sing opera. She did not disappoint them with her ethereal "Casta Diva" from Bellini's *Norma*, a role Moore never sang on stage, but which Lind did in Berlin in 1874.

The Great Ziegfeld (1936) was a more conventional, if overlong, biopic. The three-hour running time resulted in an imbalance of plot and spectacle, with the early part of the film given over to biographical details that delayed the musical sequences until Florenz Ziegfeld (1867–1932), played by William Powell, discovers Anna Held (Luise Rainer) on the London stage, brings her to New York where she becomes a sensation, and makes her his common-law wife, which the film ignores. Like other such films, The Great Ziegfeld is an amalgam of the historical and the invented. Among the former are Anna Held and Billie Burke (Myrna Loy), Ziegfeld's second wife; the well-known theatrical producers A. L. Erlanger and Charles Frohman in minor roles; and Follies performers Ray Bolger, Will Rogers, and Fanny Brice, who, sadly, sings only part of "My Man," the song she made famous. But what a joy to hear Brice sing "Yiddle on Your Fiddle" with an authentic Yiddish accent. To provide Ziegfeld with a foil, the writers created the character of Jack Billings (Frank Morgan), a rival impressario, whom Ziegfeld constantly outwitted but always in a genial way, so that they continued to be friendly enemies and ended as friends, each of whom could never admit that he lost everything in the 1929 stock market crash.

The Great Ziegfeld is more factual at the beginning than at the end. It starts with Ziegfeld informing his father—founder of the Chicago Musical College, formerly the Chicago Academy of Music—that he will not succeed him because he is drawn to popular entertainment. The historical Ziegfeld had a flair for gimmicks, as the film makes clear. When promoting strongman Eugen Sandow (Nat Pendleton) at the Chicago World's Fair, Ziegfeld chose not only to exhibit his discovery but also to allow women to feel his muscles. To publicize his next star, Anna Held, Ziegfeld attributed her creamy skin to milk baths, making certain that gallons of milk were delivered daily to her apartment. Money mattered little to Ziegfeld, who had the self-confidence of a child of fortune, knowing that funding for his shows would somehow arrive, as it invariably did.

Ziegfeld's extramarital affairs were reduced to one, involving a showgirl of modest talent (Virginia Bruce) whom he tried to make into a star. Bruce's character, Audrey Dane, is a stand-in for Lillian Lorraine, a mediocre performer with whom Ziegfeld became infatuated. It was a lifelong obsession that precipitated his breakup with Held and would have destroyed his marriage to Billie Burke had she been unable to overlook his indiscretions.

The film inverts the relationship between Ziegfeld and Dane/Lorraine, making Dane the aggressor and Ziegfeld the unwitting victim of her recklessness. Powell's Ziegfeld is so professional, and Bruce's Audrey Dane is so indiscreet, that it is only a matter of time before Dane dragoons Ziegfeld into an embrace. In the time-honored convention of the false assumption, Held sees them and, suspecting the worst, leaves Ziegfeld. Powell's Ziegfeld was too gentlemanly for a fling. To him, sex was fantasy. He had an eye for feminine beauty, as he explained when he announced his intention of "glorifying the American girl." Glorify he did, and nothing more—at least not in the film.

When it's extravaganza time, the Ziegfeld girls glide onto the screen in silvery costumes and headdresses bursting with plumage, as if they were exotic birds from a baroque aviary. The centerpiece is "A Pretty Girl Is Like a Melody" on a revolving three-tiered wedding cake, with Virginia Bruce at the top in a rhinestone-studded gown and a helmet-like headpiece. It's kitsch meets class, the latter provided by the music of Gershwin, Liszt, Johann Strauss Jr., and Dvorak; and fragments of "Un bel di" from *Madame Butterfly* and "Vesti la giubba" from *Paglicacci*.

Pseudo history returns at the end, when Ziegfeld swears that he will have four shows on Broadway in the same season, which was pretty accurate: *Rio Rita* (February 2, 1927–April 7, 1928), *Show Boat* (December 27, 1927–May 4, 1929), *Whoopee!* (December 4, 1928–November 23, 1929), and *The Three Musketeers* (March 13, 1928–December 15, 1928). Ziegfeld's death, however, was another matter. It was not as beatific as portrayed in the film, where the producer, frail and ailing in his New York apartment, dreams as his life ebbs away of another *Follies* with more steps from which the Ziegfeld girls can descend, peacock-like in synthetic splendor.

Florenz Ziegfeld Jr. died in 1932, not in New York, but in Hollywood. "No record states with certainty an official cause of death." One would like to believe that his last thoughts were of the eternal feminine, whose incarnation he had fostered in his own way.

To cinephiles, the highlight of the film is Held's phone call to Ziegfeld after reading of his marriage to Billie Burke: "Hello, Flo. Yes Yes, Anna." Her voice has the frothy sound of champagne drunk too quickly, her doleful face belying her feigned joy. It was a tour de force for Reiner, offering congratulations with tear-coated eyes, as she tries to convince him—and perhaps herself—that she is still in great demand. But just as Ziegfeld never admitted defeat, neither did Held. She toured in vaudeville, dying in 1918 at forty-five. Held's call to Ziegfeld is historically questionable. If she ever called him, it would have been after April 11, 1914, when he married Billie Burke. By then, Held was on the road. When World War I broke out that August, she returned to France to entertain the troops, often at the front lines. History has cunning corridors, and Anna Held is stranded in one of them, awaiting a film of her own. Her life was not as historically significant as Ziegfeld's, but it was engrossing in its own way.

Jerome Kern (1885–1945) was not nearly as colorful as Ziegfeld, but he made a greater contribution to the Hollywood musical, which inspired the revue, *Jerome Kern Goes to Hollywood*, which ran briefly in New York in 1986.

The critics were unimpressed, but Liz Robertson, Elaine Delmar, and the legendary Elizabeth Welch, then in her early eighties, made a convincing case for Kern as a major Hollywood composer, who enriched the American Songbook with such classics as "The Way You Look Tonight" and "A Fine Romance" (*Swing Time*, 1936); "The Last Time I Saw Paris" (*Lady Be Good*, 1941); "Dearly Beloved" and "I'm Old Fashioned" (*You Were Never Lovelier*, 1942); and "Long Ago and Far Away" (*Cover Girl*, 1944).

Arthur Freed had met Kern in 1917, a banner year for the composer who saw five of his musicals open on Broadway in a single season: *Have a Heart* (January, 76 performances), *Love o' Mike* (January, 233 performances), *Oh, Boy!* (February, 463 performances), *Leave It to Jane* (August, 167 performances); and the revue, *Miss 1917* (November, 72 performances). As a former songwriter and great admirer of Kern, Freed envisioned a tribute to the composer in the form of a biopic with strands of fact woven into a predominately musical tapestry. In 1945 Kern gave MGM permission for a biopic which, at his request, was to be called *Till the Clouds Roll By*, the title of one of his favorite songs from *Oh, Boy!* which he wrote with P. G. Wodehouse. The film had already been shot when Kern suffered a cerebral hemorrhage in November 1945, just as he was about to begin work on *Annie Get Your Gun*, which would have marked his return to Broadway. The task then fell to Irving Berlin, who composed one of his best scores, which included the show business anthem, "There's No Business Like Show Business." Copyright clearances held up the release of *Till the Clouds Roll By* until summer 1946, although it did not reach most theaters until early 1947.

Till the Clouds Roll By was a typical biopic that resorted to invention when the facts resisted dramatization. According to the credits, the Technicolor film was "based on the life and music of Jerome Kern." "Based" is the key word. Kern's life would have made dull copy if the writers, Myles Connolly and Jean Holloway, limited themselves to the facts. That same year, Warner Bros. took a similar approach to Cole Porter, resulting in the mainly fictionalized *Night and Day* (1946), "based on the career of Cole Porter." "Career" meant selectivity, adhering to a few facts (Porter's college years, his horseback-riding accident); embellishing others (his enlisting in the French army during World War I, when he was really an expatriate in Paris moving in circles that did not exist in his hometown, Peru, Indiana); ignoring the unfilmable (his homosexuality); and presenting numbers from his shows out of chronology, staged as audiences might have imagined them, not as they had been originally performed. But nothing mattered except that Cary Grant (Porter) and Alexis Smith (his wife, Linda) embraced at the fade-out, although Porter was gay and Linda knew it. However, few moviegoers then did. They may have known who Cole Porter was, but they were far more knowledgeable about Grant and Smith from the fan magazines.

They also knew the name of Jerome Kern, whose life was the opposite of Porter's, which was crammed with incident. Kern's, if faithfully presented, might have appealed to theater historians, but not to the moviegoing public. He had no private life to speak of; he was monogamous, and his only vice was betting on horses. In short, Jerome Kern's life would not a movie make. But jazz it up with a subplot and musical numbers performed by June Allyson, Lena Horne, Frank Sinatra, Marge and Gower Champion, Virginia O'Brien, and Dinah Shore and you have a movie—or rather a musical retrospective interleaved with half-filled pages from the Kern biography.

Knowing that Kern (Robert Walker) needed an arranger, the writers created the fictitious James I. Hessler (Van Heflin), a stand-in for Frank Saddler, Kern's favorite orchestrator. Hessler, a widower, has a daughter, Sally (Lucille Bremer), the name of one of Kern's greatest hits (*Sally*, 1920), in which the title character, a dishwasher, replaces a dancer one night and graduates to the *Ziegfeld Follies*. Sally Hessler also aspires to stardom. She is inexplicably cast in a show starring Marilyn Miller (Judy Garland) and given the number "Who?" The show was *Sunny* (1925), and the song was never intended for anyone but Miller, then queen of the Broadway musical. When the producers decide that "Who?" and Sally Hessler are not meant for each other, the number is given to Miller/Garland, who has to explain to the disconsolate Sally that it's not personal, just show business.

In typical biopic fashion, the writers created a scene that explained Garland's taking over "Who?" and singing it as only she could. Although Richard Whorf is credited as the director of *Till the Clouds Roll By*, Judy's then husband, Vincente Minnelli, staged "Who?" as well as her other number, "Look for the Silver Lining" from *Sally*, in which Miller gave what was arguably her best performance. *Sally* preceded *Sunny* by five years—not that chronology mattered. At least this time, there was an attempt at accuracy. Judy sang the ballad while washing dishes, which is how it was staged in the original.

Till the Clouds Roll By is a flashback beginning with the opening night of *Show Boat* (1927), or rather with highlights from the musical including Tony Martin and Kathryn Grayson as Gaylord Ravenal and Magnolia in the duet, "Make Believe"; Virginia O'Brien in a deadpan version of "Life Upon the Wicked Stage"; Lena Horne in an aching rendition of "Can't Help Lovin' Dat Man," which in a less racist age would have made her a natural for the role of Julie when MGM filmed the third version of *Show Boat* (1951); and Caleb Peterson in an emotionally controlled but deeply felt "Ol' Man River." When uncertain about a finale, create a musical montage culminating with Frank

Sinatra in a white tux singing "Ol' Man River" earnestly but without the back-story that Peterson brought to it. One might question Sinatra's white outfit, which seemed inappropriate for a song originally written for a black stevedore and generally sung by an African American, as it had been earlier in the film. But then, when Horne sang "Can't Help Lovin' Dat Man," she wore a blue-and-white gown; in the finale, she also wore white for "Why Was I Born?" At least audiences in the North saw Lena Horne. For the "Colored Upstairs" theaters in the South, her numbers were cut.

Till the Clouds Roll By was hugely profitable; it cost $3.316 million and brought in twice that much.

Next, MGM paid tribute to Richard Rodgers (1902–1979) and Lorenz (Larry) Hart (1895–1943) in *Words and Music* (1948), best remembered for the "Slaughter on Tenth Avenue" ballet from *On Your Toes*, danced with sleek and ultimately tragic sensuousness by Gene Kelly and Vera-Ellen. "Based on the lives and music of Richard Rodgers and Lorenz Hart," the film derived from a story by Guy Bolton and Jane Holloway, the coscreenwriter of *Till the Clouds Roll By*, adapted by Rodgers's brother-in-law, Ben Feiner Jr., portrayed in the film by Richard Quine. Fred F. Finklehoffe, who had mastered the MGM musical rubric, created the screenplay. As the screenwriter of *Strike Up the Band* (1940), *For Me and My Gal* (1942), *Girl Crazy* (1943), *Best Foot Forward* (1943), and especially *Meet Me in St. Louis* (1944), Finklehoffe knew that a script for an MGM musical had to be malleable enough for the insertion of musical material to keep the plot moving; in short, a segmented narrative interspersed with musical sequences that should seem as natural as dialogue—a worthy goal but not always achievable.

A musical biopic requires a slightly different structuring. The placement of the numbers has to make some kind of narrative sense. At their first meeting, Rodgers (Tom Drake) must convince Hart (Mickey Rooney) of his compos-ing skills. Rodgers sits down at the piano and plays "Mountain Greenery" and "Manhattan," while a cigar-chomping Hart flips through the pages of a maga-zine and then rushes off to pick up some books (Hart was an avid reader), giv-ing no indication that he had even heard the melodies until their next meet-ing when he has the lyrics ready. With an erratic genius like Hart, anything is possible. And with an antic Rooney in the role, Hart's behavior is totally credible. Interestingly, Rodgers always wrote the music before Hart supplied the lyrics. It was the opposite when Rodgers collaborated with Oscar Ham-merstein II from 1943 to 1959.

That Rodgers met Hart in 1919 and "Mountain Greenery" and "Manhattan" were first heard in *The Garrick Gaieties* (1925), their first success, did not mat-ter; what did was that Hart was so taken with the music that a partnership de-veloped and a brand name, Rodgers & Hart, was forged. Something Rodgers played must have struck Hart's fancy that afternoon, so why not music that audiences might recognize?

Words and Music is more accurate than most biopics, perhaps because of Feiner's input. As a family member, Feiner would not have tolerated egregious gaffes, although he knew that a certain amount of embroidery was inevitable. The first meeting of Rodgers and Hart, as depicted in the film, is, for the most part, factual. There was such a meeting in 1919 at the Harts' home on West 119th Street in Harlem, arranged by Philip Leavitt, who had been a classmate of Mortimer Rodgers, Richard's older brother, at Columbia University, which Richard entered in 1919. When Rodgers saw Hart for the first time, he looked unkept and "gnomelike." Hart was under five feet and suffered from acute dwarfism; Rooney was a little taller, 5'2", and could at least convey Hart's feeling of inferiority about his height. Unfortunately, neither Rooney nor Drake was ideally cast, Drake more so than Rooney. Richard Rodgers was not "the boy next door" type like Drake, who looked too ingenuous to be convincing.

Rodgers may have met Hart for the first time at his Harlem home, but he had seen him earlier in performance when his brother Mortimer brought him to a Columbia University varsity show, *On Your Way*, at the Hotel Astor, in which Hart performed comic routines and impersonated Mary Pickford and Oscar Hammerstein II, who was in the same Columbia fraternity as Mortimer. The teenage Rodgers was already in love with the musical stage, thanks to his parents who took him regularly to Broadway shows. That night in the Hotel Astor ballroom, Rodgers had no idea that he would be working with two of the greatest lyricists in the American musical theater, each of whom was seven years his senior.

Although Mortimer Rodgers graduated and went on to Columbia Medical School, Richard spent only two years at the university, as did Hart. While they were on campus, Rodgers and Hart wrote for the varsity shows; so did Hammerstein, who left Columbia Law School after a year to work as assistant stage manager for his uncle Arthur's shows. The connection between Rodgers, Hart, and Hammerstein—Columbia University, varsity shows, a composer in need of a lyricist and vice versa, and a love of the Broadway musical—suggests an astral alignment that totally revolutionized an art form. However, if chance is providence in disguise, design is providence in action. There is no need for further explanations. As Hammerstein expressed it in "Some Enchanted Evening," one of the great songs from *South Pacific*: "Who can explain it, who can tell you why? / Fools give you reasons, wise men never try."

Perhaps Rodgers would have discovered Hart; or Hart, Rodgers, without Leavitt as intermediary. But one doubts if it would have been in 1919 when Rodgers was a Columbia freshman. Leavitt sensed that Rodgers needed a lyricist in love with words and their rhythmic potential (two of Hart's favorite books were a thesaurus and the complete plays of Shakespeare); and that Hart needed a composer who could set his lyrics to music. In the film, the matchmaker is Herbert Fields (Marshall Thompson), who wrote the books for several early Rodgers and Hart shows: *Dearest Enemy* (1925), *The Girl Friend* (1926), *Peggy-Ann* (1926), and *A Connecticut Yankee* (1927). Since Fields, a Columbia alumnus, played a major role in the team's lives, it made more sense for Fields to bring the two together than Leavitt—a minor alteration of fact that shouldn't even bother purists, particularly since the three had Columbia University in common.

But so did Rodgers and Hammerstein, who does not appear as a character in *Words and Music*, which, literally, is about Rodgers and Hart, ending with Hart's death, depicted melodramatically, on the opening night of the 1943 revival of *A Connecticut Yankee*. On March 31 of that year, Broadway history was made when Rodgers and Hammerstein's first collaboration, *Oklahoma!* opened at New York's St. James Theatre. The groundbreaking musical was originally to have been a Rodgers and Hart creation—or so the press claimed in July 1942. Even before the announcement, Rodgers told director George Abbott that he could no longer work with Hart, whose alcoholism, frequent disappearances, and disinterest in a musical about farmers and ranchers forced him to seek out Hammerstein, who furnished him with lyrics of eloquent simplicity and smoothly balanced phrases ("Out of my dreams and into my heart"), striking images ("There's a bright golden haze on the meadow"), and unusual comparisons ("the corn is as high as an elephant's eye"). Hammerstein also provided him with a book that took young love into a world as yet unexplored on the musical stage: the pure of heart (Curly and Laurey) threatened by a loner (Jud), yearning to belong to the community but too emotionally stunted to fit in.

In 1943, in addition to Rodgers and Hammerstein's *Oklahoma!* there was also a Rodgers and Hart show on Broadway. On November 17, a revival of the 1927 musical, *A Connecticut Yankee*, opened at the Martin Beck (now the Al Hirschfeld) Theatre. Hart had written a few new songs for the revival, the best of which was the mordantly wicked "To Keep My Love Alive," in which Morgan le Fay (Vivienne Segal) described the various ways she rid herself of troublesome suitors. The revival had a decent run (135 performances, as opposed to the original's 421). Nineteen forty-three was not a year for whimsy or homicide sweetly sung.

One would assume from *Words and Music* that Hart either had an absentee or deceased father, since he is seen throughout with his mother, to whom he was extremely devoted. Hart's father, Max, who died in 1928, was very much alive when his son met Rodgers. Max Hart was a shady character with Tammany Hall connections, who once described himself as a "commission merchant," meaning that he made money any way he could. In 1948, Max's life would have merited a movie of its own, but not at MGM. Warner's, which specialized in the dark side of urban life, would have been the right studio with Edward G. Robinson or Paul Muni as Max Hart.

But the only one with a dark side in *Words and Music* is Larry Hart. Even then, the dark was airbrushed. Hart was still portrayed as a drinker, but one would have to infer from his hospitalization at the end of the film that he was a self-destructive alcoholic. What we see is a gifted lyricist unable to find a woman who would love him.

Rodgers was more fortunate; he married Dorothy Feiner in 1930 and had two daughters, Mary, who became a composer (*Once Upon a Mattress*), and Linda, both of whom briefly appear as children in the film. There were other women in Rodgers's life before his marriage and some afterward. Rodgers was attracted to women in show business, referring to them as his "little friends," as Shirley Jones noted in the PBS Documentary, *The Sweetest Sounds* (November 4, 2001). Rodgers's first crush was Ina Claire, the doyenne of sophisticated comedy. Years later when Rodgers admitted his infatuation to her, Claire called his confession "the most crushing sentence an actress can hear." Another flame was the actress Helen Ford, with whom he spent a great deal of time when her husband was away staging Shakespeare festivals. One of the characters in *Words and Music* is the fictitious Joyce Harmon (Ann Sothern), who may have been a composite of Rodgers's amours but certainly embodied the grace and charm that attracted him to Ina Claire. At least Sothern had a chance to do a peculiarly upbeat version of "Where's That Rainbow?" in a yellow dress and rainbow-colored scarf before telling Rodgers that their ten-year age difference precluded the possibility of marriage. With Tom Drake looking like a fraternity pledge, one could understand her reasoning.

Since Larry Hart was gay, there could be no reference to his ogling chorus boys, particularly with Mickey Rooney in the role. Instead, Hart falls in love with Peggy (Betty Garrett), who is taller than he and can only accept him as a friend. Hart, perhaps the most tortured songwriter in the history of the American musical theater, actually thought he could marry. He was enamored of Vivienne Segal, who originated the role of Vera in *Pal Joey* (1940) and for whom he wrote "To Keep My Love Alive," the gleeful account of a serial murderess, for the revival of *A Connecticut Yankee*. Since Segal knew Hart was gay, he felt comfortable about coming to her apartment with his procurer. Hart saw in Segal the same qualities that Rodgers found in Dorothy. Both were women of breeding, attractive and sophisticated, and able to overlook peccadillos. If Rodgers could have Dorothy, why should he not have Vivienne? What Hart did not understand is that Rodgers's peccadillos involved women; his did not.

At the end of *Words and Music*, Hart, dying from pneumonia, drags himself over to the Martin Beck to look in at the opening night of *A Connecticut Yankee*, after which he expires in the rain in front of the shoe store where he purchased the lifts that would have made him Peggy's equal in height. It was a great ending with a kernel of truth. Hart made it to the Martin Beck for the opening, standing in the rear as was his custom. When Vivienne Segal began singing "To Keep My Love Alive," he started mumbling away and had to be removed. Hart died five days later. His death in the movie is far more dramatic, which is characteristic of biopics: What might have happened is better theater than what did.

Words and Music was a disguised revue book with biographical filler. The memorable moments have nothing to do with Rodgers and Hart, but rather with Mickey teaming up with Judy for the last time in "I Wish I Were in Love Again"; Judy belting out "Johnny One Note" with the clarion force that only Ethel Merman could surpass; Mel Tormé doing a sleepy version of "Blue Moon"; Lena Horne, in white again with lavender applique, singing "Where or When?" as if she were in a posh—and unrestricted—supper club and delivering an unapologetically sassy "The Lady Is a Tramp," proudly proclaiming her love of the bohemian life.

But the highlight of *Words and Music* is the "Slaughter on Tenth Avenue" ballet from *On Your Toes* (1936), choreographed by Gene Kelly. On an urban street beneath an elevated train a man in a black cap, purple T-shirt, and black pants (Kelly) encounters a lady of easy virtue (Vera-Ellen) in a white sweater with red stripes and a red skirt slit up the side. Their attraction is immediate and mutual. It is love at first kick. They encircle each other—she, throwing up a leg as if it were an erotic reflex response, suggesting that her legs were meant for more than walking mean streets; and he, responding with virile grace that turns sensuous as he succumbs to the magic of her movements, classically and sinuously executed. They pair up and enter a cellar cafe, strutting in like regulars. The lady's boyfriend spots them; fueled by jealousy he shoots her first, and then him. In the Broadway production of *On Your Toes*, the man (Ray Bolger) kills the boyfriend. But Kelly made the finale into a true love death, with the wounded lover carrying his beloved up the stairs, only to collapse as they lie side by side. "Slaughter on Tenth Avenue"—along with *The Red Shoes* ballet, Kelly's unsurpassed recreation of the title song in *Singin' in the Rain*, and the climax of *An American in Paris*—ranks among the greatest examples of dance in the American movie musical.

Like *Till the Clouds Roll By*, *Words and Music* ends with a memorial benefit at which Perry Como sings "With a Song in My Heart," as Rodgers recalls moments from the shows he wrote with Hart. It was an exquisite ending to a movie that promised much and delivered enough to merit the gratitude of audiences who might never have experienced the team's unique blending of words and music.

Since *Words and Music* was an expensive production, costing $3.048 million, it only registered a slight profit, $4.553 million.

Although Arthur Freed was drawn to stories about songwriters (*Lady Be Good, Till the Clouds Roll By, Words and Music*), he passed on the Bert Kalmar–Harry Ruby biopic, *Three Little Words* (1950), either because he was occupied with *Annie Get Your Gun* and *Pagan Love Song* (both 1950) and preparing for *An American in Paris, Show Boat*, and *Royal Wedding* (all 1951); or, more likely, because the screenplay reminded him of a badly glazed urn: pour in a water-logged story and it trickles out. The soggy script was the problem. Screenwriter George Wells treated Kalmar and Ruby as if they were a vaudeville act, playing their historical selves in a few skits (Kalmar, a frustrated magician; Ruby, a would-be ballplayer) and their mythologized selves for the rest of the film (composer and lyricist caught up in the spin cycle of movie time in which chronology is ignored), turning out songs performed mostly out of context. The director, Richard Whorf, should have exerted greater control over the material. Whorf was not new to the genre; a few years earlier, he directed *Till the Clouds Roll By*, which had its flaws but not as many as *Three Little Words*. The blame cannot be placed entirely on the producer, either. Jack Cummings may never have made a biopic but he had produced enough MGM musicals (*Born to Dance, Ship Ahoy, Bathing Beauty, Neptune's Daughter*) to know that a musical's rhythm is imposed externally, much like the way an editor cuts a film to create a discernible rhythm with some scenes running longer than others, some looking brighter than others, some with close-ups for emphasis, and others with long shots for distance. Audiences did not go to musicals for their plots; they expected one, but it had to be able to stop at any point for a musical number and then resume. It seemed simple: Spin a little plot, stop for a song/duet/ensemble/dance, and follow the spin/stop pattern to the end.

Wells did not understand how musical yarn is spun. He was hardly a novice, except when it came to the biopic, for which he had little affinity, as did Cummings. Wells was more successful in *Take Me Out to the Ball Game* (1949), which reflected a more traditional integration of story line and music. But he really excelled at romantic comedy, winning a best story and screenplay Oscar for *Designing Woman* (1957). *Three Little Words* needed someone who understood the evolution of American popular entertainment from 1914 to 1941 and could bring it to cinematic life by tracing the journey of two songwriters from vaudeville to Tin Pan Alley, and then from Broadway to Hollywood. Wells was not that screenwriter, nor were Whorf and Cummings the ideal director-producer combination. The Technicolor production was pure soundstage and looked it. Most of the time the actors wore costumes that were more contemporary than vintage, the exception being Debbie Reynolds, who looked as if she stepped out of the Jazz Age.

MGM justified its elastic approach to history in the credits: "Based on the lives and songs of Bert Kalmar and Harry Ruby." The prologue was more specific; *Three Little Words* was not so much "based" on their lives as about "some of their songs and their adventures." In short, mythicohistory—starting with some hard facts, after which the story line alternates with musical sequences until the plot—or what's left of it—resumes and continues to the end.

The bare bones of the story are laid out at the beginning. Kalmar (Astaire) is working in vaudeville with Jessie Brown (Vera-Ellen)—the two first seen in matching tuxes and walking sticks tapping away to "Where Did You Get That Girl?" Kalmar and Brown eventually marry, with Brown becoming the conventional good wife who gives up her career for a husband with no qualms about accepting her sacrifice. The Kalmars had two children and would later divorce, but there is no place for domesticity and a breakup in *Three Little Words*. Everything is business—show business—with Jessie embroidering while her husband writes hit after hit. What matters is the collaboration between Kalmar and Ruby, and the rupture in their friendship which their wives repair by uniting them in the finale to celebrate the completion of the title song, supposedly ten years in the making. Perhaps some in the audience knew that "Three Little Words" was composed in 1930 and that Kalmar died in 1947, three years before the film was released. But death has no dominion as far as the film is concerned; if the songs are heard, the songwriter lives through them. *Till the Clouds Roll By* at least implied at the end that Jerome Kern was no longer living, but—to use the cliché—his music lingers on. *Words and Music* showed Larry Hart collapsing in the rain. *Three Little Words* ends with Kalmar finally knocking off the lyrics to the title song, not unlike Ann Sothern and Robert Young in *Lady Be Good*, who, once they found their quadrisyllabic title, had no problem coming up with the words and music, which is the way Arthur Freed and Nacio Herb Brown worked.

Three Little Words is a weave of fact and fancy, more the latter than the former. Although Ruby—who outlived Kalmar by twenty-seven years, dying at seventy-nine in 1974—is listed as technical advisor, the facts are so skewed, and in some cases, so blatantly ignored, that Astaire and Skelton seem more like simulations of Kalmar and Ruby than their embodiments. In myth, truth is either absent, embellished, or transmuted. In *Three Little Words*, it is all three.

Since Gloria DeHaven was an MGM contract player as well as the daughter of a distinguished show business couple, someone had the idea that she should play her mother, the actress and dancer, Flora Parker DeHaven, known professionally as Mrs. Carter DeHaven. In the film, Mrs. Carter DeHaven agrees to introduce "Who's Sorry Now?" (1923), which Gloria sings with the right amount of emotional restraint and then disappears from the plot. "Who's Sorry Now?" was actually introduced by bandleader and composer Isham Jones. Ruby's marriage to Irish-born Eileen Percy is historically accurate. Percy, however, was a minor silent star, although one would never know it from the film, in which she is a screen queen played by the ravishing Arlene Dahl. To bring Percy into the script and Ruby's life, Wells has her up for a part that goes to Ruby's then girlfriend. Years later, when Percy runs into Ruby at the Broadway premiere of *Animal Crackers*, the Marx Brothers musical for which he and Kalmar provided the score, she reminds him of the incident. Ruby still cannot place her, much less know who she is, until Kalmar points to a theater marquee across the street that reads, "Eileen Percy in *The Flirt*." True, Percy starred in *The Flirt*, released on December 24, 1922; *Animal Crackers* opened on October 23, 1928. Petty cavils, perhaps, but also a complete disregard for Kalmar and Ruby's role in show business history.

Wells makes virtually nothing of the fact that Kalmar and Ruby composed the scores for such Broadway musicals as *Helen of Troy, New York* (1923), *No Other Girl* (1924), *The Five O'Clock Girl* (1927), *Top Speed* (1929), and *High Kickers* (1941–1942); or that they were the librettists of *She's My Baby* (1928) with music and lyrics by Rodgers and Hart; *Top Speed*, and *High Kickers*, to which George Jessel also contributed. Wells has Astaire and Skelton do a chorus of "Hooray for Captain Spaulding," assuming that some might know that Groucho Marx sang it in *Animal Crackers*. Whether the chaotic meeting between Kalmar and Ruby depicted in the film ever took place or whether it is Wells's invention is impossible to determine, but it seems more of a way of giving Red Skelton a chance to do what he does best: klutzy slapstick. Ruby is corraled into assisting Kalmar, who is performing his magic act under the name of Kendal the Great. With Skelton as the consummate bumbler, the rabbits that were supposed to come out of the hat scamper onto the stage, sabotaging the act but eventually leading to a partnership once Kalmar and Ruby discover the symbiosis of songwriting.

Except for two musical sequences, the production numbers in *Three Little Words* are neither as lavish nor as impressive as those in *Till the Clouds Roll By* and *Words and Music*, perhaps because Arthur Freed, who had greater control over budget, was not in charge. Compare Cummings's production of *Three Little Words* with Freed's *Annie Get Your Gun*, both of which came out about the same time in 1950—*Annie* in June, *Three Little Words* in July—and you can see the difference between a mega hit and a modest one. The Wild West Show in *Annie* was a rousing spectacle that must have been expensive to stage, but worth every cent. *Annie* also had several highlights: "There's No Business Like

Show Business," "I Got the Sun in the Morning," and "Anything You Can Do I Can Do Better," and the "Show Business" reprise at the end. Both films did astonishingly well at the box office, proving that musicals still mattered to the public—at least for the time being. *Three Little Words* cost $1.470 million and brought in three times that amount. *Annie*, a more expensive production, was budgeted at $3.734 million and made $7.756 million.

The highlights of *Three Little Words* are, first, the so-called inspiration for "I Wanna Be Loved by You" (1928). Kalmar and Ruby are walking down the street working on the song when they see a piano being delivered. Ignoring the movers, Ruby starts playing, and Kalmar starts singing, when a young flapper (Debbie Reynolds) ambles over, adding "boop-boop-a-doop" after each stanza. The flapper is Helen Kane, soon to be known as the "boop-boop-a-doop girl," who, in record time, is transported from a New York street to Hammerstein's Theatre on Broadway and 53rd Street as the star of *Good Boy* (1928) singing the song that made her famous. In the film, Reynolds, whose voice was unmistakably dubbed by Kane, sings it to Carleton Carpenter, a clueless Joe College type, as she runs her fingers up his shirt, stopping short of unbuttoning it.

The incident on the street with the piano was a clever way of introducing Kane into the plot, but it never happened that way. Helen Kane was not an overnight sensation, nor was she a Kalmar and Ruby discovery. She started out in vaudeville in 1920 and was a headliner by the time she appeared in *Good Boy*.

The second highlight of *Three Little Words*, the only number in the tradition of the classic MGM musical, also has "love" in the title. Arlene Dahl as Eileen Percy—or, rather, Arlene Dahl sans character—in a silver gown with a pink-trimmed bodice, brandishing a feathery pink fan as if it were an instrument of enticement, descends a staircase thronged by adoring men in tuxedos as she sings "I Love You So Much" (1928). Eileen Percy neither sang the song nor appeared in the film in which it was introduced—the Bert Wheeler and Robert Woolsey farce, *The Cuckoos* (1930), for which Guy Bolton, Kalmar, and Ruby shared writing credit. It was sung by Dorothy Lee, who was no Arlene Dahl. Forget the fabrication and just watch Dahl glide among the men, holding the fan in front and in back of her and bringing the only touch of class to a movie that was generally lacking in it.

Arlene Dahl is the case of a performer with a flair for musicals that MGM never exploited. "In my heart I always wanted nothing else but to be a musical comedy star," she told an interviewer. Janis Paige felt similarly, but Warner Bros. thought otherwise and cast her in comedies and melodramas. MGM did the same to Dahl, who was an excellent foil for Red Skelton in *A Southern Yankee* (1948) and *Watch the Birdie* (1950), in which she was a true costar, not a line feeder to a great clown. It was not until 1972 that Dahl achieved her dream when she replaced Anne Baxter (who had replaced Lauren Bacall) on Broadway in *Applause!*

Sigmund Romberg (1887–1951) was a late addition to the MGM pantheon, which by 1954 was running out of musical icons. In 1949 Eliott Arnold's Romberg biography, *Deep in My Heart*, was published, the title deriving from a similarly entitled song from the composer's operetta, *The Student Prince*. Arnold's biography sometimes reads like a novel with dialogue that was either invented or reworked from his interviews with Romberg. And if they were Romberg's direct quotes, they were recollections of a man in his early sixties that could hardly have been verbatim. The 1954 movie version with the same title, dedicated "To All Those Who Loved the Music of Sigmund Romberg," is also flawed, but no more than most biopics and vastly superior to Warner Bros.' *Night and Day* (1946), which still infuriates Cole Porter fans. The ideal producer of *Deep in My Heart* would have been Joe Pastnerak, who, like Romberg, was Hungarian born and had a distinct feeling for operetta as he revealed in *The Merry Widow* (1952) and *The Student Prince* (1954), and musicals built around the stock themes of operetta (deception, disguise, misunderstanding, misjudgment, and reconciliation) such as *Anchors Aweigh*, *A Date with Judy*, *The Kissing Bandit*, and *Nancy Goes to Rio*. Perhaps because Pasternack was occupied at the time with *The Student Prince* and *Athena*, Roger Edens became the producer. *Deep in My Heart*, filmed in Eastman Color, was Edens's first producing credit, although he had been associate producer of several Arthur Freed musicals, sometimes credited (*Good News*, *The Harvey Girls*, *The Barkleys of Broadway*, *The Band Wagon*), but more often not. Although he was billed as associate producer of other films (MGM's *The Unsinkable Molly Brown* and *Billy Rose's Jumbo*, and Twentieth Century–Fox's *Hello, Dolly!*), he only received sole credit for one other production, *Funny Face* (Paramount, 1957), his masterpiece. Set against the New York–Paris fashion world, *Funny Face* had a starry cast headed by Fred Astaire and Audrey Hepburn, music by George Gershwin, costumes by Edith Head, and a rare screen appearance by the soignée Kay Thompson (who also did the vocal arrangements), setting the bar in the eye-catching opener, "Think Pink!" a tribute to haute couture that was one of the numbers Edens wrote especially for the film. *Funny Face* was a better fit for Edens. There was no baggage from the past to weigh him down, no Arthur Freed tradition to uphold, and above all, no sentimental kitsch. *Deep in My Heart* at least allowed him to step out of Freed's shadow and show that he had learned enough from the master to replicate his formula with its mix of real and invented characters, a plot that alternates between fiction and fact, and excerpts from Romberg shows that may have been out of chronology (and sometimes not even from the musicals in which they originated) and staged as audiences would have imagined them, but not necessarily as they were originally performed.

While Arthur Freed used familiar MGM actors for his biopics (Robert Walker as Jerome Kern in *Till the Clouds Roll By*, Tom Drake and Mickey Rooney as Rodgers and Hart in *Words and Music*), Edens cast the stage actor, José Ferrer, as Romberg, and the Wagnerian soprano, Helen Traubel, as the fictitious Anna Mueller, owner of the equally fictitious Café Vienna where Romberg worked as a pianist. Ferrer was an extremely versatile actor, who was as much at home in Shakespeare (*Othello*) as he was in classic farce (*Charley's Aunt*). He scored a major success on Broadway in 1946 with Rostand's *Cyrano de Bergerac*, winning an Oscar for his interpretation of the title character in the 1950 film version. By the time Ferrer had stepped before the cameras as Romberg, he had appeared in other movies such as *Joan of Arc* (1948), *Crisis* (1950), and *Moulin Rouge* (1952) in his Oscar-nominated role as the painter Toulouse-Lautrec. Still, Ferrer was not a household name, nor was Helen Traubel, except to operagoers. *Deep in My Heart* was not only a case of casting against type; it was casting against audience recognition. The film would succeed or fail (it cost $2.540 million and made $3.918 million) on the basis of its musical numbers with well-known performers (Ann Miller, Cyd Charisse, Jane Powell, Vic Damone, Tony Martin, Howard Keel) and some unknowns (Joan Weldon, William Olvis, and James Mitchell).

Casting Ferrer as Romberg was a gamble. Although he sang decently enough and evidenced a flair for mimicry and madcap, Traubel was the true revelation. Sporting an authentic German accent from her years of singing Wagner, Traubel performed a nimble turkey trot with Ferrer, "Leg of Mutton," as if the two of them were a seasoned vaudeville team. She had an opera singer's diction without the affected pronunciation that so many of her colleagues brought to popular song. Edens made sure she had her share of numbers: "You Will Remember Vienna," "Softly, as in a Morning Sunrise," "Auf Wiedersehen," and a robust "Stouthearted Men," in which she sounded as if she could head a regiment.

Screenwriter Leonard Spiegelgass gave Romberg's life a familiar arc: composer succeeds by adapting to current musical styles (ragtime, jazz), creates hit shows, finds the woman of his dreams, endures his share of failures, and performs his music in Carnegie Hall. That much is true. As the credits come on the screen, Romberg is shown conducting an orchestra in a medley of his songs, as he had done on various occasions and even on radio; the film ends with him doing the same in Carnegie Hall toward the end of his life. The place is right; the time is not. Romberg conducted his own orchestra in Carnegie Hall on September 13, 1943, in a sold-out performance, although this was not the one depicted in the film, at the end of which a graying Romberg justifies his style of composing as "middlebrow" and proceeds to deliver a reflective "When I Grow Too Old to Dream," which some might have remembered from MGM's *The Night Is Young* (1935).

Other factual details in *Deep in My Heart* include Romberg's writing for Shubert revues; partnering with Dorothy Donnelly (Merle Oberon), his librettist and lyricist for *Blossom Time, The Student Prince, My Maryland*, and *My Princess*; and courting Lillian Harris (Doe Avedon), whom he eventually married. The circumstances under which they meet in the film roughly correspond to real life but altered so that Ferrer can do a solo. In 1924, Romberg was busy working on the Al Jolson musical *Bombo*, with lyricist B. G. "Buddy" DeSylva and librettist Harold R. Atteridge. Determined to finish the show on time, the men retire to a cabin in the Adirondacks, vowing that they will not shave until their work is done. Lillian, vacationing nearby, encounters the bearded Romberg. It is love at first sight. Eager to make a good impression, he has violets sent to her at her hotel. Jolson, a practical joker, had the florist send violets to all the women at the hotel. Lillian is furious, but Jolson's joke was no impediment to true love, and the couple married in March 1925.

In the film, Romberg and two fictional characters take the same vow and rent a cabin to complete a musical for Al Jolson, who does not appear in the film. After inviting Lillian and her straight-laced mother to lunch, Romberg enacts the ridiculous plot, playing all the roles and ending by blackening his face in the Jolson tradition. The amazing Ferrer channels the Jolson persona, complete with Jolson's applause-begging shtick. Mrs. Harris is unimpressed, as is the fictitious Bert Townsend (Paul Stewart), the Shuberts' representative. Although the sequence seems an occasion for a Ferrer one-man show, there is some truth to the incident or at least to the cabin sequestration and the creation of *Bombo*, which was a hit for Jolson. But it was basically a set piece demonstrating the art of José Ferrer.

So much for cinematic truth. *Deep in My Heart* has its share of omissions and reimaginings. Romberg was Hungarian by birth; in the film, he is Viennese. It is true that he came of age in Vienna, where he grew to love operetta, a musical form he never abandoned and, in fact, perfected, proving that audiences could enjoy shows like *Maytime* and *The Desert Song* as musicals, and not as Broadway's answer to Old Vienna. Quite possibly, Spiegelgass decided to omit any reference to Romberg's Hungarian heritage because in 1954 Hungary was a satellite of the Soviet Union and a restless one at that, proved by the abortive uprising two years later. For the record, Lillian Harris was not Romberg's first wife; there had been another, the enigmatic Eugenia, whom he may have divorced. If Spiegelgass knew about Eugenia, he did not consider her worth bothering about, thinking it was better to omit rather than invent.

There is enough invention in some of the musical numbers in *Deep in My Heart*. Early in the film, the French dancer Gaby Deslys (Tamara Toumanova) requests a song from Romberg to perform in her show. Deslys is a historical figure, and the song, "Softly, as in a Morning Sunrise," is Romberg's, but it comes from *New Moon* (1928), which had yet to be written. Looking vampiristic, Toumanova turned it into an exotic solo with pelvic gyrations. That Deslys never performed "Softly, as in a Morning Sunrise" is less significant than its misuse. To hear it performed properly, listen to Helen Traubel sing it or watch the movie version of *New Moon* (1940), in which Nelson Eddy does full justice to the song.

Edens and Spiegelgass exercised their share of poetic license. At the time, Ferrer was married to the great pop singer Rosemary Clooney, who had made her film debut in Paramount's *The Stars Are Singing*, followed by *Here Come the Girls* (both 1953). In 1954, in addition to *Deep in My Heart*, Clooney could be seen in Paramount's dismal *Red Garters* and the studio's popular *White Christmas*, the most memorable of her handful of films. In *Deep in My Heart*, Romberg goes on for an indisposed performer in *The Midnight Girl* (1925), an excuse for a Ferrer and Clooney duet, "Mr. and Mrs.," that the two perform like a couple in love, as they were at the time. Ferrer and Clooney radiate such charm that only pedants would quibble about the source, *The Blushing Bride* (1925). Similarly, Ann Miller does a bump-but-no-grind version of "It," supposedly from *Artists and Models* (1924), although "It" originated in *The Desert Song* (1926) where it was not performed like a routine on a burlesque runway. The most unusual recreation involved Cyd Charisse and James Mitchell in a dance sequence, presumably from *The Desert Song*, or so the music—"One Alone" with some of "If One Flower Grows Alone in Your Garden" thrown in—would lead one to assume. That there was no such dance in the original did not matter. It was choreographed love making. Mitchell encircles Charisse, who throws up a leg in response, signaling availability. When the foreplay is over, she puts on her emerald-green cloak, adjusts the hood, strikes a dramatic pose in the doorway, and disappears into the night. Let deconstructionists interpret the dance. For the audience, it was a stunning exercise in controlled eroticism.

Some of the other excerpts were more conventional: Jane Powell and Vic Damone in "Will You Remember" from *Maytime*, Howard Keel in "Your Land and My Land" from *My Maryland*, Tony Martin and Joan Weldon (a gifted soprano whom sci-fi buffs will remember from *Them!*) in "Lover, Come Back to Me" from *New Moon*; and operatic tenor William Olvis in a superb rendition of "Overhead the Moon Is Beaming" ("Serenade") from *The Student Prince*. Director Stanley Donen could not do much with this embarrassment of riches that ran 132 minutes, a good twenty minutes longer than it should.

The screenplay was overloaded with biographical detail, real and transmuted. There was a stretch in the middle that was completely given over to plot—Romberg's courtship of Lillian Harris and his one-man version of Jolson's show—so that when it is time for music, a montage of excerpts arrives, each introduced by a title on a marquee. Arthur Freed would have spaced the numbers and ended with a grand finale. There is no such coda in *Deep in My Heart*, which ends with Romberg in Carnegie Hall, singing "When I Grow Too Old to Dream" as if he felt time's winged chariot at his back. Romberg died three years before the release of *Deep in My Heart*. He passed away from a stroke in 1951 at sixty-four. Roger Edens died of lung cancer in 1970. He was also sixty-four.

The year 1955 saw the release of two MGM biopics, both in Eastman Color and CinemaScope. Each was taken seriously by both critics and the Academy of Motion Picture Arts and Sciences, which in the past rarely acknowledged musical biographies. First, there was the moderately accurate *Interrupted Melody*, the story of operatic soprano Marjorie Lawrence (Eleanor Parker), who was stricken with polio at the height of her career; then *Love Me or Leave Me*, the largely fictionalized life of singer Ruth Etting (Doris Day) and her fractious relationship with Matt "the Gimp" Snyder (James Cagney). Each went into release in May 1955—*Interrupted Melody* early in the month, although in some parts of the country audiences might have seen *Love Me or Leave Me* first. *Interrupted Melody* won an Oscar for William Ludwig and Sonya Levien's story and screenplay, and a nomination for Eleanor Parker, who lost to Anna Magnani for *The Rose Tattoo*. Daniel Fuchs was Oscar nominated for the story that became the basis of the *Love Me or Leave Me* screenplay, which he coauthored with Isobel Lennart; and Cagney was nominated for best actor. Fuchs won, but Cagney lost to Ernest Borgnine for *Marty*.

Marjorie Lawrence and Ruth Etting were, roughly, contemporaries, Etting (1897–1978) being a decade older than Lawrence (1907–1979). They probably never met, although Lawrence, who enjoyed popular music, would have known who Etting was, while Etting may only have learned about Lawrence from news stories about the opera star whose career was derailed by polio. Each singer inspired Oscar-worthy screenplays—a rarity for a musical biopic. The scripts were atypical in their intelligence and refusal to mythologize the protagonists. Lawrence does not face polio with saintly resignation, nor is Ruth Etting beyond playing along with a shady character like "Gimp" Snyder to further her career.

Neither is a typical MGM musical. While the producers, Jack Cummings (*Interrupted Melody*) and Joe Pasternak (*Love Me or Leave Me*), were familiar MGM names, the stars and directors were not. Eleanor Parker began her career at Warner Bros., winning an Oscar nomination for *Caged* (1950) as a sweetly vulnerable inmate who becomes so disillusioned by the dithering of an indifferent parole board that she joins the criminal gang that facilitates her release. Like so many actors in the 1950s who sensed the twilight of the studio system, Parker found a safe haven in freelancing. MGM beckoned, and she accepted, appearing in *Above and Beyond* (1952), *Scaramouche* (1952), *Escape from Fort Bravo* (1953), *Valley of the Kings*, and *The Naked Jungle* (both 1954), which were all resume filler. *Interrupted Melody* was something else.

Parker's costar, Glenn Ford as Lawrence's husband, started at Columbia, where among his better known films were those he made with Rita Hayworth: *Gilda* (1946), *The Loves of Carmen* (1948), and *Affair in Trinidad* (1952). He also worked at other studios such as Twentieth Century–Fox (*Follow the Sun* and *The Secret of Convict Lake* [both 1951]), Paramount (*Plunder of the Sun* [1953]), and especially MGM where he made two of his best films: *The Blackboard Jungle* and *Interrupted Melody* (both 1955). "MGM" evoked names like Mickey Rooney, Judy Garland, Cyd Charisse, Gene Kelly, Katharine Hepburn, Spencer Tracy, Donna Reed, and Esther Williams; not Eleanor Parker and Glenn Ford, or James Cagney and Doris Day. Cagney was a Warner Bros. tough guy; Doris Day also started at Warner Bros. in a string of unmemorable musicals, with occasional forays into drama (*Storm Warning, Young Man with a Horn*). She could project an innocence that had reached the stage between cluelessness and experience. In *Love Me or Leave Me*, she played a woman who knew the score, but could affect a girlish air to get ahead. Each actor brought a bit of the Warner Bros. brass to their roles, Cagney more than Day. The result was not the usual MGM biopic.

The directors were also an alien breed. A refugee from Nazi Germany, Curtis Bernhardt (*Interrupted Melody*) began his American career at forty-one, first at Warner Bros., where he directed Humphrey Bogart in *Conflict* (1945), Bette Davis in *A Stolen Life* (1946), Barbara Stanwyck in *My Reputation* (1946), and Joan Crawford in *Possessed* (1947). He then began to freelance, choosing multipicture deals at various studios, including MGM, where his films included *The High Wall* (1947), *The Doctor and the Girl* (1949), *The Merry Widow* (1952) remake with Lana Turner and Fernando Lamas, and *Beau Brummell* (1954) with Stewart Granger and Elizabeth Taylor. The Hungarian-born Charles Vidor (*Love Me or Leave Me*) had a tenuous association with MGM, where he directed his first American feature, *The Mask of Fu Manchu* (1932). For the rest of the 1930s, he worked at other studios, producing nothing of consequence, until he came to Columbia in 1939 where he provided Rita Hayworth with her signature film, *Gilda* (1946). Contemptuous of Harry Cohn and tired of his obscenities, he was forced to pay Columbia $78,000 to be released from his contract, relocating first at Paramount (*Thunder in the East* [1952]) and then MGM (*Rhapsody* [1954], *Love Me or Leave Me, The*

Swan [1956]). Unlike Bernhardt, Vidor was familiar with the biopic tropes, having made the pictorially stunning but dramatically lifeless *A Song to Remember* (1945) at Columbia with Cornel Wilde as Frederic Chopin and Merle Oberon as Georges Sand. Oddly, his last film was another "song," *Song without End* (1960), a life of Franz Liszt. Vidor suffered a fatal heart attack during the shoot, and George Cukor completed the film.

For *Love Me or Leave Me*, Fuchs and Levien strung together a couple of facts about Ruth Etting and the gangster Moe "the Gimp" Snyder, who managed her career and later became her first husband. Because one of Etting's best-known songs was "Ten Cents a Dance," they decided to open the film with Etting working in a Chicago dance hall in the 1920s, where Snyder spots her after she's fired for kicking an overly friendly patron. In Etting, Snyder saw a fellow member of the disillusioned crew as well as a commodity he could sell and a property he could control. Cagney repeated his Cody Jarrett characterization from *White Heat* (1949), sociopathic and potentially lethal, replacing Jarrett's Oedipus complex with a paranoid personality.

It was not surprising that Cagney was nominated for another Oscar. (His first was for *Yankee Doodle Dandy*, which he won.) Unlike Cody Jarrett, Snyder is capable of tenderness; which he can only express in the same way that he barks orders and cuts deals. When he is able to express his true feelings for Etting, he is almost pitiful—until his next tantrum. If the writers adhered to the facts, Etting's life would have been a black-and-white melodrama with a few songs and a husband-wife-lover plot, in which Etting married Snyder, enduring his explosive outbursts for eighteen years, until she finally divorced him after she became involved with her accompanist, Merl Alderman. Still obsessed with Etting, Snyder shot Alderman, but not fatally. Snyder spent a year in jail. Alderman later had the charges dropped, and he and Etting retired to a farm in Colorado—a sunny ending after some pretty stormy weather.

The writers stuck to a handful of facts: Snyder discovers Etting in a Chicago club, becoming her unofficial manager, and later her husband. She enjoys a successful radio and recording career and appears on Broadway in the *Ziegfeld Follies of 1927*, where she introduces "Shaking the Blues Away." Their marriage is accurately portrayed as tension-ridden, with Snyder alternately tender and crazed. Etting is drawn to Alderman (a sympathetic Cameron Mitchell), whom Snyder shoots in a jealous rage. Then myth takes over for a (somewhat) happy ending complete with music. Snyder, still in love with Etting but envious of her fame, lavishes all his money on a Los Angeles nightclub, hoping to establish himself as a West Coast honcho. The notoriety from the Alderman affair threatens his enterprise, but, unbeknown to him, Etting comes to his aid and performs at the opening, singing—what else?—"Love Me or Leave Me."

Vidor was determined to give *Love Me or Leave Me* a hard edge, as he did *Gilda*, bringing out the dark side of show business brightened by splashy production numbers with Doris Day singing some of Etting's standards in Percy Faith's arrangements tailored to Day's voice that was warmer than Etting's. Even when Day sang "Ten Cents a Dance" in a black slip dress, affecting a "come hither" stance, she did not sound like someone who had incurred life's slings and arrows, but who only suffered a few nicks.

What is peculiar about the ending is that unlike "Ten Cents a Dance," in which Day is photographed singing the number in its entirety, she is not the sole attraction in the finale. We see her singing some of "Love Me or Leave Me," but then hear the rest from Snyder's point of view as he watches admiringly from the bar. Vidor does not allow Day to have the final number to herself, despite the billing in which her name precedes Cagney's. By bringing Snyder into the action, Vidor moves from Etting's world to his, which seems to be the only one in which Vidor is interested.

One expected a powerhouse performance from Cagney, whose oversize persona tended to dwarf his costars, so that you sometimes have to jog your memory to recall their names. (I keep forgetting that the fine character actress Margaret Wycherly played his mother in *White Heat*, or that Sylvia Sidney was his costar in *Blood on the Sun*.) In *Love Me or Leave Me*, there was no such problem. Day and Cagney were equals, even though he received an Oscar nomination and she did not. Her Ruth Etting was so determined to move out of the chorus and into the limelight as a singer that she used Snyder's infatuation with her to advance her career, only to discover that he had uncontrollable mood swings—volatile at one moment, childishly apologetic at another. Day had done her share of musicals at Warner Bros., beginning with her debut film, *Romance on the High Seas* (1948). Although she proved she could affect the charisma of a Broadway star in *Lullaby of Broadway* (1951), she never had the chance to display her art as actor, singer, and dancer until *Love Me or Leave Me*, or exhibit her command of different musical styles. In one sequence, she followed the jazz standard, "Everybody Loves My Baby" with "Mean to Me," sung simply and without the throb of self-pity. In the lavish production number "Shaking the Blues Away," Day wore an appropriately blue gown slit up the side. Surrounded by tuxedo-clad men, she literally shook the blues away in high kicking style, showing that she could have been a great musical comedy performer if had she chosen Broadway over Hollywood. For what she might have been like on the stage, take a look at *The Pajama Game* (Warner Bros., 1957), in which she assumed the role created by Janis Paige, with John Raitt from the Broadway production as her costar. If you didn't know the facts, you would think that Doris Day was part of the original company. A few years later, she moved into romantic comedy, receiving her only

Oscar nomination for her performance opposite Rock Hudson in *Pillow Talk* (1959).

Love Me or Leave Me proved what Doris Day could do with the right material; she had already revealed what she could do in non-singing roles (*Storm Warning, Young Man with a Horn*). *Love Me or Leave Me* gave her the opportunity to say it with music. It also brought two artists together for the first and only time in their careers in arguably Hollywood's best musical biopic.

Musicals about opera singers are a special case; there must be something unique about the subject to appeal to the non-opera-going public. The story should either be edifying (triumph over adversity) or archetypal (obscurity to fame), with the selections familiar enough to sustain audience interest in an art form that was alien to many of them. Even as a straight biopic, *Interrupted Melody* would have been an inspiring story of recovery in which Australian opera singer Marjorie Lawrence managed to resume her career, however briefly, after contracting polio. But a movie about an opera singer requires arias in context, and MGM had no intention of disappointing the public, even if it meant showing Lawrence in operas that were not in her repertoire such as *Carmen, Samson and Delilah, Don Carlo*, and *La Bohème*. Since Lawrence was a leading Wagnerian soprano, her fans at least heard her in excerpts from *Die Götterdämmerung* and *Tristan und Isolde*.

Lawrence's comeback was not as spectacular as depicted in the film, in which she returns to the Met in the taxing role of Isolde in *Tristan und Isolde*, staged so that she would not have to assume a standing position. At the end of the climactic "Liebestod," Lawrence, as if by sheer willpower or divine assistance, raises herself up and is rewarded with a rousing ovation. It never happened that way. The real-life Lawrence did return to the Metbut in a smaller role: Venus in another Wagner opera, *Tannhaüser*, which she performed convincingly while seated. Venus does not require much singing; since her business is sex and, in particular, keeping the hero in Venusberg, she has no reason to stand. Venus was an ideal comeback role for Lawrence, who brought the character to life solely through her voice. Later, Lawrence sang a recumbent Isolde and Amneris in *Aida*, even performing the title role in Richard Strauss's *Elektra* to great acclaim in 1947.

Interrupted Melody recreates Lawrence's Australian tour during World War II. In the film's most moving scene, the wheelchair-bound Lawrence entertains hospitalized servicemen with a lusty rendition of "Waltzing Matilda." Lawrence was also a hit in France, which awarded her the Légion d'Honneur medal in 1946 for her contribution to the war effort. Like many great opera singers, she did not regard pop music as lowbrow. Lawrence sang a bouncy "Don't Sit under the Apple Tree" to her fellow Australians, much to their delight.

Moviegoers in 1955 would not have been interested in the way operas were restaged for the disabled. But they heard some great singing, not by Eleanor Parker, who had never even seen an opera before she made the film, or Lawrence herself, but by the formidable Eileen Farrell, who dubbed Parker's voice.

Richard Strauss's *Capriccio* is essentially about the nature of opera. Which is more important, the words or the music? Is it a matter of *Primo, la musica, e poi le parole* ("First the music, then the words") or vice versa? In *Capriccio*, there is no resolution. In the musical biopic, there is no problem: first the story, then the music to go with it. In the case of *Interrupted Melody* and *Love Me or Leave Me*, filmgoers liked both story and music, as the box office receipts showed: $4.028 million for *Interrupted Melody*; $5.6 million for *Love Me or Leave Me*.

While *Interrupted Melody* told an uplifting story, MGM's *The Great Caruso* (1951) did not. The title indicated as much. Caruso achieved greatness in the "It's not where you start, it's where you finish" tradition. He started in a church choir, earned money singing in restaurants, and sang professionally for the first time in 1895 when he was twenty-two. After scoring major successes at La Scala and Covent Garden, he made his Met debut in 1903 as the Duke of Mantua in *Rigoletto*. That much is true, but little of it appears in the film.

Caruso may have been the most celebrated tenor of his generation, but his personal life was far from exemplary and unsuited to a 1951 film when the Production Code was being enforced. Caruso had a mistress, operatic soprano Ada Giachetti, who was already married and a mother when they began their affair around 1897. They had four sons together, two of whom died in infancy. The others, Rodolpho and Enrico Jr., died at forty-nine and eighty-three, respectively. Enrico Jr. did not live to finish his father's biography, which was completed by Andrew Farkas. The tenor's life has the makings of a steamy melodrama, with Ada betraying Caruso with his own chauffeur and then running off with him. Keeping his liaisons within the family and profession, Caruso was also involved with Ada's sister, Rina, also an opera star. Such a story has yet to be told on the screen, but if it were, Caruso's greatness would be limited to his art, not his life.

Naturally, *The Great Caruso* did not even suggest that the tenor had another life. In the film, Caruso (Mario Lanza), who had a fictitious girlfriend back in Naples by the name of Musetta (shades of *La Bohème*), marries Dorothy Park Benjamin (Ann Blyth), who was Caruso's real wife and twenty years his junior. In a movie dominated by tenor arias, Blyth had a chance to show off her soprano in the non-operatic "The Loveliest Night of the Year," which became hers by default when Lanza refused to sing it, considering it unworthy of him, although he later recorded it after it became a hit.

Mario Lanza was indisputably the film's star. Like his idol, Caruso, Lanza traveled the obscurity to fame route, from Philadelphia truck driver to MGM contract player given the star buildup in his first film, *That Midnight Kiss* (1949). Although *The Great Caruso* reportedly inspired Placido Domingo and Jose Carreras to pursue operatic careers, the film abounds in so many biographical inaccuracies that it emerges as a 109-minute operafest rather than a fully developed account of a life. For some reason, Caruso is shown making his Met debut in *Aida*, not *Rigoletto*, and having a throat hemorrhage (he was a heavy smoker) during a performance of *Martha* at the Met, not during the first act of *L'elisir d'amore* at the Brooklyn Academy of Music. Seeking treatment in Rome, he died in a hotel room in Naples, his home city, in 1921 at the age of forty-eight—information that the film does not include, perhaps because the writers, Sonia Levien and William Ludwig, believed that an onstage death was more dramatic than one in a hotel, even though it would have brought his life full circle, beginning and ending in his birthplace.

What is truly puzzling about *The Great Caruso* is its portrayal of Caruso's colleagues, played by Met Opera sopranos Dorothy Kirsten and Jarmila Novotna. Although Eduard Franz and Alan Napier appear, respectively, as the innovative Met general manager Giulio Gatti-Casazza and the renowned tenor Jean de Reszke, Kirsten and Novotna have been given the invented names of Louise Heggar (Kirsten) and Maria Selka (Novotna). Exactly whom Kirsten and Novotna were supposed to represent is unclear, since Caruso sang with a number of acclaimed sopranos such as Marcella Sembrich, Frances Alda, Emma Eames, Lillian Nordica, Olive Fremstad, Lina Cavalieri, and Emmy Destinn, none of whom bore any resemblance to the fictitious Heggar and Selka. Kirsten was at least heard in excerpts from *Aida*, *Lucia di Lammermoor*, and *Martha*, but Novotna—a celebrated Violetta, Manon, and Octavian—did not sing a note. Perhaps at one point she was scheduled to sing with Lanza, but then her character was reduced to a speaking part. It was just as well. Novotna's continental style with its musical refinements would have been at odds with Lanza's "skip the nuance and sing from the gut" school of performance. Novotna had shown earlier that she did not have to sing to be an effective actress. Cast in a straight role in Fred Zinnemann's *The Search* (1948), she movingly conveyed the anxiety of a mother looking for her son in postwar Berlin.

The Great Caruso may have disappointed musicologists, but it was a feast for the ears and a box office bonanza ($9.269 million).

As long as Lanza was under contract to MGM, he was expected to sing a mix of arias and popular songs in each of his subsequent films, none of which approximated the universal appeal of *The Great Caruso*. In *Because You're Mine* (1952), Lanza, as an opera singer drafted into the army, sang two complete arias, "Addio alla madre" (*Cavalleria Rusticana*) and "O Paradiso" (*L'Africaine*), along with excerpts from *Lucia*, *Il Trovatore*, and *Otello*. But what really excited audiences were his renditions of the title song, "Granada," and "The Lord's Prayer." *Serenade* (Warner Bros., 1956), a bowlderization of James Cain's novel, had Lanza as a vineyard worker who becomes the protégé of a wealthy socialite (Joan Fontaine) and finds redemption along with his voice through the ministrations of a Mexican bullfighter's daughter (Sarita Montiel). Neither a worthy recreation of the original nor vintage Lanza, *Serenade* is significant for two reasons: the Act III duet from *Otello* with Lanza as the tragic Moor and Licia Albanese as Desdemona, the only time the beloved soprano appeared in film; and the director, Anthony Mann (*Raw Deal*, *Winchester '73*, *The Glenn Miller Story*), who elicited a performance from Lanza that suggested there might be an actor inside the tenor, if the right property came along, which, at this point, seemed to be on the operatic stage where he felt he belonged.

Lanza had gained too much weight to play opposite Ann Blyth again in *The Student Prince* (1954). The strikingly handsome Edmund Purdom assumed the role of Prince Karl, lip-synching to Lanza's voice. By 1954, MGM realized it had gotten all it could out of Lanza, who first went over to Warner Bros. for *Serenade* (1956) and then moved to Rome in 1957. His last two films were made abroad and only distributed by MGM. In *The Seven Hills of Rome* (1957), filmed on location in Rome and at Titanus studios on the Via Tiburtina, Lanza sang "Questa o quella," the Duke's first aria in *Rigoletto*, and the now classic "Arrivederci Roma." His last film bore the ironic title *For the First Time* (1959), a German-Italian coproduction shot on location in Capri, Salzburg, Berlin, and Rome with MGM again as distributor. At least he ended his movie career playing an opera singer performing excerpts from *Rigoletto*, *Otello*, *Aida*, and *Pagliacci*. More memorable than any of these were his fervent "Ave Maria" and full-voiced "O Sole Mio."

Lanza was a true opera singer who might have had a career if he had curbed his appetite for food, drank moderately, and emulated his idol by making the operatic stage his habitat instead of MGM. Two months after the release of *For the First Time*, Mario Lanza died of a heart attack on October 9, 1959, at age thirty-eight. Enrico Caruso at least managed to last until forty-eight.

Despite its appeal, *The Great Caruso* is more of a period piece than a biopic. So many liberties had been taken with Caruso's life, and so many invented characters added to it, that the film is not so much a life told through music as a life refracted through a musical prism that bends it out of shape. While Parker's Marjorie Lawrence and Day's Ruth Etting are realistic portrayals, Lanza's Caruso is a tenor with a great voice impersonating another tenor with a great voice.

MGM's best musical biopic is unquestionably *Love Me or Leave Me*, with *Interrupted Melody* as runner-up. The others—*The Great Ziegfeld, Till the Clouds Roll By, Words and Music, Three Little Words, The Great Caruso, Deep in My Heart*—appeal mostly to the eye and the ear, but never get to the heart.

- 11 -

THE WHOLE CONSORT DANCING TOGETHER

By the 1940s, MGM had assembled a dazzling array of musical talent, both first and second tier, most of whom could also be cast in straight acting roles. MGM's was the most variegated repertory company in Hollywood: dancers who could sing (Gene Kelly, Fred Astaire, Ann Miller, Marge and Gower Champion, Leslie Caron) or seemed to when dubbed (Vera-Ellen, Cyd Charisse); singers who could dance (Judy Garland, June Allyson, Gloria DeHaven, Debbie Reynolds, Jane Powell, Frank Sinatra); actors who could sing and dance with some degree of professionalism (Ricardo Montalban, Van Johnson); comics who act and sing (Red Skelton, Rags Ragland); singers and dancers who could act (practically all of them); sopranos and tenors (Kathryn Grayson, Jane Powell, Lauritz Melchior, Mario Lanza) who could toss off arias, making them seem like popular songs; Broadway transplants for the long or short term (Howard Keel, June Allyson, Betty Garrett, Jules Munshin, Joan McCracken, Nanette Fabray); the resident mermaid (Esther Williams), who, when necessary, could act in an unaffected way; a concert pianist (Oscar Levant), a pianist/conductor (Jose Iturbi), and a bandleader (Xavier Cugat), who sometimes figured in the plot (Levant in *An American in Paris* and *The Band Wagon*, Iturbi in *Anchors Aweigh* and especially *Three Daring Daughters*, Cugat in *A Date with Judy*); the transients, good for one or two pictures (Ginger Rogers in *The Barkleys of Broadway*, Mitzi Gaynor in *Les Girls*, José Ferrer and Helen Traubel in *Deep in My Heart*, Doris Day in *Love Me or Leave Me* and *Billy Rose's Jumbo*; and the anomaly, Elvis Presley, who displayed an unusual sensitivity in *Loving You* and *King Creole* (both Paramount) but got caught in the MGM spin cycle when the studio made a last-ditch attempt to keep the musical from going the way of the kiwi bird with less than memorable results.

At MGM, Kathryn Grayson and Jane Powell had few opportunities to display whatever dramatic flair they had, but the same was true of both Jeanette MacDonald, who had a modest talent as an actress as she revealed in *Smilin' Through* (1941) and her last film, *The Sun Comes Up* (1949), with her co-star, Lassie. Cyd Charisse, the studio's prima ballerina, also proved herself an actress in *East Side, West Side* (1949), *The Wild North* (1952), and *Party Girl*

(1958). Although Esther Williams's home was Stage 30, the steel swimming pool that once was Johnny Weissmuller's jungle lake in the Tarzan movies, she is surprisingly effective in *Dangerous When Wet* (1953) when she must tell her father (William Demarest) that he is too old to swim the English Channel, a task for which she alone is suited. Every parent should hear bad news delivered so compassionately.

June Allyson, who sang, danced, and acted in the movies and returned to the stage in 1970, replacing Julie Harris in the Broadway production of *Forty Carats*, held her own with Humphrey Bogart in the Korean War drama, *Battle Circus* (1953). Allyson's portrayal of Claudette Colbert's suicidal stepdaughter is also the chief reason for watching *The Secret Heart* (1946). Gloria DeHaven also showed she could do more than sing and dance when she played a surgeon's daughter who dies from a botched abortion in *The Doctor and the Girl* (1949). Unfortunately, she had few such opportunities to display her acting ability. Like Judy Garland, DeHaven had a mature voice that belied her years and would have served her well on the musical stage. Oddly, DeHaven did not arrive on Broadway until 1955 in the short-lived *Seventh Heaven* with a score by the eminent movie composer Victor Young ("Stella by Starlight," "Love Letters," "My Foolish Heart") and costarring Ricardo Montalban, another MGM stalwart, who could sing (*Neptune's Daughter*), dance (*The Kissing Bandit*), and act (*Border Incident*).

There was a performers' hierarchy at MGM, but it was fluid, depending on who had reached his or her potential, was in the process of reaching it, or had exhausted or failed to achieve it. Popularity was the determinant; thus when Esther Williams lost her aquatic aura after *Jupiter's Darling* (1955), her days on Stage 30 were over. Judy Garland remained at the top until her emotional problems interfered with her work; she could only be replaced so often—in *The Barkleys of Broadway* (1949) with Ginger Rogers, *Annie Get Your Gun* (1950) with Betty Hutton, and *Royal Wedding* (1951), in which she was slated to replace the pregnant June Allyson and ended up being replaced herself by Jane Powell. Fred Astaire was always top tier during the decade he spent at MGM and shone as a dramatic actor in the nuclear holocaust film, *On the Beach* (1959). Gene Kelly also occupied a high place in the pantheon, able to take on serious roles in *The Cross of Lorraine* (1943) and *The Black Hand* (1950) and channel his inner Douglas Fairbanks in *The Three Musketeers* (1948). Although Ann Miller had leading roles in the Columbia musicals, *Reveilie with Beverly* (1943), *Eadie Was a Lady* (1945), and *Eve Knew Her Apples* (1945), she was always supporting cast at MGM. Yet whenever she was featured in a musical, her dance numbers were showstoppers.

For a time, Van Johnson was A list, but not in the same way as Astaire and Kelly. Johnson, who began in the chorus of Rodgers and Hart's *Pal Joey* (1940), is best remembered for classic World War II war movies like *Thirty Seconds over Tokyo* (1944) and *Battleground* (1949). He had a pleasant enough voice to play opposite Esther Williams in *Thrill of a Romance* (1945), *Easy to Wed* (1946), and *Duchess of Idaho* (1950), even though she was the star attraction. Once Mickey Rooney made *Girl Crazy* (1943), his eighth and last film with Judy Garland, except for a brief reunion in *Words and Music* (1948), he went back to playing Andy Hardy for a while (*Andy Hardy's Blonde Trouble* [1944], *Love Laughs at Andy Hardy* [1946]). His best performances during the war years were in *The Human Comedy* (1943), in which he had to deliver a "We regret to inform you" telegram to Frank Morgan about the death of his son; and *National Velvet* (1944) as a former jockey who helps Elizabeth Taylor, dressed as a boy, win the Grand National only to be disqualified when her gender is accidentally revealed. After *Summer Holiday* (1948), Rooney and MGM parted ways; he would not return to the studio again until *Andy Hardy Comes Home* (1958), which brought the series to a long-overdue end.

In addition to a hierarchy of actors, there was also one of producers at MGM—Arthur Freed, Jack Cummings, and Joe Pasternak in descending order, all of whom occupied the second floor of the Thalberg Building. Freed had the biggest office, as befitted the head of his own unit. They all had access to the same talent pool, but each had his favorites. Fred Astaire's best films came from the Freed Unit, as did Judy's. Jane Powell's was *Seven Brides for Seven Brothers*, produced by Jack Cummings, although most of her others were for Pasternak. She was never supposed to be in *Royal Wedding*, a Freed Unit movie, but ended up in it when Judy had to bow out.

Jack Cummings was the son of Louis B. Mayer's older sister, Ida. Unlike Universal's Carl Laemmle, who was known for nepotism, Mayer was not interested in establishing a dynasty, which would have been difficult with two daughters: Irene, who married producer David O. Selznick and became a notable theatrical producer herself (*A Streetcar Named Desire*; *Bell, Book and Candle*; *The Chalk Garden*). Edith, his favorite, married aspiring producer William Goetz, whom Mayer liked initially but grew to despise as much as he did Selznick. At first, relations between Mayer and Goetz were amicable. Knowing Goetz's desire to be part of the industry, Mayer agreed to finance the new company that Darryl F. Zanuck and Joseph Schenck had formed, Twentieth Century Pictures, little knowing that in 1935, Twentieth Century would merge with Fox Film Corporation to form a rival studio, Twentieth Century–Fox. Goetz wanted more than just being vice president of studio operations at Twentieth Century–Fox. Eager to run his own studio, he joined forces with Leo Spitz, former president of RKO, to create International in 1943, bankrolled by Mayer, who preferred that his son-in-law not be part of MGM.

But International was short lived, merging with Universal in 1946 to become Universal-International.

In his will, Mayer indicated what he thought of Edith and her husband. He left them nothing. However, he bequeathed $400 a month for life to his sister, Ida Mayer Cummings. If this seemed like a paltry sum, it was because Ida, known as a philanthropist for her tireless work on behalf of the Jewish Home for the Aged, really did not need it. She died in 1968, eleven years after her brother, and was buried above him in the crypt at Home of Peace Cemetery. He left Ida's son, Jack, $100,000. Mayer had high hopes for his nephew, who lived up to his uncle's expectations.

Since Cummings began in the short subject unit, directing Three Stooges comedies, he was a natural for MGM's premier clown, Red Skelton (*Ship Ahoy* [1942], *I Dood It* [1943], *Bathing Beauty* [1944], *Neptune's Daughter* [1949], *Duchess of Idaho* [1950], *Texas Carnival* [1951]). Apart from *Du Barry Was a Lady* (1943) and a sketch in *Ziegfeld Follies* (1946), Skelton was not a Freed type. His brand of humor was not to the producer's taste.

Since Cummings was married to Jerome Kern's daughter, Betty, he was the perfect choice to produce *Lovely to Look At* (1952), an overhauling of Kern's *Roberta* (1935). Both Cummings and Pasternak produced Esther Williams movies: *Bathing Beauty, Easy to Wed, Fiesta* with Williams in a virtually non-swimming role, *Neptune's Daughter*, and *Texas Carnival* (Cummings); *Thrill of a Romance, This Time for Keeps, On an Island with You, Duchess of Idaho*, and *Easy to Love* (Pasternak). Except for *Take Me Out to the Ball Game* and *Pagan Love Song*, Arthur Freed showed no interest in her films with their water ballets. If *Pagan Love Song* proved the exception, it was because the title came from a song of the same name that Freed wrote with Nacio Herb Brown, which Howard Keel sang and to which Williams swam. In fact, the entire sound track, with the exception of "Pagan Love Song," consisted entirely of songs by Freed and Harry Warren: "The House of Singing Bamboo," "Singin' in the Rain," "Etiquette," "Why Is Love So Crazy?" and "The Sea of the Moon." *Pagan Love Song* was in every sense an Arthur Freed Production.

Although Frank Sinatra appeared in Freed, Cummings, and Pasternak films, the two he made for Freed consisted of a classic, *On the Town*, and an enjoyable period piece, *Take Me Out to the Ball Game*. *It Happened in Brooklyn* (Cummings), his only MGM movie filmed in black and white, is remembered for the hit song, "Time after Time." Three years after Sinatra made his original MGM debut in *Anchors Aweigh* (Pasternak), he starred in another Pasternak musical, *The Kissing Bandit* as a mild-mannered dude in the early nineteenth century, forced to live up to his father's reputation as a womanizing bandit. One could see why Pasternak wanted to make *The Kissing Bandit*, which, despite its failure, he considered "an amusing picture." The plot bore a vague similarity to his 1939 film, *Destry Rides Again* (a Candide-like sheriff who cleans up the town), which Pasternak produced for Universal. *The Kissing Bandit*, which was no *Destry*, was saved by the fiery fiesta dance performed by Ann Miller, Cyd Charisse, and Ricardo Montalban.

It was only natural that Pasternak would produce most of Jane Powell's movies, hoping to do for her what he had done for Deanna Durbin at Universal. Born in Transylvania in 1901, Pasternak always considered himself Hungarian, since the region was then part of Hungary, although after World War II it became part of Romania. An early exposure to operetta made him partial to light entertainment. Pasternak started out as assistant to director Wesley Ruggles at Universal. When his friend, Henry Koster (né Hermann Kosterlitz), fled Germany after Hitler became chancellor in 1933, Pasternak looked for a way to bring Koster to Hollywood. He appealed to Universal's founder, Carl Laemmle, who was partial to emigres. But by 1936, the Laemmle era was over, and the studio was under new management. Since there had been cables from Laemmle that could be considered contractual, Universal, rather than go through litigation, was forced to honor the commitment, claiming that Pasternak and Koster had been hired "to bring the European technique of reduced dialogue and significant physical action together with a higher content and interpretative form of music into certain pictures in which Universal feels there is a strong foreign interest." Translation: movies that would appeal to a culturally diverse audience with a taste for good music, especially operetta and opera. With this goal in mind, Pasternak and Koster launched the career of Canadian soprano Deanna Durbin in *Three Smart Girls* (1936), in which Durbin showed off her range by singing "Il Bacio" and "Someone to Care for Me," the latter as a love song to her father (Charles Winninger). "Il Bacio" was something of a good luck song for Durbin, who sang it in her film debut, *Every Sunday* (1936), a short that brought even greater fame to her costar, Judy Garland.

Pasternak and Koster had created a formula: Durbin as an adolescent until she was ready for romance, singing songs that ranged from popular to classical, with an occasional operatic aria thrown in. Durbin could go from a powerful "Un bel di" in *First Love* (1939) to "Silent Night," "Give Me a Little Kiss," and "Night and Day" in *Lady on a Train* (1945). In *His Butler's Sister* (1943), she sang in English the aria now associated with the great tenor Luciano Pavarotti: "Nessun dorma" from Puccini's *Turandot*. By 1945, Durbin was the highest-paid star in Hollywood. By then, Koster was on his way to becoming one of the industry's most versatile directors (*Two Girls and a Sailor* [1944], *The Bishop's Wife* [1947], *Come to the Stable* [1949], *Harvey* [1950], *The Robe* [1953], etc.); and Pasternak was at MGM, fostering the career of the new Deanna Durbin, who, at first, was Kathryn Grayson, a true coloratura soprano. Grayson, at least one year older than Durbin, had everything Pasternak was seeking: beauty, intelligence, a crossover voice, and acting ability. What she lacked was something that Durbin had in abundance: charm. The Fall of Man seemed to have bypassed Durbin, who radiated an Edenic innocence even when she had a twinkle in her eye that suggested she had been around the garden more than once. If Durbin became an opera singer, the career to which she seemed headed, she would have been a people's diva like Beverly Sills, who never kept her fans at a distance. Unlike Durbin, Grayson performed in opera when her film career was over, singing such roles as Cio-Cio-San in *Madame Butterfly* and Violetta in *La Traviata*. She also received glowing reviews for her Sonia in *The Merry Widow* at the Chicago Lyric Opera. She did not consider Las Vegas beneath her; she and her favorite costar, Howard Keel (*Show Boat*, *Lovely to Look At*, *Kiss Me Kate*), played there on several occasions. She even ventured into melodrama (*Night Watch*) and farce (*Noises Off*). Of all the Hollywood sopranos of the period (Durbin, Gloria Jean, Susanna Foster, Jane Powell, Ann Blyth), Grayson had the most diversified career: recordings, radio, film, theater, television, cabaret, teaching. She did not have the welcoming personality of Durbin. She was a diva and played one—twice: as the historical Grace Moore in *So This Is Love*, and as stage star Lili Vanessi in *Kiss Me Kate*. Pasternak had other plans for Grayson, which included costarring with Mario Lanza in his first two MGM films, *That Midnight Kiss* (1949) and *The Toast of New Orleans* (1950).

In Jane Powell, Pasternak found the closest equivalent to Deanna Durbin. Although their voices seemed to be the same, Powell was a light soprano, while Durbin was a lyric soprano, who, if she chose to pursue a career in opera, would have excelled as Tosca, Cio-Cio San, and Leonora in Verdi's *La forza del destino*. One could see Powell as the coquettish Musetta in *La Bohème*, but certainly not as the consumptive Mimi. Grace Moore, Maria Callas, and Joan Sutherland all admired Durbin's technique. Powell could not inspire such admiration. But she did have one advantage over Durbin: She was a superb dancer, who adapted easily to the MGM musical format, which would have been alien to Durbin, whose films were, for the most part, romantic comedies with music; or in the case of *Christmas Holiday* (1944), a tragic melodrama in which she played a singer in a dive who performed two numbers (no arias) and attended a Christmas eve midnight Mass where she wept so convincingly that it was apparent there was an actress behind that extraordinary voice. But the actress was never to emerge again. Frustrated by the lack of variety in the films she was offered, Durbin left Hollywood in 1949 and went off to Paris with her third husband, director Charles David, where she enjoyed relative anonymity, or as much as a star with an international reputation could.

In Jane Powell, Pasternak had the new Durbin, but without her vocal range, which did not matter, since no one else at MGM had it either. Since MGM had already gone through its operetta phrase with Jeanette MacDonald and Nelson Eddy, Jane Powell musicals would be operetta-like—baubles about nothing more serious than a teenager's realization that her infatuation with a famous pianist is just a crush and that her true love is a boy her own age (*Holiday in Mexico* [1946]); or that her father is not cheating on his wife with a dance instructor but only taking lessons so he would not embarrass himself on the dance floor at their anniversary celebration (*A Date with Judy* [1948]). In all of her films for Pasternak, Powell was someone's daughter; or, in the case of *Athena*, granddaughter. Her parents could be a typical Mom and Dad (*A Date with Judy*). Her father could be a rancher (*Rich, Young and Pretty* [1951], a judge (*Small Town Girl* [1956], best remembered for Bobby Van's hopping around town on a pogo stick as if he were part kangaroo); or an admiral (*Hit the Deck* [1953]). He could even be a widower (an ambassador in *Holiday in Mexico* [1946], a cruise ship captain in *Luxury Liner* [1948]); her mother, a divorced magazine editor (*Three Daring Daughters*), an actress (*Nancy Goes to Rio* [1950]), or a free spirit who left her husband to live a glamorous life in Paris (*Rich, Young and Pretty*).

The plot complications in Pasternak's MGM movies came straight out of Screenwriting 101: Powell jumps to the wrong conclusion when she discovers her father with a dance instructor, who is simply doing her job (*A Date with Judy*). She and her two siblings try to effect a reconciliation between their divorced parents, not knowing that their mother has found someone else (*Three Daring Daughters*). Eager for an operatic career, she becomes a stowaway on her father's cruise ship after learning that two opera stars are on board (*Luxury Liner*). Even without playing matchmaker, she knows that she will have a stepmother when her widowed father reconnects with an old flame (*Holiday in Mexico*) or meets a recent widow (*Luxury Liner*). To Pasternak, Powell was Daddy's Little Girl. Powell thought of herself as a young woman.

The closest any of her Pasternak films came to sophistication, or some semblance of it, was *Nancy Goes to Rio* (1950), a reworking of an earlier film Pasternak had produced for Universal, *It's a Date* (1940), in which Deanna Durbin, more mature than she was in *Three Smart Girls*, played Kay Francis's daughter. Like her mother, Durbin is a stage actress who finds herself cast in a role that her mother had expected to play. Durbin books passage to Honolulu, hoping to master the script during the voyage but not counting on becoming infatuated with an older man (the urbane Walter Pidgeon), who is destined for mother, not daughter. Pidgeon proposes to Francis, who accepts, leaving her daughter free to star in a play about St. Anne. And what a more fitting finale than Durbin singing Schubert's "Ave Maria" with such devotion that one could easily imagine her as a saint.

Nancy Goes to Rio turns on the same plot pivot—mother (Ann Sothern) and daughter (Powell) up for the same part—with some delightful double entendre added when Nancy uses the trip to South America to prepare for her role as a pregnant woman deserted by her husband. When Barry Sullivan overhears Nancy reading her lines, he assumes she is pregnant, which becomes a running gag, possibly inspired by *Kiss and Tell* (Columbia, 1945), which had a similar plot complication, although one with potentially damaging consequences. In *Kiss and Tell*, Corliss Archer (Shirley Temple) accompanies a pregnant friend to an obstetrician. The local gossip spots them and assumes Corliss is an expectant mother and that her clueless boyfriend, whose reaction to everything is "Holy cow!" is the father. In both movies, the plot line runs its course, and the truth comes out. Once Nancy's "pregnancy" is clarified, Sothern decides that marriage to Sullivan is preferable to doing eight performances a week and relinquishes the role to her daughter.

Pasternak expected Powell to replicate Durbin's repertoire or develop one that was similar but without arias that would tax her vocal resources. Just as Durbin sang "Musetta's Waltz" from *La Bohème* in *It's a Date* (1940), so did Powell in *Nancy Goes to Rio* (1950). But Pasternak decided not to have Powell perform "Ave Maria" in *Nancy Goes to Rio*, since she already sang it in *Holiday in Mexico*. Powell was often given songs and arias that Durbin had performed. In *Holiday in Mexico*, her renditions of "Les filles de Cadiz" ("The Maids of Cadiz") and "Juliet's Waltz" from Gounod's *Roméo et Juliette* lacked the freedom and spontaneity that Durbin brought to them in *That Certain Age* (1938), partly because Durbin had a better command of French. Still, Powell did not embarrass herself. While Durbin could deliver a Met-worthy "Vissi d'arte" in *The Amazing Mrs. Holliday* (1943) and a "Pace, pace mio dio" in *Up in Central Park* (1948), Powell could not have subjected her gossamer soprano to such emotionally demanding music; she could, however, offer a heavenly "Ave Maria." Powell knew her limitations, as did Pasternak, who never let her exceed them.

Since Powell played a typical teenager in *A Date with Judy*, she was not given anything to sing that was even remotely operatic. But that did not stop her from throwing herself into "Love Is Where You Find It" and then returning to her age bracket with "It's a Most Unusual Day," suggesting that innocence is the flip side of experience. In her films, an aria was the equivalent of an insert: Add one to the mix, regardless of whether or not it fits. "Juliet's Waltz" in *Three Daring Daughters* (1948), the Gavotte from Massenet's *Manon* in *Luxury Liner* (1948), and "Musetta's Waltz" from Puccini's *La Bohème* in *Nancy Goes to Rio* (1950) are interchangeable. Powell could have sung the Gounod in *Nancy Goes to Rio*, the Massenet in *Three Daring Daughters*, and the Puccini in *Luxury Liner* for all it mattered.

After *Nancy*, Powell, then twenty-one, confronted Pasternak about the formulaic films that he has devised for her: "To you I'm still a little girl. . . . I've grown up. I'm married. I've got children. I'm a woman, it appears, to everybody in the world but to you." Pasternak agreed: "I had not let her grow up. She was a woman and I still insisted on treating her as a child." But it was not Pasternak who provided her with her two best films, in which she was anything but a teenager who could hit high C's. The producers were Arthur Freed and Jack Cummings.

Operetta was alien to Freed, who only used Powell once, and that was by default, in *Royal Wedding* (1951) when Fred Astaire needed a costar who could sing and dance after June Allyson had to bow out because she was pregnant, and Judy Garland, next in line, had to be replaced because she was emotionally unstable. The only other possibility was Jane Powell, who was an accomplished dancer. To costar with Fred Astaire, one had to be if not his equal, at least his partner. Powell proved to be both.

Royal Wedding was difficult to cast; Tom and Ellen Brown (Fred Astaire and Jane Powell) were a brother and sister act, inspired by the real-life team of Fred and Adele Astaire. Ellen could not possess the cool glamour of Ginger Rogers or Lucille Bremer. Powell was perfect; while one could envision Allyson in the role, Garland would have been miscast. Garland could no more play Astaire's sister than she could Annie Oakley in *Annie Get Your Gun* (1950). The few scenes that were shot before she was replaced by Betty Hutton showed a great talent struggling through "Doin' What Comes Natur'lly" and looking totally bewildered in "I'm an Indian, Too." *Annie* needed the hyperkinetic Betty Hutton, who, in the absence of Ethel Merman, could put the songs over with gusto, if not with Merman's seismic sound.

In *Royal Wedding*, the Browns' show has been booked in London at the time of Elizabeth II's wedding to Prince Philip in 1947. That each sibling will pair off with a Brit is inevitable with Sarah Churchill and Peter Lawford in the cast. Tom is taken with Ann Ashmond (Churchill, the prime minister's daughter,) when she shows up for an audition. Churchill executes a few turns like a dance class novice, but no matter. She gets cast. Since we never see her perform, she presumably improved by opening night. Ellen is pursued by a lord with only a title (Lawford). Since Adele Astaire gave up show business when she married Lord Charles Cavendish in 1932, Ellen should do the same. And if she does, what will happen to the act? Alan Jay Lerner's screenplay was hardly a study in invisible plotting; once Ann's estranged parents are brought into the story, a spoiler alert is unnecessary. The Ashmonds will reconcile,

Ellen resolves the career-vs.-marriage dilemma by choosing the latter, and Tom must wring a lily out of an acorn if Ann is to become his new partner. Mercifully, the audience is spared Ann's metamorphosis.

What matters are the musical numbers, the most famous of which (for all the wrong reasons) is Astaire's dancing on the wall and ceiling of his hotel room. The number has its admirers, but their admiration is more for the special effects than Astaire's art. Astaire could use objects, especially his cane and hat, the way Chaplin did by making them seem other than what they are. When he must rehearse without his sister, Astaire grabs hold of a hat rack and makes it his partner. All Astaire needs is an object that he can bring to life. One thinks of Chaplin as a starving prospector in *The Gold Rush* (1925), salting a candle as if it were a stalk of celery, slicing the sole of a shoe as if it were a roast, and winding the shoelaces around a fork like spaghetti. In 1951 few moviegoers knew how the number was filmed. "Trick photography" was the standard explanation. A Turner Classic Movies article solved the mystery: "The furniture and fixtures were all nailed down, and the room was placed in the middle of a rotating barrel. Cameraman Robert Planck was strapped to a large ironing board, along with the camera, so he could rotate with the room. Then Astaire simply danced right-side-up as the room revolved around him." The sequence is impressive at first viewing; revisiting it makes one long to see Astaire in his signature tux, turning the room into a stage and making his cane an extension of himself, as if it were an appendage granted him by special permission of Terpsichore.

Powell proved herself an able partner in her one and only movie with Astaire. They performed a specialty number with the longest song title on record—"How Could You Believe Me When I Said I Love You When You Know I've Been a Liar All My Life?"—with faux Brooklyn accents as if they had been coached by the Dead End Kids. Astaire was a low life; and Powell, a moll, beating on each other (one suspects they had their share of bruises) with Powell coming off as the winner and Astaire left with a battered hat. A hat also figures in "I Left My Hat in Haiti," the highlight of the London revue. Give Astaire a song with a Latin beat—like "Heat Wave" in *Blue Skies*—and his body absorbs the rhythm, causing his hips to swerve sinuously, as if he is responding to a siren song of the past when he left his hat in a "flat"—or so he claims—although the flat seems more like a bordello. But this is a brother-sister number, so everything is encoded sex—dance as foreplay. Director Stanley Donen created the illusion of a stage performance, beginning with Astaire in a gleaming white suit and tie in an enclosed space, setting the scene with sexy assuredness as if he were the master of ceremonies at a reenactment of a day in the tropics. Donen expands the frame, revealing a scrim behind which a village square comes to life. Everything is moving, even the top of the wall on which

Astaire glides. The stage itself moves along with the performers, as Astaire mingles with the natives, sometimes engaging them, at other times pursued and even ignored by them when he inquires about his hat. Out of the chorus emerges a dusky woman (Powell with subtly applied dark makeup) looking as if she could take on any gringo. Was it in her "flat" that he left his hat, or is she merely responding to the mood of the moment? It was a difficult number for Powell, who—to use D. H. Lawrence's distinction—had to be sensuous, not sensual. She is, after all, dancing with her brother. She encircles him as they face off, each trying to outdo the other like finalists in a dance competition in which there is no winner, but only two performers flashing radiant smiles as they acknowledge the well-deserved applause.

The number was brilliantly choreographed by Nick Castle, who knew that Powell and Astaire had to preserve the illusion of siblings generating a PG heat wave, thus downplaying the eroticism that could have erupted if Astaire's partner were Cyd Charisse. Astaire might have gotten the best remembered scene, but Powell had the best song, Burton Lane and Allan Jay Lerner's "Too Late Now," which she sang to Peter Lawford, meaning every word of it when he suggests that she could do better than a Brit with a meaningless title and an ancestral home with sheets on the furniture. At Oscar time, "Too Late Now" was nominated for best song, losing to Johnny Mercer and Hoagy Charmichael's "In the Cool, Cool, Cool of the Evening" from *Here Comes the Groom*. The latter may have been the more popular, but "Too Late Now" remains a poetic declaration of love by a master lyricist and the composer with whom he collaborated one last time on the Broadway musical, *On a Clear Day You Can See Forever* (1965), whose title song has become a perennial.

Royal Wedding grossed $3.902 million, about twice what it cost to produce.

Jane Powell's best remembered performance was in the previously discussed *Seven Brides for Seven Brothers*, which would have established her as the queen of operetta if operetta had still been in vogue. She did two more films for MGM: *Athena* (1954) and *Hit the Deck* (1955). *The Girl Most Likely* (1958)—the musical version of *Tom, Dick and Harry* (RKO, 1940), with Powell in the role originated by Ginger Rogers—was shot at RKO in 1956. When RKO ceased production a year later, MGM released *The Girl Most Likely*, which, understandably, looked like a transplant. Except for Powell, neither the director (the great Mitchell Leisen) nor costars (Cliff Robertson, Keith Andes, Tommy Noonan) had an MGM pedigree.

Powell's star began to fade after *Seven Brides for Seven Brothers*. Although opera singers can perform into their sixties, Hollywood sopranos usually lasted a decade, sometimes less (Susanna Foster, Anna Maria Alberghetti). Powell would always have the look of an ingenue, even in middle age. In MGM's *Two Weeks with Love* (1950), she was eclipsed by Debbie Reynolds in the movie's highlight, "Aba Daba Honeymoon," a novelty song by Arthur Freed and Walter Donovan that Reynolds and Carleton Carpenter sang totally deadpan as they recounted the courtship ritual of a monkey and a chimpanzee. The number might have offended animal activists, particularly simian lovers, but it was the one audiences remembered, even if they forgot the plot which centered around the heroine's obsession with owning a corset as a mark of her incipient womanhood.

Powell was the quintessence of operetta; Reynolds, of musical comedy. Reynolds had a versatility that could outlast a star whose voice might eventually lose its luster—and MGM knew it.

Whenever Reynolds was in a film with Powell, she could not help upstaging her and pretty much everybody else. She looked considerably younger than Powell, even though there was only a three-year difference between them. MGM never intended Reynolds to be Powell's replacement—Powell and Grayson were the last of the studio's sopranos—but instead, a new breed of star who could sing, dance, and act in romantic comedy or, if necessary, drama. (Reynolds was especially convincing as the daughter of a Bronx couple in *The Catered Affair* [1956], holding her own with such pros as Bette Davis and Ernest Borgnine.)

In *Athena* (1954), Pasternak's oddest movie, Powell played the title character, a numerologist supposedly able to spot a prospective mate from his birthdate, astrological sign, or even his license place. There is a bizarre meet cute when Athena informs an attorney and congressional aspirant (Edmund Purdom, looking as if he would rather be back in the ancient world as Sinue in *The Egyptian*) that she can revive his ailing peach trees with her own special brand of mulch. Athena, the oldest of seven sisters all named after Greek goddesses, belongs to a family of health fanatics and fitness enthusiasts. The film capitalized on two current fads: health food and bodybuilding, the latter being the subject of the subplot about the Mr. Universe contest, featuring 1950's Mr. Universe himself, Steve Reeves, in the minor role of Ed Perkins, who, obviously, wins the title.

Powell, who did not have the opportunity to perform any operatic selections in *Rich, Young and Pretty*, *Royal Wedding*, *Small Town Girl*, and *Seven Brides for Seven Brothers*, proved that she could still sing coloratura when she tossed off an effortless "Chacun le sait" from Donizetti's *Daughter of the Regiment*, even though there was no call for it. Reynolds stole the movie from everyone, including the muscle-bound Reeves. Although she was twenty-one, she looked like a teenager, leaping over furniture in "I Never Felt Better," and swinging on a chandelier as if it were an exercise ring. Ralph Blane and Hugh Martin, who created the memorable score of *Meet Me in St. Louis*, could not accomplish the same in *Athena*. The best number is the gender-changed

"The Boy Next Door" from *Meet Me in St. Louis*, sung at the beginning by Vic Damone about "the girl next door." Feminists might be interested in *Athena*, because it reverses the male-female dynamic of screwball comedy. Although Powell is the aggressor, Purdom, who resists her intrusions on his privacy with her makeover mania, finally comes around to her way of thinking. Usually, it is the woman who puts her career aspirations on hold to ensure a happy ending. Whether the attorney will realize his political ambitions is unresolved. The ending implies that he now prefers clean living to dirty politics. If he runs for Congress, it will probably be on the fitness ticket, although it is hard to imagine any member of Congress adopting the lifestyle of Athena's family, who behave as if they had emigrated from Mount Olympus, spending their evenings on a California hillside like figures on a Grecian urn.

One doubts that *Athena*, a box office failure, would have worked as a vehicle for Esther Williams, as had originally been planned, with Williams swimming where Powell sang. Williams's maternity leave necessitated a radical reworking of the script, in which Athena was supposed to be "a reincarnated Greek goddess swimming her way to happiness." A year later, Williams made a similar film, *Jupiter's Darling* (1955), her last for MGM. It was a George Wells production that vied with *Athena* for the dubious distinction of MGM's weirdest musical. It even fared worse at the box office than *Athena*.

Jupiter's Darling was haphazardly adapted from Robert E. Sherwood's play, *The Road to Rome*, which had a decent run on Broadway during the 1927–1928 season and marked Sherwood's emergence as a future Pulitzer Prize–winning playwright and Oscar-winning screenwriter. The play, set in Rome 216 BC, was a drawing-room comedy without a drawing room or even a salon. There were trickles of wit and a good deal of not-so-subtle moralizing about the folly of war, prefiguring similar sentiments in Sherwood's later plays such as *Idiot's Delight* (1936) and *There Shall Be No Night* (1940). Sherwood subverted the conventions of high comedy by rewriting the second Punic War, in which Hannibal routed the Roman armies at Canae, but never really took possession of Rome. In Sherwood's version, Hannibal spares Rome after a tryst with Amytis, the wife of dictator Fabius Maximus, who finds her lover preferable to her stodgy husband. Although Hannibal had once threatened to kill Amytis, he changes his mind after spending the night with her and offers her two choices: go off to Carthage with him or remain in Rome with her husband, reminding her that Rome will be destroyed no matter what she chooses. Amytis, like the all-knowing Cassandra, replies that in either case Rome will destroy itself. As a Greek, whose country was subjugated by Rome, she could care less about the decline and fall of the Roman empire. It is a bittersweet ending, in which two lovers who seemed to complement each other must part because honor, both military and domestic, must be upheld.

Whether New Yorkers in 1927 knew their Roman history is unimportant. This was history as myth, or as Sherwood put it, the "offspring of the union between fiction and fact." That Hannibal never took possession of Rome, despite the disastrous Roman defeat at Canae, did not matter. What mattered was that war was averted. That was Sherwood in 1927. A decade later, with World War II on the horizon, he wrote *Idiot's Delight*, which ends with the leads—a hoofer and a bogus white Russian—singing "Onward, Christian Soldiers" as the bombardment begins.

The Road to Rome was played as urbane comedy, as one would expect from Jane Cowl, one of the leading exponents of the genre, as the love-deprived Amytis; and Philip Merviale as the enticeable Hannibal. In the preface, Sherwood acknowledges their contribution, praising Cowl "for the graciousness, the gaiety and tenderness, that she has given to the character of Amytis"; and Merviale "for his fine, sturdy, and sympathetic impersonation of Hannibal." Sherwood's model was Shaw's *Caesar and Cleopatra*, with two articulate people sparring in high style. Shaw's Caesar, however, never succumbs to Cleopatra, while Sherwood's Hannibal cannot resist the charms of a witty woman because he is not really the Carthaginian general but a leading man in a pseudo-historical comedy playing opposite Jane Cowl, who is not really Amytis, since the name of Fabius Maximus's wife is unknown. Sherwood's Amytis is an Athenian; his choice of name may have been inspired by that of the daughter of the Persian king, Xerxes the Great, who was known for her promiscuity. Jane Cowl's Amytis is the embodiment of urbanity, dispensing wit and wisdom as she moves gracefully from the stage to the pulpit. Her Amytis is not exactly oversexed, although she is hardly a model of marital fidelity.

MGM bought *The Road to Rome* before it opened on Broadway as a vehicle for Greta Garbo, who, if she costarred with John Gilbert, would have imposed her languid and eroticized persona on Amytis and made her as sphinx-like as Garbo herself. *The Road to Rome* lay buried among unproduced properties for almost three decades, until it was finally resurrected for Esther Williams, then in her early thirties, and not up to doing two of the feats required of her: riding off a cliff on horseback straight into a lake in central Florida that doubled as the Tiber; and engaging in an underwater free-for-all with Hannibal's minions before reaching the shore. Instead, Al Lewin rode off the cliff and broke his back. Mary Zellner doubled for Williams in the underwater melee, leaving Esther free to finish the sequence by meeting up with her horse and returning to Rome.

In addition to eliminating the play's moralizing, screenwriter Dorothy Kingsley made two significant changes. In the film, Amytis is the fiancée of Fabius Maximus, not his wife, which makes it possible for Amytis to offer

herself to Hannibal in return for sparing the city. It was not much of a sacrifice; Hannibal was the incarnation of the perfect lover, which Fabius Maximus
was not. With a lighter touch, the film might have worked as a romp through
the backroads of Roman history, but it was derailed by someone's decision
(Wells's perhaps) to make it a hybrid of operetta and action movie with singing Carthaginians ("We love to fight for Hannibal") marching on Rome with
an elephant brigade. In high-concept terminology, *Jupiter's Darling* is *Naughty
Marietta* meets *Conan the Barbarian*. The "treat 'em rough" males in the audience were not disappointed when Hannibal (Howard Keel) kept tossing
Amytis (Williams) on the ground, as if she loved every minute of it, which
Williams seemed—or was directed—to convey.

MGM's resident (but not for long) mermaid had one decent but creepy
swimming sequence at the beginning of *Jupiter's Darling* when Amytis expresses her desire for a *real* man, which Fabius Maximus (a sexually depleted
looking George Sanders) is not. She plunges into the pool and swims underwater where chalk white male statues come to life, as if offering their services to the love-deprived Amytis. That was the high point. Now for the low:
the banal lyrics ("Let's keep the Romans wondering / How soon we will be
plundering"); the misuse of Marge and Gower Champion as Meta, Amytis's
slave, and Varius, a Carthaginian captive, respectively—the latter becoming
so smitten with Meta that he delivers an ode to slavery which, if it were heard
in 1863, would have delayed the Emancipation Proclamation indefinitely ("If
this be slav'ry, hooray for slavr'y / I don't want to be free"); the pervasive sex-
ism exemplified by Howard Keel's Hannibal, who is always threatening to slit
Amytis's throat when he isn't throwing her on the floor; and the exploitation
of the elephants (you can't have a movie about Hannibal without elephants).
In "The Life of an Elephant," perhaps the most supremely ridiculous number
in any musical, Gower and Marge frolic amid the elephants, with Marge at
one point simulating the walk of a baby pachyderm. When Amytis remarks to
Hannibal that his elephants need some color, one was hardly prepared for the
end in which the poor creatures have been sprayed with oil paint, looking as
if they had just returned from beyond the rainbow.

How the National Legion of Decency, which was always concerned about
"suggestive situations," managed to award *Jupiter's Darling* an A-II rating
(Morally Unobjectionable for Adults and Adolescents) is hard to explain, particularly after a scene in which the camera tracks back from Hannibal's tent
where he and Amytis are locked in an embrace—code for consummation, except that in the next scene, Amytis is in her own tent, as if to assure the Legion
that nothing happened except a good-night kiss. But with the two looking
radiant the next morning, the code breakers knew better. The end of the play's
second act makes it clear there was consummation. When Hannibal threatens

(again) to kill Amytis, she says, "Yes—I'm going to die . . . but not until tomorrow." The stage directions call for Hannibal to "seize" her in his arms and kiss her. Curtain.

The time to have made *The Road to Rome*, minus the antiwar rhetoric, was in the 1930s when MGM had William Powell and Myrna Loy, Rosalind Russell and Franchot Tone, and particularly Melvyn Douglas and Greta Garbo under contract. *The Road to Rome* would have been a high-gloss sophisticated comedy, as opposed to the witless musical into which it devolved.

- 12 -

THE LIFE AQUATIC WITH ESTHER WILLIAMS

Jupiter's Darling and *Kismet*, released in early and late 1955, respectively, marked the end of several MGM affiliations, including its premier baritone, Howard Keel, who had an impressive resume before he landed in Hollywood. As Harold Keel, he replaced John Raitt as Billy Bigelow in *Carousel* for three weeks in 1945 and then took over the role of Curly in *Oklahoma!* He endeared himself to British audiences when he played Curly again in the 1947 London production. Keel had no difficulty shuttling back and forth between film and theater. Even when he appeared in low-budget westerns like *Red Tomahawk* (1967) and *Arizona Bushwhackers* (1968), he never made it seem that he was slumming. Although *Saratoga*, the stage musical based on Edna Ferber's novel *Saratoga Trunk*, lasted a mere eighty performances during the 1959–1960 season, Keel and his costar, Carol Lawrence, did justice to the Harold Arlen–Johnny Mercer score. When Keel compared love to a game of poker ("Game of Poker"), you could imagine him with one eye on a woman and the other on his cards. Keel rarely was without work. A generation that never heard his rich baritone learned his name when he joined the cast of the popular television series *Dallas* in 1981 as Clayton Farlow, the oil baron and rancher, who became such an audience favorite that he stayed on for a decade, even though Farlow was originally intended to replace Jock Ewing, whom Jim Davis had played until he succumbed to multiple myeloma in 1981.

Careers rarely end in a blaze of glory, and Esther Williams's at MGM was no exception. She would make a few more movies (*The Unguarded Moment*, *Raw Wind in Eden* at Universal-International), but none with the appeal of her MGM Technicolor spectaculars. Although critics were unimpressed with Esther's acting ability, she was judged "The World's Most Popular Actress" in 1951. What critics failed to recognize is that she did a good deal of acting through swimming; while on land, she stuck to the script, which only required her to deliver her lines convincingly, which she was quite capable of doing. Esther might have been an Olympic champion, had not World War II intervened. At sixteen, she won the women's outdoor nationals in Des Moines, making her eligible for the 1940 Olympics to be held in Helsinki, but were

canceled when the Nazis invaded Poland in September 1939. Her extraordi-
nary performance in the nationals did not escape the attention of impresario
Billy Rose, who made her the star attraction of his Aquacade at the 1939–1940
Golden Gate International Exposition in San Francisco.

When MGM beckoned a year later, Esther made her film debut in *Andy
Hardy's Double Life* (1942), in which she awakened a sleeping Mickey Rooney
with a kiss as his eyes opened to see her in a two-piece white bathing suit. She
generated enough attention from moviegoers to win the female lead opposite Red Skelton in *Bathing Beauty* (1944), filmed in Technicolor and the first
of her water ballet extravaganzas, which, according to the *Los Angeles Times*
(July 16, 1944), were filmed with a bakelite camera with special lenses that allowed the water to separate for close-ups.

Since most 1944 moviegoers knew nothing about college administrators,
no one seemed to mind that *Bathing Beauty* presented a distorted picture of
life at a (primarily) women's college, or that the dean and faculty would con-
spire to rid the campus of a male who enrolled after discovering that the charter did not designate the college a single-sex institution. The student, Steve
Elliot (Skelton), a songwriter, hopes to win back Caroline Brooks (Esther), a
swimming instructor, who was about to become his bride when the wedding
was sabotaged by an unscrupulous producer (Basil Rathbone), eager for Elliot
to complete the songs for his show. Since *Bathing Beauty* is a musical, Victoria
College comes off as a haven for jive-happy females who would rather sing
and dance away the hours than crack a book.

The situation is perfect for Skelton, who gives the equivalent of a master
class in physical comedy, including miming the way women awake in the
morning, apply their makeup, and wiggle into a girdle. In eurythmics class,
he is literally the odd man out. Forced to wear a pink tutu, he is mocked by
the sadistic instructor (Ann Codee), does some pratfalls, and flits around to
music from *The Nutcracker*. The timing is meticulous. While prancing about,
Skelton picks up a sticky candy wrapper and, realizing it could result in a
demerit, passes it on to a student, who initiates a round robin, as the wrapper
goes from one to the other until it comes back to Skelton, who accidentally
slaps it on Esther's forehead as she enters the room. When he shows no interest in a music professor's lecture on "Loch Lomand" as folk song, he is told to
present his version for the next class, which he does with the aid of a fellow
student (Jean Porter, a wonderfully talented singer and dancer, who, sadly, did
little of either in her career). Skelton and Porter perform a hepcat version, "I'll
Take the High Note" (rather than "I'll take the high road, and you take the low
road"), and, as can only happen in an MGM musical, they are backed up by
Harry James and his Orchestra with Ethel Smith on organ, her fingers gliding
over the keys that seem to respond gleefully to her feather-light touch.

The film itself is a novel spin on the boy/girl template: boy loses girl, gets her back, and nearly loses her again until a deus ex machina arrives that mirrored the start of Esther's own career: Caroline becomes the star attraction of an aquacade. *Bathing Beauty* may have introduced Esther as the title character, but it was really Skelton's film, with a surfeit of guest appearances to fill in the script's empty spaces and satisfy audiences who would rather hear Harry James on trumpet than see Esther Williams doing the 100-meter breaststroke. The film was top heavy with talent, as if MGM did not trust Esther to carry a movie on her own and felt she needed outside help. Later films proved she didn't, but in 1944, MGM was uncertain, so they filled in the interstices of the story with guest appearances by Harry James and his Orchestra, Ethel Smith tickling "Tico-tico" out of the organ, Helen Forrest doing a restrained but soulful "I Cried for You"; Carlos Ramiriz crooning "Magic Is the Moonlight" in Spanish; the Spanish American bandleader Xavier Cugat cradling his signature Chihuahua, and singer Lina Romay adding a Latin touch to the lunatic plot. With so many specialty numbers and a top-heavy script, Esther had only two swimming sequences, which were enough to establish her as a true bathing beauty. In the first, wearing a fuchsia bathing suit, she dived into a pool of Technicolor blue, at one point logging in and out of the water like a porpoise, as a bevy of bathing beauties in fuchsia and green offered a lesson in choreographed geometry. In the finale, Esther, now queen of the deep and clad in a silver-white bathing suit, rises out of the water on a pedestal, framed by decorative sea horses. To show that one can waltz in water, she swims to the *Die Fledermaus* prelude, doing breaststrokes and backstrokes, as if the pool had become a Viennese dance floor. As the ladies of the aquatic chorus swim within circles of water lilies, jets of water shoot up, illuminated from within by flares, until the entire set is concealed behind a watery curtain, signaling the end of the performance.

Esther was sanguine about her tenure at MGM. When Art Buckwald interviewed her for the *Beverly Hills Citizen* (October 11, 1957), she was quite candid: "I enjoyed my years at MGM but they would never let me out of the tank. I decided I had to move on. I've been treading water long enough." She had expressed the same sentiments earlier to Hedda Hopper (*LA Examiner*, August 18, 1945): "I wanted something more. Even 'Bathing Beauty' didn't satisfy me. Because I wanted to get away from the swimming pool and really act." A year later, she had the opportunity, as she told the *Saturday Evening Post* (April 12, 1947): "[*Easy to Wed*] gave me my first real characterization, plus a chance to sing and dance."

Then, she would have considered *Easy to Wed* (1946) the best of her first four musicals—the others being *Bathing Beauty*, *Thrill of a Romance* (1945), and *This Time for Keeps* (1947). In *Thrill of a Romance*, Esther is a swimming instructor courted by Van Johnson in her husband's absence. Marriage—or what passed for it—is treated lightly in *Thrill of a Romance* and *Easy to Wed*. So are engagements. But how else could writers get Esther out of a pre- or post-marital predicament except with a plot twist that spared her the stigma of promiscuity or adultery? Since it all seemed so wholesome, the National Legion of Decency registered no objections to *Thrill of a Romance* and *This Time for Keeps*, which it classified as A-II (Morally Unobjectionable for Adults and Adolescents). In *This Time for Keeps*, Esther is the star of an aquacade in a recycled boy-girl plot in which girl learns that boy is engaged to another, leading to misunderstanding, confusion, and a happy ending—plus Jimmy Durante, a water ballet choreographed by Stanley Donen, and the Wagnerian tenor, Lauritz Melchior, in arias from operas ("La donna e mobile" from *Rigoletto*, "M'appari" from *Martha*) in which he was better heard than seen.

The Legion felt differently about *Easy to Wed*, which it labeled B (Morally Objectionable in Part for All) because of "light treatment of marriage." The rating did not deter the moviegoers; the box office had spoken: $5.638 million. Esther may have preferred *Easy to Wed* because she only had two swimming scenes, neither of which was balletic. Since she was not confined to a seventy-foot-deep pool with hydraulic lifts and cranes for overhead shots, she could concentrate on creating a character. *Easy to Wed* was a plot-heavy remake of *Libeled Lady* (1936) in which an heiress, Connie Allenbury (Esther), lodges a $2 million libel suit against a newspaper. To save the paper from bankruptcy, Haggerty (Keenan Wynn), the business manager, talks ex-reporter Bill Chandler (Van Johnson) into a bogus marriage with Haggerty's fiancée, Gladys (Lucille Ball). Then Chandler is to woo Connie and set her up for a love nest exposé in which the aggrieved "wife" barges in, threatening Connie with alienation of affection, as a photographer takes a tabloid-worthy picture that will make her drop the suit. The plot is screwy, but so was *Libeled Lady*. Esther had to do more acting than swimming, first playing the spoiled heiress, aloof and imperious, and then warming to Johnson while implying that she is not entirely convinced of his sincerity. Connie is well aware of how the game of love is played. When Chandler invites her to his room for drinks, she sends a social climbing mother and her mousy daughter in her place.

Unfortunately, an inordinate part of this 106-minute movie is taken up with a duck-hunting sequence. To ingratiate himself with Connie and her father (Cecil Kellaway), a duck-hunting enthusiast, Chandler passes himself off as a pro. Some may find humor in the scenes with Chandler on a boat in the Canadian marshes with a dog that looks as perplexed as he. Others might wonder how long it will take him to shoot the bloody duck or eat crow. He manages to bring one down, Connie cooks it, and face is saved—temporarily.

Turning *Libeled Lady* into a musical softened the pervasive cynicism of a story in which people are basically pawns. Once Chandler realizes he is in love with Connie, he feigns affection for Gladys to distract her from the alienation of affection scenario. In a scene that would have struck a responsive chord in many women, Gladys does a 180-degree turn. Previously she was a wisecracking nightclub performer, still in love with Haggerty even though a scoop takes precedence over her. Now, she drops the comic persona and bitterly expresses her resentment at being used by men to further their own ends. Oddly, Connie did not question the "marriage." Cleverly, she proposes to Chandler, insisting they marry immediately, knowing that if he hesitates, he must be hiding something. Chandler is enthusiastic, which is all the proof she needs.

There is a charming interlude in this hectic film that is not dictated by plot. At a fiesta, Esther and Van do a samba to "Boneca de Pixe" (literally "black doll" in Portuguese, or "tar baby" in the American vernacular), singing the tricky lyrics in their own voices and in the original Portuguese (Carmen Miranda was the language coach), even trilling the "r's." Ethel Smith practiced her usual wizardry at the organ, her fingers barely touching the keys as Esther and Van performed a song that, in a later age, would have been deemed politically incorrect. But they sang it so beguilingly that "Boneca de Pixe" provided a welcome break in a movie about people manipulating each other.

Easy to Wed gave Esther an opportunity to sing and dance, which she did with a professionalism that would have eluded an ordinary swimmer. But one of Esther's rarely tapped talents was her ability to treat lyrics as dialogue, which she did expertly in *Neptune's Daughter* (1949), whose best-remembered number is Frank Loesser's Oscar-winning "Baby, It's Cold Outside," a call-and-response duet, in which the first singer says something that prompts a response from the second as if they were conversing in song. In the film, Ricardo Montalban tries to persuade Esther to spend a romantic evening with him, although he clearly has more on his mind than conversation. Esther is conflicted, finding it hard to resist him while at the same time trying to maintain a sense of propriety. Whenever Esther says she must leave, Ricardo counters with, "But baby it's cold outside." When she agrees to "half a drink more," he tells her to "put some music on while I pour."

It is the most innocent attempt of seduction ever shown on the screen, with the lyrics implying more than they state. Esther and Ricardo perform the duet as musically interdependent dialogue with separate vocal lines—seduction as counterpoint. But dialogue, musical or spoken, must be acted, which is precisely what Esther and Ricardo do: they act out the lyrics. Esther does not want to leave but feels she must offer excuses. Ricardo applies the velvet touch that is soft enough to persuade her to linger a bit. But just when it seems there will be a slow backward tracking shot away from the two of them on the sofa—a familiar metaphor for off-camera sex during the Production Code era—the scene shifts to Betty Garrett and Red Skelton performing the same number, this time with Garrett as the aggressor putting the moves on a befuddled Skelton, pulling his jacket over his head and turning the duet into a literal battle of the sexes with Garrett as victor. The difference between the two renditions is the difference between musical dialogue and musical comedy, sophistication and slapstick, and ultimately connotation and denotation. Ricardo charmed Esther into spending the evening—as opposed to the night—with him; instead of breaking down her resistance, he lets her play coy until she feels it is time to stop feinting and enjoy whatever lies ahead. Garrett viewed Skelton as a steer to be roped. Same duet, two versions—one, musical conversation; the other, musical competition.

Jack Cummings and Joe Pasternak produced most of Esther's musicals: *Bathing Beauty, Easy to Wed, Neptune's Daughter,* and *Texas Carnival* (Cummings); *Thrill of a Romance, This Time for Keeps, On an Island with You, Duchess of Idaho, Skirts Ahoy,* and *Easy to Love* (Pasternak). *Dangerous When Wet* and *Jupiter's Darling* were produced by George Wells; *Million Dollar Mermaid* (1952), Esther's favorite, by Arthur Hornblow Jr., who had virtually no experience with musicals when he came from Paramount to MGM in the early 1940s.

Ordinarily, Esther would never have appeared in an Arthur Freed film. She was not the kind of performer to whom he would be drawn. To him, she was a decent enough actress, a passable singer and dancer, but essentially a swimming pool ballerina. Esther ended up in his productions, *Take Me Out to the Ball Game* (1949) and *Pagan Love Song* (1950) the same way Jane Powell did in *Royal Wedding*: as a replacement. *Take Me Out to the Ball Game* started as an original story idea by Gene Kelly and Stanley Donen about a trio of ballplayers—Kelly, short stop; Frank Sinatra, second baseman; and Leo Durocher, at the time manager of the New York Giants (and husband of actress Laraine Day), first baseman—who trade their jerseys for red-and-white-striped suits in off-season to work in vaudeville until they discover that their ball club, the Wolves, has been taken over by a C. B. Higgins, who happens to be a woman. Kelly envisioned Kathryn Grayson, his costar from *Anchors Aweigh*, as Ms. Higgins. Freed thought differently. In 1948, Grayson struck him as a lightweight, although after seeing her play opposite Mario Lanza in *That Midnight Kiss* (1949) and *Toast of New Orleans* (1950), he felt differently and cast her as Magnolia in his truncated version of *Show Boat* (1951).

For *Take Me Out to the Ball Game*, Freed, suspecting that the one-joke plot could not succeed on its own, wanted a forty-carat cast: Garland as C. B. Higgins, along with Kelly, Sinatra, and Betty Garrett as another man-hungry female, this time setting her sights on Sinatra. Since Durocher could never have managed the musical numbers, Jules Munshin, who had appeared in the New York production of *Call Me Mister* (1946) with Garrett, inherited the part of first baseman Goldberg. Durocher would have been out of his element in "O'Brien to Ryan to Goldberg," in which the three enact a double play in a restaurant, doing everything from step dancing and tap to stomach slides.

When *Take Me Out to the Ball Game* was going into production, Judy was so heavily medicated that she had become unpredictable. By October 1948, just as the film was nearing completion, she had recovered, however temporarily, to start work on *In the Good Old Summertime* (1949), the musical remake of *The Shop around the Corner* (1940). *Take Me Out to the Ball Game* would have been a mistake for Judy; only those with overreaching imaginations would find her convincing as a ball club owner. *In the Good Old Summertime* was her kind of film; she could be funny and poignant, even dance around the floor singing Eva Tanguay's declaration of insouciance, "I Don't Care." Both films made money. *Take Me Out to the Ball Game* earned $4.344 million; *In the Good Old Summertime*, $3.534 million. *In the Good Old Summertime* may be lesser Garland, but *Take Me Out to the Ball Game* is lesser Freed, Kelly, and Sinatra.

As Judy's replacement, Esther was worked into the script and, because of her already established screen persona, had to be given one swimming scene, in which she sang the title song. It was an unhappy experience for practically everyone. Kelly did not consider Esther an equal and treated her accordingly. He was used to working with Judy, Rita Hayworth, Vera-Ellen, and Kathryn Grayson. To him, Esther was just a swimmer, although to her credit she was perfectly credible as Ms. Higgins. Esther brought a naturalness to all her roles; one might be able to dismiss the plot but not her performance. In *Dangerous When Wet*, you believed she was a farmer's daughter from Arkansas; in *Easy to Wed*, a pampered heiress; in *Neptune's Daughter*, a swimming star about to enter the swimwear business. In *Take Me Out to the Ball Game*, Esther wore the period costumes well and behaved with enough self-assurance to show that she was perfectly capable of running the ball club she inherited. Esther also knew it was Kelly's picture when he sang and danced "The Hat My Dear Old Father Wore on St. Patrick's Day." In a gray-and-white-striped jacket, a white turtleneck, and matching pants, he did everything from an Irish jig in which his legs barely seemed to leave the floor, often with one behind the other, and a George M. Cohan imitation with legs apart and body thrust forward, to a tap routine and even a march that began slowly and ended with a patriotic flourish. He seemed so miraculously loose, even though the ease with which he danced was the result of intense discipline. The chemistry between himself and Esther was what one would expect of two ill-suited professionals;

they smile and even kiss in the fade-out, but that is what the script called for, and that is what they delivered.

The finale is a vaudeville sketch, "Strictly U.S.A.," in which Kelly and Sinatra, dressed in identical blue jackets, white pants, and red-and-white-striped bow ties, simplified the denouement: "Sinatra gets Garrett, / Kelly gets Williams, / For that's the plot the author wrote, / So we'll turn this duet / Into a quartet / And end on a happy note." Garrett comes on, dancing a jig; Esther joins her, blending in easily with three extraordinary dancers. The four of them look as if they could have played the Orpheum circuit. At the end, it is evident from the red, white, and blue costumes and Roger Edens's lyrics celebrating the Fourth of July, apple pie, hot dogs, little red schoolhouses, circus parades, and ice cream cones that "Strictly U.S.A." and the film itself are a tribute to both the Great American Pastime and an America where a woman can own a ball club, ballplayers can be vaudevillians, a Jew can be a first baseman at the turn of the twentieth century, and anyone messing with the team gets his comeuppance.

Gene Kelly was a great artist and an equally great narcissist. Even when he had partners like Rita Hayworth, Cyd Charisse, and Vera-Ellen, he seemed to be dancing by himself. To be noticed, the partner had to muster up hidden resources to hold her own, as Leslie Caron did in *An American in Paris*. That she and the others succeeded is a tribute to their art, which had to compete with an ego in overdrive. Gene Kelly once remarked that if Fred Astaire is the Cary Grant of dance, he is the Marlon Brando. Kelly stayed within his own spotlight, expecting his partners to find their own. What he didn't realize is that when they found it—as Vera-Ellen did in *Words and Music*, Rita Hayworth in *Cover Girl*, Judy in *Summer Stock*, Cyd Charisse in *Brigadoon*—they could hold it. In their own way, they became his equal by forcing their art to reach a level that matched his.

Kelly underestimated Esther, as did Freed. Her popularity rose from twenty-fourth place in 1947 to eighth in 1949 and 1950. She even did better in Britain, where she and Bob Hope were voted the two most popular stars of 1950. Esther's popularity meant little to Freed when he was contemplating a musical version of William S. Stone's novel, *Tahiti Landfall*, to be called *Tahiti* and filmed on location. Then the changes began: *Tahiti* became *Pagan Love Song* (1950), inspired by the title of the song that Arthur Freed wrote with Nacio Herb Brown and that Ramon Navarro introduced in *The Pagan* (1929). The Hawaiian island of Kaua'i stood in for Tahiti; the original stars went from Van Johnson and Cyd Charisse, to Howard Keel and Ann Miller, to Howard and Esther. Charisse was pregnant; Johnson was booked solid: *Mother Is a Freshman* (loan-out to Twentieth Century–Fox); *Scene of the Crime, In the Good Old Summertime, Battleground* (MGM, all 1949), *The Big Hangover*, and

Duchess of Idaho (MGM, both 1950). Keel was suited to the role of a former Ohio schoolteacher, who discovers the good life on a Polynesian island, but Ann Miller in brown body makeup as the half Caucasian, half Tahitian Mimi Bennett would have been high camp, as Freed must have realized. Keel stayed on, and with a title like *Pagan Love Song*, with its evocation of coconut trees and moonlit beaches, who would be a better costar than Esther Williams?

When Esther heard that the director would be Stanley Donen, she wanted no part of the film, citing the snide remarks she had to endure about her performance in *Take Me Out to the Ball Game*, on which Donen functioned as Kelly's assistant. Freed replaced Donen with Robert Alton, a fine choreographer with limited experience as a director. The direction was not the problem; nothing except a complete rewrite could save the film, which might have worked better as a straight romantic comedy with socially conscious overtones.

Freed was apparently fond of his "Pagan Love Song" lyrics that conjured up an earthly paradise "where moonbeams light the Tahitian sky / and the starlit waters linger in your eyes." Hearing it sung with a bit of crooning, as Keel did in the film, one can indeed envision lovers on a tropical isle at sunset. *Pagan Love Song* had a South Seas lushness that showed itself periodically in an over-plotted story that portrayed Polynesian culture as quaint. That the movie ran a mere seventy-nine minutes suggests that Freed only thought of it as a way of extending his song's longevity. If the Jerry Davis–Robert Nathan screenplay were just another variation on boy meets girl, it might have been less tedious—the boy in question being Hazard Endicott (Keel), who inherits his uncle's plantation that is in utter disrepair; and the girl, Mimi Bennett (Esther), part white, part Tahitian, who lets him think she's a servant when she really leads a charmed life. Mimi plays another trick on Hazard by inviting him to a party that he assumes is for the natives and dresses accordingly, but discovers to his embarrassment that everyone is formally attired. This is the stuff of screwball where a chance meeting turns into a romantic game, in which there can be no winner, regardless of who is ahead. Love is the great equalizer, and once Hazard realizes Mimi is not a self-effacing native, love can bloom along with the other exotic flowers on the island. The writers wanted to retain some sense of social consciousness by having Hazard adopt some Tahitian children as he grows to understand a culture that was at first alien to him. He finally decides to go native and remain in Tahiti with Mimi, who, until his arrival, was eager to leave for America. The plot had the makings of a clash of cultures film that a politically savvy director might have explored—but not in a 1950 musical, in which cultural differences (a pig given as a gift) are played for laughs.

There is a ridiculous fantasy sequence in which Hazard, hearing ethereal voices, looks up and sees Mimi in a silver bathing suit, swimming in the bubbly blue sky amid random clouds. The scene shifts to an island grotto, with Mimi rising out of the water like a sea goddess, draped in shimmering chiffon. Surrounded by her handmaidens, she lip-synchs "The Sea of the Moon" to Betty Wand's vocal ("Come with me to the sea of the moon / To the sea that was named for the moon."). She then plunges into the water, swimming amid coral and lush vegetation, as Keel sings the title song. He tosses a coin into the water, which she retrieves. (The coin bit was a reenactment of their first meeting when Hazard thought Mimi was a non-English-speaking native in need of loose change.) Hazard—or rather Keel's double, as the long shots indicate—dives off the cliff and joins Mimi/Esther in the water. She does a backstroke as he swims toward her, both of them behaving as if they would rather be recumbent on land. At the end he holds her up triumphantly, her body pressing against his, as he kisses her welcoming lips. "The Sea of the Moon" with its sappy lyrics that made little sense was deleted after a preview, but can be seen when the film is aired on Turner Classic Movies.

Whether the sequence, which took place in Hazard's imagination, was an attempt at high art that turned into high kitsch or had some deeper meaning (his succumbing to the island's sensuality as embodied by Mimi) is hard to determine, especially since Keel had the same perplexed look at the end of the fantasy that he had at the beginning. If this was an attempt to suggest that the combined forces of Mimi and Tahiti had an unsettling effect on him, leading to sexual culture shock, it succeeded, but only for those who interpreted Keel's puzzled expression as a metaphor for the Western mind forced to confront a culture that stirs up emotions which had previously lay dormant.

Keel had another such fantasy in the eighty-minute *Texas Carnival* (1951), in which he imagined Esther swimming about his bedroom in a diaphanous negligee that looked as if she had nothing on underneath. Screenwriter Dorothy Kingsley, who also wrote the original story, was aware of *Pagan Love Song*, which was a minute shorter than *Texas Carnival*, and knew that, in the absence of any physical attraction between the leads, the movie needed a shot of sex, as if Ann Miller belting out "It's Dynamite" while dancing on a xylophone was not enough.

When Esther was making *Neptune's Daughter* (1949), she was well aware of Annette Kellerman (1887–1975), the Australian English Channel swimmer, but had not seen the 1914 movie of the same name, to which MGM's film owes nothing but the title. There was little any screenwriter could do with a plot that had Kellerman playing a sea deity's daughter, appropriately named Annette (no one even bothered to come up with a mythological name), who uses a magic shell to transform herself into a mortal so she can avenge the death of her younger sister. She falls in love with the man supposedly responsible for her sister's death, who is really a king in disguise. When the shell breaks, Annette realizes she cannot return to her kingdom beneath the sea and decides that being a queen on earth is better than being a goddess full fathoms five. As hokey as the plot seems, *Neptune's Daughter*, filmed in Bermuda at a cost of about $50,000, proved a hit with audiences, who were fascinated by Kellerman's swimming, just as a later generation was by Esther's.

Kellerman also had a body that she was not averse to baring—and did in *The Daughter of the Gods* (1916), in which she played Anitria, the title character, whose nemesis is the Witch of Badness (there is a corresponding Witch of Goodness, à la *The Wizard of Oz*), who will bring the sultan's dead son back to life if he helps her destroy Anitria. Again, no one cared about the fairy-tale plot; the main attraction was a nude Kellerman with her long hair strategically arranged. When Esther played Kellerman on the screen in *Million Dollar Mermaid* (1952), there was about as much exposed flesh as the Production Code allowed, which was very little.

Since Kellerman's life was lacking in drama, the water ballets had to outdo anything yet seen on the screen, and with Busby Berkeley in charge, they were. The plot is the usual triumph over disability tale with the young Kellerman overcoming rickets by learning to swim and then going on to become a champion swimmer, who caused a scandal when she wore a one-piece bathing suit. Kellerman meets and falls in love with promoter James R. Sullivan (Victor Mature), but theirs was a rocky relationship, far different from that of the historical Kellerman and Sullivan, who married in 1912 and remained together for sixty-three years, he predeceasing her by six days in October 1975. In the film, Annette has an accident on a soundstage that leaves her hospitalized with a broken back, so that the film can end with a bedside reconciliation.

There actually was such an accident, but not as depicted in the film. In early February 1914, Kellerman was in Bermuda giving an exhibition in a tank filled with eight thousand gallons of water when the glass suddenly cracked, leaving her with a severe spinal cord injury and a prognosis that her career was over. She proved the doctors wrong by continuing to swim and making five more movies between 1916 and 1924. Sullivan obviously visited her during her hospitalization, but there was no reconciliation since there was never a breakup. He and Kellerman had been married for two years when the accident occurred.

To evoke the ambience of a Kellerman performance, Berkeley went from his usual excess to surfeit. Jets of pink-colored water shoot upward and then subside, revealing clouds of red and yellow smoke billowing in the background. Women slide down chutes straddled by men, passing between their legs and into the pool. A crowned Esther in a red bathing suit slides down a ramp and into the water, with the men swinging on trapezes and dropping into the pool. And as the pièce de la résistance, Esther, hoisted up on a ring above the swimmers, who have formed a wheel with their bodies, dives into their midst, emerging on a glittering platform—a triumph of sublime glitz and a testament to Esther's ability to display her art in all its glory and maintain a radiant smile under circumstances that would have taxed a mere mortal. But she was, as the title indicated and as the public acknowledged, a million-dollar mermaid.

Less gaudy but more impressive athletically was the Cypress Gardens waterskiing spectacle in *Easy to Love* (1953). Usually, Esther's character is manipulated by one patriarchal male, but as Julie Hallerton in *Easy to Love*, she is besieged by three: her employer Ray Lloyd (Van Johnson), who, when she isn't performing in the Cypress Gardens aquacade, is forced to pose for ads and function as his secretary; her costar Hank (John Bromfield), who wants both of them to get out of the water and relocate in his home state of Texas; and "charm boy" singer (Tony Martin), who envisions Julie as a Broadway attraction. Masochist that she is, Julie chooses her slave master employer, which is inevitable since Williams and Johnson had paired off in three other films, *Thrill of a Romance* (1945), *Easy to Wed* (1946), and *Duchess of Idaho* (1950). But it's also the kind of movie in which no one is left without a partner: Her roommate and fellow performer (Edna Skinner) gets Hank, and the singer spots an attractive brunette in a bathing suit and immediately makes a play for her. The brunette is the unbilled Cyd Charisse, who had been married to Tony Martin since 1948 and remained his wife until her death in 2008 at the age of eighty-seven. It was a lovely *entre nous* touch in a film that is chiefly remembered for the finale, a water skiing sequence that could never have been staged at Cypress Gardens but only through the combined efforts of the second unit director and editor Gene Ruggiero, who had to forge a sense of continuity from the scenes of the skiers engaged in different formations and activities. Esther, all in pink with scarf flying behind her, skis down a ramp and into the water, joined by men behind her in V-formation. The swimmers grow into teams, often resembling human flotillas, which, when filmed from on high, seem to span the entire body of water. The swimmers, especially Esther, maneuver around jets of water that suddenly gush forth, but mermaids never show discomfort or fear, and Esther kept her smile intact, even with a sprayed face.

The finale of *Easy to Love* required another feat of fearlessness, as Esther was hoisted up by a helicopter, kicking off her skis and grabbing on to a ring before taking the great plunge. It was Esther holding onto the ring, all right, but it is not Esther doing the diving. Pregnant at the time, Esther insisted that

Berkeley, who choreographed the sequence with considerable help from Robert J. Eastman, the aquatic technical advisor, use her double, Helen Crelinkovich, who in long shot looked so much like Esther that the result was a perfect match cut: a close-up of Esther about to dive, followed by a wide shot of the dive. Helen was rewarded, thanks to Esther, who insisted she be paid $3,000 for each take. Helen made $9,000 for about a minute of screen time.

Although Cyd Charisse had opportunities at MGM to display her dramatic side, Esther did not until she left the studio and did *The Unguarded Moment* (1956) at Universal-International. The film originated as a script entitled "Teach Me to Love," written by C. A. McKnight (pseud. Rosalind Russell) and Larry Marcus in 1951. Influenced by *The Accused* (Paramount, 1948) in which Russell's close friend, Loretta Young, played a psychology professor who befriends a troubled student and then kills him in self-defense when he tries to rape her, Russell and Marcus created a similar character, Lois Conway, a high school math teacher, harassed by a student who convinces the authorities that she is pursuing him.

As the years passed, Russell triumphed on Broadway in *Wonderful Town* (1953) and then became occupied with bringing Patrick Dennis's *Auntie Mame* to the stage in 1956. Marcus and Herb Meadow took over the script and retitled it *The Unguarded Moment*. Russell received story credit under her own name, and Lois Conway (Esther) became a music teacher. The plot, considerably more violent, has Lois contending with a potentially lethal student (John Saxon), the school's top athlete, whose misogynistic father (Edward Andrews) is unmasked at the end as a rapist-murderer. Lois believes the student can be rehabilitated, even after a near rape and rumors that the two are lovers. When the father targets Lois as another of his victims, she is saved by a quick-thinking police lieutenant. The student is rid of his lunatic father, who dies of a heart attack, and Lois gets the lieutenant. Although *The Unguarded Moment* disappointed some of Esther's fans who were used to her in a bathing suit, she did remarkably well, particularly in the scene when the father bolts out of the closet while she is undressing and attempts to do to her what he had done to others. At least Esther proved to herself, and those willing to overlook the absence of a petal-strewn pool, that she was indeed an actress.

Her films are often shown on Turner Classic Movies where they attract a new generation of viewers, who never experienced the art of synchronized swimming and water ballet. Despite a stroke in 2007, Esther Williams did not rage against the day but went gentle in her sleep in 2013 at ninety-one.

- 13 -

EXIT ALL

Screenwriter-producer George Wells thought Marge and Gower Champion had the makings of a dance team on the order of Fred Astaire and Ginger Rogers. Believing he could elevate the Champions from supporting cast to leads, he fashioned a screenplay for them with a title that came from a popular Burton Lane and Harold Adamson ballad, "Everything I Have Is Yours." The title has a double meaning. The Champions play a dance team making their Broadway debut. Every time Marge develops a symptom, the hypocondriacal Gower does, too—except that he cannot become pregnant, as he discovers Marge is when she collapses after a triumphant opening night. The run continues with the understudy (Monica Lewis), while Marge retires to Connecticut to raise their daughter. While Marge is tending to the garden, the understudy is making a play for Gower. Sensing competition, Marge expresses a desire to return to show business, only to encounter flack from Gower. Determined to show her rival that she still has star power, she dances across the patio as if it were a stage, at one point high-stepping on the wall in the film's best number, "Derry Down Dilly" by the two Johnnys, Green and Mercer. Unable to resolve the career vs. marriage dilemma, the couple begin divorce proceedings just as Marge is out of town with a new show that is foundering. In true Hollywood fashion, Gower comes to the rescue, joins the company, and what was half becomes whole again.

Wells, who also produced *Everything I Have Is Yours* (1952), was familiar enough with the Champions' professional life to incorporate some of it into the script. Partnership always played a role in their careers. Gower started out as part of a team, Gower and Jeanne (Tyler), making their film debut in a musical short, *Projection Room* (1939). Gower and Jeanne soon went their separate ways, with Gower arriving on Broadway in the revue, *Streets of Paris* (1939), with a cast that included the comedy team of Bud Abbott and Lou Costello and Carmen Miranda, the "Brazilian bombshell," both of whom made their movie debuts the following year—Abbott and Costello in Universal's *One Night in the Tropics*, Carmen in Twentieth Century–Fox's *Down Argentine Way* (both 1940). Next came a small part in a forgettable musical,

The Lady Comes Across (1942), which lasted a mere three performances. Since revues were popular at the time and always in need of good dancers, Gower went immediately into *Count Me In* (1942), which starred Jean Arthur and ran longer: fifty-one performances.

Gower met Marge (née Marjorie Belcher) in 1945 when she was on Broadway in *Dark of the Moon* under the name of Marjorie Belle. He sensed he had found a team mate, something Jeanne Tyler never was. He and Marge formed a supper club act, Gower and Bell. Marge preferred "Belle" for the stage, appearing under that name as the lead dancer in the much underrated Duke Ellington musical, *Beggar's Holiday* (1946). Once they married in 1947, they were always known as Marge and Gower Champion until their divorce in 1973.

The first few years of their marriage were hectic. Gower had already become bicoastal. He had a bit part in *Rhapsody in Blue* (Warner Bros., 1945) and danced with Cyd Charisse in the "Smoke Gets in Your Eyes" sequence in *Till the Clouds Roll By* (1946). Apparently, no one at MGM knew what a potent combination they had in Gower and Cyd. But Gower was meant for Marge, and Cyd for Astaire and Kelly.

In 1946, Gower did not believe his future lay in Hollywood. He had not gotten Broadway out of his system and never would. When it came to theater, Gower was more interested in choreographing and directing than performing. He choreographed the musical revues *Small Wonder* and *Lend an Ear* (both 1948)—the latter, a personal triumph for Carol Channing, who achieved stardom the following year as Lorelei Lee in *Gentlemen Prefer Blondes* (1949).

Wells introduced enough personal material into *Everything I Have Is Yours* to make it an alternate version of the Champions' own story, which, minus the specifics, was the familiar Broadway to Hollywood journey; in *Everything I Have Is Yours*, it's from supper clubs to Broadway, doing the same act on a bigger stage for more money. It wasn't quite than smooth, but who cared? The film might have worked better if Wells had stuck more closely to the facts. The Champions sensed their future lay in the movies, appearing together for the first time in the Bing Crosby musical, *Mr. Music* (Paramount, 1950), which brought them to MGM, a better fit, where they were supporting cast until *Everything I Have Is Yours*. Elevating their status was one thing; starring them in a clichéd musical that perpetuated all the myths naïve moviegoers have about Broadway was something else. Any stage revue that had as many pedestrian numbers as *Everything I Have Is Yours* would have closed out of town. There was no evidence in the film that anyone in the cast could have moved on to Broadway, except the Champions. Even though Gower and Nick Castle staged the dance sequences, only one, "Casbah," evidenced the kind of sophistication for which revues were famous. "Casbah" was a spoof of *Algiers* (1938), with

Marge as a bespectacled tourist wandering around the ancient part of Algiers, when a black shirted Gower, evoking Charles Boyer's Pepe le Moko, encircles her, as she grows more uninhibited, keeping the same innocent face, while her body yields to a rhythm she had never felt back home.

"Casbah" did not redeem the film, which tanked at the box office. The $1.46 million production lost $458,000. The title song, the best known in the film, is sung once by Monica Lewis and danced by the Champions amid swirling smoke as Marge's character fantasizes about a reunion with her husband.

Although the Champions ended up starring in *Give a Girl a Break* (1953), that was never MGM's intention. The musical had been planned as a vehicle for a formidable quartet: Judy Garland, Fred Astaire, Gene Kelly, and Ann Miller—someone's idea of a dream cast, probably Arthur Freed's—in 1949 or 1950. Even if the four were available, they would have canceled each other out unless the roles were equally apportioned, and the musical numbers staged so that no one usurped the spotlight. Billing aside (alphabetical order would have solved the ego problem), circumstances arose that conspired against such a production. Garland left MGM after *Summer Stock* (1950); Astaire was occupied with *The Belle of New York* (1952) and later *The Band Wagon* (1953); Miller, with *Lovely to Look At* (1952) and *Kiss Me Kate* (1953). Kelly was a possibility since *Brigadoon* (1954) was still a year away. But the story line would have to be revised if Kelly were to star. Even if some form of planetary alignment allowed the film to be made with that cast, it would have been an Arthur Freed production. Who else could have brought it off? It would also have been more lavish than the scaled-down entertainment it became.

When *Give a Girl a Break* was released in December 1953, Debbie Reynolds was not a major star. She was third billed after the Champions—first Marge, then Gower. And yet *Give a Girl a Break* is *her* movie. In the best number, "In Our United State," set in MGM's idea of New York's Central Park, Reynolds and Bob Fosse—he as a moonstruck lover, she as his spunky intended—added some impressive athleticism to a courtship ritual, with Fosse's doing a back flip, and Reynolds a somersault, as they hoofed away into the night, which ended with Fosse falling into the lake. That number alone makes the movie worth viewing, along with the finale in which Reynolds dances with Gower Champion—no mean feat. Reynolds, who had now danced with Gene Kelly, Donald O'Connor, Bob Fosse, and Gower Champion, would never have such partners again. In fact, Reynolds would only appear in a few more musicals (*Athena, Hit the Deck*, and *The Unsinkable Molly Brown*, for which she received an Oscar nomination). By reinventing herself as an actress specializing in romantic comedy but also capable of doing a serious movie when the opportunity arose (e.g., *The Catered Affair, The Rat Race*), she had a much longer career than any of her MGM peers.

In *Give a Girl a Break*, two newcomers (Reynolds, Helen Wood, later known as the notorious porn queen Dolly Sharp) and one former star (Marge Champion) are up for the lead in a "new musical review [*sic*]." One expected Marge to outshine them as the former dancing partner of the director (Gower), who left the business and is now prepared to return. A two-year absence from the stage means she must audition for the part. There was no way Marge Champion, then thirty-one, could look like Reynolds and Wood, who were nine and thirteen years younger, respectively. Marge looked her age; in short, she was no "girl." Her designer wardrobe and beauty parlor hairdo gave her the aura of a Broadway diva with a Park Avenue penthouse. (Unlike the others, she takes a cab to the audition.)

The plot took on some unusual permutations. First, Wood gets the lead, relinquishing it when she becomes pregnant (no eyebrow raising; she's married). Marge is clearly not right for the part, which eventually goes to Reynolds, who scores a sensation, as if there was any doubt. *Give a Girl a Break* is noteworthy for another reason: Before she became a porn star, Helen Wood had featured roles in the Broadway musicals *Gentlemen Prefer Blondes* (1949), *Seventeen* (1951), and the historic 1952 revival of *Pal Joey*. In 1952, Wood's star was in the ascendant. She was named one of *Theatre World*'s "most prominent personalities of the stage," along with Audrey Hepburn, who made her Broadway debut in *Gigi* (1951). Wood was also an amazing contortionist, as she demonstrated scarily in *Give a Girl a Break* when she lifted a leg above her head. There seemed no end to her talents. She was an accomplished violinist and a ballerina. She appeared in Las Vegas, in stage shows at the Roxy and Radio City Music Hall, and on *The Ed Sullivan Show*. Although stardom eluded her, she never lacked for work. Her last Broadway credit as Helen Wood was in *Ziegfeld Follies of 1957*, in which she was billed as "Dancer," "Singer," and "The Girl"; her last film credit as Helen Wood was "Minsky Girl" in *The Night They Raided Minsky's* (United Artists, 1968).

Beginning in 1970, the former Helen Wood was known as Dolly Sharp after she answered an ad for "adult film" performers. Helen Wood would have balked at having sex on camera, but Dolly Sharp had no qualms about it. After her days in "adult films" were over, her career ended, and her life went into free fall. In 1998, she died of colon cancer at sixty-three.

One wishes *Give a Girl a Break* would be remembered as the only time Debbie Reynolds danced with Bob Fosse and Gower Champion, instead of the movie debut of the fresh-eyed Helen Wood, who bore a resemblance to the young Mitzi Gaynor, and turned to hardcore when she could have been a lady of the chorus, if nothing better materialized.

Give a Girl a Break was a box office failure, resulting in a loss of $1.156 million. It was obvious that the Champions' name could not sell a movie. After

Jupiter's Darling (1955) and *Three for the Show* (Columbia, 1955)—the latter, a musical remake of *Too Many Husbands* (Columbia, 1940) with Betty Grable and Jack Lemmon—the Champions returned to Broadway in the revue, *3 for Tonight* (1955), with Harry Belafonte, which only lasted for eighty-five performances.

For Gower, it was not the beginning of the end, but the end of one career and the beginning of another. Gower established himself as a major Broadway director with *Bye Bye Birdie* (1960), with its extraordinary "Telephone Song" sequence, as teenagers in bedroom cubicles phoned each other. You never thought about choreography, only the energy emanating from that honeycombed set. Gower achieved his greatest Broadway success with *Hello, Dolly!* (1964), which provided Carol Channing with her best role. There was a string of misses (*The Happy Time, Sugar, Mack and Mabel*), until he made a spectacular return to Broadway in 1980 with the stage version of the Warner Bros. classic, *42nd St.* (1933). Diagnosed with a rare form of blood cancer, Gower was determined to have the show ready for its opening on August 25, 1980. Gower Champion died earlier that day, as producer David Merrick announced at the curtain call to a stunned audience and a devastated cast that had not been informed.

Marge also found a new life after Hollywood. Among her other accomplishments was teaching Maureen Stapleton how to dance in the television movie *Queen of the Stardust Ballroom* (1975). In 2001, at age eighty, she appeared on Broadway in a revival of Stephen Sondheim's *Follies*. Despite Gower's preeminence as a choreographer and director, Marge had the satisfaction of knowing that, when they were a team, it was always Marge and Gower Champion, not the reverse.

Nineteen fifty-five was a crucial year not just for Esther Williams, Howard Keel, and the Champions but also for the leads—Jane Powell, Tony Martin, Vic Damone, and Ann Miller—of *Hit the Deck*, released in early February. After almost a decade at MGM (1946–1955), Powell left the studio. *Hit the Deck*, however, was not her last musical. She went over to RKO for its last film, *The Girl Most Likely*, shot in 1956 and released through MGM in 1958 after RKO ceased production. Except for Gower Champion's choreography, *The Girl Most Likely* had a generic, but decidedly non-MGM, look.

The studio also bid adieu to Tony Martin, who appeared regularly in Twentieth Century–Fox musicals in the 1930s and intermittently in MGM's between 1941 and 1955 (*Ziegfeld Girl, Till the Clouds Roll By, Easy to Love*, and *Deep in My Heart*). His acting was rudimentary, although he was convincing as a sleazy nightclub singer in *Easy to Love* (1953). It was also the end of Vic Damone's brief hour, which concluded with *Kismet*, released eight months after *Hit the Deck*. Neither Martin nor Damone was what one would call a movie star. Martin made a number of hit records ("To Each His Own," "It's Magic," and especially "There's No Tomorrow") and had a successful nightclub act with his wife, Cyd Charisse. Vic Damone had a major recording career before his film debut in *Rich, Young and Pretty* (1951). He continued making records after he left MGM ("On the Street Where You Live" made the top ten) and appeared frequently on television and in Las Vegas.

Since MGM was no longer making the kind of musical that allowed Ann Miller to tap up a tempest, she, too, was about to exit. Miller made two more movies before leaving the studio. First, was *The Opposite Sex* (1956), a quasi remake of that classic of feline feminism, *The Women* (1939). What was unusual about the original is that it lived up to its title: There was not a male in the cast. One had to imagine the character of the philandering husband who cheats on his model wife (Norma Shearer) with a crass gold digger (Joan Crawford). In *The Opposite Sex*, the wife is now a former singer (June Allyson), whose husband (Leslie Nielsen) is all too visible. Ann was fifth billed without an opportunity to do a single tap. Even more sobering was that Ann Sheridan, once a major Warner Bros. star who began in the business in1934, was fourth billed after newcomers Joan Collins and Dolores Gray. After *The Opposite Sex*, Sheridan worked sporadically in television. In 1966, CBS offered her a series, *Pistols 'n' Petticoats*, in which she starred until she died of cancer the following year.

Ann Miller's fans would rather forget that in her last MGM film, *The Great American Pastime* (1956), she played a widow eager to get her son into the local Little League. Again, not a single tap. Miller had more success—television; tours, especially in Cole Porter's *Anything Goes*; and finally Broadway, when she replaced Janis Paige (who replaced Angela Lansbury) in the musical *Mame*, with a tap routine added for her fans. Miller's greatest post-Hollywood triumph was also on Broadway in *Sugar Babies* (1979), in which she and Mickey Rooney recreated classic sketches from vaudeville and burlesque for audiences who either had never encountered that kind of entertainment or wished to relive it. *Sugar Babies* played for over one thousand performances at New York's long-gone Mark Hellinger Theater. Although Miller and Rooney did not sign on for the entire run, the show still drew audiences eager for a taste of yesterday. Miller was one of the cohosts of MGM's *That's Entertainment! III* (1994) and returned to the screen one last time as Naomi Watts's landlady in David Lynch's mind-teasing *Mulholland Drive* (Universal, 2001). Ann Miller, too, died of cancer in 2004.

At least Miller had a decent part in *Hit the Deck*, although why MGM decided to dredge up a property that had already gone through several iterations is hard to fathom. Since it was a Joe Pasternak production, the producer may have felt he needed an extravaganza to compensate for the public's indifference to *Athena*. *Hit the Deck* was not the answer. Neither a critical nor a commercial success, it, too, failed at the box office. Budgeted at $2.3 million, it incurred a loss of $454,000.

What became the Broadway musical *Hit the Deck* (1927) began as Hubert Osborne's *Shore Leave* (1922), the story of lonely dressmaker and a sailor that was staged by David Belasco and premiered at New York's Lyceum Theater on August 8, 1922. A movie version with Richard Barthelmess and Dorothy Mackaill arrived three years later. Osborne's plot remained pretty much intact. Mackaill played Connie Martin, the daughter of a deceased sea captain, whose ship had capsized somewhere in South Asia. Desperate to have it restored so that the sailor (Barthelmess) she loves can have a ship of his own, she manages to have it brought back to New England. Knowing only that the sailor's name is "Bilge" Smith, Connie celebrates the arrival of the refurbished ship by staging a party for all sailors named "Smith," hoping that the love of her life will be among them. When "Bilge" and Connie connect, he assumes that she is flaunting her wealth to snare him until he learns the truth, which is the only way this improbable yarn can end happily.

Vincent Youmans and his librettist Herbert Fields thought *Shore Leave* had the makings of a musical, which it did, although not a great one. *Shore Leave* spawned *Hit the Deck* (1927), whose score included two perennials, "Sometimes I'm Happy" and "Hallelujah!" The story line remained the same, except that Connie was renamed Loulou, the owner of a dockside cafe in love with "Bilge" Smith, who is averse to commitment and leaves her with a parrot that motivates the song "Lucky Bird." Fields replaced the abandoned ship with a bejeweled elephant pendant that Loulou sells for enough money to pursue Bilge to China for some second-act chinoiserie. When Loulou locates Bilge, his pride prevents him from marrying a wealthy woman until she informs him that her money is in trust for her first child, provided the child bears the name of "Smith." The revelation bolsters his ego. In effect, Bilge is marrying a trust fund, but after two and a half hours, few theatergoers would have questioned the implications of such a union.

For what was basically an average Broadway musical, *Hit the Deck* proved eminently adaptable, inspiring a 1930 RKO movie of the same name, with Jack Oakie as Bilge and Polly Walker as the rechristened Looloo, who now runs a diner and remains stateside. Although Looloo does not take a side trip to China, she still sells the pendant so she can buy a ship for Bilge, who initially is too proud to accept her gift but then relents. Some of the songs from the original made it to the screen ("Sometimes I'm Happy," "Harbor of My Heart," "Join the Navy," and of course, "Hallelujah"), others were dropped ("Lucky Bird," "Why, Oh Why?") and new ones added ("Keepin' Myself for You," "An Armful of You," and "Nothing Could Be Sweeter"). Critical indifference did not deter audiences seeking light entertainment in a year that would not inspire anyone to shout, "hallelujah!" *Hit the Deck* made a profit of $145,000, not bad for 1930.

Since RKO owned the rights to *Hit the Deck*, it was determined to extend its shelf life—not as the Youmans original or even as the 1930 movie, but as one with a vaguely similar plot: *Follow the Fleet* (1936) with Fred Astaire and Ginger Rogers, singing and dancing to a score by Irving Berlin. The screenplay by Allan Scott and Dwight Taylor preserved the maritime setting of Osborne's play, but without the characters' names, which would be ill suited to America's newest dancing team. There was no way that Astaire could play someone nicknamed "Bilge." Astaire and Rogers are now "Bake" Baker and Sherry Martin, a former dance team. "Bilge" and Connie Martin survive as the names of the secondary characters, Randolph Scott as Bake's best friend and Harriet Hilliard as Sherry's sister, whose thorny romance parallels that of "Bake" and Sherry. Astaire and Rogers perform the final number, "Let's Face the Music and Dance," with such romantic fatalism that, except for the battleship setting, they seem to have stepped out of *Follow the Fleet* and into another, more sophisticated musical.

RKO was not finished with *Hit the Deck*. In 1941, the studio announced a remake with Ray Bolger, whose lovably goofy Scarecrow in *The Wizard of Oz* would have made him the perfect "Bilge" Smith. And if Ann Miller would sign on as Connie/Loulou/Looloo, the two stars, both superb dancers, would have been a vast improvement over Jack Oakie and Polly Walker. For some reason—World War II, perhaps—the remake never materialized, and never would, at least at RKO. In 1947, RKO, having no further use for *Hit the Deck*, sold the rights to MGM. Nineteen forty-seven would have been the right year for a remake; MGM had stars of the caliber of Judy Garland, Peter Lawford, Gene Kelly, Mel Tormé, June Allyson, Van Johnson, Gloria DeHaven, and Vera-Ellen under contract. But MGM looked elsewhere for musical properties until early 1953 when the studio announced that Martin Racklin and Herbert Baker had been assigned to write the screenplay for a *Hit the Deck* update.

In 1953, MGM could no longer boast of having more stars than there are in the heavens, at least not in the musical galaxy. Judy Garland had left the studio; followed by June Allyson a few years later. "JUNE ALLYSON QUITS M-G-M," a *Los Angeles Examiner* headline (May 1, 1953) announced. Allyson stressed that she was not leaving because she was dissatisfied with her roles or her salary. She was more specific when she told the *LA Daily News* (June 29, 1953) that "MGM was my home for 10 years . . . I've made some very good friends there—lifetime friends—but staying too long in one place can result in everyone taking you for granted." Instead, the paper reported that she would be going to Universal-International for *The Glenn Miller Story* (1954) opposite James Stewart, who had also left the studio to have the freedom to pick and choose his own projects. Thus Stewart could return to MGM for *The Naked Spur* (1953) and Allyson for *The Opposite Sex* (1956).

Esther Williams was swimming her last laps; and Lucille Bremer had danced her last dance with Fred Astaire in *Ziegfeld Follies* and made her last musical appearance in *Till the Clouds Roll By* (1946). Before she retired from the screen in 1948, she appeared in four melodramas, *Dark Delusion* (1947), the last of MGM's Dr. Gillespie series, as an heiress whose mental stability is questionable. *Dark Delusion* gave Bremer her first dramatic role; it was also her last film for MGM, which satisfied its contractual obligations by loaning her to Eagle-Lion for three films: *Adventures of Casanova* (1947); filmed in Mexico which would soon become Bremer's new home; Edgar G. Ulmer's *Ruthless* (1948), in which she showed a genuine flair for melodrama, particularly when she mocks her husband (Sydney Greenstreet) because of his obesity, pointing to his image in a full-length mirror; and Budd Boetticher's *Behind Locked Doors* (1948), her last film, in which she had top billing as a reporter out to expose a former judge posing as an inmate in a mental institution. Although Lucille Bremer's movie career only lasted four years—six, if you count *Penny Arcade*, a short she made in 1942—she had no intention of returning to Broadway, where she started, or continuing in B movies on Poverty Row. Instead, she married a Mexican millionaire and died in 1996 at seventy-nine.

Vera-Ellen's last MGM musical was *The Belle of New York* (1952), her second pairing with Fred Astaire. It was not a milestone for either of them and may rank as Astaire's weakest. It was a *Guys and Dolls* knockoff, with Vera-Ellen as a stand-in for Sarah Brown, beating her drum and shaking her tambourine as a Daughter of Right, a street corner evangelist, whose mission is neither woman suffrage nor salvation, but an excuse for an encounter between her straight-laced self and playboy Astaire. Since Arthur Freed's big 1952 musical was *Singin' in the Rain*, he may have had little interest in *The Belle of New York*, which cost $2.5 million and lost $1.57 million. For an Arthur Freed production, only the costumes had a genuine turn-of-the-twentieth-century look. Otherwise, it was soundstage New York. Freed thought little of the film, which only ran eighty-two minutes and, in the absence of anything resembling a plot, was filled with such gimmickry as Astaire dancing on ledges and at one point atop the Washington Square Arch that looked like the mockup it was. Even Astaire believed the Washington Square Arch number, "Seeing's Believing," was a failure in terms of both photography and story line. Astaire and Vera-Ellen performed a delightful but totally unmotivated Currier and Ives salute to the seasons with the two even skating in waltztime in the winter segment. Although her voice was dubbed by Anita Ellis in "Naughty but Nice," Vera-Ellen proved she could still kick a mean leg. But it was Astaire who saved a minor musical from oblivion with Johnny Mercer and Harry Warren's "I Wanna Be a Dancin' Man," turning it into a personal statement: "I wanna be a dancin' man / While I can, / Gonna leave my footprints on the sands of time." He was the ultimate "dancin' man," whose every step spelled "class" in all caps. He sang Johnny Mercer's lyrics with a casualness that implied his dancing was effortless, although his fans knew he was demonstrating the art of concealing an art.

To compensate for the slim plot and the low-tech special effects in *The Belle of New York*, including the final scene in which Astaire and Vera-Ellen defy gravity and float into space, the stars did some elegant if decidedly impersonal dancing. Only once in her career did Vera-Ellen explode in sensuality: when she danced "Slaughter on Tenth Avenue" with Gene Kelly in *Words and Music*. Her response to Rodgers's feverish score and Kelly's sexually charged movements allowed her to play a lady of the streets as if her usual stand was against a lamp post. Her perfectionism and discipline turned sleaze into art and sex into sensuality, so that the ballet was not so much erotic as sexy. Sexy, Vera-Ellen could manage; the erotic, she left to Cyd Charisse.

While Vera-Ellen enjoyed working with Kelly in *Words and Music* and Astaire in *The Belle of New York*, she believed she was at her best in *Call Me Madam* (Twentieth Century–Fox, 1953), in which she and Donald O'Connor (an astonishingly good dancer) partnered in Irving Berlin's "Something to Dance About," an evocation of young love in a movie that had nothing to do with it. She and O'Connor danced around a pool like two young people discovering the poetry of first love and expressing it not in verse, but in dance— O'Connor looking like a kid in his first tux at the senior prom; Vera-Ellen, resplendent in a white gown, alternately kittenish and teasing, and at one point supporting herself on one leg and extending the other behind her in a perfect arabesque. "Something to Dance About" represented the fusion of Broadway and ballet, beginning as highly refined ballroom dancing and ending in exquisitely choreographed courtship, reminiscent of the halcyon days of Astaire and Rogers.

Vera-Ellen departed MGM after *Big Leaguer* (1953), her only nonmusical, in which she played Edward G. Robinson's niece and appeared perfectly comfortable in a role that did not require her to sing or dance. She then freelanced, first in *Call Me Madam*, then in her best-known movie, *White Christmas* (Paramount, 1954) with Bing Crosby, Rosemary Clooney, and Danny Kaye, and finally in *Let's Be Happy* (Allied Artists, 1957) with Tony Martin, in which she looked unhealthily thin. Vera-Ellen did not enjoy a serene retirement. Plagued by anorexia and later arthritis, and severely depressed by the death of her infant daughter, she succumbed to cancer at age sixty in 1981.

That left Kelly, Astaire, and Charisse, who, when their dancing days were over, proved that they could do straight acting in both film and television. Since Charisse had already acted in several MGM dramas (*East Side, West Side, Tension, The Wild North*), she had no problem giving her legs a rest after *Silk Stockings* (1957), her last screen musical. She was still available; if a musical came along, all the better. Charisse often toured in musicals but never played Broadway until 1992 when, at seventy, she replaced Lilliane Montevecchi in *Grand Hotel*. Kelly played Father "Chuck" O'Malley on ABC-TV's *Going My Way* (1962–1963) in the role created by Bing Crosby in the film of the same name. Kelly then tried his hand at directing: Rodgers and Hammerstein's *The Flower Drum Song* (1958) on Broadway; and the films *Gigot* (1962), *A Guide for the Married Man* (1967), *Hello, Dolly!* (1969), and *The Cheyenne Social Club* (1970). Astaire was the host and sometimes star of ABC's *Alcoa Premiere* (1961–1963) that showcased his acting skills, which were rarely utilized in Hollywood. He was a Golden Globe nominee for *On the Beach* (1959) and an Oscar nominee for *The Towering Inferno* (1974). Although their post-MGM work was hardly their most memorable, Charisse, Kelly, and Astaire achieved longevity in a business in which forty marks the onset of old age.

None of them, however, would have been right for *Hit the Deck*, which Pasternak desperately wanted to make in the old MGM tradition—top-tier stars in a high-class production in CinemaScope and Eastman Color. Filming *Hit the Deck* in wide screen and color was not a problem; casting it with big names who had the youthful ebullience the movie needed was. Pasternak only had Jane Powell for the role of Susan Smith, formerly Connie/Loulou/Looloo/Sherry. Since the script now revolved around three couples, one more than *Follow the Fleet*, he needed a costar for Powell and for each of the other performers. Names started appearing in the trades; under consideration were George Murphy, Vera-Ellen, and Bobby Van. Murphy, then in his early fifties, had left MGM after *Talk about a Stranger* (1952) and would have been out of place in a film where the accent was heavily on youth, unless he played somebody's father. Vera-Ellen was then at Paramount, making *White Christmas*. On the other hand, if Bobby Van could hop down streets on a pogo stick in *Small Town Girl*, he might be a sprightly sailor. But that did not happen. For a while, it even seemed that Powell might have to be replaced.

When news leaked out that Powell was carrying on a not-so-private affair with Gene Nelson, whom she met while they were making *Three Sailors and a Girl* (Warner Bros., 1953), Powell was between marriages, while Nelson was still married but in the midst of a divorce. MGM panicked, temporarily dropped Powell, and began testing a bevy of unknowns, including Ann Crowley, who may have been an unknown in Hollywood, but not on Broadway, where she had appeared as Laurey near the end of the run of *Oklahoma!* and replaced Jan Clayton as Julie Jordan in *Carousel*. Next, she took over the role of Jennifer Rumson from Olga San Juan in Lerner and Loewe's *Paint Your Wagon* and starred as Lola Pratt in the musical version of Booth Tarkington's *Seventeen* (1951). Crowley was a lyric soprano with impeccable diction, whose voice had an endearing quality well suited to Youmans's score. But that was not enough to get her the role. After Nelson's divorce went through, he and Powell chose not to marry, leaving the scandal mongers with no gossip and MGM with no reason to replace her. That so much time and effort was spent on casting a minor musical was typical of Hollywood at sunset, proving that even studio executives lead lives of quiet desperation.

Sonya Levien and William Ludwig replaced Racklin and Baker as the screenwriters of the reconstituted *Hit the Deck* (1955), which bore no resemblance to either the 1927 musical or the 1930 movie. Since the story line had been expanded from a one- to a three-couple romance, there was no way MGM could assemble an A-list cast. B was the best it could manage, particularly since the musical contingent had seen its share of attrition and defection. The *Hit the Deck* update was not about a sailor and a dressmaker/waitress/ cafe or diner proprietor but about (1) Susan and Danny Smith (Jane Powell and Russ Tamblyn), the daughter and son of Rear Admiral Smith (Walter Pidgeon), and their problems, domestic and romantic. The admiral expects Danny to uphold the family tradition and enroll at West Point after his discharge from the navy; Susan is determined to become a musical comedy star, even if it means auditioning for a womanizing producer (Gene Raymond) in his hotel suite; (2) Danny, on shore leave, is immediately smitten with Carol Pace (Debbie Reynolds), who is rehearsing for the producer's new musical appropriately called *Hit the Deck*, while Danny's friend Rico (Vic Damone) is equally taken with Susan; (3) Chief Boatswain's mate, William Clark (Tony Martin), is trying to avoid marriage to Ginger (Ann Miller), a nightclub performer to whom he has been engaged for six years. When Danny learns about his sister's unorthodox audition, he and his friends rough up the producer who presses charges but later withdraws them for fear of his wife's learning about his philandering. The admiral sighs, "Hallelujah!"—the cue for the finale, which the cast performs on the deck of a battleship—a stirring climax without any connection to the plot.

Since Levien and Ludwig added a subplot (a florist's courtship of Rico's widowed mother) to their already crammed screenplay, Pasternak came up with the idea of casting another pop singer, Kay Armen, as the widow. The multitalented Armen was both a singer and composer, known to radio audiences for her fifteen-minute show on NBC Blue (which became ABC in 1945), and to early television viewers for her appearances on ABC-TV's *Stop the Music.* Although *Hit the Deck* was Armen's film debut, most moviegoers would have recognized her name.

Billing in *Hit the Deck* had less to do with order of importance than with contract stipulations and MGM's idea of who ranked where in the popular hierarchy. Jane Powell and Tony Martin headed the cast, followed by Debbie Reynolds (third billed again), Walter Pidgeon, Vic Damone, Gene Raymond, Ann Miller, Russ Tamblyn, J. Carol Naish, and "Introducing Kay Armen." Pidgeon's days costarring with Greer Garson were over, and his few scenes could have been played by anyone able to affect an air of gravitas. That Raymond should be billed above Miller when he had so little screen time may have been the studio's way of bolstering the sagging career of an actor better remembered as Jeanette MacDonald's husband than for any of his films.

Not all of the songs from the original made it to the screen. "Lucky Bird," "Join the Navy," "Looloo," "Why, Oh Why?" and "Sometimes I'm Happy" did. And, of course, "Hallelujah!" without which *Hit the Deck* would not be *Hit the Deck*. "Hallelujah!" is performed twice—once, as Tamblyn juggles eggs, while he, Martin, and Damone clean up the kitchen; and again in the battleship finale. Powell sings "Lucky Bird," the least memorable song in the show, to a toy penguin that replaced the parrot in the original. Reynolds performs "Looloo," never much of a song, in the rehearsal scene.

Levien and Ludwig were obviously thinking of Nathan Detroit and Miss Adelaide from *Guys and Dolls* when they created the characters of William Clark and Ginger, who is pressing her "fiancé" to put a ring on it after a six-year engagement. Martin and Miller behave very much like the reluctant Detroit and the marriage-minded Adelaide in *Guys and Dolls*, except that, unlike Adelaide, Ginger is not prone to allergies. But when Clark finally proposes, it is to the romantic ballad "More Than You Know," an interpolation from *Great Day* (1929). Powell's "Sometimes I'm Happy" is remarkable for her thoughtful phrasing of the lyrics, especially the dilemma of being caught "between the devil and the deep blue sea." Another interpolation, "I Know That You Know," was introduced by Beatrice Lillie in the stage revue "Oh, Please" (1926). Lillie played with the lyrics, but Powell and Damone sang them straight, turning a snappy song with repeated notes ("I know that you know / That I'll go where you go") into a literal statement of shared devotion. Miller was given a sizzler, "Lady from the Bayou," turning on the heat in a sparkling low-cut red outfit that gave her legs enough room for kicking and teasing men in blue T-shirts who collapse in exhaustion, as if felled by her awesome power.

While "Hallelujah!" was conceived as the grand finale, sung by the entire company, with Miller tapping in and out of rows of sailors, the most memorable moment in *Hit the Deck* is Kay Armen's rendition of a song that was not written by Youmans: "Chiribiribin." As Damone plays the accordian, Armen with her mellow contralto turns what in the past was a showpiece (compare Grace Moore's semi-operatic delivery in *One Night of Love* (Columbia, 1934) into a folk song about a gondalier and his beloved, as the couples—Powell and Damone, Miller and Martin, and Reynolds and Tamblyn—waltz around the living room. It was a short-lived moment in an anxiety-ridden story that made one realize that singers like Kay Armen, whom the public took for granted, were really artists working under the radar. Like "Let's Face the Music and Dance" in *Follow the Fleet* (1936), "Chiribiribin" seems to belong in another musical, perhaps an unmade Mario Lanza one with an Italian setting, but not in *Hit the Deck*, however welcome.

Pasternak would make a few more musicals (e.g., *Billy Rose's Jumbo* [1962], *Girl Happy* [1965]), none of which had much distinction. With a cast headed by Dan Dailey and Cyd Charisse, *Meet Me in Las Vegas* (1956) seemed the exception until the film began to roll. Then it was apparent it was a high-concept ode to Las Vegas, specifically to the mob-financed Sands Hotel, then Frank Sinatra's and the Rat Pack's playground. If LasVegas had become a fabled kingdom in the desert, the story that transpired there was equally fabulous. It was a place where prima ballerina Maria Corvier (Charisse) and rancher-gambler Chuck Rodwell (Dailey) could work out an arrangement where she would spend six months touring the world's capitals, and six as Mrs. Rodwell at his Nevada ranch. The term "magic realism" was not yet in vogue, but the plot depended heavily on it. Discovering that he can win at roulette every time he holds Maria's hand, Chuck is convinced that she is his lucky star. When she visits the ranch, chickens that never laid eggs do so in profusion; a cow, supposedly ill, gives birth; and oil gushes forth from a hole in the ground. Chuck's winning streak peters out when Maria's manager (Paul Henreid) arrives and joins them at the roulette table. And when it seems that the two will go their separate ways, a reconciliation occurs behind Maria's dressing room door, a convenient way of ending the tedium without increasing the 112-minutes running time. The film is worth seeing for Charisse, who had been a member of the Ballet Russe de Monte Carlo and whose dancing en pointe makes it clear she could have become the world-class ballerina she portrayed if she continued in professional ballet. To dance lovers, she was a star, even though she only had leading roles in *Brigadoon*, *Meet Me in Las Vegas*, *It's Always Fair Weather*, and *Silk Stockings*.To others, she was supporting cast with the longest legs in film. And to moviegoers with an aversion to musicals, she was a convincing dramatic actress. But little in *Meet Me in Las Vegas* was worthy of her; it was the kind of movie in which Frank Sinatra and Peter Lorre pop up in cameos; and Lena Horne, Jerry Colonna, and Frankie Laine appear at the Sands' Copa Room. The film might have worked with Fred Astaire as Rodwell, but Dailey with his broad grin seemed more like a big brother than a potential husband. That left Cyd to hold up the musical end in a hip version of "Frankie and Johnny" with updated—and now just dated—lyrics by Sammy Cahn, sung by the cool cat himself, SammyDavis Jr.

By the end of the 1950s, there was a final blaze of glory, *Gigi*, followed by a few adaptations: *Bells Are Ringing, Billy Rose's Jumbo*, and *The Unsinkable Molly Brown*. MGM had pretty much ignored the classic Broadway musicals: Twentieth Century–Fox released *Gentlemen Prefer Blondes* (1953), *The King and I* (1955), *Carousel* (1956), *South Pacific* (1958), and *Can-Can* (1960); Warner Bros., *The Pajama Game* (1957), *Damn Yankees* (1958), and *The Music Man* (1962); Universal, *The Flower Drum Song* (1961) and *Sweet Charity* (1969); Columbia, *Pal Joey* (1957) and *Bye Bye Birdie* (1963); Samuel Goldwyn, *Guys and Dolls* (1955), distributed by MGM.

The year 1955 was critical for the stars of *It's Always Fair Weather*, an ironic title for a downbeat musical that starred three extraordinary dancers—Gene Kelly, Dan Dailey, and Michael Kidd—appearing together for the first and only time. It was also Kelly's last dance-driven musical. *Invitation to the Dance* (1956), in which Kelly functioned as both director and star, may seem the exception. However, *Invitation to the Dance* was ready for release in 1952, but MGM, suspecting it would be a prestige film but a financial flop, kept delaying until, finally, in May 1956, it became a question of then or never. Ballet lovers adored it, but the public did not, and the film lost a whopping $2.5 million.

Invitation to the Dance consists of three stories told solely in dance (there were originally four) with Kelly appearing in each of them with such renowned ballet dancers as Igor Youskevitch and Tamara Toumanova, "The Black Pearl of Russia." In "Circus," with music by Jacques Ibert, Kelly makes his first appearance in a white costume and black skullcap, looking like Marcel Marceau. He is the Pierrot figure, a soulful clown in white face and painted lips, forced to play the fool. At the end of *The Pirate*, Kelly and Judy urged the audience to "be a clown" because "all the world loves a clown." The world indeed may, but Pierrot pines for his Columbine; and this circus clown pines for a fellow performer in love with a tightrope walker (the great Youskevitch). Since Kelly walked a tightrope in *The Pirate*, it was a feat that he could negotiate. In "Circus," the clown tries, balancing himself with outstretched arms as he inches his way along the high wire. Unlike Kelly, the clown is not an aerialist.

"Circus" was a response to Cole Porter's "Be a Clown" that promises comics in baggy pants will find romance and a buffoon will make the ladies swoon. Pierrot plays the clown and experiences only disappointment; when he ventures out of his element, he encounters death. "Circus" proved that Kelly was a master of mime, an art that he had little opportunity to display, although one can see hints of it in the *American in Paris* ballet. Kelly may have been a stern taskmaster who suffered neither fools nor folly. But he was also the greatest dancer in film history.

"Ring around the Rosy"—the second story in dance with music by André Previn, who wove dissonant fragments of the nursery rhyme into the orchestration—was inspired by Arthur Schnitzler's *La Ronde*, with its round of seductions. Here, it is a bracelet, a husband's gift to his wife, that keeps changing hands until it reverts to the husband, who gives it back to his wife. "Ring around the Rosy" features some accomplished ballet dancers—Youskevitch, Toumanova, Diana Adams, and Tommy Rall. Kelly only danced the minor role of the marine, but he had the opportunity to partner with Toumanova as a prostitute. By this time, the marine is in possession of the bracelet, which he gives to the prostitute for services rendered. Their brief dance recalls "Slaughter on Tenth Avenue" with Toumanova, sinuous and leggy, using her body to suggest her profession in case her rose-colored shirt and dark-red dress, appropriately slit up the side, failed to make the point. But she did not mind taking a walk on the wild side, a far cry from the world of classical ballet, and raising a leg that may not have been as long as Cyd Charisse's but registered the same effect.

The final sequence, "Sinbad the Sailor," set to the music of Nicolai Rimsky-Korsakov's *Scheherazade*, is a clever amalgamation of live action and Hanna-Barbera animation, with Kelly as a sailor who buys a magic lamp, rubs it, and finds a genie whom he makes into an alter ego, a boy in a matching sailor suit. Here, Kelly dances with his younger self, unlike the spectral image he sees of himself in the "Alter-Ego Dance" in *Cover Girl* (Columbia, 1944).

There are two outstanding sequences in "Sinbad the Sailor," the first of which is Kelly's dance with an animated Scheherazade to the music of "The Young Prince and Princess," the third movement from Rimsky-Korsakov's symphonic suite. The animators superimposed the movements of Carol Haney, a fine dancer and Kelly's assistant on the film, on to Scheherazade. Kelly and Haney/Scheherazade capture the onrush of sudden attraction as they glide across the screen, and at times are transported to the heavens. The wittiest is Sinbad's encounter with an animated dragon, who is not the retiring kind like the one in Disney's *The Reluctant Dragon* (1941). In *Anchors Aweigh*, Kelly danced with Jerry, the animated mouse from the *Tom and Jerry* cartoons, but here it is just himself and the dragon, who, we discover, is female. When the dragon encoils Kelly with her tail, the genie charms her with a flute, causing her to become coquettish, fluttering her eyelashes and going into an exotic dance, with Kelly as partner. But the dragon is best doing her own thing, and is so delighted at having an audience that she goes back up the winding path to her lair, waving a last good-bye. It was a charming end to a film that is to dance what *Fantasia* (Disney/RKO, 1940) is to music. *Fantasia*, a flop in its day, is now regarded as a masterpiece. But *Invitation to the Dance* is an all but forgotten film. It is available in its entirety on YouTube, and balletomanes should not miss the opportunity to sample this relatively unknown masterpiece by an artist, who despite his ego, which was warranted, and his perfectionism, which could irk those who found it excessive, was a genius when it came to the art of the dance. In "Circus," he left no doubt that he could easily have become a ballet dancer as he performs half turns and jumps with his fellow clowns; and in "Sinbad," that he could even get a dragon to behave like one of the girls.

If Kelly was testy during the filming of *It's Always Fair Weather*, which ruptured his friendship with director Stanley Donen, it was partly due to his realizing that, by October 1954, when the film went into production, MGM had still not released *Invitation to the Dance* and perhaps never would. Because it was *his* film, he must have inquired, but in 1954, MGM was under new leadership, and Dore Schary was not Louis B. Mayer, who loved musicals. Schary preferred issues movies like *Bad Day at Black Rock* (racial prejudice that leads to murder) and *The Blackboard Jungle* (teaching in the urban trenches). Kelly, then forty-two, knew he had not changed, but MGM had. The musical had become obsolescent. After *It's Always Fair Weather*, he would star in one more musical, *Les Girls*, in which he did some dancing, but not the kind for which he was famous. And the title implied that he was not the film's centerpiece.

It's Always Fair Weather was not a pleasant experience for Kelly. For the first time, he was dancing with two extraordinary men, one of whom was an award-winning choreographer. It was not like dancing with Sinatra and Munshin in *On the Town*, in which he had the best numbers. Dan Dailey, known for his Twentieth Century–Fox musicals with Betty Grable (*Mother Wore Tights*, *When My Baby Smiles at Me*, *My Blue Heaven*, *Call Me Mister*), had a two-picture deal with MGM (the second was *Meet Me in Las Vegas*). He, too, was nearing the end of his musical career. From then on, it would be straight acting. One would rather remember Dailey in *It's Always Fair Weather* than in his last musical, the flaccid biopic *The Best Things in Life Are Free* (Twentieth Century–Fox, 1957), the flip side of *It's Always Fair Weather*, both of which revolved around trios (former army buddies in the one, songwriters in the other) and the tensions that can either doom or alter such relationships. *The Best Things in Life Are Free* was inspired by the songwriting and music publishing team of Ray Henderson (Dailey), Buddy DeSylva (Gordon MacRae), and Lew Brown (Ernest Borgnine). Although MacRae was top billed, Dailey had a few numbers to himself ("Lucky Day," "You're the Cream in My Coffee") and a duet with MacRae ("Button Up Your Overcoat"). Dailey could share the spotlight with Betty Grable, Ethel Merman (*There's No Business Like Show Business* [1954]), and even with James Cagney in the *What Price Glory?*

remake (1952), but had difficulty holding his own with MacRae and Borgnine, who had the meatier roles.

Michael Kidd—one of Broadway's greatest choreographers, as anyone who saw the original productions of *Guys and Dolls* and *Can-Can* can attest—made his film debut in *It's Always Fair Weather*. Believing, as did Kelly, that dance is a form of storytelling, Kidd turned movement into characterization in *Seven Brides for Seven Brothers*, in which mountain men, in town for a barn raising, beat out their rivals for the local girls by engaging in some exuberantly virile dancing that seemed totally natural, as if dance was another way of socializing. In both the stage and screen versions of *Guys and Dolls*, "Luck Be a Lady" begins as a craps game in a sewer, starting as stylized movement and swelling to a feverish climax with the gamblers moving around restlessly as if they cannot wait to see what the throw of the dice will bring. Kidd knew how to translate the kinesis of dance into story.

Betty Comden and Adolph Green regarded *It's Always Fair Weather*, originally intended for the stage, as the continuation of, not the sequel to, their 1944 Broadway show and 1949 movie, *On the Town*, in which three sailors on a twenty-four-hour leave have a series of adventures in New York before returning to their ship the next morning. The three may have been close friends in the service, but would they feel the same about each other as civilians ten years later? That was the question posed in *It's Always Fair Weather*. The innocence of *On the Town* had dissipated; innocence had yielded to experience, optimism to cynicism.

In the prologue, three recently discharged GIs—Ted Riley (Kelly), Doug Hallerton (Dailey), and Angie Valentine (Kidd)—celebrate in a Third Avenue bar on October 11, 1945, vowing to meet there again on the same day in ten years when each will have fulfilled his dream: Doug, a famous painter who had studied in Paris; Ted, a lawyer; and Angie, a master chef at a four-star restaurant. Historically, much had happened in the intervening decade. The movie industry and the State Department were being purged of so-called Communist subversives; the Korean War ended in an armistice, proving that unconditional surrenders went out with World War II; the Cold War kept heating up and cooling down; television had replaced movies as the mass medium; Dore Schary had replaced Louis B. Mayer at MGM, signaling the gradual deemphasis on musicals in favor of message pictures; the dance cards of Gene Kelly and Fred Astaire only had a few signatures; Cyd Charisse decided to wait until her contract expired, knowing that it would not be renewed; and the Freed Unit was good for a few more pictures before it shut down.

It's Always Fair Weather is not exactly musical noir (Martin Scorsese's *New York, New York* [1977] deserves that title), but it did address subjects more suited to drama (the fraying of friendships, marital unhappiness, fight fixing) than musicals. After the prologue, the years fly by in a typical montage until it is October 11, 1955. When the three return to the bar, the owner does not recognize them. They have all changed. Doug, the would-be Picasso, creates ad campaigns that are unworthy of him; Ted has forsaken law for the rackets and is now managing a boxer, Kid Mariacchi, who has been paid to throw a fight; Angie, the only one married with children, confines his cooking to his roadside diner pretensiously called Le Cordon Bleu. They barely recognize each other. Doug has grown a mustache and acts like a big spender; Ted is dressed like a promoter; and Angie, who has come down from Schenectady, New York, behaves like a tourist. An attempt to cheer up the despondent Ted, who has received a "Dear John" letter from his fiancée, is just an excuse to bond over booze, as if alcohol can restore their wartime friendship. The drinking spree ends with their monopolizing the street and dancing in, on, and out of taxi cabs. One could argue that the sequence is a representation in dance of their inebriated state. But it's really a showcase for three dancers in peak form. On the other hand, if three drunks prevented you from hailing a cab, you would be too frustrated to find their antics humorous. But a musical is not life, but a simulacrum of it, an alternate world where speech is song, mobility is dance, eccentricity is normality, and liberty is license. If seven men abducted seven women in real life, a manhunt would have ensued, and the perpetrators prosecuted. In *Seven Brides for Seven Brothers*, the men are "lonesome polecats" looking for wives and regard kidnapping as the equivalent of a hasty courtship.

There is a strained alliance of music and story in *It's Always Fair Weather*. Sometimes they're in synch, as in the "Blue Danube" parody. Doug, the most successful of the three, invites the others to lunch at a posh restaurant, where it dawns on them how little they have in common. Each expresses his inner thoughts to the music of the "Blue Danube Waltz." Ted is first, mimicking the opening five notes with "I shouldn't have come." Angie thinks similarly ("This thing is a frost."), as he bites into a celery stalk. Doug regrets inviting a "crook" like Ted and a "hick" like Angie to a restaurant where he is known ("This thing's a bad dream.").

When it's time to pick up the story, Comden and Green tie together two seemingly unrelated plot threads—a fixed fight and the 1950s version of reality TV—whose interconnection allows for a few numbers that are not wholly out of place, but not as seamlessly integrated as those in *Singin' in the Rain* and *Seven Brides for Seven Brothers*. Ted and Angie are introduced to Doug's world, when they are invited to a rehearsal of a television show, *Midnight with Madeleine*, sponsored by Kleezrite, a detergent for which Doug has created the commercial. *Midnight with Madeleine* was a send-up of *This Is Your Life*, which premiered in 1952, hosted by Ralph Edwards, who would come up to a person, usually a celebrity, and announce, to his or her amazement (and sometimes embarrassment), "This is your life." If the guest of honor was not in the studio, he or she would be escorted there and asked to identify the offstage voices of friends recalling incidents from the past. The program had a bogus sincerity, but audiences loved it, and it stayed on the air for nine seasons.

Midnight with Madeleine works from the same premise. Some unsuspecting audience member, usually with a hard-luck story, is spotlighted and forced to endure Madeleine's (Dolores Gray) unctious condescension. Program co-ordinator Jackie Leighton (Cyd Charisse) decides that Ted, Doug, and Angie would make perfect surprise guests, unaware of their abortive luncheon. Cyd, as a woman with an encyclopedic mind and a trove of boxing trivia, has her only opportunity to display her classy legs when she accompanies Ted to a gym where Kid Mariacchi is training. The setting explains the number, "Baby, You Knock Me Out," which makes it seem that every time Cyd/Jackie enters a gym, she goes into a dance. Dressed in a form-fitting green sweater and long skirt, she offered another exhibition of disciplined dancing, throwing baby punches and reveling in being the only woman in a man's world. Cyd Charisse had one last moment of screen glory in her best film, *Silk Stockings* (1957), which gave her a chance to act and sound more Russian than Garbo in *Ninotchka*.

Unlike the honorees on *This Is Your Life*, who, if they felt uncomfortable about the hoopla, behaved otherwise, Ted, Doug, and Angie want no part of a show that peddles phony humanitarianism. Their refusal to play the game turns into unscripted TV, which reaches a new level when the mob barges in, intending to make Ted pay for knocking out Kid Mariacchi to prevent him from throwing the fight. Realizing that Ted is in danger, Jackie instructs the camera operator to focus on the mob leader (Jay C. Flippen), making him part of the telecast, so Ted can trick him into disclosing information about the fix in an on-air confession. A happy ending, perhaps, but at the fade-out, Ted and Jackie go off in one direction, Doug and Angie in another. A second reunion? Not very likely. Christmas cards, maybe.

It was courageous of Arthur Freed to produce an antimusical with characters that are either career-driven (Jackie, Doug, Madeleine), careerless (Ted), or career-deprived (Angie). To compensate for a story in which no one is especially empathetic, Kelly, the codirector and star, went for bravura, performing "I Like Myself" on roller skates—which may not have topped sloshing around in the rain and holding on to a lamp post with one arm and brandishing an umbrella in the other, but it came close. The number was not so much motivated as occasioned by Ted's ducking into a roller rink to avoid the mobsters. When the coast is clear, he skates onto the street, at times gliding on one leg with the other behind him like a figure skater. He even tap dances on skates. Ted—really Kelly—shamelessly plays to the crowd that has gathered, even though his hogging the street forces drivers and pedestrians to fend for themselves. If a song title could characterize a singer, "I Like Myself" characterized Gene Kelly.

The one solo Kidd had, "Jack and the Space Giants," was deleted at Kelly's insistence, despite Donen's urging that it be kept. Donen, who directed *Seven Brides for Seven Brothers*, knew that the barn-raising sequence, carefully choreographed by Kidd, was the film's highlight, and believed that audiences deserved to see Kidd in performance. A space-age retelling of Jack and the Beanstalk, in which Kidd danced out the story in front of three children (who did not look amused), would have been out of place in a movie about broken dreams, hypocrisy, and fight fixing. Viewers can decide for themselves; it is included as an outtake on the *It's Always Fair Weather* DVD and adds nothing to the plot, except ten minutes. Kidd could have been asked to come up with a new idea, perhaps a fantasy in which he is a chef in a French restaurant, which at least would have been in character. To Kelly, Kidd may have been a newcomer, but to theatergoers and balletomanes, he was a star. Kidd danced the lead in Aaron Copland's *Billy the Kid* and was one of the sailors in Leonard Bernstein's ballet, *Fancy Free*, the precursor of *On the Town*. He received a Tony for the first musical he choreographed, *Finian's Rainbow* (1947), and a second for *Guys and Dolls* (1950). Kidd was every bit Dailey's and Kelly's equal when they danced with one foot under the handle of a trash-can lid or performed a soft shoe with lighted cigarettes as they meditated on dreams that went up in smoke ("Once upon a Time").

Kelly could not keep Dailey, second billed, from having a solo, "Saturation-Wise," which spoofs the way "-wise" had become an all-purpose suffix. The events of the day—the disastrous reunion, his wife's filing for divorce, a lucrative but dead-end career—have become too much for Doug, who gets drunk at his boss's dinner party and launches into "Saturation-Wise," an eruption of self-loathing that is quite the opposite of the self-enraptured "I Like Myself." Mocking advertising jargon and trashing the living room, he ruins the party. Any boss would not only have fired him but also sued for damages. But this is a musical, albeit a sour one, and Doug is too talented an ad man to let go. And no one would fire Dan Dailey, another case of an actor who can play an unlikable character and at the same time endear himself to audiences because of his "nice guy" persona.

It's Always Fair Weather cost $2.771 million and lost $1.675 million. The profitable musicals of 1955 were light-hearted: *Daddy Long Legs* (Twentieth Century–Fox), *My Sister Eileen* (Columbia), *Guys and Dolls* (Goldwyn), and *Oklahoma!* (Magna). There was also a problem with André Previn's score, which had no memorable songs. "The Time for Parting" with its friends-to-the-end theme came close but could not compete with the familiar classics from *Guys and Dolls* and *Oklahoma!* and the Oscar-nominated "Something's Gotta Give" from *Daddy Long Legs*. Perhaps *It's Always Fair Weather* would have worked better as a stage musical. Theatergoers can accept a show about unsympathetic characters. Cynicism pervades *Pal Joey* (1940), whose title character is a heel and a boy toy. Stephen Sondheim's *Sweeney Todd* ran for 557 performances during the 1979–1980 season. The movie version was a failure. Moviegoers prefer popcorn to meat pies made of human flesh.

Les Girls (1957), Kelly's last MGM musical, was also a financial disappointment, despite its creative team. John Patrick wrote the screenplay from a story by Vera Caspary, whose only contribution was the title. The producer, Sol Siegel, had been at Twentieth Century–Fox before coming to MGM in 1956, the year Dore Schary was fired. Upon his arrival at MGM, he commissioned the same writer-composer team of John Patrick and Cole Porter, who contributed to the success of his production of *High Society* (1956), expecting that their script and score—along with Gene Kelly and (originally) Cyd Charisse, Leslie Caron, and Carol Haney as "Barry Nichols and Les Girls"—would ensure another hit. That was not the case. Kelly was the constant; les girls were the variables. The original choices—Charisse, Caron, and Haney—either proved unavailable or unacceptable, even though, as professionals, they could all have adapted to Jack Cole's choreography.

Except for Kelly and the director, George Cukor, there was little about *Les Girls* that suggested it was an MGM musical. Cukor was MGM's premier director, whose films included such classics as *Camille* (1936), *The Women* (1939), *The Philadelphia Story* (1940), *Gaslight* (1944), and *Adam's Rib* (1949). Although musicals were not Cukor's forte, he directed the musical remake of *A Star Is Born* (Warner Bros., 1954) from Moss Hart's screenplay with its unsentimental depiction of the ebb and flow of stardom (husband falls while wife rises). *A Star Is Born* was essentially a drama with music, just as *Les Girls* was an epistemological comedy about a dance troupe, one of whose members, now a peer's wife, publishes a memoir that leads to a libel suit. Like Akira Kurosawa's *Rashomon* (1950), which presents three conflicting accounts of a murder, *Les Girls* operates on the same "What is truth?" premise. In her memoir Lady Sibyl Wren (Kay Kendall in the role that may have been intended for Cyd Charisse or perhaps even Jean Simmons) wrote that Angèle (Taina Elg in the role intended for Leslie Caron) attempted suicide out of unrequited love for Nichols (Gene Kelly in a role intended for no one but himself) by trying to asphyxiate herself. Angèle takes the stand and swears that it was really Lady (then just Sibyl) Wren, who tried to end her life that way. Finally, Nichols testifies, claiming that a loose connection in the heater was the culprit and that both women would have died of carbon monoxide poisoning if he had not broken into the flat and saved their lives. Whether Nichols has told the truth or lied to save the reputations and marriages of his two "girls" is never resolved. In the final shot, a man wearing a "What Is Truth?" sign walks into the frame, signaling "The End." At least in *Rashomon*, the woodcutter, the sole witness to the event, explains what actually happened, which is far from a simple case of rape and murder and, in fact, is downright ludicrous.

Although Cukor would later direct one of the world's best-loved musicals, *My Fair Lady* (Warner Bros., 1964), a brilliant stage-to-screen transplant, he was primarily interested in the development of Patrick's script, which posed two intriguing questions: Is truth relative, absolute, or indeterminate? And is testimony under oath any guarantee of veracity? No musical ever explored such issues. Patrick's screenplay did not go into the deeper implications of the event remembered vs. the event itself; or the event itself vs. the event mythologized. When Pilate asked Christ, "What is truth?" (John 18:38), Christ would not answer. Nor did John Patrick.

Cukor worked well with Patrick, a well-known playwright (*The Hasty Heart, The Curious Savage, The Teahouse of the August Moon*, for which he won a Pulitzer and a Tony) and screenwriter (*Look Out, Mr. Moto, Mr. Moto Takes a Chance, High Society*). Cukor respected a well-crafted script, and that is exactly what Patrick provided with a frame narrative beginning and ending in a courtroom with three flashbacks depicting three conflicting accounts of a "suicide attempt." Cukor was especially pleased with Patrick's revision of the final testimony, "the new last episode," as he called it. Cukor was also obsessed with details. For the Paris exteriors, taxis must have false license plates, and there must be no shots of advertisements or theater marquees. Cukor looked at several theaters that would have been appropriate for Nichols's troupe and settled on the Théâtre d'Atelier in the eighteenth arrondissement.

The choice of locations was easy compared to the casting. Although *Les Girls* did not seem difficult to cast, it proved otherwise. At some point Jean Simmons was considered for the role of Lady Wren. Cukor had directed her in *The Actress* (MGM, 1953), based on Ruth Gordon's autobiographical play, *Years Ago* (1946), in which Simmons gave one of her usual vibrant performances, although perhaps not with the Yankee feistiness that the role required. Kay Kendall, the British actress who could combine whimsy and zaniness into a comedic anomaly, was eventually cast as Sibyl and walked off with the movie. Playing an alcoholic who hides liquor in perfume bottles, she does a hilarious version of the "Habanera" from Bizet's *Carmen* while in a drunken stupor. Yet Kendall was Cukor's last choice. In August 1956, Cukor was courting Gina Lollobrigida, who wired him and Siegel, "Am trying hard to be in your picture." The only role she could have played was Sibyl Wren, which would have required a name and/or nationality change, and an explanation as to how she went from Barry Nichols's lover to a peer's wife. It is tempting to envision the tempestuous Gina in the role, which would have forced Cukor to calibrate her performance, which, if left unchecked, could throw the film off balance. Gina wanted $500,000, and before negotiations had even begun, informed the Venice press that she would be in the film. At this point, the telegrams and memos cease, and the paper trail ends.

Cukor was conflicted about the French performer in the troupe, Angèle. First, it was Leslie Caron, then Jeanmaire, and finally Taina Elg, the Finnish actress and dancer who had made a strong impression in MGM's *Diane* and *Gaby* (both 1956).

That left the role of the American showgirl, Joy Henderson, once envisioned for Carol Haney, and now marked for Mitzi Gaynor. Choreographer Jack Cole had no problem with Gaynor, but for some reason, Cukor did, either because he could not imagine her as the character or regarded her as a dancer with great legs but not an actress of depth, as if any depth was required to portray a character as "normal as blueberry pie" like *South Pacific's* Nellie Forbush, which Gaynor played with bubbly ingenuousness in the 1958 movie until the plot turned serious and she did the required turnaround and proved to be a sensitive actress. Cukor, in fact, was so dead set against Gaynor, whom he had never directed, that he threatened to leave the production, only to be told that if he did, he would go on suspension.

The reason for Cukor's animus against Gaynor will probably never be known. It was not as if she were the star; hers was almost a supporting role with one good number, a take-off on Marlon Brando's biker movie, *The Wild One* (Columbia, 1954), with Kelly in a black leather jacket and white scarf, strutting into a soda fountain with his entourage. Gaynor was the waitress, who swiveled around from stool to stool, kicking up a leg in Cyd Charisse fashion that was now code for availability. Kelly sings "Why Am I So Gone about That Gal?" one of Porter's weakest lyrics, as if he were a charter member of Hell's Angels. The dancing is what mattered; Kelly choreographed the number, which allowed himself and Gaynor to return to the palmy days of the sexy pas de deux when he and his partners, Vera-Ellen in *Words and Music* and Tamara Toumanova in *Invitation to the Dance*, turned every movement into desire. But Kelly, the leader of the pack, would rather be with his fellow bikers than with a lonely waitress, whom he leaves with a white handkerchief as a memento of the visit.

Kelly had more numbers than any of the others in *Les Girls*, none of which were on a par with those in *The Pirate, Singin' in the Rain*, and *It's Always Fair Weather*. In the title song, he captured the debonair style of Maurice Chevalier, honoring the great French entertainer as well as acknowledging his own past as a song-and-dance man. Kelly was always a class act, even when he was forced to play the equivalent of a strolling player. He and Kendall had fun with "You're Just Too Too!" but the best song in the show, "Ça, c'est l'amour," is sung, or rather lip-synched, by Taina Elg to a vocal by Thora Mathison. It is a dreamier version of "C'est magnifique" from *Can-Can*, sung as Angèle and Nichols float down the Seine in a canoe—a tranquil moment in a less-than-tranquil movie.

"Ladies in Waiting" is the highlight, with Les Girls in Marie Antoinette wigs and period gowns, each with an exposed backside decorated with a bow. After enumerating the various ways they serve the king, each returns from his chamber with the bow resting in her wig. It was certainly one of the raciest bits in any musical, but Queen Elizabeth II enjoyed it immensely when *Les Girls* was screened at a royal command performance.

- 14 -

THE MUSICAL MOVIE

There is a subgenre, the reverse of the movie musical, which might be called the musical movie, in which songs were inserted into a narrative that could either have unfolded on its own with the right kind of plotting or needed a series of musical jolts to keep it from losing momentum. The former, which could have functioned just as well as a nonmusical, is rare. If anything, it would have been a "B" movie at best. It is hard to imagine most musicals commanding attention solely on the basis of their story lines. Universal's teenage musicals of the 1940s with Donald O'Connor, Peggy Ryan, Grace McDonald, Susanna Foster, and Gloria Jean—which, for contrast, also included mature performers like Allan Jones and Jane Frazee—were programmers with more music than story. In *What's Cookin'?* (1942), Donald O'Connor's first film for Universal, a group of talented youngsters are eager to break into radio. Of course, they'll succeed, but for the next seventy minutes, audiences can also enjoy performances by the Andrews Sisters, Gloria Jean, Jane Frazee, the Jivin' Jacks and Jills, Woody Herman and his Orchestra, Donald O'Connor, Peggy Ryan, and Grace McDonald tapping her way down the stairs—all of them filling in the gaps of a script whose conclusion is known from the outset. The formula was simple: If the story is weak, shore it up with music; or, the weaker the story, the stronger the musical charge.

The story line in *Variety Girl* (Paramount, 1947) was so weak that practically all the Paramount contract players had to hold it up, turning out en masse to help newcomer Mary Hatcher become a star, which, historically, never happened. After a while, it did not make any difference. You were too distracted by cameo appearances by Bing Crosby, Bob Hope, Dorothy Lamour, Paulette Goddard, Alan Ladd, Pearl Bailey, Gary Cooper, and a host of others including directors Cecil B. DeMille and Mitchell Leisen to care. Paramount even threw in a George Pal *Puppetoon* in Technicolor, *Romeow and Julie-cat*, for those suffering from star surfeit. At the end, it seems that Mary Hatcher will be a new addition to the Paramount pantheon. After *Variety Girl* was completed, Paramount loaned her to the Theatre Guild to make her Broadway debut as Laurey opposite Harold (later Howard) Keel in *Oklahoma!* toward the end of the run. Keel had a major career; Hatcher did another Broadway musical, *Texas L'il Darlin'* (1949), and made a few more films, none of them significant, before leaving Hollywood in 1952. *Variety Girl*, which was nothing other than a Paramount variety show, did Mary Hatcher a disservice. She was unquestionably talented, but setting her on the obscurity-to-fame route set her up for disappointment. In the late 1940s, Paramount was not making musicals for sopranos nor was it in the market for ingenues.

Musical sequences should either advance or enhance the plot; in *Variety Girl*, they were an excuse for one. Similarly, Paramount's *Road* movies with Bing Crosby, Bob Hope, and Dorothy Lamour were too lame to carry the weight of a plot that had the trio circling the globe from Singapore, Zanzibar, and Morocco to Alaska, Rio, and Bali. But add music to madcap—particularly Hit Parade songs like "You're Dangerous" (*Road to Zanzibar*); "Moonlight Becomes You" (*Road to Morocco*); "Sunday, Monday and Always" and "Personality" (*Road to Utopia*); "You Don't Have to Know the Language" and "But Beautiful" (*Road to Rio*)—and audiences will ignore the silly scenarios. In fact, they will get used to them and go just for the laughs and the songs. The musical movie was a Paramount specialty; the studio applied the same formula to the Dean Martin and Jerry Lewis films. Martin could sing, and Lewis could clown. What the two of them needed was a film in which they could do both, beginning with *My Friend Irma* (1949) and ending with *Hollywood or Bust* (1956), after which they went their separate ways. Elvis Presley's first Paramount film, *Loving You* (1957), only needed songs because Presley played a delivery man catapulted to fame as a country-western singer. If Presley had been unavailable, the script could have been refashioned as a nonmusical with the main character a writer, actor, or athlete—the story line being simply the discovery and exploitation of an unknown.

MGM, like all the studios, made its share of movies with slender plots hidden under layers of music. *Two Girls and a Sailor* (1944), in which two sisters working at a World War II canteen are in love with the same man, could easily have been a nonmusical. The two women/same man theme is a familiar one; the rivals can be siblings (*A Stolen Life*), cousins (*The Old Maid*), even mother and daughter (*Mother Is a Freshman*). But when the sisters (June Allyson and Gloria DeHaven) and the man (Van Johnson) can sing and dance, and MGM had Harry James and his Orchestra, Jose Iturbi, Lena Horne, and Xavier Cugat at its disposal, it was up the ante all the way. The film was a big moneymaker and is worth viewing for Lena Horne's "Paper Doll" and Allyson and DeHaven's heavenly harmonizing in "Sweet and Lovely."

It was the same with *Two Sisters from Boston* (1946), with Kathryn Grayson as an aspiring opera singer forced to make a living by performing in a Bowery saloon. Audiences expected to hear Grayson in both low- and highbrow entertainment. She obliged, but for some reason the opera selection was from the fictitious *Marie Antoinette* set to the music of Mendelssohn's Violin Concerto. The only real opera came from MGM's resident tenor, Lauritz Melchior, who sang a bit of Wagner. The film made a modest profit, but anyone expecting a full-scale musical would have been disappointed; it was another deception movie with music. *New York Times* critic Bosley Crowther devoted most of his review (June 7, 1946) to Jimmy Durante, "the funniest man in the world" who "boldly but benignly runs away with the show," implying that *Two Sisters from Boston* was designed as a vehicle for Kathryn Grayson and June Allyson, who could sing; and Durante, who could pick up the slack when the plot began to drag. You really cannot call such films musicals; they are neither song- and/or dance-driven nor show business sagas in which the production numbers do not so much advance the plot as reflect the kind of entertainment depicted in it.

If a movie is entitled *Music for Millions* (1944), the audience expects music, even though the story—a pregnant woman (June Allyson) with a husband missing in action (who turns out at the end to be alive)—could easily have been a wartime drama like *Since You Went Away* (1944), which ends with a wife's being informed that her husband, from whom she has not heard, will be coming home. But since Allyson plays a member of a symphony orchestra, the slender plot is larded with selections by Debussy, Chopin, Dvorak, Grieg, and Handel; and for less discerning tastes, Jimmy Durante singing his popular "Umbriago," about a fellow who "can make your life so mellow," very much like Durante himself. Calling *Music for Millions* a musical is like calling *Meet Me in St. Louis* a period piece with musical interludes.

MGM conceived *Living in a Big Way* (1947) as a musical movie or at least a quasi-musical. Photographed in black and white, and lacking in strong production values, *Living in a Big Way* was the flip side of *The Clock*. Imagine what would have happened if Robert Walker returned from the war unharmed and discovered that his wife, who had been a secretarywhen they married after knowing each other for only forty-eight hours, is really an heiress who wants no part of him. That is the premise of *Living in a Big Way*, another movie about a wartime romance that led to a quick marriage, after which the groom (Gene Kelly) ships out, leaving his new bride (Marie McDonald) to, presumably, continue working as a model. Upon his return to civilian life, he finds that his wife is not only fabulously wealthy but also prefers life without him. A divorce would have made sense. Kelly should have found himself a young working-class woman; and McDonald, a polo-playing lawyer. *The Best Years of Our Lives* (1947) took a far more realistic view of a marriage that was probably crumbling when the husband (Dana Andrews) went off to war and came back to find his faithless wife (Virginia Mayo) stepping out with her employer.

When Andrews meets the radiantly innocent Teresa Wright, his marriage is ready for the landfill.

But MGM was not willing to go the divorce route with Gene Kelly in the lead, his first film after being discharged from the navy. With another actor in the role, for example, Robert Walker, there would have been no need for musical numbers. But Kelly had to dance a few times—and on one occasion brilliantly, as he plays Pied Piper to a group of children at a construction site, anticipating the "I Got Rhythm" sequence in *An American in Paris*. To wrest a happy ending out of intractable material, director-coscreenwriter, Gregory La Cava, has the wife give up her selfish ways so she can be worthy of her egalitarian husband. La Cava, who made one of Hollywood's greatest social satires, *My Man Godfrey* (1936), might have hoped that *Living in a Big Way* with its skewering of the idle rich would be its companion piece. It might have at another studio, but not MGM.

After Leslie Caron became an audience favorite in *An American in Paris*, she was cast in two more MGM films in quick succession, *The Man with a Cloak* (1951) and *Glory Alley* (1952). Ideally, Vincente Minnelli should then star her in a musical, perhaps not as elaborate as *An American in Paris*. Minnelli, however, was preoccupied with *The Band Wagon*, which left the director's chair open for Charles Walters. Helen Deutsch put together a screenplay from Paul Gallico's *Saturday Evening Post* story (October 28, 1950), "The Man Who Hated People," inspired by the popular children's puppet show, *Kukla, Fran, & Ollie*, which premiered in 1948 and ran for nine seasons. It was an unusual show in two respects: like *Sesame Street*, it attracted adult viewers; it was also unscripted. Fran Allison, the host and only live member, would ad lib with the puppets voiced by puppeteer Burr Tillstrom, who made certain that whatever was "said" was in character. Kukla was a chronic worrier; Ollie, a one-toothed, non-fire-breathing dragon. Some of the others included Fletcher Rabbit, the droopy-eared mail carrier; Ophelia Oglepuss, a former opera diva; Beulah Witch; and Ollie's mother.

Deutsch kept the idea of a woman's spontaneous interaction with puppets, but created a markedly different screenplay that resulted in *Lili* (1953). Lili (Caron), a French orphan, is attracted to a magician (Jean-Pierre Aumont) on the carnival circuit, but finds employment with a misanthropic puppeteer (Mel Ferrer), who hires her because of her ability to draw crowds by singing a folk song, "Hi-Lili, Hi-Lo," and conversing with the puppets as if they were human. Audiences are fascinated by Lili's disarming way of communicating with inanimate objects that have taken on distinct personalities and voices provided by Paul the puppeteer. The puppets—a con artist fox (Reynardo), a mischievous red-haired boy (Carrot Top), a self-absorbed ballet dancer (Marguerite), and a cowardly giant (Golo)—become her family. Paul, whose dancing career was cut short by a war injury, is too consumed with self-pity to declare his love for Lili, driving her away instead. When Lili realizes that Paul is her true love and the magician, an infatuation—and a married one at that— the film gets back on the road to happiness after a detour into the crepuscular side of life.

It is difficult to think of *Lili* as a musical. If anything, it is a one-song romantic drama with two fantasy sequences. In the first, Lili imagines herself as part of the magician's act, dressed in the same red-sequined gown as his assistant, who is really his wife; in the second, Lili leaves Paul and is proceeding along a desolate road, when she imagines herself surrounded by the puppets, who keep turning into Paul. Once she understands that the song of love may be a sad song, as "Hi-Lili, Hi-Lo" maintains, but love itself is not sad, she rushes back into Paul's welcoming arms.

MGM did not hold much hope for the film; the producer was not Freed, Cummings, or Pasternak, but Edward H. Knopf, the brother of publisher Alfred Knopf, whose credits at the time consisted mostly of dramas (*The Seventh Cross; The Secret Heart; Edward, My Son; Malaya*). *Lili*'s running time, eighty-one minutes, was shorter than the usual MGM musical, but it was enough time for the story to unfold. Yet it proved to be an audience favorite, grossing $5.393 million, which is impressive for a film without major stars. Caron gave a lovely, elfin performance, for which she received an Oscar nomination. But a full-fledged musical *Lili* was not. It became one in 1961 when it was reborn on Broadway as *Carnival!* with book and lyrics by Michael Stewart and music by Bob Merrill, starring Anna Maria Alberghetti as Lili and Jerry Orbach as Paul. "Love Makes the World Go Round" replaced "Hi-Lili, Hi-Lo"; Stewart fleshed out the roles of the magician and his assistant, now his mistress, and under Gower Champion's direction, Lili and Paul emerged as wounded people who managed to heal each other through love. Late in his career, Arthur Freed contemplated bringing *Carnival!* to the screen, but it never came to pass.

The musical movie blurs the distinction between the integrated and nonintegrated musical, suggesting that the dichotomy is, for the most part, academic. In true integration, like Wagnerian music drama, the written text (libretto, book, screenplay) takes on musical life when it meshes so perfectly with the score that the two become inextricable, which is not often. Even in an opera as well constructed as Mozart's *Don Giovanni*, Donna Elvira sings her aria, "Mi tradi," in the first act in some productions; in the second act, in others. In Wagner, the wedding of libretto and score is indissoluble. A conductor can make cuts, but there can be no rearrangement. Since operas are known primarily for their music, less so for their libretti, and rarely for the synergistic union of the two, the same is true of the film musical, in which a seamless blend of screenplay and score may be something devoutly to be wished but only occasionally achieved, except in such classics as *Meet Me in St. Louis, Seven Brides for Seven Brothers, West Side Story, Oklahoma!* and *My Fair Lady*—the last three, adaptations of already integrated Broadway musicals,which in turn derived from well-crafted plays—Shakespeare's *Romeo and Juliet*, Lynn Riggs's *Green Grow the Lilacs*, and G. B. Shaw's *Pygmalion*, respectively. An integrated Broadway musical should result in a similarly integrated movie musical such as *Guys and Dolls* and *The King and I*. I once saw a production of *Guys and Dolls* at London's National Theater in the 1970s, which was like watching a play set to music. When the actress playing Adelaide sang her "Lament," she performed it as a monologue, sung softly, introspectively, but not as a showpiece, which is how it usually comes off. In the London production, the performer worked from the text to its musical setting. First the words, then the music.

In film, it is difficult to use song and dance propulsively, so that the audience thinks of them as the equivalent of narrative. One wonders, for example, how many moviegoers thought of the opening of *West Side Story* (United Artists/Mirisch, 1961) as a prologue, setting the tone for the story that follows. Usually, musical numbers are functional; they do not so much advance the plot—and, in fact, may even slow it down—as heighten it, raising it to a level higher than it would have reached otherwise. That is pretty much the case in *Anchors Aweigh* (1945), which is overlong at 142 minutes, but the musical numbers are so entertaining that they divert attention from the hackneyed story of two sailors, Joe (Gene Kelly) and Clarence (Frank Sinatra), on leave in Los Angeles, who become involved with Susan Abbott (Kathryn Grayson), a movie extra and aspiring concert artist, and her young nephew Donald (Dean Stockwell), a first grader determined to join the navy.

If non-singing actors like Tom Drake and Robert Walker had been cast as the sailors in *Anchors Aweigh*, the plot would have remained intact, but the music would have consisted of Grayson performing a few arias and José Iturbi playing some classical selections. But once MGM decided that *Anchors Aweigh* would be a traditional musical, Kelly, Sinatra, and Grayson would have to sing; Kelly and Sinatra, sing and dance; and Iturbi, play the piano and hear Susan's great voice, so that she can go professional and give up her evening job singing for enchiladas at a Mexican restaurant. The plot gets a bit complicated when Joe claims that Clarence knows Iturbi and can arrange for an audition at MGM, thus allowing the audience to see what a back lot and soundstage look like. Susan gets her audition, Joe gets Susan, Clarence gets a waitress from Brooklyn (Pamela Britton), and the audience gets to hear Iturbi play "The Donkey Serenade," Liszt's Hungarian Rhapsody No. 2, and the opening of Tschaikovsky's First Piano Concerto.

Anchors Aweigh could never have become the megahit that it did if it were merely a movie with a couple of musical numbers. With producer Joe

Pasternak's knack for bridging the cultural divide by combining highbrow (classical music) and middlebrow (popular song), *Anchors Aweigh* grossed $7.45 million. It was also released at the right time—a month before the end of World War II, when audiences wanted a feel-good movie, regardless of its length.

Anchors Aweigh is buoyantly optimistic; there are no villains, only God's helpers. There are also three outstanding sequences which are peripheral to the plot and, if excerpted, make sense on their own.

In the first, when Joe visits Donald's class, the students ask him how he received his Medal of Honor. Rather than tell them the truth, he invents a story about a mouse king who has plunged his kingdom into gloom, forbidding singing and dancing because he can do neither. The set-up was an excuse for a delightful blend of animation and live action, which originally called for Kelly to dance with Mickey Mouse. But Roy Disney, Walt's brother and the Disney Studios' unofficial CEO, did not want to lease Mickey to a rival studio. Instead, Kelly dances with Jerry, the mouse in MGM's *Tom and Jerry* cartoons, created by William Hanna and Joseph Barbera. The coordination of Jerry's movements with Kelly's is faultless. The point is that Joe won his medal by making the world dance, as did Gene Kelly.

(MGM attempted something similar in the Esther Williams movie, *Dangerous When Wet* [1953], in which Esther dreams she is swimming with Tom and Jerry, pursued by a shark, followed by sea horses, and nearly caught up in the tentacles of an octopus. The dream is symbolic; her kid sister's reference to Tom and Jerry triggers the dream, which Esther has on the eve of her swimming the English Channel. The octopus represents her suitor [Fernando Lamas], whose charm is proving a distraction. Esther manages to swim the Channel and get Lamas in both the film and real life.)

In the second, Clarence (one should really say Sinatra) is at a restaurant, meditating on the nature of love in the Sammy Cahn–Jule Styne ballad, "I Fall in Love Too Easily." In a nonmusical, it would have been a soliloquy in voiceover. Here, Sinatra sings it reflectively, but within hearing distance of a waitress from his hometown, Brooklyn. The song could easily have become a soul-searcher, except that Sinatra, who knew how to probe lyrics for their deeper meanings, realized that the context required that it be sung like a confession not meant for the ears of others but only for the waitress, as if telepathically, so that she could be introduced into the plot.

In the third, Joe spots a lonely child (seven-year-old Sharon McManus) in the square and together they perform "The Mexican Hat Dance." At first she is clumsy, but soon catches on, and the two make a delightful but short-lived couple. Since McManus could not dance, Stanley Donen was hired to teach her. It was an ordeal for both of them, but the number succeeded as a bitter-sweet interlude that left the girl as forlorn as she had been before.

The only motivated song in the film is "If You Knew Susie," which Joe and Clarence sing to Susan's prissy suitor (Grady Sutton) to dissuade him from courting her. The Breen Office was concerned that one of Eddie Cantor's sig-nature songs was "sex-suggestive." "Ask her and she won't refuse-y" must be excised. To Breen, "the song still reveals a girl who is promiscuous." Mayer would bend only so much. He retained, "She's not so choosy. / No, not our Susie." When speaking of his girlfriend, Lola, Joe sighs, "After eight months at sea, all I want to do for a long, long time is—just look at her." Breen informed Mayer that "there must be no suggestive break in the line." Some moviegoers may have dirty minds, but few could match Breen's.

Sinatra did not have as long an association with MGM as did Kelly and Grayson. Sinatra had already made *Higher and Higher* (1943) and *Step Lively* (1944) at RKO, when Louis B. Mayer heard him sing "Ol' Man River" at a ben-efit for the Jewish Home for the Aged, Mayer's sister's favorite charity. Mayer was impressed and offered Sinatra a five-year contract at $260,000 a year with a less stringent morals clause than usual to accommodate his peccadillos. *Anchors Aweigh* was his first MGM film, followed by an appearance in the finale of *Till the Clouds Roll By* (1946), in which he reprised "Ol' Man River"; the undistinguished *It Happened in Brooklyn* (1947); the ridiculed *Kissing Bandit* (1948); the entertaining *Take Me Out to the Ball Game* (1949) dominated by Gene Kelly; and the classic *On the Town* (1949). Mayer did not renew Sinatra's contract in 1950, and it was not until 1955, after Mayer had left the studio, that Sinatra returned for *The Tender Trap*, followed by *High Society* (1956), a far better film than *Anchors Aweigh* with a superior script and score. Yet *Anchors Aweigh* is more typical of the Golden Age musical in which the numbers are ornamental rather than functional. But few musicals revealed the faithful al-liance of text and music as did the best of the MGM canon: *Meet Me in St. Louis* (1944), *An American in Paris* (1951), *Singin' in the Rain* (1952), *The Band Wagon* (1953), *Seven Brides for Seven Brothers* (1954), and *Gigi* (1958).

- 15 -

ALL OVER

Arthur Freed's last musical was the 1960 film version of the Broadway hit, *Bells Are Ringing* (1956), for which the star, Judy Holliday, won a Tony for her performance as a switchboard operator at an answering service who plays nursemaid to her clients: a dentist-songwriter; a method actor; and her favorite, Jeff Moss, a playwright unable to finish his play. She affects a maternal voice when speaking to Moss, who calls her "Mom," assuming she is a sweet-natured grandmother type, while she is really Ella Peterson, who has a crush on him, although they have never met. It was reunion time for Holliday and Betty Comden and Adolph Green, who wrote the book and lyrics. Before Comden and Green began writing Broadway musicals, and Holliday became a movie star, they were The Revuers, who performed comedy sketches and songs at the Village Vanguard. Hollywood soon beckoned, but after most of what The Revuers did in *Greenwich Village* (Twentieth Century–Fox, 1944) ended up on the cutting-room floor, Comden and Green headed back to New York where they wrote the book and lyrics for Leonard Bernstein's first musical, *On the Town* (1944). Holliday appeared fleetingly in *Greenwich Village*, *Winged Victory*, and *Something for the Boys* (Twentieth Century–Fox, all 1944) before returning to New York as Billie Dawn in Garson Kanin's *Born Yesterday*, scoring a triumph on opening night, February 4, 1946. Three years later she was back in Hollywood for MGM's *Adam's Rib* (1949) and repeated her Oscar-winning characterization of a junk dealer's mistress in Columbia's movie version of *Born Yesterday* a year later.

Bells Are Ringing had three Jule Styne–Betty Comden and Adolph Green songs that became cabaret staples, "The Party's Over" and "Just in Time," which were retained in the film; and "Long Before I Knew You," which was omitted in favor of "Better Than a Dream," understandably dropped during tryouts. Styne's score and Comden and Green's book dovetailed to showcase Holliday's skill at blending vulnerability and brassiness, which even comes across in the original cast recording, revealing her range that extends from the rueful ballad, "The Party's Over," to the eleven o'clock song, "I'm Going Back." Alone on the stage, Ella, tired of mothering her clients, decides to leave

Susanswerphone and return to her former job: "I'm going back where I can be me / Back to the Bonjour Tristesse Brassiere Company." Holliday's delivery, which recalls Al Jolson's way of mesmerizing an audience by sheer force of personality, is, thankfully, preserved in the film, which suffers from the same defect as the original: the flimsy story line of someone falling in love with a voice. (One thinks of the pen pals in *The Shop around the Corner*, who do it far more realistically, epistolary style.) Then, too, anyone who grew up with voicemail would consider an antiquated system like an answering service a relic of the past. The original ran for 533 performances; a 2001 revival with Faith Prince, doing her best to convince audiences that the show was still relevant, lasted a mere 68. There was no attempt to update the book. Although the Playbill for the revival gave the time as 1956, audiences were not interested in going back to the past, not even to the Bonjour Tristesse Brassiere Company.

Vincente Minnelli directed the movie version of *Bells Are Ringing*, which is so faithful to its source that it seems like a hybrid—half Broadway, half Hollywood. Some of the songs that theatergoers would have enjoyed, but not necessarily movie audiences, were dropped such as "Salzburg," a parody of operetta schmaltz; and the hilarious "Is It a Crime?" in which Ella explains to a skeptical police officer that she works for a legitimate business, not an escort service, which, if it had been available to Romeo and Juliet, "those two kids would be alive today." Other songs were added, resulting in a disparity between the quality of those retained and the mediocrity of the ones added. Some members of the original cast reprised their roles, including Jean Stapleton in her pre–*All in the Family* days.

What is immediately striking about the film, particularly for those who grew up with MGM musicals, is that, except for the director and the screenwriters (Comden and Green, who executed a smooth stage-to-screen transfer), the stars were not from the old MGM. If *Bells Are Ringing* does not seem like a typical MGM musical, it is largely because Judy Holliday and her costar, Dean Martin, were not MGM talent. Holliday first attracted attention in MGM's *Adam's Rib* (1949) but then moved over to Columbia where she made six films, including her most famous, *Born Yesterday* (1950), in which she surprised everyone by winning a Best Actress Oscar, beating out Bette Davis (*All about Eve*) and Gloria Swanson (*Sunset Boulevard*). Martin began his film career at Paramount as Jerry Lewis's straight man. When he and Lewis parted ways after *Hollywood or Bust* (1956), Martin's career entered a new phase; he was now an actor with no need of a partner, which he proved in Minnelli's *Some Came Running* (MGM, 1958) and Howard Hawks's *Rio Bravo* (Warner Bros., 1959). Martin, a natural for the role of Jeff Moss, enjoyed the experience of making a real musical, instead of another comedy with music, Paramount style. Minnelli also enjoyed making *Bells Are Ringing*, as he wrote in his autobiography. Holliday felt differently; she was unhappy with the script and its close adherence to the play. *Bells Are Ringing* was her last film. A year after its release, she was diagnosed with cancer, to which she succumbed in 1965 at the age of forty-two.

When *Bells Are Ringing* began filming on October 8, 1959, most of the supporting cast came from the Broadway original, in which Sydney Chaplin, Charlie Chaplin's son by Lita Grey, was Holliday's costar. Chaplin had a decent voice, not particularly robust like Howard Keel's but engagingly mellow, which he displayed effectively in *Subways Are for Sleeping* (1961), another Styne–Comden and Green musical, and particularly in *Funny Girl* (1963), with a Styne score, a book by Isobel Lennart, and a star turn by Barbra Streisand as Fanny Brice. A Holliday-Chaplin combination, however potent on the stage (he also won a Tony), would not have drawn moviegoers. Wisely, Minnelli cast Dean Martin as the playwright Ella cures of writer's block. Martin was surprisingly suave and urbane, qualities not usually associated with him.

The production itself seemed to have landed on that bifurcating road with Broadway in one direction and Hollywood in another. Although some of the scenes were shot on location (e.g., the "Just in Time" number in a private park on Sutton Place), the production is very much studio bound, with Minnelli doing his best to create a New York that exists primarily in the minds of those who never or rarely visited the city. But he did create a brilliant moment in "I Met a Girl," in which Dean Martin is "the central dot in a pointillist sea" of New Yorkers and tourists that, under ordinary circumstances, would have terrified any pedestrian, but in Minnelli's hands, becomes the perfect setting for a man's discovery of "a fabulous creature, without any doubt," aka Ella, whom he knows only as the elusive Melisande Scott.

For Minnelli, *Bells Are Ringing* must have been an anticlimax after *Gigi*. But the show was never much to begin with and succeeded largely on the basis of Styne's score, Comden and Green's lyrics, and Holliday's performance.

When Hollywood made a movie out of a Broadway musical, the format was pretty much the same: a few members of the original cast or sometimes none at all; often, one of the leads, but rarely both—plus Hollywood types familiar to moviegoers. Thus in *Damn Yankees* (Warner Bros., 1958), Gwen Verdon and Ray Walston returned as Lola and the Devil, with Tab Hunter filling in for Stephen Douglass, whose name would have meant nothing to movie audiences, although he was a fine stage performer with a thrilling voice. Walston also took over the role of Luther Billis in *South Pacific* (Twentieth Century–Fox, 1958), which Myron McCormick created in the original production with Mitzi Gaynor and Rossano Brazzi as Nellie Forbush and Emile de Becque in the roles that Mary Martin and Ezio Pinza had made famous. Even if Pinza had been alive (he died in 1957 of a stroke), he and

Martin could never have worked the same magic on the screen as they did on stage. Pinza made a few forgettable movies (MGM's *Strictly Dishonorable* and *Mr. Imperium* [both 1951]) but he was never as successful in film as he was in opera and on Broadway in *South Pacific* (1949) and *Fanny* (1954). It was the same with Martin, who was a stage creature to the core. Since the role of Emile required a basso like Pinza, Met opera star Giorgio Tozzi did the dubbing for Brazzi.

John Raitt, the original Sid in *The Pajama Game*, was recruited for the film (Warner Bros., 1957), but his Broadway costar, Janis Paige, was passed over in favor of Doris Day, which is ironic, since Paige was a featured player at Warner Bros. from 1944 to 1950 and had to go to Broadway to show that she was a natural musical comedy performer. *The Pajama Game* at least made it possible to see three of the original's supporting cast: Eddie Foy Jr., Reta Shaw, and the extraordinary dancer, Carol Haney. Warner Bros. wisely had Robert Preston repeat his Professor Harold Hill in Meredith Willson's *The Music Man* (1962), with Shirley Jones in the role of Marion the librarian in place of the inestimable Barbara Cook. Jones sang with purity of tone, but not with Cook's crystalline clarity that could be both limpid and plangent.

In 1964, two movies opened—one, a faithful transcription of a frequently revived classic; the other, a less-than-faithful one of a crowd-pleaser that has not had a major revival. If you did not know that *My Fair Lady*, directed by George Cukor, was a Warner Bros. film, you would have sworn it was produced by MGM because of its impeccable visual style; if there is such a thing as flawless mise-en-scène, in which every facet of the production blends harmoniously into a glorious totality, it is *My Fair Lady*. The crowd-pleaser, both onstage and screen, was Meredith Willson's *The Unsinkable Molly Brown*. The only thing the movies had in common was the gross: each was a moneymaker: $17 million (*My Fair Lady*), $11 million (*The Unsinkable Molly Brown*).

Warner Bros. would have been the natural home for *The Unsinkable Molly Brown*, especially with the success of the earlier Meredith Willson musical. While *The Music Man* had a tuneful but not a great score, it is remembered for the love duet, "Till There Was You"; Preston's revival-style "Trouble"; and "Seventy-Six Trombones," which was so infectious that you almost wanted to join the band. On Broadway, *The Unsinkable Molly Brown* (1960) had a career-defining performance by Tammy Grimes in the title role; a hummable but undistinguished score, and a rags-to-riches book that was an abbreviated version of the life of Margaret Tobin Brown, best known as the *Titanic* survivor played by Kathy Bates in the 1997 film of that name. Born to Irish immigrant parents, Margaret longed at an early age for social status, which she acquired when she married James Joseph ("J.J.") Brown, a mine supervisor, who was originally as poor as herself until he struck it rich after gold and copper deposits were discovered in the Little Jonny Mine in Leadville, Colorado. For his efforts, he was rewarded with 12,500 shares of stock, which enabled him to buy a Denver mansion, so that he and Margaret could live in style.

As melodious as Willson's score is, and as vital as the cast made it sound—especially when Tammy Grimes, imagining herself as a grand dame, grabbed a broom for a scepter, a tablecloth for a cape, and tin pail for a crown, and paraded around the kitchen, singing the anthem of empowerment, "I Ain't Down Yet"—*The Unsinkable Molly Brown* brought back memories of other shows in which the main character traverses the poverty to wealth route. Fifteen years earlier, *Molly Brown* would have been a natural for Ethel Merman, who went from a nobody sharpshooter to a star in Buffalo Bill's Wild West Show in *Annie Get Your Gun* (1946).

Shirley MacLaine was originally scheduled to play Molly, until producer Hal Wallis decided not to release her from her contract. Doris Day also coveted the role, but the poor box office for *Billy Rose's Jumbo* (1962) did not work in her favor. Debbie Reynolds, an MGM stalwart since 1950, inherited the role. She at least could handle the songs—the few that remained. The director was a familiar MGM name, Charles Walters; despite his and Reynolds's long association with MGM, *The Unsinkable Molly Brown* did not look like an MGM musical; in fact, it did not look like a musical at all, even though the rich-voiced Harve Presnell repeated his "Leadville" Johnny Brown, now given a mere two songs. Only four songs remained from the original seventeen: the song of the self, "I Ain't Down Yet"; "I'll Never Say No"; the boisterous "Belly Up to the Bar, Boys"; and "Colorado, My Home." "He's My Friend," which was not in the original production, was either discarded before the Broadway opening or composed especially for the film.

What struck movie buffs about *The Unsinkable Molly Brown* was the producer. He was none of the big three—Arthur Freed, Jack Cummings, or Joe Pasternack. Freed's last film for the studio was not a musical, but a drama, *Light in the Piazza* (1962), with Olivia de Havilland as a mother with a grown daughter who has the mentality of a twelve-year-old as the result of a freak accident. Pasternak's last MGM musical—excluding the inconsequential Elvis Presley films, *Girl Happy* (1965) and *Spinout* (1966), which were movies interspersed with musical numbers—was *Billy Rose's Jumbo* (1962), a critical and financial failure. Cummings was producing his last film for MGM, *Viva Las Vegas* (1964), with Presley and Ann-Margret, who looked as if they were performing in Vegas rather than in a movie. Rather, the producer of *The Unsinkable Molly Brown* was Lawrence Weingarten, who, except for *The Broadway Melody* (1929), was primarily known for MGM's comedies (*Adam's Rib*, *Pat and Mike*, *The Tender Trap*) and dramas (*The Actress*, *I'll Cry Tomorrow*, *Cat on a Hot Tin Roof*). Perhaps it was his decision to eliminate most of the score and emphasize the drama. Regardless, the result was an Oscar nomination for Reynolds, who lost to Julie Andrews in *Mary Poppins*, which was pure Disney and could boast of a more enduring score. Reynolds had the more difficult job. With just a few songs, she had to act the part, which she did by making Molly a social climber without the obsessiveness of Joan Crawford in *Flamingo Road* (Warner Bros., 1949). Reynolds was an upwardly mobile Tammy, the character she portrayed in *Tammy and the Bachelor* (1957); you could believe Molly wanted the amenities that came with a better life when she expressed her longing for a brass bed, which, if she had been allowed to sing "My Own Brass Bed," as Grimes did in the original, would have made the character even more sympathetic. Still, *The Unsinkable Molly Brown* was the third-highest-grossing film of 1964, and Reynolds had the satisfaction of being recognized by her peers, even though Walters would have preferred Shirley MacLaine, who was better suited to the role of the dance hall worker, Charity Hope Valentine, in *Sweet Charity* (Universal, 1969).

When *The Unsinkable Molly Brown* was released in June 1964, Arthur Freed was still at MGM. He had just succeeded Wendell Corey as president of the Academy of Motion Picture Arts and Sciences (1963–1967). He could have rested on his laurels: the Irving G. Thalberg Memorial Award (1951) for producers "whose bodies of work reflect a consistently high quality"; Best Picture Oscars for *An American in Paris* and *Gigi*; and an honorary Oscar in 1967 for "distinguished service to the Academy and the production of six top-rated Awards telecasts." But even in his early seventies, Freed was planning new productions, among which were an adaptation of the Broadway musical *Carnival!* and his dream project, *Say It with Music,* the life of Irving Berlin with Fred Astaire, presumably as Berlin (odd casting, indeed) and Julie Andrews. He was still trying to get the biopic made as late as 1969. The problem was the script; nothing satisfied him, not even the contributions of Leonard Gershe, Betty Comden and Adolph Green, and George Wells. The directors also kept changing; first it was Vincente Minnelli, then Blake Edwards. Berlin was the constant; he had even composed some new songs for the film. But MGM was not what it was when the Freed Unit was at its height. An Elvis Presley movie passed for a musical. Sometimes there was a blast from the past—Robert Taylor in *Return of the Gunfighter* (1960); Debbie Reynolds, Ricardo Montalban, and Greer Garson in *The Singing Nun* (1966). Otherwise, stars came and went. Seven-year contracts were relics.

In 1969, the end had come. MGM was a losing proposition as a studio; by the end of 1969, its losses totaled $35.4 million. But it had other assets: property and a wealth of auctionable memorabilia for those who could afford a nostalgia trip. Kirk Kerkorian, "an Armenian farm boy with an eighth grade education" and a prescient entrepreneur, made his initial fortune flying high rollers to Las Vegas in the post–World War II years. Kerkorian then began buying up property in Vegas, eighty-two acres of which became a hotel, the International, which opened in 1969 with Barbra Streisand as the main attraction in the enormous showroom. A year later it became the Las Vegas Hilton and is currently the Las Vegas Hotel and Casino.

Kerkorian's reasoning was simple: Why stop with entertainment in the desert when an ailing movie studio is up for grabs? Kerkorian did everything in a big way, including buying MGM, in which he was a major stockholder. To him, the studio was real estate, not movies. Yet MGM was still in the movie business, and Kerkorian needed someone to run the studio. He chose Princeton-educated James Aubrey, who had been president of CBS-TV from 1965 to 1968 and who revitalized the network with such series as *Gilligan's Island*, *The Dick Van Dyke Show*, *Green Acres*, *Petticoat Junction*, and *The Beverly Hillbillies*, which pretty much indicated where he stood when it came to mass entertainment.

Nicknamed "The Smiling Cobra," Aubrey showed no mercy when it came to slashing budgets and firing employees. His policy was simple: fewer movies to be filmed on location rather than on soundstages, which would be used primarily for television production, except for those that could be sold as real estate; and pickups rather than in-house movies, which would make MGM a distributor rather than an old-style movie studio. Since the pipeline had to be filled, it made no difference where the product came from.

To Aubrey, Arthur Freed was expendable. In 1971 Aubrey asked Roger Mayer (no relation to Louis B.), "Why do we need that old man in that office for?" Mayer was then assistant general manager of the Culver City studios and later a leading advocate of film preservation. It was his job to break the news to Freed, then wheelchair bound and arthritic. For Arthur Freed, it was the beginning of the end. He died of a heart attack at seventy-eight on April 12, 1973, a year after he was inducted into the Songwriters Hall of Fame. He is buried in the Garden of Memories in the Hillsdale Memorial Park and Mortuary in Culver City, along with many notable Jews from the entertainment world, including Jack Benny, Milton Berle, Theodore Bikel, Eddie Cantor, Al Jolson, Leonard Nimoy, George Jessel, LewWasserman, and Shelley Winters. For Arthur Freed, it was the ideal location—a few miles from the old MGM studios that occupied the northwest corner of Washington Boulevard and Overland Avenue, now the headquarters of Sony Pictures Entertainment, the parent company of Columbia Pictures. He could not have wanted a more fitting resting place, although he would have questioned the credentials of the new owners of the former MGM lot.

Unfortunately, Arthur Freed lived to see the notorious twenty-day MGM auction in May 1970, which the *Los Angeles Times* (May 4, 1970) described as the selling off of "the things dreams were once made of" and of part of the Culver City lot where the dreams were made. Since annotated screenplays, props, and costumes were considered "impedimenta," their removal would allow for a streamlined MGM. A collector of costumes could have his or her pick of, among other items, Clark Gable's trench coat from *Comrade X*; the loin cloth Johnny Weissmuller wore as Tarzan; Bert Lahr's Cowardly Lion costume from *The Wizard of Oz*; John Barrymore's exquisitely embroidered jacket from *Marie Antoinette*; Elizabeth Taylor's wedding gown from *Father of the Bride*; a Susan Hayward dress from *I'll Cry Tomorrow*; Charlton Heston's tunic and robe from *Ben-Hur*; Audrey Hepburn's dress and hat from the Ascot scene in *My Fair Lady*; Greta Garbo's cape from *Queen Christina* or Stewart Granger's from *Young Bess*; Gene Kelly's sailor hat and scarf from *On the Town*; and Fred Astaire's dress shirt and trousers from *Royal Wedding*. A pair (several were used in the film) of the ruby slippers from *The Wizard of Oz* went for $15,000. Jack Haley Jr., the son of the actor who portrayed the Tin Man in *The Wizard of Oz*, purchased William Wyler's shooting script of *Mrs. Miniver* for twelve dollars.

If you had a penchant for boats, there was the *Bounty* from *Mutiny on the Bounty* (1935) and the *Cotton Blossom* from *Show Boat*. For *Ben-Hur* fans, there was Charlton Heston's chariot; and for anyone who, like Molly Brown, longed for a brass bed, there was the one from *The Unsinkable Molly Brown*. "One could bid on an entire ship's lavatory or a wide array of antique organs and other musical instruments." Debbie Reynolds bought up as much as she could, and over the years acquired costumes and artifacts from other studios including the iconic white dress that Marilyn Monroe wore in *The Seven Year Itch* (Twentieth Century–Fox, 1955) that billowed when she stood over the subway grating, revealing much less on the screen than what onlookers saw during the various takes. Reynolds had hoped for a museum to house her collection, but that did not happen. A considerable part of the collection was auctioned off at the Paley Center for Media in Beverly Hills in 2011.

Having divested itself of its impedimenta, MGM decided in May 1974 to generate more income by celebrating its fiftieth anniversary with the release of *That's Entertainment!* a cinematic scrapbook of sequences from its musicals. Since MGM had entered the hospitality business in December 1973 with the opening of the MGM Grand in Las Vegas, there was only one way it could attract attention—and it was not by its paltry slate of 1974 films that consisted of a grand total of five, including *That's Entertainment!* MGM had to showcase its glorious past, albeit in fragmentary form. MGM's present was its past, which was all that mattered to moviegoers willing to pay for a trip down memory lane, but not to suffer through the studio's other 1974 offerings: *The Super Cops*, *Kazabian*, *Mr. Ricco*, and Michelangelo Antonioni's *The Passenger*, a Carlo Ponti production distributed by MGM. An existential masterpiece with no connection to the studio, *The Passenger*, attracted the art house crowd but would have baffled the average moviegoer.

That's Entertainment! was an enticing sampler that appealed to audiences who had seen the sequences in context and wanted to relive the experience even in montage form; and those who were too young to have seen the originals but were now sitting in the dark, awed by the kaleidoscopic outpouring: Gene Kelly literally singing (and dancing) in the rain; the climactic *An American in Paris* ballet; Louis Jourdan professing his love for Gigi in various parts of Paris; Judy Garland and the cast of *The Harvey Girls*, imitating a chugging locomotive in "On the Acheson, Topeka and Santa Fe"; Fred Astaire and Eleanor Powell dancing to "Begin the Beguine" in *Broadway Melody of 1940*; Debbie Reynolds and Carleton Carpenter doing the simian "Aba Daba Honeymoon" in *Two Weeks with Love*; Judy's "Over the Rainbow" and "Mack the Black," the latter looking weirdly ritualistic out of context; and June Allyson's "Thou Swell" from *Words and Music*, which brought out the wit in Larry Hart's lyrics that were a mix of archaic English and American slang—and much more for a total of 134 minutes. Budgeted at $3.2 million, *That's Entertainment!* grossed $19.1 million. The 1976 and 1994 sequels were less successful. It was not a matter of surfeit, but the musicals were being shown on television, and by the third installment, the gold had been mined. *That's Dancing!* (1985), MGM's documentary on the history of dance in film, is not, strictly speaking, part of the *That's Entertainment!* series, since it includes excerpts from other studios' films such as *42nd St.* (Warner Bros., 1933), *Roberta* (RKO, 1935), *Down Argentine Way* (Twentieth Century–Fox, 1940), *Cabaret* (Allied Artists, 1972), and *Saturday Night Fever* (Paramount, 1977).

MGM may have lost its stars in the heavens, but the musicals are still shining in a different firmament. To paraphrase Humphrey Bogart's famous line to Ingrid Bergman in *Casablanca*, "We'll always have MGM," thanks to DVDs, BluRays, and Turner Classic Movies, which premiered in 1994 and regularly shows MGM films as well as those of other studios.

As Bette Davis said to Paul Henreid in *Now, Voyager* (Warner Bros., 1942), "Don't let's ask for the moon. We have the stars."

NOTES

INTRODUCTION

3   "Nick sings": Vocal Selections, *Something Rotten!* Music and Lyrics by Wayne Kirkpatrick and Karey Kirkpatrick (Victoria, Australia: Hal Leonard Corporation, 2015).

CHAPTER 1: THE MUSIC MAN OF MGM

6   "Arthur's life": I have reconstructed Arthur Freed's early life from material obtained from ancestry.com, the Seattle Genealogical Society, the Phillips Exeter Academy archives, and the Arthur Freed clippings file at the Margaret Herrick Library.

9   "At least one critic": Gary Marmorstein, *Hollywood Rhapsody: Movie Music and Its Makers, 1900–1975* (New York: Shirmer Books, 1997), 241.

10   "His grades": e-mail to author, June 8, 2015.

11   "Laemmle started in exhibition": Bernard F. Dick, *City of Dreams: The Making and Remaking of Universal Pictures* (Lexington: UP of Kentucky, 1997), 15–16.

11   "He first found a job": Dennis Lee Gatling, "Arthur Freed," *Films in Review*, November 1964, 521.

12   "assumed responsibility": hollywoodart.blogspot.com/2006/03/with-a-song-in-his-heart.

12   "Arthur remained stateside": "Freed, Arthur," in Thomas Hischak, *The Oxford Companion to the American Musical* (New York: Oxford UP, 2008), 264.

14   "'Louisiana' is typical": halcyonmusic.com/1920s-songs-louisiana-song.php.

14   "the recording center of the West Coast": Kenneth Marcus, *Musical Metropolis: Los Angeles and the Creation of a Musical Culture, 1880–1949* (New York: Palgrave Macmillan, 2004), 135.

15   "became a successful tailor": Nancy Capace, *Encyclopedia of New Mexico* (Santa Barbara: Somerset, 2001), 162.

15   "a network of informers": Scott Eyman, *Lion of Hollywood: The Life and Legend of Louis B. Mayer* (New York: Simon & Schuster, 2005), 2.

16   "The sight of his organ": Bruce Handy, "The Art of the Creep: When Good Movies Happen to Bad People," February 11, 2014, Vanity Fair.com/2014/-02-honor-art-without-honoring-artist.

CHAPTER 2. ALL TALKING, ALL SINGING, ALL DANCING, ALL EVERYTHING

18   "There were eight sequences": *The Jazz Singer*, edited with an introduction by Robert L. Carringer, Wisconsin/Warner Bros. Screenplay Series (Madison: U of Wisconsin P, 1979), 143–46.

19   "first full-length talking picture": Ronald Flamini, *Thalberg: The Last Tycoon and the World of M-G-M* (New York: Crown, 1994), 113.

20   "playback": ibid., 114.

21   "Thalberg was eager": Charles Higham, *Merchant of Dreams: Louis B. Mayer, M.G.M., and the Secret Hollywood* (New York: Laurel/Dell, 1993), 230.

21   "great style, presence, and reserve": ibid., 234.

21   "insisted [he] was the actual director": Patrick McGilligan, *George Cukor: A Double Life* (New York: St. Martin's, 1991), 71.

24   "a second father": Lorna Luft, *Me and My Shadow: A Family Memoir* (New York: Simon & Schuster, 1999), 206.

24   "Edens was gay": ibid., 206.

25   "Arthur Freed, along with many others": Hugh Fordin, *The World of Entertainment: Hollywood's Greatest Musicals* (New York: Avon, 1975), 8–29.

26   "as a transition," "full of crescendos": ibid., 15.

26   "first draft screenplay": ibid., 12–13.

26   "scene-by-scene summary": The greatest films.filmsite.org/The Wizard of Oz.

28   "screenplay by many hands": see *The Wizard of Oz* credits at imdb.com.

28   "for no good reason": Eyman, *Lion of Hollywood*, 10.

28   "Freed and Mayer": ibid., 328–29.

CHAPTER 3. "I WANNA BE A PRODUCER"

29   "a slob": Gerald Clarke, *Get Happy: The Life of Judy Garland* (New York: Dell/Random House, 2000), 194.

29   "Arthur approached Mayer": Fordin, *The World of Entertainment*, 18.

32   "That was the version": lorenzhart.org/babes.

34   "In his autobiography": Vincente Minnelli, with Hector Arce, *I Remember It Well* (Garden City, NY: Berkeley/Doubleday, 1975), 121.

36   "$10 million deficit": Richard B. Jewell, with Vernon Harbin, *The RKO Story* (New York: Arlington House, 1982), 44.

36   "Ginger, I love you": Ginger Rogers, *Ginger: My Story* (New York: HarperCollins, 1991), 89–90.

36   "a bad drunk": Eyman, *Lion of Hollywood*, 407.

38   "When I held the C note": Ethel Merman, with George Eells, *Merman: An Autobiography* (New York: Simon & Schuster, 1978), 40.

CHAPTER 4. JUDY WITHOUT MICKEY

41   "Paging Mr. Greenback": YouTube/"Paging Mr. Greenback."

41   "if it had been made in 1938": tcm.com/Ziegfeld Girl/articles.

43   "much to the displeasure of Joseph Ignatius Breen": Breen to Mayer, October 23, 1940, MPA Production Code Administration Records, Margaret Herrick Library.

44   "the most terrible event": Clarke, *Get Happy*, 59.

44   "Lana herself was discovered": *Spokane Daily Chronicle*, May 5, 1941, 16.

46   "When Stella Adler": tcm.com/For Me and My Gal/articles.

48   "MGM bought the rights": Minnelli, *I Remember It Well*, 47.

49   "Benson had been assigned": Fordin, *The World of Entertainment*, 91n.1.

49   "Howard Lindsay and Russel Crouse": Gerald Kaufman, *Meet Me in St. Louis*, BFI Film Classics (London: British Film Institute, 1994), 11.

50   "Judy's then lover": Fordin, *The World of Entertainment*, 95.

50 "according to Minnelli": Minnelli, *I Remember It Well*, 134.

50 "I've taken this boy": Clarke, *Get Happy*, 193.

50 "Neither [Finklehoffe nor Brecher]": Aljean Harmetz, *The Making of the Wizard of Oz* (New York: Knopf, 1977).

51 "she missed seventeen days": Clarke, *Get Happy*, 197.

51 "emergency appendectomy," "sinusitis," "nervous spells": Kaufman, *Meet Me in St. Louis*, 20–21.

51 "an unprecedented jolt of Americana": Richard Barrios, *Dangerous Rhythm: Why Movie Musicals Matter* (New York: Oxford UP, 2014), 70.

51 "Arthur Freed wanted deleted": Kaufman, *Meet Me in St. Louis*, 217.

CHAPTER 5. THE ACTRESS

56 "Drive-In": oldtimeradiodownloads.com/drive-in-judy-garland.

57 "Judy went to Arthur Freed": Clarke, *Get Happy*, 213.

57 "Having made his reputation in New York": Minnelli, *I Remember It Well*, 57–114.

58 "Boy-Girl story": Minnelli to Thau, November 5, 1945, *The Pirate*, Vincente Minnelli Collection, Box 7, Margaret Herrick Library.

59 "causing her to miss ninety-nine": Clarke, *Get Happy*, 225–26.

61 "She and Minnelli had violent rows": YouTube/The Pirate: A Musical Treasure Chest, 2007.

61 "the best thing": Minnelli to Freed, September 23, 1947, Vincente Minnelli Collection, Box 7, #118, Margaret Herrick Library.

61 "violent emotional transitions": ibid., #117.

CHAPTER 6. JUDY'S LAST YEARS AT MGM

63 "conversation set to music": Laurence Bergreen, *As Thousands Cheer: The Life of Irving Berlin* (New York: Da Capo Press, 1996), 316.

65 "She informed Arthur": Clarke, *Get Happy*, 237.

68 "we made her feel wanted": TCM.com/In the Good Old Summertime/articles.

69 "When Charles Walters informed Judy": Clarke, *Get Happy*, 266.

CHAPTER 7. THE REVUE, HOLLYWOOD STYLE

71 "A revue": William A. Everett, *Sigmund Romberg* (New Haven: Yale UP, 2007), 47.

73 "Don Brown's Body": Jean Kerr included the sketch in her collection of essays, *Please Don't Eat the Daisies* (New York: Doubleday, 1957).

76 "paid the American Theatre Wing": AskPlaybill.com/A question about Broadway's historic Stage Door Canteen.

77 "Kelly's admission": Fordin, *The World of Entertainment*, 129.

77 "*Ziegfeld Follies*": Production details and script revisions derive from the MGM Legal Department Records, MGM Script Dept. #185, Margaret Herrick Library.

81 "book revue": Ethan Mordden, *Beautiful Mornin': The Broadway Musical in the 1940s* (New York: Oxford UP, 1999), 187.

85 "showed the lyric": Thomas S. Hischak, *The Jerome Kern Encyclopedia* (Lanham, MD: Scarecrow Press, 2013), 108.

87 "her feet bled": Esther Williams, with Digby Diehl, *The Million Dollar Mermaid: An Autobiography* (New York: Simon & Schuster, 1999), 184.

CHAPTER 8. THE MGM ORIGINALS

91   "In his autobiography": Minnelli, *I Remember It Well*, 245.
97   "not stop": "Introduction," *Singin' in the Rain*, story and screenplay by Betty Comden and
      Adolph Green, the MGM Library of Film Scripts (New York: Viking, 1972), 4.
97   "how illusions are created": Earl J. Hess and Pratibha A. Dabholkar, *Singin' in the Rain: The
      Making of an American Masterpiece* (Lawrence: UP of Kansas, 2009), 106.
98   "twenty-five feet of voile": ibid., 164.
102   "Although Mervyn LeRoy is credited": Stephen Harvey, *Directed by Vincente Minnelli*
      (New York: Museum of Modern Art/Harper & Row, 1989), 111.
104   "was courting her": Eyman, *Lion of Hollywood*, 317.
105   "the result of plastic surgery": ginnysimms.com.

CHAPTER 9. FILM AS THEATER, THEATER AS FILM

118   "the cinematic equivalent of *My Fair Lady*": Harvey, *Directed by Vincente Minnelli*, 145.
121   "the rights were cheap": ibid., 40.
121   "arguing that the title implied": Fordin, *The World of Entertainment*, 75.
127   "hash," "souffle": Bill Rosenfield, album notes, *Silk Stockings*, original cast recording, RCA
      Victor, 1102-02-RG.
130   "with song and dialogue added": Clive Hirschorrn, *The Hollywood Musical* (London: Oc-
      topus Press, 1981), 27.
131   "Dunne toured": Hischak, *The Jerome Kern Encyclopedia*, 186.
131   "original London cast recording": ibid., 188.

CHAPTER 10. LIVES IN MUSIC

137   "No record states": Ethan Mordden, *Ziegfeld: The Man Who Invented Show Business* (New
      York: St. Martin's, 2008), 292.
137   "She toured in vaudeville": ibid., 77–78.
138   "Copyright clearances": Hischak, *The Jerome Kern Encyclopedia*, 221.
141   "unkept and 'gnomelike'": Richard Rodgers, *Musical Stages: An Autobiography* (New York:
      Random House, 1975), 126–27.
141   "brought him to a Columbia varsity show": David Ewen, *Richard Rodgers* (New York: Holt,
      1957), 72.
141   "commission merchant": Frederick Nolan, *Lorenz Hart: A Poet on Broadway* (New York:
      Oxford UP, 1994), 4.
142   "the press claimed in July 1942": Frederick Nolan, *The Sound of Their Music: The Story of
      Rodgers and Hammerstein* (New York: Applause, 2002), 2.
143   "the most crushing sentence": Meryle Secrest, *Somewhere for Me: A Biography of Richard
      Rodgers* (New York: Knopf, 2001), 24.
143   "Another flame": ibid., 54.
143   "enamored of Vivienne Segal": Samuel Marx and Jan Clayton, *Rodgers & Hart: Bewitched,
      Bothered, and Bewildered* (New York: Putnam's, 1976), 210.
144   "When Vivienne Segal began singing": Nolan, *The Sound of Their Music*, 145.
148   "in my heart": James Robert Parish and Ronald L. Bowers, *The MGM Stock Company: The
      Golden Era* (New York: Bonanza Books, 1972), 157–58.
150   "conducted his own orchestra": Elliott Arnold, *Deep in My Heart* (New York: Duell, Sloan
      & Pearce, 1949), 450.

151 "he had violets sent": William A. Everett, *Sigmund Romberg* (New Haven: Yale UP, 1997), 16–17.

158 "Caruso had a mistress": Enrico Caruso Jr. and Andrew Farkas, *Enrico Caruso: My Father and My Family*, abridged edition (Portland, OR: Amadeus Press, 1997), 56–61.

158 "Enrico Jr. did not live": ibid., 7.

159 "As long as Lanza was under contract": Derek Mannering, *Mario Lanza: Singing to the Gods* (Jackson: UP of Mississippi, 2005), 97.

CHAPTER 11. THE WHOLE CONSORT DANCING TOGETHER

165 "In his will": Eyman, *Lion of Hollywood*, 501.

166 "an amusing picture": Joe Pasternak, as told to David Chandler, *Easy the Hard Way* (New York: Putnam's, 1956), 254.

166 "to bring the European technique": Dick, *City of Dreams*, 212.

170 "To you I'm still a little girl": Pasternak, *Easy the Hard Way*, 246.

171 "solved the mystery": tcm.com/Royal Wedding/articles.

174 "a reincarnated Greek goddess": tcm.com/Athena/articles.

174 "the offspring of the union": Robert E. Sherwood, *The Road to Rome* (New York: Scribner's, 1927), preface, xlii.

174 "Sherwood acknowledges": ibid., xliv.

174 "broke his back": Williams, *The Million Dollar Mermaid*, 261.

174 "Mary Zellner doubled for Williams": Regina Ford, "Stand-in for a Star: Esther Williams' Double Still a Water Babe," *Green Valley News*, June 8, 2013, rford@gvnews.com.

CHAPTER 12. THE LIFE AQUATIC WITH ESTHER WILLIAMS

183 "original story idea by Gene Kelly and Stanley Donen": Fordin, *The World of Entertainment*, 240–41.

184 "forty-carat cast": ibid., 241.

184 "Kelly did not consider Esther an equal": Williams, *The Million Dollar Mermaid*, 167–69.

185 "Gene Kelly once remarked": Christopher Walken, TCM interview, YouTube.

185 "the two most popular stars of 1950": *Sydney Morning Herald*, December 14, 1950, 3.

188 "There actually was such an accident": bernews.com/2010/12/video-neptunes-daughter-resurfaces, December 14, 2010.

190 "Helen was rewarded": Williams, *The Million Dollar Mermaid*, 250–51.

CHAPTER 13. EXIT ALL

194 "the former Helen Wood": therialtoreport . . . whatever-happened-to-deep-throats-dolly-sharp.

198 "*Hit the Deck* made a profit": Richard Jewell, "RKO Film Grosses, 1931–1951," *Historical Journal of Film, Radio and Television* 14 (1999): 56.

198 "the studio announced a remake": *New York Times*, August 18, 1941, 18.

199 "Even Astaire believed": Fred Astaire, *Steps in Time* (London: Heinemann, 1959), 299–300.

211 "believed that audience deserved to see Kidd": Hess and Dabholkar, *Singin' in the Rain*, 203–4.

213 "the new last episode": telegram from Cukor to Patrick, July 3, 1956, George Cukor Collection, #156, Margaret Herrick Library.

213 "For the Paris exteriors": ibid., Cukor to Siegel, August 2, 1956.

213 "am trying hard": ibid., Lollobrigida to Cukor and Siegel, October 13, 1956.

214 "threatened to leave the production": McGilligan, *A Double Life*, 250.

CHAPTER 14. THE MUSICAL MOVIE

223   "sex-suggestive," "no suggestive break": Breen to Mayer, June 2, 1944, *Anchors Aweigh*, MPA Production Code Administration Records, Margaret Herrick Library.

223   "five-year contract": James Kaplan, *Frank: The Voice* (New York: Doubleday, 2010), 200.

CHAPTER 15. ALL OVER

225   "Minnelli also enjoyed": Minnelli, *I Remember It Well*, 346.

226   "the central dot": Harvey, *Directed by Vincente Minnelli*, 153.

229   "by the end of 1969": Robert Stanley, *The Celluloid Empire: A History of the American Motion Picture Industry* (New York: Hastings House, 1978), 234.

229   "an Armenian farm boy": Peter Bart, *Fade Out: The Calamitous Final Days of MGM* (New York: William Morrow, 1990), 29.

230   "Princeton-educated James Aubrey": ibid., 33.

230   "Why do we need that old man": Eyman, *Lion of Hollywood*, 507.

231   "William Wyler's shooting script": Peter Hay, *MGM: When the Lion Roars* (Atlanta: Turner Publishing, 1991), 326.

231   "One could bid": Bart, *Fade Out*, 40.

FILMOGRAPHY

Unless indicated, films are MGM productions.

FILM	DIRECTOR
An American in Paris (1951)	Vincente Minnelli
Anchors Aweigh (1945)	George Sidney
Annie Get Your Gun (1950)	George Sidney; Busby Berkeley (uncredited)
Athena (1954)	Richard Thorpe
Babes in Arms (1939)	Busby Berkeley
Babes on Broadway (1941)	Busby Berkeley
The Band Wagon (1953)	Vincente Minnelli
The Barkleys of Broadway (1949)	Charles Walters
Bathing Beauty (1944)	George Sidney
Because You're Mine (1952)	Richard Thorpe
The Belle of New York (1952)	Charles Walters
Bells Are Ringing (1960)	Vincente Minnelli
The Best Things in Life Are Free (Twentieth Century–Fox, 1956)	Michael Curtiz
Bitter Sweet (1940)	W. S. Van Dyke
Blue Skies (Paramount, 1946)	Stuart Heisler; Mark Sandrich (uncredited)
Brigadoon (1954)	Vincente Minnelli
The Broadway Melody (1929)	Harry Beaumont
Broadway Melody of 1936 (1935)	Roy Del Ruth; W. S. Van Dyke (uncredited)
Broadway Melody of 1938 (1937)	Roy Del Ruth
Broadway Melody of 1940 (1939)	Norman Taurog
Broadway Rhythm (1944)	Roy Del Ruth
Cabin in the Sky (1942)	Vincente Minnelli

Cairo (1942)	W. S. Van Dyke
Call Me Madam (Twentieth Century–Fox, 1953)	Walter Lang
The Clock (1945)	Vincente Minnelli
Cover Girl (Columbia, 1944)	Charles Vidor
Dangerous When Wet (1953)	Charles Walters
A Date with Judy (1948)	Richard Thorpe
Deep in My Heart (1954)	Stanley Donen
Don Juan (Warner Bros., 1926)	Alan Crosland
Du Barry Was a Lady (1943)	Roy Del Ruth
Duchess of Idaho (1950)	Robert Z. Leonard
Easter Parade (1948)	Charles Walters
Easy to Love (1953)	Charles Walters
Easy to Wed (1946)	Edward Buzzell; Buster Keaton, Edward Sedgwick (uncredited)
Every Sunday (1936)	Felix E. Feist
Everything I Have Is Yours (1952)	Robert Z. Leonard
Follow the Boys (Universal, 1944)	Eddie Sutherland; John Rawling (uncredited)
For Me and My Gal (1942)	Busby Berkeley
For the First Time (1959)	Rudolph Maté
Gigi (1958)	Vincente Minnelli
Girl Crazy (1943)	Norman Taurog, Busby Berkeley
The Girl Most Likely (1957)*	Mitchell Leisen
Give a Girl a Break (1953)	Stanley Donen
Going Hollywood (1933)	Raoul Walsh
Good News (1947)	Charles Walters
The Great Caruso (1951)	Richard Thorpe
The Great Waltz (1938)	Julien Duvivier
The Great Ziegfeld (1936)	Robert Z. Leonard
The Harvey Girls (1946)	George Sidney
High Society (1956)	Charles Walters
Hit the Deck (1955)	Roy Rowland
Holiday Inn (Paramount, 1942)	Mark Sandrich
Holiday in Mexico (1946)	George Sidney
Hollywood Canteen (Warner Bros., 1944)	Delmer Daves
The Hollywood Revue of 1929 (1929)	Charles F. Reisner; Christy Cabanne (uncredited)
I Dood It (1943)	Vincente Minnelli

I Love Melvin (1953)	Don Weis
I Married an Angel (1942)	W. S. Van Dyke; Roy Del Ruth (uncredited)
Interrupted Melody (1955)	Curtis Bernhardt
In the Good Old Summertime (1949)	Robert Z. Leonard
Invitation to the Dance (1956)	Gene Kelly
It Happened in Brooklyn (1947)	Richard Whorf
It's a Date (Universal, 1940)	William A. Seiter
It's Always Fair Weather (1955)	Stanley Donen, Gene Kelly
The Jazz Singer (Warner Bros., 1927)	Alan Crosland
Jupiter's Darling (1955)	George Sidney
Kismet (1955)	Vincente Minnelli; Stanley Donen (uncredited)
The Kissing Bandit (1948)	Laslo Benedek
Kiss Me Kate (1953)	George Sidney
Lady Be Good (1941)	Norman Z. McLeod
A Lady's Morals (1930)	Sidney Franklin
Les Girls (1957)	George Cukor
Let's Be Happy (Allied Artists, 1957)	Henry Levin
Lili (1953)	Charles Walters
Little Nellie Kelly (1940)	Norman Taurog
Living in a Big Way (1947)	Gregory La Cava
Lovely to Look At (1952)	Mervyn LeRoy; Vincente Minnelli (uncredited)
Love Me or Leave Me (1955)	Charles Vidor
Luxury Liner (1948)	Richard Whorf
Maytime (1937)	Robert Z. Leonard
Meet Me in Las Vegas (1956)	Roy Rowland
Meet Me in St. Louis (1944)	Vincente Minnelli
The Merry Widow (1934)	Ernst Lubitsch
Million Dollar Mermaid (1952)	Mervyn LeRoy
Music for Millions (1944)	Henry Koster
My Fair Lady (Warner Bros., 1964)	George Cukor
Nancy Goes to Rio (1950)	Robert Z. Leonard
Naughty Marietta (1935)	W. S. Van Dyke
Neptune's Daughter (1949)	Edward Buzzell
New Faces (Twentieth Century–Fox, 1954)	Harry Horner, John Beal
One Hour with You (Paramount, 1932)	Ernst Lubitsch/George Cukor

On the Town (1949)	Stanley Donen, Gene Kelly
Pagan Love Song (1950)	Robert Alton
Panama Hattie (1942)**	Norman Z. McLeod; Roy Del Ruth, Vincente Minnelli (uncredited)
The Pirate (1948)	Vincente Minnelli
Presenting Lily Mars (1943)	Norman Taurog
The Red Shoes (The Archers/Eagle-Lion, 1948)	Michael Powell, Emeric Pressburger
Roberta (RKO, 1935)	William A. Seiter
Rosalie (1937)	W. S. Van Dyke
Rose Marie (1936)	W. S. Van Dyke
Royal Wedding (1951)	Stanley Donen
San Francisco (1936)	W. S. Van Dyke; D. W. Griffith (uncredited)
Sensations of 1945 (United Artists, 1944)	Andrew L. Stone
Serenade (Warner Bros., 1956)	Anthony Mann
Seven Brides for Seven Brothers (1954)	Stanley Donen
The Seven Hills of Rome (1957)	Roy Rowland
Ship Ahoy (1942)	Edward Buzzell
Show Boat (Universal, 1936)	James Whale
Show Boat (1951)	George Sidney
Silk Stockings (1957)	Rouben Mamoulian
The Sky's the Limit (RKO, 1943)	Edward H. Griffith
Stage Door Canteen (United Artists, 1943)	Frank Borzage
Star-Spangled Rhythm (Paramount, 1942)	George Marshall
Stormy Weather (Twentieth Century–Fox, 1943)	Andrew L. Stone
Strike Up the Band (1940)	Busby Berkeley
Summer Holiday (1948)	Rouben Mamoulian
Summer Stock (1950)	Charles Walters
Take Me Out to the Ball Game (1949)	Busby Berkeley
Texas Carnival (1951)	Charles Walters
Thank Your Lucky Stars (Warner Bros., 1943)	David Butler
That's Entertainment! (1974)	Jack Haley Jr.
This Time for Keeps (1947)	Richard Thorpe
Thousands Cheer (1943)	George Sidney
Three Daring Daughters (1948)	Fred M. Wilcox
Three Little Words (1950)	Richard Thorpe
Thrill of a Romance (1945)	Richard Thorpe

Till the Clouds Roll By (1946)	Richard Whorf
Top Banana (United Artists,1954)	Alfred E. Green
Two Girls and a Sailor (1944)	Richard Thorpe
Two Sisters from Boston (1946)	Henry Koster
Two Weeks with Love (1950)	Roy Rowland
The Unsinkable Molly Brown (1964)	Charles Walters
Variety Girl (Paramount, 1947)	George Marshall
What's Cookin'? (Universal, 1942)	Edward F. Cline
The Wizard of Oz (1939)	Victor Fleming; George Cukor, Mervyn LeRoy, Norman Taurog, King Vidor (uncredited)
West Side Story (United Artists,1964)	Robert Wise, Jerome Robbins
Words and Music (1948)	Norman Taurog
Yolanda and the Thief (1946)	Vincente Minnelli
You Were Never Lovelier (Columbia, 1942)	William A. Seiter
Ziegfeld Follies (1946)	Vincente Minnelli; George Sidney, Roy Del Ruth, Norman Taurog, Lemuel Ayers, Robert Lewis, Merrill Pye
Ziegfeld Girl (1941)	Robert Z. Leonard; Busby Berkeley (uncredited)

*Shot at RKO but released through MGM when RKO ceased production.
**Retakes directed by Del Ruth after the poorly received preview; patriotic finale added by Minnelli.

INDEX